THE CHANGING POLITICS AND POLICY OF AUSTERITY

Edited by
Stephen McBride, Bryan Evans
and Dieter Plehwe

First published in Great Britain in 2021 by

Policy Press, an imprint of
Bristol University Press
University of Bristol
1–9 Old Park Hill
Bristol
BS2 8BB
UK
t: +44 (0)117 954 5940
e: bup-info@bristol.ac.uk

Details of international sales and distribution partners are available at
policy.bristoluniversitypress.co.uk

British Library Cataloguing in Publication Data
A catalogue record for this book is available from the British Library

ISBN 978-1-4473-5951-7 hardcover
ISBN 978-1-4473-5952-4 ePub
ISBN 978-1-4473-5953-1 ePdf

Cover design: Andrew Corbett
Front cover image: iStock/Syldavia
Bristol University Press and Policy Press use environmentally responsible print partners.
Printed and bound in Great Britain by CPI Group (UK) Ltd,
Croydon, CR0 4YY

FSC
www.fsc.org
MIX
Paper from responsible sources
FSC® C013604

Contents

List of figures and tables

Figures

Tables

Notes on contributors

Donna Baines is Director and Professor of Social Work at the University of British Columbia (UBC). Prior to her positions at UBC she held professorial appointments at Dalhousie University and McMaster University. Her research interests focus on paid and unpaid care work, theory and practice, and social policy and austerity. Recent publications include a co-edited book, *Working Across Difference: Social Work, Social Policy and Social Justice* and a journal article, 'Nonprofit Care Work as Social Glue: Creating and Sustaining Social Reproduction in the Context of Austerity/Late Neoliberalism'.

Hans-Jürgen Bieling is Professor of Political Economy at the Institute for Political Science at Eberhard Karls University, Tübingen, Germany, where he teaches the master's degree programme 'Democracy and Governance in Europe' and other courses relating to the EU. He is (co-)editor of 12 volumes on aspects of European integration, most recently, *Neue Segel, alter Kurs? Die Eurokrise und ihre Folgen für das europäische Wirtschaftsregieren* (with S. Guntrum) (Springer 2019) and *Europäische Staatlichkeit: zwischen Krise und Integration* (with M. Grosse Huettman) (Springer 2016). His articles in scholarly journals both in English and German deal with the Eurozone crisis, the rise of right-wing populism in Europe and the crisis of transatlantic globalization policies.

Sebastian Botzem is a political scientist and organization scholar. He has published extensively on a wide range of topics in international political economy including global business regulation, transnational governance and financial market regulation. He has also contributed to critical accounting research by analyzing standard setting, resource distribution and stakeholder participation. Sebastian has been teaching at the Free University of Berlin and Bremen University, where he is currently an Associated Fellow.

Sharon Broughton is an independent research and strategy consultant with 20 years of private sector leadership experience. Her recent research on Employer Talent & Recruitment Strategies and Newcomer Employment Outcomes was funded by the Partnership for Change: The RBC Immigrant, Diversity and Inclusion Project at Ryerson University.

Siu Mee Cheng is a PhD candidate in Social Policy Studies at Ryerson University. Her doctoral research is on community-based integrated health and social care for older adult populations. She possesses a BASc in Public Health and a MHSc in Community Health, and is a Certified Health Executive Member with the Canadian College of Health Leaders. She has 25 years of leadership and volunteer experience in the health and social services and public sectors at local, provincial and national levels in Canada, and has worked across the care continuum and in various subsectors.

Ian Cunningham is Professor of Employment Relations at the University of Strathclyde. His research includes employment relations in social care, the workforce implications from moving to individualized forms of care, the employment dynamics of supply chains, the living wage, union organizing, health, absence and disability in the workplace, and employee involvement and participation.

Bryan Evans is Professor in the Department of Politics and Public Administration at Ryerson University. Prior to his appointment at Ryerson he worked as a policy advisor in the Ontario government. His research centres on co-governance, policy work and processes, policy analysis in non-government organizations, and state restructuring. Recent publications include: *The Austerity State* (ed. with S. McBride); *Austerity: The Lived Experience* (ed. with S. McBride); *The Public Sector in an Age of Austerity* (ed. with C. Fanelli); *Divided Province: Ontario Politics in the Age of Neoliberalism* (ed. with G. Albo); *Austerity: 12 Myths Exposed* (ed. with D. Plehwe, M. Neujeffski and S. McBride).

Philip James is Professor of Employment Relations at Middlesex University. His research has spanned a range of issues within the fields of employment relations and occupational health and safety. Recent themes have included the employment dynamics of supply chains, health and safety regulation, the productivity effects of employment regulation, the employment effects of social care marketization and union organizing among migrant workers.

Meghan Joy is Assistant Professor in the Department of Political Science at Concordia University. Her research interests include the politics of population ageing, theories and practice of progressive politics and policy in cities, and the political economy of the non-profit sector. Select publications include her book, *The Right to an*

Age-Friendly City: Redistribution, Recognition, and Senior Citizen Rights in Urban Spaces (MQUP 2020), and the article 'Beyond Neoliberalism: A Policy Agenda for a Progressive City' (with R.K. Vogel, *Urban Affairs Review*, 2021).

Sebastian Kramer is Trade Union Secretary for IG Metall in the field of social and labour market policy. He received his PhD in Political Science from the Free University of Berlin and worked as a research associate in the field of global and European governance at the Berlin Social Science Center. He has published on topics such as political participation, social movements, global governance and social policy.

Steffen Lehndorff is Research Fellow at the Institute for Work, Skills and Training/IAQ, University of Duisburg/Essen, Germany. Before retiring in 2012 he was Head of Department on Working-Time and Work Organisation at IAQ. His areas of comparative research include problems of European integration and national varieties of capitalism and employment relations in the EU. His latest book is *'New Deal' Means Being Prepared for Conflict: What We Can Learn from the New Deal of the 1930s* (VSA, 2020).

Stephen McBride is Professor and Canada Research Chair in Public Policy and Globalization in the Department of Political Science at McMaster University, Canada. He has published widely on issues of political economy and public policy. His most recent book, co-authored with H. Whiteside and B. Evans, is *Varieties of Austerity* (Bristol University Press, 2021).

Moritz Neujeffski is Research Fellow at the Center for Civil Society Research (WZB-Berlin Social Science Center). Previously Moritz was Project Manager at the School of Data Germany, on an educational project by Open Knowledge Foundation Germany. He has worked in the Inequality and Social Policy unit, and from July 2017 to September 2018 in the President's Research Group as Research Assistant. He studied Public Policy and Human Development (MSc) and European Studies (BA) at Maastricht University.

Dieter Plehwe is Senior Research Fellow at the Center for Civil Society Research (WZB-Berlin Social Science Center). His research interests focus on transnational varieties of capitalism, regional integration, internationalization of corporations, industrial relations, cultural political economy and studies of neoliberalism. Publications of note include *Austerity: 12 Myths Exposed* (ed. with M. Neujeffski and S. McBride) and *Liberalism and the Welfare State: Economists and Arguments for the Welfare State* (ed. with R.E. Backhouse, B.W. Bateman and T. Nishizawa).

Chandrima Roy is a Lecturer in Work, Employment and Organisation Studies in the University of Leicester School of Business, University of Leicester. She has a growing research interest in exploring work and employment in the UK social care sector in the context of social care reform activities, and increased social and political attention paid to this area. One of her recent publications informs the urgently needed rethink on job quality in social care. Her research interests also lie in examining work and employment in a digitally globalized world where production and services are increasingly coordinated across countries and firms.

Ingo Schmidt is Academic Coordinator of Labour Studies at the Centre for Interdisciplinary Studies, Athabasca University. His research interests focus on trade unions in Germany, European integration and international political economy. One of his recent publications is a book on comparative neoliberal policies across a selection of countries in the global North and South, and he is currently working on a comparative analysis of Third Way social democracy.

Joy Schnittker is a PhD student in Political Science at McMaster University. Her research interests include exploring the debates surrounding public versus private service delivery, and alternatives to privatization. Her doctoral research focuses on the re-municipalization process, and its potential as a democratic alternative to privatization and the free market system.

John Shields is Professor in the Department of Politics and Public Administration at Ryerson University. He has published extensively in the areas of immigration, the non-profit sector and public policy. His most recent books are *Immigrant Experiences in North America* (ed. with H. Bauder, 2015) and *Precarious Employment: Causes, Consequences and Remedies* (ed. with S. Procyk and W. Lewchuk, 2017). With Zainab Abu Alrob, he has recently published a major research report, 'COVID-19, Migration and the Canadian Immigration System: Dimensions,

Impact and Resilience' (July 2020), for the SSHRC Partnership Grant, Building Migrant Resilience in Cities (BMRC).

Christoph Sorg is a critical political economist and social movement scholar currently based at Ruhr-University Bochum. Prior to this he completed his PhD at Humboldt University, Berlin on social movements against debt, and spent a year as a post-doc at New York University to study the interrelations of capitalism and social movements. His research focuses on debt, work, global value chains and contentious politics. He is currently finishing an open-access book with Amsterdam University Press, tentatively titled *Social Movements and the Politics of Debt: Contentious Debt Politics on Three Continents.*

Jim Stanford is Economist and Director of the Centre for Future Work. He divides his time between Vancouver, Canada, and Sydney, Australia. He is also the Harold Innis Industry Professor in Economics at McMaster University, Canada, and an Honorary Professor in the Department of Political Economy at the University of Sydney.

Hans-Jürgen Urban is a member of the IG Metall Executive Committee in Frankfurt/Main, responsible for the fields of social, qualification and labour policy. He also teaches as a private lecturer at the Institute for Sociology, Friedrich Schiller University Jena, where he is a Permanent Fellow at the Research Group on Post-Growth Societies. Urban is co-editor of the journal *Blätter für Deutsche und Internationale Politik*. His research and publications cover a wide range of topics, including the theory of capitalism, political economy of the welfare state, union revitalization, labour policy and European integration.

James Watson completed his PhD in Sociology from McMaster University in 2020. His research interests include political sociology and social movements, and studies of work and occupations. He is currently an advisor on Public and Post-secondary Policy at New Brunswick Community College.

Heather Whiteside is Associate Professor of Political Science at the University of Waterloo and Fellow at the Balsillie School of International Affairs, Canada. Her research on the political economy of privatization, financialization and austerity has been published in journals such as *Review of International Political Economy*, *Economic Geography*, *Environment and Planning A* and *Studies in Political Economy*, and she is the author of several books including *Purchase for Profit* (2015), *Canadian Political Economy* (2020), *Capitalist Political Economy* (2020) and *Varieties of Austerity* (with S. McBride and B.M. Evans, 2021).

Acknowledgements

This volume is one product of a Canadian Social Sciences and Humanities Research Council (SSHRC) Partnership Development Grant (file number 890-2015-0025) entitled: 'Austerity and its alternatives'.

The project (Principal Investigator Stephen McBride) brought together 16 academic and community-based researchers and involved seven universities and community partners/collaborators.

Ideas and research were exchanged at a number of workshops or conferences held in Hamilton, Ottawa and Berlin. We would like to thank all participants in what turned out to be a stimulating and productive research partnership. A number of chapters in the present volume were presented in draft form at the conference 'Austerity: Coping Is Not Enough' held in Berlin, 21–22 February 2019. For hosting and organizing this event we would like to particularly thank the Friedrich Ebert Stiftung (FES).

We would also like to thank Nour Afara for her assistance in managing the preparation of this book.

Introduction

Bryan Evans, Dieter Plehwe and Stephen McBride

On 21–22 February 2019, more than a hundred university and non-government organization-based researchers from across Europe, Canada and Australia gathered in Berlin to participate in the 'Austerity: Coping Is Not Enough' conference. The chapters collected in this volume emerge from this international event which was hosted by the German Social Democratic Party's think tank, the FES. The conference itself grew out of a collaboration between FES and Stephen McBride's 'Austerity and Its Alternatives' Canadian-based project funded by the Social Sciences and Humanities Research Council of Canada. The conference participants sought to move the study of post-2008 crisis austerity forward through both a rigorous diagnosis of actually existing austerity as well as imagining the pathways out of permanent austerity. Among the key questions the conference sought to address were: how do social and economic relations change under conditions of permanent austerity? How do international, national and regional political institutions influence the development of austerity-regimes? What commonalities and differences exist between nations? And which alternatives exist to overcome the status quo of austerity politics? To analyze the causes, connections and effects of this new age of austerity-capitalism, a broad debate that questions the core ideas and dominant paradigms that animated politics, explores political alternatives and develops new and far-reaching perspectives is necessary to move beyond the contemporary stasis of coping. And coping is demonstrably not enough. The project of this book is to contribute to moving on.

In the wake of the 2008 crisis, as the 'clean-up' rolled out, critics of market liberalization, globalization and financialization saw their initial expectations dashed. Initial optimism was understandable, encouraged as it was by a rapid revival of the largely dormant 'institutional legacy of Keynesianism' (Strange 2012, 121) by governments and central banks, and doing so regardless of partisan hue. Such a coherent and broad response was seen to herald 'the end of the Reagan-Thatcher counter-revolution', nothing less than the demise of the era of neoliberalism (Collignon 2008, 8). It was a profoundly erroneous reading of the historical moment. Instead of witnessing the unravelling of a paradigm, it became an abject lesson in the stickiness of an established social order where neoliberalism, post-crisis, remained very nearly entirely intact, has even been solidified (Crouch 2011, 179; Mirowski 2013). The only way to understand this political and ideational resolve is to bring the mobilization and unity of the ruling class into perspective. The apparent equilibrium was sustained through a 'strategy of class war undertaken by the financial and political elite to hold on to the wealth and power they accumulated during the decades of market liberalism' (Quiggin 2010, 233). A brief period of stimulus packages alongside unprecedented monetary liquidity provided by the Fed in the United States and channelled to allied Central Banks in many countries turned out to stabilize the global economy (Tooze 2018). But Keynesian spending programmes were then followed by an aggressive rollback, or fiscal consolidation. Despite broad social protest, in some cases leading to electoral realignments of both the Left and Right, the crisis-ridden states in Europe and beyond returned to the primacy of balanced budgets and debt reduction. Internal competitive austerity subordinated social concerns as the orthodoxies of fiscal conservatism and consolidation imposed an austere discipline upon the range of acceptable policy alternatives. Consequences moved well beyond only a correction in the expenditure side of public finance. The provision of public goods and services, the component functions of the post-1945 welfare state, underwent processes of privatization and financialization. The end result exacerbated already existing inequalities within and between regions, states and classes, thus setting in motion a new political crisis, a crisis challenging the very legitimacy of the liberal democratic order. Right-wing populist parties have as a consequence won considerable electoral support across and beyond the European Union, and have in several cases entered into government. Their influence, whether in government or from the streets, has been felt in many different aspects of state policy. A new emphasis has been placed pursuing nationalist and hence exclusive policies which undermine international (European) solidarity, and they have made ultra-conservative attitudes including explicit racism socially acceptable. At the same time, anti-immigration policies in some European countries have now become normalized or, at best, nearly so. Solidarity must be considered under siege both nationally and internationally.

But it is the 'stickiness' of the neoliberal paradigm, as noted, which has been cause for both frustration and intrigue. In public policy studies and economics, paradigm change is explained by, among other approaches, the punctuated equilibrium model. In abbreviated form, this 'theory' poses that long periods of stability are disrupted (punctuated) at critical junctures by formative events which may take various forms – 'wars, depressions, deep recessions, or natural disasters' – and these 'give leaders the opportunity to turn policies, and sometimes polities, in new directions' (Bermeo and Pontusson 2012, 1). The blunt conclusion respecting the 2008 crisis is that 'it is the ruling classes, not the labour movements, that have seized the crisis as an opportunity' (Panitch et al 2010, x). A victory achieved despite the popular discrediting of the prior three decades of neoliberal restructuring. The Occupy movement came and went, still indelibly leaving the heuristic stamp of the '1 percent' as a political meme for the deep inequality characterizing the American landscape, and one which relayed an understanding of an elite unabatedly in pursuit of dispossession. The economic crisis had failed to spark a political crisis of sufficient breadth to transform let alone topple the cracked edifice of neoliberalism. In other words, the crisis *in* neoliberalism, in that moment, was not pushed into becoming a crisis *of* neoliberalism (Saad-Filho 2010). The financial crash of the 1930s created a crisis in economic orthodoxy and of the prevailing political order resulting in a transformation in economic thought and correspondingly in state policy. Indeed the entire post-war order, the welfare state and the political consensus, specifically the labour-capital compromise upon which that compromise was based, marked a rupture ideologically and politically with laissez-faire capitalism. The great crisis of the 1970s, the crisis of 'Fordism' (Aglietta 1979) likewise marked a rupture with Keynesian approaches like the inflation unemployment trade-off and the expanded welfare state. Stagflation and the fiscal crisis of the state ushered in monetarism and supply side economics and the era of neoliberal transformation of the welfare state into competition states at large. And yet after 2008, no such reconsideration occurred (Mirowski 2013, 2). Keynes himself understood the challenge facing him was not the complexity of his ideas but rather 'escaping from the old ones' which had the status of common sense (Keynes 1936, 4).

Paradoxically, the 'present period is one of economic turbulence but ideological stability. Despite the scale of the 2008 financial crash, there has not been' a similar fundamental reconsideration of the prevailing economic policy orthodoxy (Gamble 2013, 53). Indeed, quite the opposite occurred where, post-crisis, neoliberal ideas appear to be as or more deeply embedded. Understanding this seemingly inexplicable continuity is the task here. The keys to understanding this resiliency move beyond the impasse of 'zombie ideas' (Krugman 2009; Quiggin 2010, 1) and are situated historically in the class struggles of the 1960s and 1970s. In the following section we briefly review the history of structural crises of capitalism in the 20th century. The purpose of doing so is to illustrate, in rather stark terms, the distinctly different political impact and responses observed in each case and the consequent role of each crisis in shaping class relations and politics.

End of the post-war Golden Age

Each of the two major structural crises of 20th-century capitalism, the Great Depression of the 1930s, and the state fiscal and corporate profitability crisis of the 1970s, ended with a profound paradigm shift in political, economic and social terms. The first structural crisis of the 21st century, the Great Financial Crisis of 2008, saw nothing comparable notwithstanding ample demonstrations of resistance. The question is why? What was at play in the 1970s which was not in years following 2008?

The period 1945–1975, the alleged Golden Age of Capitalism or the 'trente glorieuses' (Fourastie 1979), was an unprecedented era in the history of capitalism where working class-based demands for re-distributional public policies, trade union rights among other labour protections, the de-commodification of various goods and services in whole or in part by the state, and regulation of markets, became defining features of the post-war welfare state. By the late 1960s and into the 1970s, amid renewed working class militancy and mobilization, expressed in the streets and at the ballot box, began to undermine profits and capital accumulate profits (Notermans 2000; Harvey 2005). The confidence derived from employment security fueled greater militancy which led to a sharp rise in money wages. Rising wages increased inflationary pressures and shrunk profits. And later, the downward pressure on profit rates would only increase as international competition became more intense. Second, Bretton Woods was undermined by a shrinking productivity gap between the United States and its key European and Japanese competitors and ultimately pushing the US into a trade deficit and inflation but particularly the rapidly rising price of oil. And third, declining labour productivity which became particularly acute after 1973 (Glyn 2007). The abandonment of fixed exchange rates in 1973 drove an explosion of activity on international currency markets, undermining government capacities to influence exchange rates.

With growth slowing, the system went into crisis; however, the Keynesian social and economic order did not collapse immediately. A shift in politics and a re-composition of the state began to unfold (Stewart and Walsh 1992). The transition from the Keynesian to neoliberal order was a project in building a different kind of state where 'the goal is no longer to protect society from the market's demands but to protect the market from society's demands' (Cohn 1997, 586). In this environment, the new right, offering an intellectually forceful critique of the Keynesian welfare state, became ascendant. New right parties arrived in office with a commitment to 'rolling back the state' through 'a major change in the dominant macro-economic paradigm from Keynesianism to monetarism and neoliberalism' (Müller and Wright 1994, 1).

The political stability of the neoliberal variant of capitalism was remarkable. That was until the 2008 financial crisis. In rapid response to an unfolding global economic catastrophe, both governments and central banks moved to intervene with an array of tools – from nationalizations to quantitative easing to bank bailouts – the world was turned upside down (Tooze 2018). The entire neoliberal project appeared to be dead. In reality it had only been suspended, and that truth became evident once governments turned to restore the status quo ante through austerity very much in line with the advocates of neoliberal renewal (Plehwe 2017). There was nothing novel about austerity in general as it was a central feature of neoliberal state policy. What was different was the severity of the post-crisis fiscal consolidation agenda and the political response this engendered. A new politics and movements of both Left and Right, sharing only a departure from post-war consensus of the centre-Right and centre-Left, sprung from this lived experience. Would a Corbyn or a Sanders ever have found the traction, however brief, if not for this historic foment? Would 'populism' have become so overworked in mainstream punditry? Likely not. While the various shades of resistance in the history of neoliberalism are more pronounced and organized than has been the case in several decades, the ease with which the restoration of the neoliberal order took place is best understood by situating the 2008 crisis as an episode in the continuity and adaptation, rather than rupture, of neoliberalism (Plehwe et al 2020).

What distinguished 2008 from other structural crises of capitalism is that 2008 was not caused by a profit squeeze or a collapse in investment from over-accumulation. Instead, its roots lay in the growing importance of US mortgage finance, which 'cannot be understood apart from the vital role of the state and the effects of the erosion of working-class strength' (Panitch and Gindin 2010, 12). The US state's longstanding promotion of home ownership combined with the stagnation of working-class incomes and the erosion of social programmes reinforced workers' dependence on the rising value of their homes. Home ownership became not a place to live but a private pension programme and savings account. When the bubble burst working-class wealth declined, undermining consumer spending. Importantly, working-class weakness, driven by the neoliberal assault on workers and unions, contributed to the crisis, unlike previous crises which partly stemmed from working-class power. Thus a clear line can be drawn from the defeat of trade unions in the 1970s and 1980s which restored profitability in part through growing consumer debt (Panitch and Gindin 2010). In the US, the rate of profit had been declining for 35 years before stabilizing in the 1980s. This stabilization occurred for two reasons. First, it was a product of the assaults on labour initiated during the Reagan presidency. This 'political' victory served to delink wage growth from increases in productivity, channeling an increasing share to capital. And second, the sharp fall in the interest rate after 1982. The low interest rate spurred borrowing, and debt burdens grew. With incomes stagnating, households were offered cheap debt to maintain consumer spending; household debt to income ratios grew dramatically. By the 1990s, debt-service began to rise, ultimately cresting at historic highs immediately before the crisis in 2007 (Shaikh 2010).

Under neoliberalism profits grew faster than wages. With wages and state spending restrained, economic expansion, profitability and capital accumulation could only be enabled through borrowing (Streeck 2017). By the early 2000s, the gap between profits and wages was so significant that consumption could only be maintained by borrowing, and one key expression of this being the housing bubble which ignited the crisis. Enter the deregulated financial sector where huge profits were rendered by lending to those with low income through subprime mortgages, demand for which was fueled by stagnating incomes (Kotz 2009, 312–13). An expansion dependent on continuous expansion of household debt was unsustainable, a crisis was inevitable once the housing bubble burst. As Canadian political economist Sam Gindin described: 'each crisis modifies the trajectory of history, the subsequent crisis occurs in a changed context and so has its own distinct features … Like the previous crisis, the 2008–09 crisis yielded more neoliberal financialization, but this time it also opened the doors to right wing populism alongside an acute disorientation of traditional political parties'. (Gindin 2020). And hence the crisis informed multiple crises.

The balance of class power was fundamentally altered through the 1970s and into the 1980s. Through 2008 and after, the political capacity of the working class to engage in even defensive battles was generally modest though with certain exceptions. In the years following 2008, the distinction between structural and conjunctural crises appears to have become blurred if not disappeared with the onset of multiple crises which are not at their point of origin economic or political. Though the implications are fundamentally concerned with the economy and political responses. The climate crisis/catastrophe and the COVID-19 global pandemic are cases in point. Such crises, while not essentially structural, ultimately bring to the fore tensions, fault lines, respecting structure and future trajectories.

The multiple crisis: the 21st century's accumulating fault lines

Crises are not aberrations but are rather endemic to capitalism. In the history of modern capitalism four significant structural crises have taken place. The 'first great depression' of the late 19th century; the 'Great Depression' of the 1930s; the 'stagflation' of the 1970s; and, of course, the 2008 'Great Financial Crisis' (Panitch and Gindin 2010, 5). Efforts to construct a general theory of capitalist crisis are problematic given the multiple potential sources where in 'one particular historical moment conditions may lead to one kind of crisis dominating, but on other occasions several forms can combine and on still others the crisis tendencies get displaced spatially … or temporally' (Harvey 2008, 25). And to further add complexity to the problem of understanding crises, the early 21st century grapples with multiple crises running historically parallel – in fact interrelated crises of the economy, climate, politics, and with COVID-19, of public health. While qualitatively distinct, each flows from or is alternatively enabled or constrained by the features of neoliberal capitalism and the neoliberal state. Employed by Walden Bello in 2004 to capture the inundation of system stressors, he took up what he saw as a rapid collapse of globalization 'triumphalism' in the 1990s, a collapse originating with the Asian financial crisis of 1997, the anti-WTO protests in Seattle in 1999 (The Battle of Seattle) and the collapse of the dot-com/Clinton boom (Bello 2004, xi–xvi). Taken together, the result is a 'crisis of legitimacy that is affecting the system of global capitalism' the most salient indication of which was the growth of the anti-globalization movement and the protests that cropped up at the meetings of multilateral organizations around the world (Bello 2004, 1). Several 'intersecting crises' are different dimensions of this broader crisis in the globalization project including multilateralism, the neoliberal order, the system of military hegemony, liberal democracy and the global production system, all of which compose the foundation for system destabilization.

Several years later, and in the aftermath of the 2008 crisis, a 2009 policy statement issued by the United Nations Environment Programme (UNEP) used the term 'multiple crises' to collect under a single rubric a broad array of global threats. Succinctly identified were several concurrent crises including: the most severe recession since the Great Depression, with unemployment levels at 50 million; severe economic inequality both within and between countries; climate change, a threat to which the world's most impoverished were particularly vulnerable; a fuel crisis threatening the ability of developing countries to afford oil imports; a food crisis wherein rising grain prices had cost developing countries the equivalent of three years of global aid (US$324 billion); the erosion of biodiversity with severe consequences for agricultural productivity in a context of rapid population growth; and a water crisis, in which one in five people in the developing world lacked access to clean water (UNEP 2009, 2). Importantly, the UNEP statement attributed these multiple crises to a common source: 'the gross misallocation of capital' (UNEP 2009, 3). In other words, more than market or government failure, these crises reflected the inadequacy of the liberalized global system of capitalism to be attentive to basic needs. While in the previous two decades significant volumes of capital had flowed into real estate, oil and gas, and complex financial assets while very little had been invested in renewable energy, public transit, sustainable agriculture and land and water conservation. In other words, capital had other interests which did not coincide with socially and environmentally sustainable development. And in a similar application of the concept of 'multiple crisis' François Houtart suggested that 'the crisis' was in fact 'a combination of various crises, which are all the fruit of capitalist logic' (2010, 10). He points to four crises in particular: the financial crisis, the food crisis, the energy crisis and the ecological crisis. Houtart describes the characteristics of the climate crisis as follows: the drastic acceleration of CO_2 emissions since the 1970s; the impact of rising sea-levels on low-lying countries and cities; the Earth's diminishing capacity to regenerate the biosphere; the potential for mass extinctions; and the likely uninhabitability of certain regions and the consequent mass migration of climate refugees. Houtart suggests that, like the other dimensions of the multiple crisis, the climate crisis is a product of capitalist logic: 'considering nature as a resource for capitalist growth, and refusing to integrate into the balance sheet the externalities of the productive system' (2010, 12). Although neoliberal economists have developed economic instruments to attempt internalization of 'external costs' since the 1970s, economic policy instrument debates advocating elegant schemes (emissions trading) have been frequently used to block precautionary and time-tested effective approaches to environmental and climate change-related problems. Neoliberal concepts that continue to drive financialization and intensify exploitation of labour and nature so far have not been able to contribute much to tackle ecological crisis. Multiple crisis of contemporary capitalism therefore translates more and more into multiple and interrelated crisis of neoliberalism.

The contribution of the multiple crisis/crises concept is that it speaks to the points of rupture or disruption, of punctuated equilibrium as the policy studies scholars call it, dotting the history of modern capitalism. Each capitalist crisis can share certain structural commonalities with other crises while possessing unique qualities and, of course, responses. As noted earlier, the 2008 crisis drew recurring comparisons to the 1930s: 'Now, as then, a relentless push to extend and de-regulate markets is every-where wreaking havoc … Now, as then, attempts to commodify nature, labour and money are destabilizing society and economy … Now, as then, the result is a crisis in multiple dimensions – not only economic and financial, but also ecological and social' (Fraser 2013, 119). However, as for 2008, the very non-Polanyian political dynamic of the struggle is explained as one where the popular opposition 'fails to coalesce around a solidaristic alternative' (Fraser 2013, 121). The COVID-19 crisis of 2020, while of an entirely different order, a crisis of public health, made clear to all what four decades of neoliberal capitalism and the consequent dismantling of key components of the post-1945 order meant in terms of social protection, and the world was reminded that 'political regulation was needed to save it' (Fraser 2013, 120). The controversies around the pandemic's merciless revelation of the status of public health infrastructures after decades of austerity capitalism and the sudden visibility of the fragility of globalized neoliberal capitalism at large at the same time help to anticipate alternative scenarios: a) another return to the status quo ante crisis, b) selective escape from the prerogatives of austerity capitalism mainly in the areas of immediate concern for public health and c) more comprehensive departures from what then could finally be understood as late austerity capitalism and post-neoliberalism.

The 'new times' of COVID-19

Conceptually, multiple crisis/crises enables us to think of the 2008 global financial crisis and 2020 pandemic as episodes in a series of crises which have been, each in its own manner, endemic to capitalist development. The aggravation of the various crises related to global warming, sea-level rise, intensification of extreme weather events, heatwaves and draughts like the recent phenomenon in Siberia seem to be conjunctural and yet cannot be understood without considering structural parameters of energy production and consumption in the now unified system of globalized capitalism. Looking at the intersections of the various elements of the multiple crisis clarifies both the enormous challenges ahead and the reason why just coping and selective dealing with any of the elements will not be enough to address the challenges. The pandemic and related economic crisis arguably have clarified the linkages between crises more in the public mind than the global financial crisis, for example. However, it is still not certain if previous strategies of defending the pre-crisis status quo will succeed again, limiting response to the bare minimum and engaging in blame games such as talking about 'the China virus'. It is also not certain that the pandemic-related economic crisis will be used to water down climate change-related policies as something 'we can no longer afford'. But let us first take a closer look at COVID-19-related strategies before coming up with three ideal type scenarios designed to strengthen analytic capacities in the coming controversies and battles, both at the level of policymaking and in the realm of ideas. The unexpected bursting of COVID-19 onto the global stage in the winter of 2020 and the ensuing pandemic clearly added one more dimension to consider, since previous pandemics remained confined to regions or did not lead to the breakdown of international travel and trade (Davis 2005). While a public health crisis, the implications for economies, workers and public finance are immense. In previous structural crises, notably the Great Depression and 2008, states intervened to re-float failing economies. It was the markets which had failed.

But COVID-19 presented an entirely different and unprecedented problem. Rather than inject new stimulus into anemic economies the task was to suspend much of the social activity necessary to routine economic function by inducing a state directed coma upon such activity to minimize the spread of the virus. Political leaders now shared platforms not with finance ministers and central bankers but with senior public health officials. The central place of protecting health in this particular version of crisis management rather than capital held other and previously unimaginable political and ideological implications. Both the official state response to COVID-19 as well as that of tens of millions of working people has pulled back the curtain to offer a glimpse of an alternative (Harvey 2020). Before the significance of the COVID-19 virus was understood, austerity was still the rule. But once the threat this virus represented was grasped, governments of every partisan hue 'magically found a way to pay for all kinds of programs and supports written off as impossible before. The sky, it seems, is the limit' (Gindin 2020). The resources to meet what was needed were released. Not for emancipation of course but to ensure that the basic structures of capitalism could be kept in place. Regardless, the curtain had been pulled back, if only slightly. The desire to go back to 'normal' was met with reconsideration of that normal because normal was the problem all along (Prashad 2020). Wage subsidies to employers and income support payments to workers raises the question: 'Is there some way to organize the production of basic goods and services so that everybody has something to eat, everybody has a decent place to live, and we can put a moratorium on evictions, and everybody can live rent free? Isn't this moment one where we could actually think seriously about the creation of an alternative society?' (Harvey 2020).

And a further glimpse of that alternative could be seen a small way in expressions of gratitude to ordinary workers. The social value hierarchy of capitalism, dominated by the celebrities of Silicon Valley, the financial magicians of New York, London, Frankfurt, Tokyo and beyond, the all-stars of professional sports and every other manner of mass entertainment, suddenly were not as 'essential' as we thought. Instead a new cast of folk heroes stepped onto the stage. Genuinely essential workers. These included health professionals of course, not just doctors but also nurses and lab technicians. In addition, less glamourous but still essential, cleaners, who wiped down every floor and surface of not just hospitals but of office towers; grocery clerks who stocked and re-stocked shelves with food items and other necessities; truck drivers who kept the supply chain functioning; and restaurant kitchen workers who continued to provide takeaway. And most of these essential workers are low-paid. And yet these invisible workers were now characterized as 'heroes'. Their contributions, unacknowledged just a short time ago, were now saluted every evening from the apartment balconies of the quarantined in cities as far removed as Toronto, Barcelona, Rome and so many more. And beyond this re-ordering of status and gratitude, something else was taking place. Cracks were appearing, at least ideationally, in the elite neoliberal consensus.

France's president Emmanuel Macron, the pre-eminent champion for free market liberalism within the European Union, pre-COVID-19 had his hands full dealing with the *gilets jaunes* (yellow vests) and workers in the street protesting his pension reforms. But in the midst of COVID-19, Macron declared 'free healthcare … and our welfare state are precious resources, indispensable advantages when destiny strikes' (Gindin 2020). And in a striking statement, the editorial board of nothing less than the *Financial Times*, appear to renounce everything President Reagan and all who followed put in place. Rather than a call for balance or pause, they call for 'radical reforms' which would achieve nothing less than 'reversing the prevailing policy direction of the last four decades' which would be replaced by what reads like a post-1945 social democratic programme where governments 'will have to accept a more active role in the economy. They must see public services as investments rather than liabilities, and look for ways to make labour markets less insecure. Redistribution will again be on the agenda; the privileges of the elderly and wealthy in question. Policies until recently considered eccentric, such as basic income and wealth taxes, will have to be in the mix' (Editorial Board, *Financial Times* 2020). To rebuild an American, European or indeed global 'common purpose' will require nothing less than such a new social contract. Andrew Yang, American entrepreneur and in 2020 a candidate for the Democratic presidential nomination, proposed that recovery from COVID-19 would require nothing less than a 'national rebuilding project at a scale that has never existed in our lifetimes' and the 'biggest battle in politics now is over who will control that project, and whom it will prioritize' (Goldberg 2020). In Europe, a recovery fund has been crafted on top of national programmes. An unprecedented amount of 750 billion Euro will be arranged, enabling a significant European strategy to rebuild following the damages caused by lockdowns in Europe and elsewhere. Although the original plan has been watered down somewhat by a group of countries ill-termed the frugal four (the Netherlands, Austria, Sweden and Denmark), the package is unprecedented both in substance and in form, a break with the dogma of restrained European public finance. The EU will be eligible to own sources of funding and the programme establishes a scheme of fiscal transfers way beyond traditional cohesion politics (relying on agricultural, structural and regional funds). While subject to ongoing controversy with regard to conditionality and democracy aspects (lack of European Parliament oversight, compare Guttenberg and Nguyen 2020), many observers consider the Recovery Fund and the changes to the medium-term budget plan significant steps towards a European federal state.

At the national level, the COVID-19 reactions likewise show significant departures from orthodox public finance in the age of austerity. Countries in North America and Europe have allowed unprecedented monetary stimulus through Central Bank interventions (backed up by the Federal Reserve) and deficit rules long considered orthodoxies have been trashed. At the same time, the fiscal capacity of the individual countries is also telling of the differences resulting from more than a generation of austerity. Winners in the global division of labour – export champions and resource-rich countries like Germany – have mobilized larger amounts of fiscal assistance to combat the economic fallout of lockdowns than was applied through the Great Financial Crisis and the subsequent recession.

And still others, less identified with the established neoliberal order, see in the pandemic recovery a historic opportunity not to go back to normal. Rhianna Gunn-Wright, director of the US think tank, the Roosevelt Institute, echoes the potential of the pandemic recovery to serve as a platform for paradigm shift. Crisis, such as that in the 1970s she says, can cause dominant beliefs about how the world works to lose currency: 'That moment opened up the space for the neoliberalism that we have now' (Goldberg 2020). Canadian economist Jim Stanford highlighted the example of the post-1945 Marshall Plan as one worthy of repeating in the post-pandemic rebuilding phase. In addition to 'massive fiscal injections' it will be necessary to draw upon other 'tools of direct economic management and regulation – including public service, public ownership and planning – to make it all happen' (Stanford 2020). And more explicitly, in terms of the United States, the policy agenda could be extended to include nationalization of major banks which could finance, at least in serious measure, a Green New Deal; introduce more stringent financial regulations; expand the unemployment insurance programme and establish Medicaid as a universal health care programme; public investment in physical and social infrastructure; and an industrial strategy for the auto sector based on the production of environmentally friendly cars (Henwood 2020). Amid the imagining of alternatives which the COVID-19 crisis has provided, there remains, as the lesson of 2008 suggests, the question of power. State deficits have increased to levels which only a short time ago would have been completely unacceptable outside of wartime. The public finances which enabled the rescue packages of 2008, as history teaches, were clawed back through austerity. It is open at this point if the pandemic crisis will lead to a revival of austerity under the pressure of financial markets and currency speculation. If social struggles to reclaim the public prevail to a greater or lesser extent, we may see some effort to reinvest in public health and the social infrastructure of the health and care sectors and some industries (such as meat packing), which demonstrated the particular vulnerability of the old, and to younger people with medical conditions and care as well as other workers in literally dangerous environments. A more profound redirection of economic and social development as expressed in high-flying plans such as a Green New Deal would require even stronger realignments of social and political forces, a surge in trade union organization and an unprecedented parallel mobilization of progressive alliances across many countries. For the time being we only know that enormous debt has been piled up, both financial debts incurred to fight the pandemic and the huge debt owed to the people, to social and public infrastructures of society neglected in the age of austerity.

Once the COVID-19 crisis subsides, those debts too will need to be reckoned with and 'choices will have to be made over who gets what; the questions of inequality and redistribution will … be intensified' (Gindin 2020). The struggles over that very question are not distant. Of course, the wealth of the global economic elite should be forced 'out of the offshore finance system and into taxable deposits and investments' (Mason 2020) but it will take more than the force of good argument to make that so. This volume explores many different angles in need of tackling to prevent another comeback of neoliberalism and austerity capitalism and a redirection of public purpose.

The chapters presented here composing *The Changing Politics and Policy of Austerity* provide a variety of approaches including national case studies, comparative perspectives, and theoretical interrogations of a specific political or economic phenomenon. All possess a polemical edge. They are organized into three distinct thematic parts. Part I is concerned with austerity-related policies and practices as a roll-out platform for private accumulation. Heather Whiteside (Chapter 1, Beyond austerity: pro-public strategies versus public-private partnership scandals) illuminates how the normalization of PPPs we have witnessed over the past decades ignores a long run, however scandalous a track record, of market monopolization by sometimes corrupt and inept private partners, and plagued by bankruptcies and bailouts. Whiteside demonstrates how PPPs serve as an instrument for national revenue extraction through private partner equity rights and offshoring practices. Alternatives to austerity require not only more spending, but also new types and sources of investment beyond private finance. How these dynamics are playing out in the context of the 2020 pandemic is explored.

Sebastian Botzem (Chapter 2, Institutionalizing austerity accounting in Europe: the implementation of European Public Sector Accounting Standards as crisis response) examines the role of public sector accounting standards in Europe. How these standards have been revised marks a shift towards an increasing influence of capital markets on public accounts. European Public Sector Accounting Standards (EPSAS) are being implemented to privilege the information needs of investors and capital providers. This provides a challenge to democratic accountability and is likely to intensify pressure for austerity politics in the future. The main actors engaged in bringing about this new managerial regime are state bureaucrats and statisticians together with accounting practitioners working in large auditing firms.

Part II shifts the focus to how austerian objectives and practices become embedded in an array of different policy fields. Steffen Lehndorff (Chapter 3, A fragile triangle: collective bargaining systems, trade unions and the state in the EU) profiles the EU's decade-long prioritization accorded to the weakening of collective bargaining systems. Based on the Stability and Growth Pact and its tightening in the course of the Eurozone crisis, decentralization and fragmentation of collective bargaining geared to promote labour cost-based competitiveness has become common standard in the 'country-specific recommendations' within the 'European Semester'. The chapter describes the different dynamics of collective bargaining systems in Spain, Italy and Greece over recent years and gives some tentative explanations for different outcomes, pointing primarily at contrasting trade union approaches. Against this background, the potential of the state at national and EU levels to act as a stabilizer, rather than a driver for weakening is taken up.

Next Donna Baines, Ian Cunningham, Philip James and Chandrima Roy (Chapter 4, Privatizing the sacrifice: individualized funding, austerity and precarity in the voluntary sector in Australia and Scotland) examine the provision of social care and specifically the conditions of social care work. This chapter explores austerity in relation to two major pieces of social policy recently introduced in Australia and Scotland, the National Disabilities Insurance Scheme (NDIS) and Personalisation Self-Directed Care. Claiming to promote human rights and consumer choice, both policies introduce cash-for-care packages that significantly changes programme delivery and work for service users, the female-majority workforce, and the organizations providing services. Consistent with austerity, the need for service outstrips supply, labour markets are being rapidly restructured to offer increasingly precarious and degraded employment, including the emergence of gig work in the Australia example, and service organizations in Scotland that are unable to remain solvent in the austerity-led funding regimes. Rather than protecting and empowering service users and workers, the government has instigated the further privatization of services, and the deepening of insecurity.

Continuing with the theme of reinventing social policy financing and delivery, Meghan Joy, John Shields, Sharon Broughton and Siu Mee Cheng (Chapter 5, Austerity and the social innovation agenda) provide a fascinating interrogation of 'social innovation'. Social innovation (SI) has been widely embraced as a pragmatic problem-solving approach to social policy challenges. While framed as apolitical, this chapter demonstrates that the dominant SI agenda, which became prominent in the wake of the 2008 crisis, is anything but. Instead, SI is illustrative of the ways in which the neoliberal project has adapted to its own crises, embracing policy ideas and processes needed to drive forward its agenda. This chapter explores the lineage of SI, including its amorphous definition, seemingly conflicting idea-sets, and associated tools and techniques to understand how it has been used to extend the neoliberal project. The authors warn against the dominant version of SI as a solution to social policy challenges in a post-pandemic era and encourage a more radical orientation towards the application of SI.

Part III moves the foregoing exploration of austerity in its many manifestations towards a consideration of real alternatives, at least as alternative possibilities if not yet alternative realities.

Stephen McBride and Joy Schnittker (Chapter 6, Politics as an alternative to constitutionalization) interrogate the impermeability of the neoliberal order. Political authority has been increasingly transferred from national to supranational or international levels, resulting in the depoliticization of certain economic issues by substituting application of neoliberal rules for normal politics. This process is termed 'constitutionalization' and is often associated with international integration which could be understood as either a framework for building cooperation and regulation (positive integration) or as a strategy of institution building and market enlargement (negative integration). Notwithstanding efforts to achieve positive integration, such as the European Social Model, the chapter concludes that the overall crisis-driven trajectory has been one of negative integration. Responses to the Global Financial Crisis (GFC) reinforced neoliberalism and though many hope that the EU's response to the pandemic will bring a change, the authors cast doubt on this optimism, arguing that the international road to replacing constitutionalism with democratic politics is unpromising. The road to more democracy may instead be through a less integrated international system with more autonomy at the national level.

Considering neoliberal impermeability from a different perspective, Dieter Plehwe and Moritz Neujeffski (Chapter 7, There could be alternatives! German economic advisory councils and the institutional reproduction of austerity economics) take up the manufacturing of policy ideas and their circulation within the policy advisory system. Economics has been considered the academic discipline most responsible for the lock-in of austerity doctrines in Germany. The authors make a strong case of hierarchy and bias in the economics profession and in the media. However, they also point to the existence of competing groups of politically relevant advisors and the diversity of economic research institutes in the country. To illustrate this proposition, they closely examine the members of four different advisory bodies in the fields of economic and social policy between 1998 and 2017. The results are not surprising where such bodies include few women, express an over-representation of individuals hailing from a small number of academic institutions and give expression to a strong bias in favour of austerity. Alternatives would in turn require modifications of advisory bodies, diversification of university chairs and the development of competitive progressive think tanks.

Bryan Evans, Stephen McBride and James Watson (Chapter 8, Negotiated austerity? A comparative survey of social concertation in Canada, Denmark, Ireland and Spain) are also interested in mechanisms where competing interests and perspectives can engage. Their chapter charts the impact of austerity on social concertation. These arrangements varied considerably between states, and were variously interpreted as providing a real voice for labour or, alternatively, representing a means by which labour might be managed and controlled. Considered as a means of expressing labour influence on policy, social dialogue or partnership has not fared well in the period of austerity. In quite diverse contexts – Canada, Ireland, Spain and Denmark – notwithstanding national differences, social concertation mechanisms have been bypassed, effectively abolished or, where they remain, reduced in scope and significance. Whatever its limitations in the past, this avenue for expressing labour's voice on policy issues is even less effective than formerly.

The resurgence of populism as a political response to austerity is taken up by Ingo Schmidt (Chapter 9, Market populism, its right-wing offspring and left alternatives). For Schmidt, populism is presented as an antithesis to liberalism, without differentiating between right- and left-wing populisms on the one hand and between liberal democracy and economic liberalism on the other. This chapter challenges such views by (1) demonstrating that economic liberalism was successfully translated into market populism that gained popular support during the economic and legitimation crises of welfare capitalism, (2) tracing the rise of right-wing populism to the failure of market populism to deliver on its promises and (3) discussing the question why the left doesn't gain more support in the face of the unpopularity of economic liberalism and widespread rejection of the new right. To explain these developments, Schmidt presents a model explaining why liberal, left-wing and right-wing ideas gain enough popularity so that historical blocs can coalesce around them but also why the same ideas fall out of favour, lead to the fracturing of existing historical blocs and create opportunities for the making of new blocs around new ideas.

Remaining on the theme of populism, but through a different analytical lens, Hans-Jürgen Bieling (Chapter 10, Austerity-induced populism: the rise and transformation of the new right) contests the academic focus, the cultural dimensions and causes of right-wing populism. In place of this, Bieling instead builds on approaches which place political economic factors at the centre and highlights the impact of the European austerity agenda post-crisis. The key contention is that austerity has stimulated not only the move towards right-wing populist parties, but also initiated their programmatic and strategic reorientation, above all in the areas of economic and social policy. So far, however, this reorientation has been disparate, selective and contradictory. This reflects the specific features of given models of capitalism and domestic political cultures as well as the particular balancing of contradictions between the bourgeois self-image of the party and the social claims of large parts of the electorate.

Anti-austerity social movements are the focus of Christoph Sorg (Chapter 11, Reducing the burden: international struggles against illegitimate debt). Austerity measures have faced one of the biggest and most dynamic waves of protest in recent decades. While a pluralism of issues converged in the occupied squares of 2011, such as stagnating wages, housing rights, political corruption and more, debt constituted one of the pivotal themes of claim-making. From the sudden contraction of financial markets precipitating household debt traps, bankruptcies and evictions, to the devastating effects of austerity justified by sovereign debt crises, the issue of debt reflected larger questions of democratic decision-making and economic life. This brief chapter aims to situate debt-centred movements and the issue of debt within more and less recent anti-austerity struggles. These movements challenge the neoliberal notion that all 'debts have to be paid' and additionally blame creditors as well as rules privileging creditors for existing debt burden instead of supposed failures by debtors. By way of observing actually existing movements and their practices we can also get a better view of existing alternatives to austerity and neoliberal debt politics in different countries.

What is to be done seems to be the abiding question of our time, and in this respect Jim Stanford (Chapter 12, The crisis next time: the GFC and the continuing fragility of capitalism) provides an analysis of the current context and identifies a political and policy platform to move beyond the impasse. A decade after the GFC of 2008–09, most Organisation for Economic Co-operation and Development (OECD) economies had still not regained normal economic and labour market conditions. Now the COVID-19 pandemic has thrown the global economy into the worst crisis since the Great Depression. The advanced capitalist economies enter this crisis in an economically and politically precarious state: financial leverage and instability, fiscal imbalances, constraints on monetary policy, and household financial fragility are all worse than in 2008–09. Perhaps most worryingly, the legitimacy and effectiveness of democratic institutions and processes have been battered by a decade of hardship, polarization and populism. In this worrying context, progressive movements must develop and fight for a response to this latest crisis that will strengthen popular economic and political capacities, instead of merely rescuing a battered, financialized regime.

With a focus on Europe, Hans-Jürgen Urban and Sebastian Kramer (Chapter 13, Austerity after COVID-19: from emergency pragmatism to inclusive economic governance in Europe) pursue imagining what a practical alternative might be achieved. Their central proposition is that the process of European integration needs to be directed towards a fundamentally new path if the EU wants to surmount the economic, social and environmental problems it is facing. On the one hand, this necessity emanates from the legacy of the damage caused by the EU's austerity and structural adjustment policies. At the same time, it is indispensable, because the growth model prevailing in the EU is reaching its social and environmental limits and has become a real obstacle to sustainable prosperity. What is needed is a transition to a mode of economic governance that not only opens up scope to overcome austerity and structural reform policies, but which also offers a functional framework for the indispensable social-ecological transformation of the economy. Such an objective calls for inclusive economic governance, which, in overcoming the austerity regime, combines environmental, social as well as democratic policy objectives.

And finally, editors Stephen McBride, Dieter Plehwe and Bryan Evans present a Conclusion that draws out the lessons from the previous chapters in terms of the imperatives of going beyond coping with austerity.

References

Aglietta, Michel. 1979. A Theory of Capitalist Regulation: The US Experience. London: Verso.

Bello, Walden. 2004. *Deglobalization: Ideas for a New World Economy*. Halifax: Fernwood Publishing Ltd.

Bermeo, Nancy and Jonas Pontusson. 2012. *Coping with Crisis*. New York: Russell Sage Foundation.

Cohn, Daniel. 1997. 'Creating Crises and Avoiding Blame: The Politics of Public Service Reform and the New Public Management in Great Britain and the United States', *Administration and Society*, 29(5): 584–616.

Collignon, Stefan. 2008. 'The Dawn of a New Era: Social Democracy after the Financial Crisis', *Social Europe*, 4(1): 9–13.

Crouch, Colin. 2011. *The Strange Non-Death of Neoliberalism*. Cambridge UK: Policy Press.

Davis, Mike. 2005. The Monster at our Door: The Global Threat of Avian Flu. New York: New Press.

Editorial Board, *Financial Times*. 2020. 'Virus Lays Bare the Frailty of the Social Contract', *Financial Times*, 3 April. www.ft.com/content/7eff769a-74dd-11ea-95fe-fcd274e920ca

Fourastie, Jean. 1979. *Les Trente Glorieuses, ou la révolution invisible de 1946 à 1975*. Paris: Fayard.

Fraser, Nancy. 2013. 'A Triple Movement? Parsing the Politics of the Crisis After Polanyi', *New Left Review*, 81: 119–32.

Gamble, Andrew. 2013. 'Neo-liberalism and Fiscal Conservatism', in V. Schmidt and M. Thatcher (eds) *Resilient Liberalism in Europe's Political Economy*. Cambridge: Cambridge University Press.

Gindin, Sam. 2020. 'The Coronavirus and the Crisis This Time', *The Bullet*, 10 April. https://socialistproject.ca/2020/04/coronavirus-and-the-crisis-this-time/

Glyn, Andrew. 2007. *Capitalism Unleashed: Finance, Globalization and Welfare*. Oxford: Oxford University Press.

Goldberg, Michelle. 2020. 'The New Great Depression Is Coming. Will There Be a New New Deal?' *The New York Times*, 2 May.

Guttenberg, Lucas and Thu Nguyen. 2020. 'How To Spend It Right. A More Democratic Governance for the EU Recovery and Resilience Facility'. Herie School Jaques Delors Centre and Bertelsmann Stiftung Policy Brief, 11 June 2020. https://hertieschool-f4e6.kxcdn.com/fileadmin/2_Research/1_About_our_research/2_Research_centres/6_Jacques_Delors_Centre/Publications/20200610_How_to_spend_it_right_Guttenberg_Nguyen.pdf. Last accessed 14 August 2020.

Harvey, David. 2005. *A Brief History of Neoliberalism*. Oxford and New York: Oxford University Press.

Harvey, David. 2008. 'Introduction', Karl Marx and Friedrich Engels *The Communist Manifesto*. London: Pluto Press.

Harvey, David. 2020. 'We Need a Collective Response to the Collective Dilemma of Coronavirus', Jacobin, 24 April. https://jacobinmag.com/2020/4/david-harvey-coronavirus-pandemic-capital-economy

Henwood, Doug. 2020. 'Now Is the Time to Fundamentally Transform America', Jacobin, 21 March. https://jacobinmag.com/2020/03/coronavirus-crisis-economic-recession

Houtart, François. 2010. 'The Multiple Crisis and Beyond', *Globalizations*, 7(1–2): 9–15.

Keynes, John M. 1936. *The General Theory of Employment, Interest and Money*. London: Macmillan.

Kotz, David. 2009. 'The Financial and Economic Crisis of 2008: A Systemic Crisis of Neoliberal Capitalism', *Review of Radical Political Economics*, 41(3): 305–17.

Krugman, Paul. 2009. 'All the President's Zombies', *The New York Times*, 23 August.

Mason, Paul. 2020. 'After the Coronavirus crisis, a new struggle against austerity will begin', *New Statesman*, 1 April. www.newstatesman.com/politics/economy/2020/04/after-coronavirus-crisis-new-struggle-against-austerity-will-begin

Mirowski, Philip. 2013. *Never Let a Serious Crisis Go to Waste: How Neoliberalism Survived the Financial Meltdown*. London and New York: Verso.

Müller, Wolfgang C. and Vincent Wright. 1994. 'Reshaping the State in Western Europe: The Limits to Retreat', *West European Politics*, 17(3): 1–11.

Notermans, Ton. 2000. *Money, Markets and the State: Social Democratic Economic Policies Since 1918*. Cambridge, UK: Cambridge University Press.

Panitch, Leo and Sam Gindin. 2010. 'Capitalist Crises and the Crisis This Time', in L. Panitch, G. Albo and V. Chibber (eds) *Socialist Register 2011: The Crisis This Time*. New York: Monthly Review Press, pp 1–20.

Panitch, Leo, Gregory Albo and Vivek Chibber. 2010. 'Preface',*Socialist Register 2011: The Crisis This Time*. London: The Merlin Press.

Plehwe, Dieter. 2017. 'Neoliberal Think Tanks and the Crisis', in R.E. Backhouse, B.W. Bateman, T. Nishizawa and D. Plehwe (eds) *Liberalism and the Welfare State: Economists and Arguments for the Welfare State*, pp 192–211.

Plehwe, Dieter, Quinn Slobodian and Philip Mirowski (eds). 2020. *Nine Lives of Neoliberalism*. London: Verso.

Prashad, Vijay. 2020. 'We Won't Go Back to Normal, Because Normal Was the Problem', *The Tricontinental Newsletter*, 26 March. www.thetricontinental.org/newsletterissue/newsletter-13-2020-new-world-order/

Quiggin, John. 2010. *Zombie Economics: How Dead Ideas Still Walk Among Us*. Princeton and Oxford: Princeton University Press.

Saad-Filho, Alfredo. 2010. 'Crisis in Neoliberalism or Crisis of Neoliberalism', in L. Panitch, G. Albo and V. Chibber (eds) *Socialist Register 2011: The Crisis This Time*. London: The Merlin Press.

Shaikh, Anwar. 2010. 'The First Great Depression of the 21st Century', in L. Panitch, G. Albo and V. Chibber (eds) *Socialist Register 2011: The Crisis This Time*. New York: Monthly Review Press, pp 44–63.

Stanford, Jim. 2020. 'We're Going to Need a Marshall Plan to Rebuild After COVID-19', *Policy Options*, 2 April. https://policyoptions.irpp.org/magazines/april-2020/were-going-to-need-a-marshall-plan-to-rebuild-after-covid-19/

Stewart, John and Kieron Walsh. 1992. 'Change in the Management of Public Services', *Public Administration*, 70(4): 499 –518. Doi.org/101111/j.1467-9299.1992.tb00952.x

Strange, Gerard. 2012. 'Understanding the Fundamentals of Capital, the Crisis and the Alternatives: Marx's Legacy Beyond Revolutionary Marxism', *British Journal of Politics and International Relations*, 15: 107–24.

Streeck, Wolfgang. 2017. *Buying Time: The Delayed Crisis of Democratic Capitalism*. Second Edition, With a New Preface. London and New York: Verso Books.

Tooze, Adam. 2018. *Crashed: How a Decade of Financial Crises Changed the World*. New York: Viking.

United Nations Environment Programme (UNEP). 2009 (March). *Global Green New Deal Policy Brief*. https://wedocs.unep.org/bitstream/handle/20.500.11822/7903/A_Global_Green_New_Deal_Policy_Brief.pdf?sequence=3&amp%3BisAllowed=

PART I

Austerity and the promotion of the private

1

Beyond austerity: pro-public strategies versus public-private partnership scandals

Heather Whiteside

Three decades of neoliberal era spending restraint have left countries around the world with a public infrastructure investment crisis. By 2030, according to one prominent estimate, the global need for infrastructure spending will total US$57 trillion (McKinsey Global Institute 2013). This infrastructure investment crisis comes at a time of renewed austerity with governments of all stripes committed to balancing budgets and paying down debt in the wake of the 2008 GFC. Recent austerity matches well-established neoliberal currents, coalescing to reconfigure sources of revenue for public works such as drawing on private finance to pay for state infrastructure through public-private partnerships (PPPs), and the further institutionalization of PPP through new generation initiatives like the Canada Infrastructure Bank.

However, as explored here, the normalization of PPPs today ignores a long run, scandalous track record: market monopolization by corrupt and inept private partners, troublesome bankruptcies and bailouts, and national revenue extraction through private partner equity rights and offshoring practices. Thus the chapter argues that alternatives to austerity require not only more spending, but also new types and sources of spending – namely, finding alternatives to private financing for public infrastructure. Alternative strategies include enacting 'pro-public' reforms to public sectors and mobilizing national sources of pooled savings for community-oriented purposes. The effects of the 2020 pandemic pandemonium are equally significant though they appear at this stage to be following familiar lines with governments encouraging PPPs despite their drawbacks, and the need for enhanced commitments to pro-public strategies being all the more dire.

Austerity and public infrastructure

Austerity is a clear example of what Jacob Hacker (2006) calls the 'neoliberal risk shift': some groups in society benefit but most are left worse off. A technical definition of austerity budgeting would refer narrowly to reductions made in the cyclically adjusted fiscal deficit; seen from a wider perspective, changes in fiscal policy greatly influence both state and society. Austerity is, as Jamie Peck (2013, 4) suggests, a strategy of redistribution that pushes 'the costs, risks, and burdens of economic failure onto subordinate classes, social groups and branches of government'. Along with cuts to public sector jobs, pensions and other forms of spending, the sale/lease of public assets is a major facet of austerity-related restructuring (Whiteside et al 2021).

After decades of market-oriented reforms, public infrastructure remains one of the principal assets held by the state. This provides the opportunity for fiscal conservatives and austerians to benefit from its sale and monetization, with creditors (investment funds, banks, wealthy individuals) all too eager to profit off the low-risk, high-return nature of public works through investment in PPP deals. Thus austerity budgeting entails not only cuts to expenditures, it can also mean lucrative opportunities for capital (Whiteside 2017).

The opportunity to profit off austerity emerges from post-2008 budgeting practices and, from a longer historical perspective, from the infrastructure gap associated with previous bouts of fiscal restraint. Well before the 2008 GFC, groups such as TD Economics (2004) and Deloitte (2006) were recommending greater use of privately financed PPPs to pay for public works. The rationale is in part ideological (that is, the perception that public debt is a sign of mismanagement) and in part practical given the presence of balanced budget legislation or other forms of spending control. More recently, McKinsey Global Institute (2016), BlackRock (2015) and other finance industry beneficiaries have continued to press the 'infrastructure gap' as one that must be filled through new, large-scale, commercialized infrastructure projects (see Krugman 2016). The supply of finance credit existed but the demand for infrastructure debt had to be created in the context of deep fiscal austerity dedicated to repaying economic stimulus and corporate bailouts. Peck (2013) argued that austerity had to be continually 'pushed' given that it is not self-evidently desirable or necessary; likewise for austerity's profitable 'alternatives' such as PPP.

PPP scandals

Over 1,500 PPP infrastructure contracts, worth over €250 billion, were signed in the EU over the 1990s and 2000s, in Australia there were over 150 contracts worth nearly A$40 billion, in Canada there were more than 200 worth C$45 billion (Kappeler and Nemoz 2010); and by 2014, the UK had over 700 operational PPP projects worth nearly £60 billion. The normalization of PPP (whether in times of stimulus or austerity) continues unabated despite ever-mounting concerns and scandals, namely: market monopolization involving corruption, bankruptcy and ineptitude, and equity sales to offshore tax haven-registered firms. The institutionalization of these and other worrisome PPP features through new-generation infrastructure banks is particularly problematic. Examples here are drawn from the well-developed Canadian PPP market.

Market monopolization

Smaller subnational contractors are often excluded from PPP markets. Not only does this create a power imbalance when a local authority is negotiating with a consortium of large private firms, such as multinational banks and construction giants, it also creates a power imbalance within the private sector. Smaller construction contractors, cleaners, caterers and the like are now hired and fired by multinational PPP private partners, a practice seldom overseen or controlled by governments, despite these companies being on the front lines of public service provision (see Whiteside 2016a).

The monopolization of Canadian PPP markets took less than a decade. By 2008, the British Columbia and Yukon Territory Building and Construction Trades Council found that PPPs were hurting small and medium-sized contractors in the province. Though the Council supports PPP in principle (being an obvious beneficiary of new construction projects), they have found that prime contractors are most often large firms, and once a contract is awarded it is entirely up to their discretion whether and how they subcontract to smaller local companies. The Council also reports that there is no official oversight into how subcontracting is done or whether it is done, and that in some cases the prime contractors are not tendering bids fairly or openly.

Similar concerns around construction industry competition (or the lack thereof) exist in the province of Ontario. The Ottawa Construction Association estimated in 2008 that only eight to ten general contractors in the province were able to take on PPP projects (Ontario Standing Committee on Government Agencies 2008). Given that PPP contracts bundle all project elements together (design, construction, financing, operations and maintenance), each company that forms a private partner must be able to bear the financial burden of surety and bonding amounting to the entire cost of a project, squeezing out smaller firms and limiting bidding to only the largest companies. In construction, this might mean a redistribution of contracts from smaller to larger firms; in services, the introduction of the PPP model has meant the creation of a subcontracting industry for the delivery of public services that is often beyond the control of public administrators.

Corruption, bankruptcy and ineptitude

Market monopolization contradicts the neoclassical argument that PPP contract competition will produce project efficiencies and generate greater value for money than public procurement; it also means locking in the activities of often corrupt or inept big players in national PPP markets.

SNC Lavalin provides engineering, financing and other project development, management and operations services in Canada and around the world. It is the central private partner in Montreal's super hospital project, the McGill University Health Centre, costing in excess of $1 billion. It has been a partner in other PPPs around the country, for example, the Canada Line, a light rail project linking Vancouver's airport with its downtown. It is also a member of 407 International Inc., which owns Ontario's Highway 407. Its PPP involvement appears unabated by a series of scandals relating to fraud, corruption and bribery accusations in projects worldwide. In 2013, it was added to the list of companies banned from bidding on World Bank projects, and in that same year it admitted to Quebec's Charbonneau Commission of Inquiry into provincial corruption that it made illegal political donations.

EllisDon, another Canadian construction sector giant and a partner in 20 PPP deals (and counting) since 2004, is an important player in Canada's PPP industry and internationally, from courthouses and hospitals to public transit. It is a member of the country's largest PPP project – the Eglinton Crosstown Light Rail Transit project in Toronto, which is touted to create thousands of jobs and provide transit services through 25 stations and stops. EllisDon is a major financial contributor to the Ontario Liberal Party and has had family connections to the party in the past. In 2013 it attempted to circumvent the Ontario

Labour Relations Board by gaining political support to end its legally binding commitment to unionized workers dating back to a 1958 closed-shop working agreement. The controversial bill (74 – *the Fairness and Competitiveness in Ontario's Construction Industry Act*) was ultimately defeated but the effort is instructive.

Carillion LPC, a British construction and maintenance and operations service provider of global note, filed for bankruptcy protection in London, England on 15 January 2018. With over 400 contracts in Britain, and 43,000 employees, its collapse is of significance for the homeland of PPP and the model worldwide. Some 7,500 Canadian jobs in health care and transportation were immediately put at risk, along with associated services on highways and in hospitals and airports in Ontario, Saskatchewan, Alberta and Northwest Territories (Waldie 2018). Initially downplaying the implications of its bankruptcy in the UK, Carillion Canada filed for creditor protection in Ontario ten days later. Fairfax Financial Holdings Ltd. would come acquire most of Carillion Canada's construction and facility services in February 2018. A Toronto-based investment company, Fairfax was implicated in the Paradise Papers for its ultimate ownership of two offshore Jersey-registered companies (International Consortium of Investigative Journalists (ICIJ) nd). The deal with Fairfax did not include highway sanding and snow removal services in Ontario and Alberta. With Carillion Canada responsible for nearly half of all highways in Alberta, the provincial government stepped in, thus far providing $12 million in financing to support Carillion Canada employees, services and operations in that province (Heidenreich 2018).

Bombardier, manufacturer of planes and trains, and serial contract winning firm in Canadian transportation, is not a PPP private partner but its activities affect infrastructure service delivery and PPP obligations given that it is a significant provider of transit-related rolling stock in communities across Canada. Grand River Transit (a public authority overseeing transit in Kitchener-Waterloo, Ontario) contracted Bombardier to deliver all 14 light rail vehicles to serve the region's new ION LRT PPP by the end of 2016. Bombardier delayed each delivery of ION rolling stock, and a project that was supposed to reach substantial completion by 1 July 2017 was not operational for another two years, on 21 June 2019; yet, given that it is a PPP, the region nevertheless continued to owe monthly operations and maintenance payments to GrandLinq, the PPP private partner (Desmond 2016; Eppel 2020). The region promised that once the LRT was operational, it would consider pursuing damages from Bombardier, until then paying GrandLinq to maintain non-functioning track (Ferrier and Lam 2018), but one year into the operational phase, by July 2020, damages had not been recovered. Instead, damages of another sort were reported: three quarters of the ION fleet would need special repairs by Bombardier (Thompson 2020).

Despite these serious delays, Bombardier was shortlisted for a LRT PPP project in Hamilton, Ontario and secured a contract with Metrolinx (a public authority overseeing Toronto transit) for its aforementioned Eglinton Crosstown PPP project, originally for 182 light rail vehicles but more recently renegotiated to 76 after many vehicles had been sent back to Bombardier due to quality-related concerns; the new agreement adds greater penalties with respect to delivery- and quality-related stipulations (Craggs 2018). TransLink (transit authority for Vancouver, BC) is also owed rolling stock for its SkyTrain extension. In the midst of all these new deals, repairs and delays, Bombardier announced in February 2020 that it would be selling its transportation division to French multinational corporation Alstom, adding an international dimension to market monopolization in Canadian PPP markets.

Equity sales and offshoring

Not only can we identify troublesome activities with PPP private partners, signatories to the project agreement, along with actors like Bombardier who are crucial for the functioning of PPP operations, there is now a flourishing – and worrisome – secondary market for infrastructure equity. Whitfield's (2016) report on the topic reveals a £17.1bn industry churned up by the buying and selling of equity in PPP infrastructure project companies, with rates of return on investment coming in at upwards of 50 per cent (five times the amount typically agreed to in the average PPP business case). These earnings flow to the original private partner, the secondary market investors re/selling equity in the project company and associated shareholders. Staggering returns generated off public infrastructure are private profiteering by any measure yet Whitfield's report also exposes the increasingly offshore nature of this secondary market. Many associated companies are registered in tax havens meaning none of their revenue recycles in the domestic market through redistributive taxation. Sizable profits abound, with the five largest listed offshore infrastructure funds making a total profit of £1.8bn from 2011 to 2015, monies that would be of great benefit to struggling cash-strapped governments, particularly the municipalities that are home to these infrastructure projects.

In Canada, where more than 200 PPPs have been developed since the late 1990s, over 20 equity sales occurred by the end of 2016. Given that most Canadian PPPs have only been developed in the past 5–10 years, and are typically social (not commercialized) infrastructure, this secondary market in equity sales is set to grow. Along with its growth comes revenue loss through offshoring. Already we see tax haven-registered companies buying and selling Canadian public infrastructure assets: Bilfinger Berger Global Infrastructure (registered in Luxembourg), HICL Infrastructure Company Limited (registered in Guernsey) and John Laing Infrastructure Fund Limited (registered in Guernsey) (Whiteside 2016b).

Beyond austerity

PPP-led stimulus?

The recently created, US$100 billion, Asian Infrastructure Investment Bank (AIIB), will soon target PPP infrastructure in Asian emerging market economies, an ambition both rivalling and supporting similar longstanding efforts by the World Bank's Public Private Infrastructure Advisory Facility (PPIAF) within the global South. The OECD and G20 countries have spent years promoting and supporting PPP as avenues for institutional investors to access public infrastructure projects in an era of low-growth austerity. Similarly, touted as a 'win-win', the Canada Infrastructure Bank intends to attract institutional investors' sizeable supply of capital by 'identify[ing] a pipeline of potential projects and identify[ing] investment opportunities that provide the biggest economic, social and environmental returns' (cited in Whiteside 2018). Public infrastructure will be reconfigured: revenue-generating infrastructure projects – those 'commercializable' through tolls and user fees – will be targeted, and equity investments will be offered. Canadians' stimulus will now come with a price tag of at least 7–9 per cent return on investment for private equity holders.

Pro-public strategies

Resisting the lure of consultants pushing private finance 'alternatives' must be made a priority (see Whiteside 2018). Infrastructure funding-specific alternatives that would allow for greater democratic control and a wider range of policy options in the future include drawing on revenue from the activities of (as opposed to the sale of) state-owned enterprises, sovereign wealth funds composed of natural resource revenues, pooled savings like insurance and pensions, and public bond debt. Revenue bonds, the form of public debt most suited for infrastructure because it links debt repayment to public works activities, in particular, could be more widely used in countries like Canada where they are rare.

More than merely a fiscal matter, recent academic literature on the subject of public services and public ownership, such as *Making Public in a Privatized World* (2016) by David McDonald, focuses attention on how alternatives to privatization must take into account the transformation of the public sector over the neoliberal period. McDonald suggests we need to develop a pro-public position rather than merely an anti-privatization one. The pro-public position that he articulates is based on a normative ideal that promotes the idea of 'publicness' and establishes measures that public service providers must aim to achieve – access, affordability, quality, equity, efficiency, environmental protection, solidarity, accountability, participation, and quality of workplace. Similarly, Andrew Cumbers, in his book *Reclaiming Public Ownership*, observes that 'left thinking on the forms that public ownership might take in the context of globalization and neoliberalism has scarcely advanced since the last time nationalization was on the agenda in the economic crisis of the 1970s' (2012, 2). His vision of reform emphasizes the importance of democratic forms of ownership, including forms of public property that do not involve the state but rather favour communities or collectives less tethered to neoliberal capitalism. Pro-public and democratically oriented infrastructure strategies, such as those articulated by Cumbers and McDonald, are needed to move beyond austerity and defeat the push for scandal-ridden PPP-led stimulus.

Pandemic-driven pandemonium

If the 2008 GFC was one of finance (and later the 'real economy'), the crisis of 2020 is in some ways qualitatively different given its twin crises of reproduction and production – a virus-driven health crisis amid simultaneous economic collapse due to government lockdown measures to address a novel pandemic. With vaccines distributed incrementally and unevenly in 2021, the health crisis will continue for some time albeit with hope on the horizon. As for the economy, predictions are more dire, with many economists warning of dramatic inflation, evoking comparisons with the Great Depression of the 1930s in terms of growth and employment concerns, or, more specifically for the US: 'the household fiscal cliff, the great business die-off, the state and local budget shortfall, and the lingering health crisis' (Lowrey 2020). Governments around the world have enacted stimulus and income support measures of various sorts (International Monetary Fund (IMF) 2020). Stalwarts of neoliberal governance quickly became bastions of state intervention: from stimulus and neo-mercantilism to seizing the means of production, nationalization and interfering with circulation and accumulation (International Labour Organization (ILO) 2020). What this all means for PPP as infrastructure finance and public services is at present unknown. In America, the Biden administration will likely unroll trillions in infrastructure stimulus over the coming years; in the UK, the Private Finance Initiative continues to be modified by Johnson. More concretely, and again taking Canada as an example, the fate of future Canadian PPPs, given their normalization as de facto go-to public policy, appears tethered to the health of 1) construction sector projects and 2) the politicization of public service provision.

For construction sector projects, aside from some temporary worksite closures due to generalized lockdown initiatives, it is full steam ahead in Canada given that infrastructure is, like after 2008, being turned to as a stimulus measure. However, by 6 July 2020, industry was nevertheless reporting an historic low for infrastructure investment in Canada due to the global economic downturn (Hixson 2020). In populous (and populist) Ontario, the government had two days later (8 July) announced an omnibus bill (with multiple pieces of legislation) designed to spur economic recovery from the pandemic slump (2020 – *COVID-19 Economic Recovery Act*). Construction-related changes include: streamlining the Building Code development process, consolidating the approval process for environmental infrastructure projects, reducing timelines for environmental assessments, creating a new Invest Ontario agency as a 'one stop shop' for business and investors, and other matters like accelerating highway and transit projects, zoning changes, and greater flexibility for municipalities to levy a community benefits charge to fund services (DCN-JOC News Services 2020).

In terms of the politicization of public service provision, it is clear that privatized health service issues have been brought to the fore during the pandemic, with respect to for-profit nursing homes in particular. On 6 May 2020, the Ontario Health Coalition (OHC) released a report uncovering the correlation between the type of long-term care facility (public versus private) and rates of COVID-19 mortality. The report establishes that there is 'a significantly higher death rate as a result of COVID-19 in long-term care homes that are owned by for-profit corporations compared to non-profit and public (municipal) homes'

(OHC 2020). How or whether this taint will affect PPPs is a question mark. Given that PPPs are often presented as public ownership by governments seeking to occlude their privatization dimensions, it is entirely likely that PPPs will continue to fly under the radar. What Canada desperately needs now is a similar study analyzing PPP hospitals and their relevant COVID-19 experiences since PPP hospitals involve for-profit operations for non-clinical support services like cleaning, food and laundry, and their management.

Beyond Canada, a few realistic possible scenarios for global/national PPP markets in general are: heightened global turbulence assuaged through international PPP-promoter support, market winnowing in favour of public sector options, and/or the nationalization of 'business as usual' after an initial period of turmoil (business as usual, as this chapter has detailed, nonetheless features a scandalous track record of market monopolization by corrupt and inept private partners, troublesome bankruptcies and bailouts, and national revenue extraction through private partner equity rights and offshoring practices).

Global turbulence

International PPP promoters like the World Bank's PPIAF have identified serious global disruption to PPP markets given the impact of the economic crisis (demand and supply issues) on infrastructure. The PPIAF is at the ready, however, to bolster privatization through its Rapid Response Programme accessible to national PPP units, ministries and other agencies that need technical advice, assessments and legal opinions (PPIAF 2020). The AIIB is similarly providing 'COVID-19 Response' loans worth USD billions for national projects linked to pandemic-related social and physical infrastructure (see AIIB 2020a). The programme operates as part of the AIIB Crisis Recovery Facility created to support members from April 2020 to October 2021 (US 5–10 billion) facing adverse risks due to the pandemic (AIIB 2020b). Thus global turbulence is, as of July 2020, being largely addressed through the leading PPP promoting institutions internationally. Whether this will be successful in the long run remains to be seen.

Market winnowing

PPP risk transfer provisions often mean the public sector retains responsibility for 'force majeure' or catastrophic unpredictable risks like natural disasters. To the extent that fears and lockdowns lead to plummeting demand for infrastructure, revenue like transit fares and highway tolls will collapse too. Should this lead government to reassess the risk profile of PPPs and their exposure to now unsustainable commitments to repay private partners through user fees, value for money calculations could quickly favour the public option with infrastructure procurement. Options appraisals may also dovetail with growing public sentiment and government proclamations that for-profit involvement in areas like health care can easily lead to perverse results and incentives. In the area of soft infrastructure like health and welfare provision, and social infrastructure like hospitals and schools, market winnowing could be significant depending on the specific nature of the pandemic-related impact on public opinion and government action.

Nationalization

Only a few months into the pandemic response and it is obvious that market-oriented governments are tethering their economic recovery plans to infrastructure-led stimulus. For example, in reference to a transit PPP project pre-dating the pandemic, the Transportation Minister of Ontario stated on 2 June 2020 that the province was 'one step closer to realizing our transit vision and helping to generate economic activity and create tens of thousands of jobs as the province recovers from COVID-19' (Spurr 2020). Though the announcement was in fact informing audiences of a delay to the schedule, the connection between infrastructure and stimulus is notable. The question becomes, however, to what extent PPP private actors from within-jurisdiction will be in some way favoured. The provincial Premier has spoken many times over the course of the pandemic about how this moment illustrates the importance of domestic capacity and made-at-home responses. For example, in reference to touring a local N95 mask-making facility: 'Thanks to the incredible businesses like this one, Ontario will never again be left at the mercy of other countries and leaders when it comes to vital Personal Protective Equipment (PPE) and medical equipment … We can make anything here in Ontario, we have the people, the expertise, the manufacturing might to build anything right here on our soil' (Wilson 2020). Statements such as these could be chalked up to empty and easy populist tropes on the road; however, they could equally signal a more fundamental reconsideration of how public works and services are procured for local use and needs.

As mentioned, alternatives to austerity involve not just more money for public infrastructure and services, but also new types and sources of spending beyond private financing for public infrastructure. Updating Whiteside (2018) on 'Alternatives to PPP Financing' in light of the pandemic (here offering 'pandemic era predictions' written in July 2020) we see potential variation in the impact of the 2020 crisis on sources identified in Table 1.1.

To the extent that governments are willing and able to use public infrastructure and service procurement as a form of pandemic-era stimulus, infrastructure investment funds and other forms of PPP equity will be as attractive to pension funds and sovereign wealth funds as after 2008. Economic crises expose investors to market volatility, and this degree of turbulence is likely beyond many institutional investors' risk thresholds. Government-backed projects are guaranteed safe and offer relatively high-return investments. Similarly, when economic crises are dealt with through easy monetary policy (low interest rates), returns on public infrastructure become all the more attractive to investors. For government bond-related investment as an alternative to profiteering by the private sector, as long as the demand is there, this remains a viable option in the future – tempered, however, by the nature and arrangements of public debt loads that have emerged during the pandemic, and by the possibility of interest rate creep in response to looming inflation. Using other means of pooled savings like employment insurance might not be feasible for the foreseeable future given the serious problems that currently exist in labour markets. Taxation levels and the fiscal capacities of municipalities during this difficult period will be something to watch for. The creation of new state-owned enterprises, or repurposing of existing ones, would help with institutionalizing a pro-public infrastructure and service programme.

Conclusion

PPP projects are subject to regular failures and notable scandals. Markets are largely monopolized in countries like Canada, and ripe with corruption, bankruptcies and ineptitude that only make matters worse. Offshoring and equity sales proceed largely beyond government regulators' view or approval, despite involving significant losses in fiscal revenue and control. The 2008 GFC temporarily stalled PPP market investments, but government support through infrastructure-led stimulus created space for investors amid generalized retrenchment through austerity imposed on other aspects of government service and procurement. For their part, institutional investors like pension funds and sovereign wealth funds get the best of both worlds from PPP debt and equity markets: not only are these safe investments in a time of turbulence, they are also lucrative in comparison with

Table 1.1: Alternatives to PPP financing

Forms	Examples	'Publicness' and economic democracy? (Pros and cons)
Drawing on new or existing forms of pooled savings	Pension and superannuation funds Employment insurance Sovereign wealth funds Credit union funds Public banks People's Quantitative Easing	Pro: worker and natural resource savings directly link Canadian services and infrastructure to its land and people Con: demographics (repayment concerns?), environmental concerns (for example carbon-based wealth funds), inflation? Pandemic-era prediction: these remain viable sources of funds for public infrastructure projects, with services covered in-house by government
Income remitted through the activities of Crown corporations	Sales, dividends, and expansion into new revenue-generating markets	Pro: profit captured and controlled directly by the state, not by the private sector or indirectly through taxes Con: corporatized Crown corporations? Pandemic-era prediction: new or repurposed state-owned enterprises would help institutionalize pro-public approaches
Issuing debt	Federal bonds dedicated to vital infrastructure	Pro: finance provided by the jurisdiction best able to shoulder debt and ensure pan-Canadian service equity Con: credit rating downgrades? Pandemic-era prediction: the capacity for public sectors to issue debt is highly government-specific, reliant largely on the nature and arrangements of public debt loads that have emerged during the pandemic and on how interest rates change in response to future economic recovery
User fees	Funds for 'revenue bond' repayment or direct financing for services	Pro: ensures intergenerational repayment equity Con: regressive Pandemic-era prediction: with the collapse of household savings, incomes and jobs, user fees will become all the more regressive
Creating a more progressive taxation system	Greater corporate tax, wealth tax, tax on higher income earners Better rule enforcement and monitoring Banning offshore and tax haven practices	Pro: redistributes 'dead money' hoarded by wealthy individuals and institutions and allows municipalities to collect more and new forms of tax revenue beyond the current reliance on property taxes Con: capital flight? Pandemic-era prediction: recovering offshore income and establishing a more progressive taxation system are desperately needed now more than ever given that government debt incurred with the 2020 crisis is in some cases over ten times the amount taken on after 2008, and that a middle class-funded revenue base has collapsed amid high joblessness

Source: Adapted from Whiteside (2018)

low prime rates on government bonds. Market, government and household pandemonium created through the 2020 pandemic has once more rocked global and local political economies, this time with consequences both wider and deeper for lives and livelihoods. The impact of 2020 on PPPs is of course uncertain. However, if the familiar pattern of government support for, and industry promotion of, PPPs endures through infrastructure-led stimulus and an austerity-generated squeeze on public works and services provision, we will likely see the endurance if not enhancement of corruption, bankruptcies, ineptitude and market monopolization.

Hope for a pro-public approach to public services has also expanded as of late. The consequences of the 2020 health crisis may be dire in many ways, but they could also usher in a new period of public finance, broad cynicism with profiteering off public works and governments of all stripes recognizing the advantages of local control. Changes such as these would support fiscal tools like opening space for public investment in public infrastructure, recovering foregone revenue via stringent penalties on tax avoidance and evasion and re-establishing healthy fiscal balances through progressive taxation. Reinvigorating the tradition of state-owned enterprises in countries like Canada would provide an institutional vehicle for policy learning, revenue capture and pro-public service provision. Whatever the exact details and make-up of the recovery, if communities want to move beyond lurching from crisis to crisis (whether in health, global capitalism or PPP markets), wealth through well-being must be privileged.

References

Asian Infrastructure Investment Bank (AIIB). 2020a. *News*. www.aiib.org/en/news-events/media-center/news/index.html. Last accessed 15 July 2020.

Asian Infrastructure Investment Bank (AIIB). 2020b. *COVID-19 Crisis Recovery Facility*. www.aiib.org/en/policies-strategies/COVID-19-Crisis-Recovery-Facility/index.html. Last accessed 15 July 2020.

BlackRock. 2015. *Infrastructure Rising: An Asset Class Takes Shape*. April. www.blackrock.com/investing/literature/whitepaper/infrastructure-rising-an-asset-class-takes-shape.pdf

British Columbia and Yukon Territory Building and Construction Trades Council. 2008. Submission to Hon. Colin Hansen, Minister of Finance.

Craggs, Samantha. 2018. 'Bombardier, Late in Delivering Waterloo's LRT Cars, Is on Hamilton's Shortlist Too'. *CBC News*. 13 April. www.cbc.ca/news/canada/hamilton/lrt-bombardier-1.4618827

Cumbers, Andrew. 2012. *Reclaiming Public Ownership: Making Space for Economic Democracy*. London: Zed Books.

DCN-JOC News Services. 2020. 'Omnibus Ontario Bill Aims to Spur Economic Recovery,' *Daily Construction News*. 13 July. https://canada.constructconnect.com/dcn/news/government/2020/07/omnibus-ontario-bill-aims-to-spur-economic-recovery

Deloitte. 2006. *Closing the Infrastructure Gap: The Role of Public-Private Partnerships*. www2.deloitte.com/content/dam/Deloitte/ie/Documents/Finance/Corporate%20Finance/2006_closing_infrastructure_gap_deloitte_ireland.pdf

Desmond, Paige. 2016. 'LRT Rollout Delayed, Bombardier Blamed', *The Record*. 24 May. www.therecord.com/news-story/6677484-lrt-rollout-delayed-bombardier-blamed/

Eppel, Ben. 2020. 'Bombardier Negotiations Continue, Compensation Timeline for ION Delivery Delays Still up in the Air', *Kitchener Today*. 19 February. www.kitchenertoday.com/local-news/bombardier-negotiations-continue-compensation-timeline-for-ion-delivery-delays-still-up-in-the-air-2103857

Ferrier, Melanie and Peggy Lam. 2018. 'Bombardier Says It's "Doing Everything" to Finish Waterloo Region's LRT Order'. *CBC News*. 17 April. www.cbc.ca/news/canada/kitchener-waterloo/bombardier-says-it-s-doing-everything-to-finish-waterloo-region-s-lrt-order-1.4623798

Hacker, Jacob S. 2006. *The Great Risk Shift*. Oxford: Oxford University Press.

Heidenreich, Phil. 2018. 'Government Makes "Additional $3.1M Available" to Financially Troubled Carillion to Maintain Alberta Highways'. *Global News*. 11 May. https://globalnews.ca/news/4204020/alberta-transportation-highways-carillion-canada-business-insolvent/

Hixson, Russell. 2020. 'Canada Sees Historic Drop in Construction Spending', *Daily Commercial News*. 6 July. https://canada.constructconnect.com/dcn/news/economic/2020/07/canada-sees-historic-drop-in-construction-spending

International Consortium of Investigative Journalists (ICIJ). nd. *Fairfax Financial Holdings Limited*. Offshore Leaks Database. https://offshoreleaks.icij.org/nodes/80064053

International Labour Organization (ILO). 2020. *Country Policy Responses*. www.ilo.org/global/topics/coronavirus/regional-country/country-responses/lang--en/index.htm. Last accessed 14 April 2021.

International Monetary Fund (IMF). 2020. *Policy Response to COVID-19*. www.imf.org/en/Topics/imf-and-covid19/Policy-Responses-to-COVID-19#S. Last accessed 16 July 2020.

Kappeler, Andreas and Mathieu Nemoz. 2010. *Public-Private Partnerships in Europe: Before and During the Recent Financial Crisis*. European Investment Bank. www.eib.org/attachments/efs/efr_2010_v04_en.pdf

Krugman, Paul. 2016. 'Infrastructure Build or Privatization Scam?' Krugman Blog. *The New York Times*. 19 November. http://krugman.blogs.nytimes.com/2016/11/19/infrastructure-build-or-privatization-scam/?_r=0

Lowrey, Annie. 2020. 'The Second Great Depression'. *The Atlantic*. 23 June. www.theatlantic.com/ideas/archive/2020/06/second-great-depression/613360/

McDonald, David A. (ed). 2016. *Making Public in a Privatized World: The Struggle for Essential Services*. London: Zed Books.

McKinsey Global Institute. 2013. *Infrastructure Productivity: How to Save $1 Trillion a Year*. January. www.mckinsey.com/industries/capital-projects-and-infrastructure/our-insights/infrastructure-productivity

McKinsey Global Institute. 2016. *Bridging Global Infrastructure Gaps*. June. www.mckinsey.com/~/media/McKinsey/Industries/Capital%20Projects%20and%20Infrastructure/Our%20Insights/Bridging%20global%20infrastructure%20gaps/Bridging-Global-Infrastructure-Gaps-Full-report-June-2016.ashx

Ontario Health Coalition (OHC). 2020. *COVID-19 Death Rates in Ontario Long-Term Care Homes Significantly Higher and Increasing in For-Profit Homes vs. Non-Profit and Publicly-Owned Homes: New Data Analysis*. 6 May. www.ontariohealthcoalition.ca/index.php/death-rates-in-long-term-care-by-ownership-release/

Ontario Standing Committee on Government Agencies. 2008. *Agency Review: Ontario Infrastructure Project Corp. (Infrastructure Ontario)*. Hansard Committee Transcripts. 17 September.

Peck, Jamie. 2013. 'Pushing Austerity: State Failure, Municipal Bankruptcy and the Crises of Fiscal Federalism in the USA', *Cambridge Journal of Regions, Economy and Society*, 6(2): 17–44.

Public-Private Infrastructure Advisory Facility (PPIAF). 2020. *COVID-19 PPP Rapid Response Umbrella Program*. https://ppiaf.org/covid-19-ppp-rapid-response-umbrella-program

Spurr, Ben. 2020. 'Ford's $11B Ontario Line Likely Won't Be Completed By 2027, Source Says'. *The Star*. 2 June. www.thestar.com/news/gta/2020/06/02/fords-11b-ontario-line-likely-wont-be-completed-by-2027-source-says.html

TD Economics. 2004. *Mind the Gap: Finding Money to Upgrade Canada's Aging Public Infrastructure*. TD Bank Financial Group.

Thompson, Catherine. 2020. 'Three-quarters of Ion fleet to Undergo Unexpected Repairs'. *Cambridge Times.* 8 July. www.cambridgetimes.ca/news-story/10071876-three-quarters-of-ion-fleet-to-undergo-unexpected-repairs/

Waldie, Paul. 2018. 'Carillion's Canada Branch Files for Bankruptcy Protection'. *The Globe and Mail.* 25 January. www.theglobeandmail.com/report-on-business/carillions-canadian-branch-files-for-creditor-protection/article37731988/

Whiteside, Heather. 2016a. *About Canada: Public-Private Partnerships.* Halifax: Fernwood.

Whiteside, Heather. 2016b. *Austerity Infrastructure: Financializing, Offshoring, and Tax Sheltering Public-Private Partnership Funds.* Summary Report for SSHRC Partnership Development Grant on 'Austerity and Its Alternatives'. 14 December.

Whiteside, Heather. 2017. 'Profiting Off Austerity: Private Finance for Public Infrastructure', in S. McBride and B. Evans (eds) *The Austerity State.* Toronto: University of Toronto Press.

Whiteside, Heather. 2018. 'Public Works: Better, Cheaper, Faster Infrastructure', *Studies in Political Economy*, 99(1): 2–19.

Whiteside, Heather, Stephen McBride and Bryan M. Evans. 2021. *Varieties of Austerity.* Bristol: Bristol University Press.

Whitfield, Dexter. 2016. *The Financial Commodification of Public Infrastructure.* European Services Strategy Unit. October. www.european-services-strategy.org.uk/publications/essu-research-reports/the-financial-commodification-of-public-infras/financial-commodification-public-infrastructure.pdf

Wilson, Codi. 2020. 'Ont. Company Planning to Manufacture up to 1 million N95 Masks Per Week, Province Says'. *CP 24.* 14 July. www.cp24.com/news/ont-company-planning-to-manufacture-up-to-1-million-n95-masks-per-week-province-says-1.5023187

2

Institutionalizing austerity accounting in Europe: the implementation of European Public Sector Accounting Standards as crisis response

*Sebastian Botzem**

Accounting for public finances is always political, even more so in times of crises. Material resources are core to allow for short-term crisis relief but, more fundamentally, they are necessary for the provision of public services more broadly. In this regard, health crises are not much different from earlier financial crises, as states need substantial amounts of money, both short and long term for effective crisis response. In 2020, as well as ten years earlier after the financial crisis, public expenditures sky-rocketed and public debt increased substantially. While it is still way too early to make predictions on how COVID-19 will develop and how public finances will be affected, a look back at the global financial crisis of 2007/2008 provides some insights on how austerity policies were introduced in Europe. This chapter does not focus on any particular policy field. Instead, I analyze the implementation of a new set of accounting rules that enable austerity politics as part of comparing and streamlining public accounts.

I argue that the implementation of such standards can be interpreted as the institutionalization of an austerity infrastructure. I suggest that an austerity infrastructure is the institutional and the socio-legal context in which a specific accounting constellation flourishes. Critical scholars interpret an accounting constellation as a relational field of institutions, economic and administrative processes, bodies of knowledge, systems of norms, practices of measurement and classification techniques in

* I thank Columba Krieg for excellent research assistance and support in aggregating the data.

accounting (Burchell et al 1985; Botzem 2012, 22). In that sense, an austerity infrastructure is the expression of and a tool for an accounting constellation that is dominated by neoliberal thought in general and investment logics in particular.

In this chapter, I will provide an analysis of how the European Union reacted to the global financial crisis of 2007/2008 by tightening the budgetary requirements for its member states. At the core is an institutionalist analysis of how market-oriented public sector accounting standards become the law of the land. Behind the apparently dry issue of implementing novel European budgetary standards lies a political battle in which neoliberals have achieved a great victory by implementing an unlevel playing field through the introduction of an austerity-prone budgetary and calculatory infrastructure. Europe's new standards for national accounts privilege capital providers as they primarily require the provision of financial information that is relevant for investors. Other stakeholders, such as taxpayers or the public at large are becoming less important as addresses of national account information. European Public Sector Accounting Standards (EPSAS) are the tool for harmonizing national accounts and align them with capital market information requirements.

The European Union reacted with determination to the financial crisis of 2007 that later morphed into a banking, sovereign debt and Euro crises. A number of European legal statutes (Sixpack, Twopack, fiscal compact, all implemented between 2011 and 2014) have significantly increased the European Commission's macroeconomic oversight and the budgetary surveillance of individual member states. These legal revisions build on, specify and tighten the Maastricht Criteria and introduce harmonized European standards as a tool set for strict supervision. This attempt of European harmonization, however, coincides with introducing new principles of market-orientation of public sector accounting that have a much longer history. By looking at the background of EPSAS introduction, it becomes clear that the trend of orientating public accounts towards financial markets reflects a larger trend of financialization (see Epstein 2005; Krippner 2005; Davis and Kim 2015). Nevertheless, the increasing relevance of financial actors, financial logics and financialized practices – all subsumed under the concept of financialization – does not lead to any predetermined state of affairs. The role and effect EPSAS have in furthering financialization, and their relevance for European austerity more precisely, needs closer scrutiny. Therefore, this chapter focuses on the institutionalization of EPSAS in Europe and discusses the broader organizational configuration of standard setting in Europe. It also contains an analysis of actor constellations to identify individuals and organizations that occupy a prominent role in public sector accounting. As the implementation of EPSAS is a recent phenomenon, much is still in flux. It will therefore not be possible to show in detail how EPSAS drive austerity. Nevertheless, the chapter shows how an infrastructure of austerity accounting emerges around EPSAS.

Accounting standardization in an interconnected world

EPSAS are developed to provide rules for the preparation of public accounts of European member states as well as for the European Community as a whole. The purpose of a harmonized set of rules for public accounts is to provide a uniform basis for planning activities and to ensure a transparent allocation of resources. Similar to private sector accounting standards, which determine the external relations between firms and their environment with regard to accountability and flow of profits, public accounts also determine the relation between the state as an accounting entity and its stakeholders. As such, public sector accounting rules show the distribution of money and provide an overview of public assets and liabilities. In advanced economies, the soundness of public finances has been a political issue for some time (Streeck 2017). Moreover, states' creditworthiness have been particularly prominent with regard to developing countries and their account liberalization (see Moschella 2009). So, while the distributional nature of public finances is a given, the harmonization of the standards that are used for the preparation of state budgets has received much less attention.

Public budgets are essential for holding governments accountable. In liberal democracies, budgetary control is a cornerstone of parliamentary oversight and a key element of public accountability. EPSAS – as any other set of standards – are therefore more than 'technical' prescriptions to present apparently 'neutral' information. Just like standards for private firms (see Botzem 2012), EPSAS present financial information according to the principles on which they are based.

Traditionally, public sector accounts were provided on a cash basis. This method recognizes a public entity's revenues and expenses at the time cash is received or paid out. Cash-based accounting is relatively easy to do but always strongly connected to effective cash transfers. In contrast, for some time, now, an alternative method is on the rise: accrual-based accounting, which is particularly strong in

Anglo-American countries, seeks to implement the application of business-style accounting practices to all government activities (see Biondi 2014; Robb and Newberry 2007). Accrual-based accounting is also promoted by international donor organizations, such as the IMF, that argue that accrual-based accounting delivers higher-quality information making public accounts more transparent, reliable and accessible (see Cavanagh et al 2016). Unlike the cash method, the accrual method records revenue when a political decision is legally decided, not when a payment is due. This concerns both assets, such as public property and state-owned companies, and liabilities, essentially public debt and future payment obligations. Both assets and liabilities are increasingly accounted for at market values, showing the potential price of public assets such as land, real estate or publicly owned corporations. At the same time, liabilities – most importantly debt and other contractual obligations – are shown at current values effectively treating jurisdictions as if they were corporate entities. This has immediate consequences for a state's accountability relations. It is less the citizenry or the population that can call for democratic accountability. Instead, it is creditors and debt holders who are able to measure public entities according to their investment logic. Essentially, accrual-based accounting provides financial market actors with a toolbox that it easily extendable to austerity politics. Effectively, EPSAS co-determine *how much* can be spent by *whom*, in *what way* and under *which conditions*.

Detailed accounts of the material content of EPSAS cannot be considered here, because it is a comprehensive set of standards which is currently under consideration.[1] However, EPSAS are not only a European endeavour. They are based on International Public Sector Accounting Standards (IPSAS) of which currently 42 exist as well as International Financial Reporting Standards (IFRS) which regulate the financial reports for private corporations. In both cases, the principle of Fair Value Accounting (FVA) plays a crucial role. Essentially, FVA suggests that any activity or asset is worth whatever a market actor is willing to pay (Botzem 2012). Under FVA, price and value are identical which gives investors and other capital providers a central role in all market activities. The following section discusses the introduction of EPSAS in Europe, the attempts for harmonization and the role exercised by different actor groups.

[1] https://circabc.europa.eu/faces/jsp/extension/wai/navigation/container.jsp

European budgetary surveillance in the name of financial markets

Activities to harmonize EU budgetary rules picked up steam after the financial crisis of 2007. However, attempts to harmonize budgetary rules for EU member states go back further. Already in the early 2000s, in a desire to update the EU's internal accounting system, the Commission sought to reach harmonization through implementing an accounting system which supports the production of 'reliable and complete accounts' (European Commission 2002). More importantly, as stated by the Commissioner for Budget at the time, the EU used the modernization of its accounting system to move away from cash-based accounting towards the more future-oriented accrual accounting: '[T]he Commission's accounting framework is based on cash accounting and is moving, in common with public administrations in some member states, towards more commercial-style (accrual) accounting practices required by the new Financial Regulation to be put in place for the year 2005' (European Commission 2002).

Since 2005, the EU applies accrual-based accounting for its internal budgeting procedures. The shift is considered an improvement of the Union's management activities, precisely because the EU embraces a new managerial culture that is in line with the information needs of capital market actors: 'This [the shift from cash-based to accrual accounting, SB] is not merely a technical change. It is a profound change in management culture, vital to ensure effective scrutiny over spending, minimize the risk of errors, and improve the day-to-day management of EU funds' (European Commission 2008).

Based on these changes for internal account keeping, the implementation of EPSAS goes further as harmonization entails a stringent top-down oversight of member states by the European Commission. For all aspects – the compilation of statistical information, policy planning as well as fiscal and budgetary oversight – a new and coherent set of accounting rules is deemed necessary by the Commission in order to apply uniform rules across the EU. This issue emerged with great force when the EU decided to implement stricter macroeconomic oversight for the Economic and Monetary Union (EMU), and toughened rules for the Stability and Growth Pact (SGP). As part of the Sixpack, Europe-wide accrual accounting was introduced via Council Directive 2011/85/EU. Article 3 of the directive states:

> As concerns national systems of public accounting, Member States shall have in place public accounting systems

> comprehensively and consistently covering all subsectors of general government and containing the information needed to generate accrual data with a view to preparing data based on the ESA 95 [European system of national and regional accounts 1995, SB] standard. (European Commission 2011)

In the eyes of the European Commission and its statistical unit Eurostat (a Directorate-General in its own right) the sovereign debt crisis has 'underlined the need for more rigorous, transparent and comparable reporting of fiscal data' (Biondi and Soverchia 2014). A useful occasion to argue for the need to harmonize member state accounts arose shortly after the crisis when it became evident that the Greek authorities had been tampering with official statistics. A Commission report of 2010 noted that Greece had falsified data about its public finances in 2009 and allowed political pressures to obstruct the collection of accurate statistics. Moreover, the report also detailed problems with statistical data and fiscal information by Greece in the early 2000s (European Commission 2010). While there is little doubt that manipulation occurred, the report states no evidence that a particular type of accounting logic favoured fraudulent statistical representation. Nevertheless, the Greek case was discussed publicly as an instance of unlawful application of standards and it provided a window of opportunity to implement a new, accrual-based system of accounts (Oulasvirta and Bailey 2016, 659). Despite the fact that there is no obvious relation between the plurality of accounting practices in Europe before the crisis and the manipulation and mishandling of Greek data that was transmitted to the Commission, EPSAS were praised as the solution to bring about uniform standards and hamper future fraudulent behaviour. It is important to point out, however, that the decision to implement accrual accounting by no means pre-determines the selection of a particular set of standards. As stated earlier, accrual accounting is a method, not a standard. Advocating for the introduction of EPSAS as one version of accrual-based accounting standards is therefore a political decision, especially as EPSAS' implementation has the potential to reshape public policies and to alter the modes of operation of public administrations (see Biondi 2014; Bracci et al 2015).

As mentioned earlier, EPSAS are not intended to be a stand-alone European set of standards; rather, they are derived from international standards for public accounts. IPSAS are a set of standards the global auditing profession has been developing for many years. Its professional body, the International Federation of Accountants (IFAC) has been at the forefront of global harmonization and played a crucial role in developing IPSAS (Humphrey et al 2009). IFAS was also engaged in bringing the United Nations to turn to IPSAS as a new global standard for the harmonization of public accounts (Chow and Aggestam 2019). From the beginning, IPSAS were sought to be compatible with the global standards for corporate accounting. In their development, IPSAS have been closely aligned with IFRS for listed corporations, which primarily address the information needs of capital providers (Botzem 2014). In this context, the introduction of accrual-based accounting for budgeting within the EU was also a significant step to bring legitimacy to IPSAS (Grossi and Soverchia 2011).

There is a distinct hierarchy of norms in international accounting using company accounts as the primary benchmark (IFRS) to which international standards (IPSAS) are made compatible. The later serve as blueprints for European rules. IFRS follow accrual-based accounting and their fair value-orientation clearly reflects the primacy of the information needs of capital market actors. In short, the European Union's decision to rely on EPSAS as a basis for the harmonization of member states public accounts draws a direct line to the accounting standards of large corporations. By making IFRS and IPSAS the guiding principles for public accounts, the EU is prioritizing and legitimizing the information needs of capital providers as primary stakeholders. In addition to 'simply modernizing' public accounts and to make them comparable, drawing on EPSAS establishes a direct line between capital market actors and public budgets. Member states' public accounts are to be brought in line with the dominant information needs of the corporate world. EPSAS express accounting norms on which all EU countries have to rely. Their implementation greatly facilitates the introduction of austerity politics because EPSAS make public assets visible and allow for pricing public debts according to market logics. All of this unfolds against the background of substantial differences in accounting practices of member states, some of which have implemented accrual accounting while others still apply cash-based accounting and/or a mixture of both. The next section takes a closer look at the introduction of EPSAS in Europe's regulations and at the institutionalization of the standard setting procedures.

EPSAS as a tool for budgetary governance

One of the notable facts about EPSAS introduction in Europe is that the decision to adopt the standards was effectively taken at a point in time when the governance structure on how to develop EPSAS was not yet clear. This is particularly relevant because accounting standards rely on continuous deliberation, reworking and incremental development in which the due process is decisive for the prescribed outcome (Botzem 2014). The dynamics are noteworthy to understand how EPSAS became EU rules: on the one hand, at the level of regulatory content, it was clear that the method of accrual accounting was preferred, even though neither EPSAS nor the EPSAS framework, a document summarizing underlying accounting principles, were precisely defined at the time (see EU 2019, 2). On the other hand, the EU's push for post-crisis harmonization reflects the desire for budgetary transparency and account comparability. As a consequence, the EU and member states were willing to effectively implement a black box – a set of standards which were not fully developed and a governance regime that was decided upon only after implementation was decided.

As indicated earlier, the development of accrual-based accounting standards in Europe has long been in the making. The breakthrough for EPSAS came about when accrual-based accounting was accepted as an instrument to tighten budgetary surveillance. Table 2.1 gives a brief overview of the core policy decisions to introduce accrual-based accounting in the EU. Three phases can be distinguished: an initial preparatory phase opening Europe to accrual accounting by linking up with the global regime for corporate standards (up to 2005); a second phase when the adoption of EPSAS was initialized (up to 2012); and thirdly, the effective introduction of EPSAS into EU law.

An essential aspect of harmonization, in particular during phases II and III, was 'downloading' the normative content from IPSAS into EPSAS. However, as the private, association-based governance structure to develop IPSAS could not be used in the European context, decisions were needed to come up with a due process that is in line with European accountability requirements. At the same time, IPSAS and EPSAS are intended to be as similar as possible to ensure global homogeneity. This indicates an ambitious plan to effectively square the circle: subscribe to internationally accepted market-oriented budgetary standards while implementing an independent governance arrangement that follows European accountability expectations of stakeholder participation, due process and transparency.

This approach led to a number of complementing legal and administrative decisions that used the financial and economic crises as a catalyst to further drive harmonization. The first official step towards EPSAS was taken with the Budgetary Frameworks Directive 2011/85/EU which states that '[r]ecent economic developments have posed new challenges to the conduct of fiscal policy across the Union and have in particular highlighted the need for … having uniform requirements as

Table 2.1: Chronology of EPSAS introduction in Europe

Phase	Date	Decision
I. Preparatory decisions	2001	Establishment of the European Financial Reporting Advisory Group (EFRAG) for IFRS implementation
	9/2002	Regulation 1606/2002 on the implementation of international accounting standards for private entities
	3/2005	Introduction of accrual accounting for the EU internal General Accounts
II. Initializing budgetary control via EPSAS	11/2011	Budgetary Frameworks Directive 2011/85/EU 'On Requirements for Budgetary Frameworks of the Member States'
	12/2011	Reform of the Sixpack is adapted by EC and EP with the aim to improve fiscal surveillance
	2–5/2012	Public Consultation 'On the Suitability of the International Public Sector Accounting Standards for EU Member States'
	2012	Official announcement of EPSAS in the report 'Towards Implementing Harmonised Public Sector Accounting Standards in Member States'
III. Introducing EPSAS	10/2013	First meetings of the Task-Forces 'EPSAS-Governance' and 'EPSAS-Standards'
	11/2013–2/2014	Public Consultation on future EPSAS governance principles and structures
	2014	Last update of European System of Accounts, ESA10
	9/2015	Establishment of the EPSAS Working Group
	6/2019	Report on the progress of EPSAS

Source: Author

regards the rules and procedures forming the budgetary frameworks of the Member States' (Council of the European Union 2011).

To bring about uniformity, the EU chose the Union's statistical unit to administer the process of harmonizing European budgetary rules (Biondi 2014, 167). In order to pave the way for EPSAS, Eurostat launched a number of public consultations that invited public and private stakeholders to comment on the suitability of IPSAS for member states (Eurostat 2012). The consultations explicitly asked for input from the interested public to gather evidence but also to provide legitimacy for the entire process. In addition, the European Commission (EC) commissioned studies on the state of public sector accounting in the EU to assess the status quo of accrual accounting, cash-based accounting and hybrid forms in the public sectors of the member states. These studies were conducted by PricewaterhouseCoopers (PwC) and Ernst & Young (EY), two of the Big Four auditing firms from which a large number of individuals are recruited to develop IPSAS under the auspices of the global auditing profession. Finally, in 2012 EPSAS were officially announced in a Commission document ('Towards Implementing Harmonised Public Sector Accounting Standards in Member States') that was presented to the Council and the European Parliament (European Commission 2013). Eurostat became the primary political and administrative entity to foster EPSAS implementation and the establishment of a European governance regime.

Currently, Eurostat is actively engaged in developing EPSAS. The organization serves both as an actor advancing the harmonization and implementation of standards as well as a venue facilitating the interest representation of other actors. To that end, a number of working groups and task forces were established to administer the dual process of standard development and of institutionalizing standardization arrangements. The first body, the 'EPSAS Task Force' was set up in 2013. In 2015, the 'EPSAS Working Group' replaced the task force and was established as a permanent forum of experts meeting bi-annually (European Commission 2019, 2).

A more detailed analysis of the different steps of EPSAS establishment indicates the relevance of Eurostat: in 2011, a Council directive requested the European Commission to conduct a study to assess the suitability of the IPSAS for European member states through public consultation.[2] The consultation was carried out by Eurostat and included 68 responses (mostly from financial and statistical authorities of EU member states) of which 38 per cent considered IPSAS to be suitable for implementation in EU member states, 31 per cent deemed them to be partly suitable and 28 per cent rated IPSAS unsuitable as a basis for EPSAS. Despite mixed results, Eurostat continued to lead the process by drafting reports, organizing conferences and engaging with member states. In 2013, Eurostat conducted a second public consultation ('Towards Implementing EPSAS for EU Member States – Public Consultation on Future EPSAS Governance Principles and Structures')[3] inviting comments on governance principles. This was the starting point for a long-term engagement of different stakeholders which will be analyzed in the following section. Consensus emerged

[2] https://ec.europa.eu/eurostat/about/opportunities/consultations/ipsas

[3] https://ec.europa.eu/eurostat/about/opportunities/consultations/epsas

that IPSAS provided a starting point for the development of EPSAS but could not simply be adopted as such.[4]

Agents of austerity accounting

In the initial four years of developing EPSAS, from 2011 to 2015, two task forces with specific mandates were established: first, the EPSAS Governance Task Force was created to exchange views with authorities from European member states on possible future governance arrangements and underlying principles of EPSAS. This task force should assist Eurostat in identifying the key issues for EPSAS governance, discuss how to balance those issues and thereby assist Eurostat to develop a model for the EPSAS governance structure. Second, the EPSAS Standards Task Force was created to exchange views with authorities from European member states on technical aspects of the EPSAS standards. The group's mission was to assist Eurostat in identifying the most contentious IPSAS, address the concrete difficulties encountered with some of the IPSAS in practice and find ways to overcome them.

Following the initial stage, the institutional setting of a formalized EPSAS governance arrangement was modified: four bodies were created to advance with more stringency and to secure the input of selected private organizations and some international organizations such as the World Bank. This paved the way for an expertise-based regime to develop EPSAS. Currently, an institutional arrangement is being put in place in which seemingly apolitical European bureaucrats are engaged with EPSAS development while European authorities organized accountability which is formally provided on the basis of national delegation. The four entities that were set up, a primary working group as central decision-making body and three smaller bodies (so called 'cells') to address specific matters:

- The Working Group on EPSAS was established in September 2015 and serves as a permanent body to develop and implement EPSAS. Its task is to serve as core unit to administer the institutionalization of a firm governance arrangement.[5] The Working Group consists of delegates of the member states as well as observers from other private and public bodies. The group's official mandate is to 'advise the

[4] https://ec.europa.eu/eurostat/about/opportunities/consultations/epsas

[5] https://ec.europa.eu/eurostat/web/epsas/expert-groups

Commission on issues relating to the area concerned and establish close cooperation between the Commission and the authorities responsible for public sector accounting in member states, in order to facilitate the exchange of information, experiences and good practices'.[6] Primarily, the group seeks to identify key issues for EPSAS governance and standards and discusses how to develop and introduce durable EPSAS governance arrangements.
- In addition, three smaller expert groups ('cells') were established to address issues concerned with first-time implementation of EPSAS, governance principles and principles-related standards.

Each group met about five times between June 2015 and October 2016. An empirical analysis shows who is effectively engaged in defining the content and governance of European accrual accounting. Formally, all bodies consist of delegates from national authorities, observers from EU bodies and other private or public sector organizations. As shown in Table 2.2, the primary difference is in the entities' size: the Working Group, where final decisions are taken, is much larger and roughly two thirds are delegates from member states. The cells, where relevant decisions on the content of rules are taken, 30 to 44 per cent delegates from member states. Cells have much more influence on experts from the private sector and other representatives from international organizations.[7]

A more detailed look at the bodies' composition with regard to the organizational origins of its members shows how the field of European accounting standardization is internally structured and unveils who the central players are. The number of individuals involved in the four distinct bodies over the last four years is 183 in total, of which 175 have attended one or more of the Working Groups' meetings. There is significant personal continuity between the Working Group and the cells. Of the 175 individuals, 105 were member states' representatives, the large majority of them delegated from national finance ministries and, to a much lower degree, representatives of the national Court of Auditors.

[6] http://ec.europa.eu/transparency/regexpert/index.cfm?do=groupDetail.groupDetail&groupID=2989

[7] All information of the analysis presented here can be accessed via Eurostat's website. https://ec.europa.eu/eurostat/web/epsas/expert-groups. It includes a list of attendees (including their names and the organizations they represent), dates and protocols of meetings. Last accessed 4 June 2019.

Table 2.2: Delegates and observers attending meetings convened by Eurostat

	Working group	Cell 1: First time implementation	Cell 2: Governance principles	Cell 3: Principles related to EPSAS
In operation	Since 2015	6/2015–10/2016	12/2015–3/2017	3/2016–10/2018
Number of meetings	7	5	4	6
Number of members attending each meeting	47–65	3–6	4–9	2–9
Average number of members per meeting	50	5	5	5
Number of observers attending each meeting	18–28	4–8	6–12	8–13
Average number of observers per meeting	26	6	8	11

Source: Author

With regard to the organizational origin of the 183 individuals, it can be said that the vast majority (75 per cent) is delegated by member states: 137 individuals engaged in the establishment of EPSAS represent public entities of member states, predominantly finance ministries. With regard to country representation, Germany is the country with the most delegates. A total of 16 persons have been attending one or more of the meetings. In part this is a reflection of German federalism (six of the 16 represent federal German states) but it also indicates a more fundamental aspect which is Germany's reluctance to adopt accrual-based accounting rules. Other countries which send an above-average number of individuals to the Working Group and the cells are Greece and Italy (nine persons each), UK and Malta send eight individuals and Austria seven delegates.

A closer look at the individuals who do not fall in line with the patterns of national representation is also instructive. A quarter of all the individuals engaged in one of the four bodies (47 of 184) do not represent a specific national jurisdiction. All of these individuals act as observers from European institutions, the private sector or other international organizations. Nearly half of all 47 non-jurisdictional members are from European institutions; 23 observers are engaged in EPSAS development (most notably Eurostat (ten persons), European Court of Auditors (five persons) and DG budget (three persons)). The second largest group of observers are from the Big Four auditing firms (12 individuals), followed by International Organizations (World Bank seven individuals, OECD one person) and four individuals from professional bodies.

Perhaps more striking is the involvement of large auditing firms. Two of the large firms send 12 different individuals to observe and advise the Working Group. Of the 12 individuals, seven are on EY's payroll (Hendrik Bartsch, Franck Chevalier, Jens Heiling, Ozgur Ererdem, Georges Ortmann, Luc Veyssiere and Joke Wiercx) while five work for PwC (Anton de Greef, Fabrice Francillon, Romain Reus, Jean-Louis Rouvet and Patrice Schumesch). The role of these firms is particularly remarkable because these two auditing firms have helped initiate the entire process by writing two significant reports each in 2011 and 2013.

With regard to selected individuals who have been engaged in EPSAS development, it becomes clear that only a relatively small group has participated over the entire process: only 14 individuals of the entire group of 183 persons have attended at least half of the 22 cell and Working Group meetings. Of the 14 individuals, seven are Eurostat staff members, four are employees of national finance ministries And the remaining three people are Andreas Glöckner, an observer from the Court of Auditors of the German federal state of Hesse, Thomas Müller-Marqués Berger and Ian Carruthers. The last two have attended 20 of the 22 meetings and merit special attention.

A closer look at two of the core individuals reveals some striking features: both persons are intricately involved with auditing practice and global professional bodies. Müller-Marqués Berger is listed in the official EU document as representing the European professional body Accountancy Europe (until 2016: Fédération des Experts Comptables Européens – FEE). It is the Brussels-based umbrella organization advocating for the professional interest and engaged in advocating harmonization at the European level. Moreover, Müller-Marqués Berger is also heavily engaged in international standard-setting at other venues. For example, since 2011, he is Chair der Public Sector Group von Accountancy Europe or FEE. From 2009 to 2014 he was the German representative at the IPSAS-Board, and since 2013 he has been advising the European Commission in the European Accounting Advisory Group. Moreover, since 2016 Müller-Marqués Berger is member and now also head of IPSAS-Board's Consultative Advisory

Group. He is a senior partner with EY in Germany's Stuttgart office where he has been Global Leader of International Public Sector Accounting since 2005.[8]

Ian Carruthers is a similarly networked individual. He first joined the EPSAS activities in his capacity as Policy and Technical Director of the Chartered Institute of Public Finance and Accountancy (CIPFA) of the UK. In addition to this position, he has long been a member of the International Public Sector Accounting Standards Board (IPSASB) with a focus on aligning IPSASs and Government Finance Statistics. He was also working for HM Treasury and was involved in the UK's transition from cash to accrual budgeting and reporting until 2006 when he joined CIPFA. In addition, since 2010, Carruthers has been a board member of the IPSASB which he has chaired since 2016.

Both Müller-Marqués Berger and Carruthers are engaged in a number of activities and events to which they contribute in a number of functions. The relations to the IPSASB are the most striking. In fact, they can be interpreted as an expression of the desire to link EPSAS as closely as possible to IPSAS thus making a unique European set of standards unlikely. In conceptual terms, these two individuals reconfirm an observation already made with regard to the IASC in the late 1990s: high-profile individuals are often engaged in a variety of settings and organizations. It is therefore difficult to assess whose interests they are effectively representing. They wear different hats at different times (Tamm Hallström 2004) which makes it difficult to trace their loyalties and – equally problematic – assess the political nature of the advice they provide. For instance, is Müller-Marqués Berger speaking for IPSASB, Accountancy Europe or perhaps for EY when he participates in discussions? It is important to note that EPSAS is no exception. Blurred identities allow 'experts' to speak in the name of different constituencies while also pursuing commercial interests. This pattern is also common for financial reporting standardization under the auspices of the IASB (Botzem 2014) and can also be seen at IFAC (see Loft et al 2006).

Conclusion

European harmonization of public accounts is a result of different dynamics for which accrual accounting is the common denominator:

[8] www.ey.com/Publication/vwLUAssets/ey-cv-mueller-marques-berger/%24FILE/ey-cv-mueller-marques-berger.pdf.

ongoing harmonization of statistical information at international and EU levels took hold, accrual-based accounting was enshrined in IPSAS and EPSAS became the benchmark for EU internal accounts as well as for EU member states. Accrual-based accounting privileges the information needs of capital market actors and establishes an immediate link between state budgets to large capital providers by synchronizing their accounting systems. At all levels, the principles of accrual-based accounting cement an unlevel playing field on which it is increasingly difficult to argue on behalf of societal needs.

It is too early to assess the impact of EPSAS as their implementation is currently underway. However, as their primary purpose was to strengthen budgetary oversight and they primarily cater to the information needs of capital providers, essentially investors and creditors, it can be expected that EPSAS reinforce austerity policies. In case of the EU, EPSAS are being introduced top-down from the European level to national governments. EPSAS is more than a set of standards, however. This chapter has indicated that EPSAS are embedded in an institutional and socio-legal complex that establishes an austerity infrastructure. It provides an unlevel playing field on which neoliberal pro-market actors can unfold their full potential. With regard to possible effects regarding the current pandemic, it is likely that EPSAS will put pressure on public actors through making liabilities visible and showing the value of assets which can be sold in order to plug budget holes. After all, EPSAS were introduced by the EU in response to the last financial crisis roughly ten years ago. EPSAS and COVID-19 might be a toxic combination because the standards will soon be implemented and can reveal their full potential to compare member states and to bring the logics of financial investments to public budgets.

As the chapter shows, there is no simple one-way relation between accrual-based accounting, EPSAS and austerity. However, the logic of fair value, measuring and assessing the value of everything according to what a potential buyer is willing to pay, is a powerful frame that enjoys recognition almost worldwide: accrual-based accounting is fully implemented for large firms, it is embedded in the UN framework, it is promoted internationally through IPSAS and it has now been made mandatory in Europe. There are a few countries not yet fully on board with accrual-based accounting, among them Germany, the Netherlands, Greece and Italy, which are fighting an uphill struggle that even Germany, the EU's largest and most powerful member state, is likely to lose.

Austerity accounting also points to another aspect of international harmonization: the relevance of technocrats, experts and large auditing firms. Their role has been discussed at length in the critical accounting literature (see Botzem 2012; 2014). What is new in this case is that seemingly apolitical bureaucrats play a key role. Eurostat, the EU's statistical unit, is effectively in charge of developing EPSAS. The strongest voices from outside the public sector are auditing practitioners who earn their money by preparing and assessing the accounts of private and public entities. And they work for large auditing firms. Accounting professionals have a primary interest in pushing for market-oriented accounting because it has become a universal language only they fully understand and because they earn their money in auditing and consulting. So, while austerity might be devastating for citizens who depend on a functioning state and public services, austerity can also be good business for those who assess public activities and arrange the sale of public assets. Globally active auditing firms and the practitioners on their payrolls are among the great beneficiaries of austerity politics.

EPSAS solidify a new paradigm of accountability: in the future, the state is linked much more directly to the financial expectations of capital providers – and perhaps less focused on democratic accountability. Assets and liabilities are brought in line with market expectations while the democratic demands of citizens are becoming less pressing. Precisely because accounting standards appear to be neutral and apolitical it is not always easy to document the distributive effects they have. However, critical discussions and a changing discourse on austerity help make the distributional effects of certain standards visible which might lead to discussions about the value of state activities – not only in a pecuniary sense of investing capital.

References

Biondi, Yuri. 2014. 'Harmonising European Public Sector Accounting Standards (EPSAS): Issues and Perspectives for Europe's Economy and Society', *Accounting, Economics and Law*, 4(3): 165–78.

Biondi, Yuri and Michela Soverchia. 2014. 'Accounting Rules for the European Communities: A Theoretical Analysis', *Accounting, Economics and Law*, 4(3): 179–214.

Botzem, Sebastian. 2012. *The Politics of Accounting Regulation: Organizing Transnational Standard Setting in Financial Reporting*. Cheltenham: Edward Elgar.

Botzem, Sebastian. 2014. 'Transnational Standard Setting in Accounting: Organizing Expertise-Based Self-Regulation in Times of Crises', *Accounting, Auditing & Accountability Journal*, 27(6): 933–55.

Burchell, Stuart, Colin Clubb and Anthony G. Hopwood. 1985. 'Accounting in Its Social Context: Towards a History of Value Added in the United Kingdom', *Accounting Organizations and Society*, 10(4): 381–413.

Bracci, Enrico, Christopher Humphrey, Jodie Moll and Ileana Steccolini. 2015. 'Public Sector Accounting, Accountability and Austerity: More Than Balancing the Books?', *Accounting, Auditing & Accountability Journal*, 28(6): 878–908.

Cavanagh, Joe, Suzanne Flynn and Delphine Moretti. 2016. *Implementing Accrual Accounting in the Public Sector (Technical Notes and Manuals, TNM/16/06)*. Washington, DC, US: International Monetary Fund Fiscal Affairs Department.

Chow, Danny and Caroline Aggestam. 2019. 'The United Nations' (UN) Decision to Adopt International Public Sector Accounting Standards (IPSAS)', *Journal of Public Budgeting, Accounting & Financial Management*, 31(2): 285–306.

Council of the European Union. 2011. 'Council Directive 2011/85/EU of 8 November 2011 on Requirements for Budgetary Frameworks of the Member States', *Official Journal of the European Union (306/41)*, updated 8 November 2011.

Davis, Gerald F. and Suntae Kim. 2015. 'Financialization of the Economy', *Annual Review of Sociology*, 41(1): 203–21.

Epstein, Gerald. 2005. 'Introduction: Financialization and the World Economy', in G. Epstein (ed) *Financialization and the World Economy*. Cheltenham and Northampton: Edward Elgar, pp 3–16.

EU. 2019. *Commission Staff Working Document. Reporting on the Progress as Regards the European Public Sector Accounting Standards (EPSAS)*. Brussels, SWD(2019) 204 final.

European Commission. 2002. *Modernisation of the Accounting System: The Way to an Integrated Accrual Accounting Framework System*. Press Release. IP/02/1136. Brussels.

European Commission. 2008. *Modernising the EU Accounts: Enhanced Management Information and Greater Transparency: Your Guide to the EU's New Financial Reporting*. Luxembourg: Office for Official Publications of the European Communities.

European Commission. 2010. *Report on Greek Government Deficit and Debt Statistics. COM(2010) Greek Report*. Brussels. European Commission. 2011. *Council Directive 2011/85/EU of 8 November 2011 on Requirements for Budgetary Frameworks of the Member States*. Brussels.

European Commission. 2013. *Towards Implementing Harmonised Public Sector Accounting Standards in Member States: The Suitability of IPSAS for the Member States*. Report from the Commission to the Council and the European Parliament. Brussels.

European Commission. 2019. *Reporting on the Progress as Regards the European Public Sector Accounting Standards (EPSAS)*. Commission Staff Working Document (Brussels), updated 5 June 2019.

Eurostat. 2012. *Public Consultation Paper: Document Accompanying the Public Consultation on the Suitability of the International Public Sector Accounting Standards for EU Member States*. https://ec.europa.eu/eurostat/documents/10186/752720/IPSAS_stakeholders_consultation_paper.pdf, updated 15 February 2012. Last accessed 4 June 2019.

Grossi, Giuseppe and Michela Soverchia. 2011. 'European Commission Adoption of IPSAS to Reform Financial Reporting', *Abacus*, 47(4): 525–52.

Humphrey, Christopher, Anne Loft and Margaret Woods. 2009. 'The Global Audit Profession and the International Financial Architecture: Understanding Regulatory Relationships at a Time of Financial Crisis', *Accounting, Organizations and Society*, 34(6–7): 810–25.

Krippner, Greta. 2005. 'The Financialization of the American Economy', *Socio-Economic Review*, 3(2): 173–208.

Loft, Anne, Christopher Humphrey and Stuart Turley. 2006. 'In Pursuit of Global Regulation: Changing Governance and Accountability Structures at the International Federation of Accountants (IFAC)', *Accounting, Auditing & Accountability Journal*, 19(3): 428–51.

Moschella, Manuela. 2009. 'When Ideas Fail to Influence Policy Outcomes: Orderly Liberalization and the International Monetary Fund', *Review of International Political Economy*, 16(5): 854–82.

Oulasvirta, Lasse O. and Stephen J. Bailey. 2016. 'Evolution of EU Public Sector Financial Accounting Standardisation: Critical Events That Opened the Window for Attempted Policy Change', *Journal of European Integration*, 38(6): 653–69.

Robb, Alan and Susan Newberry. 2007. 'Globalization: Governmental Accounting and International Financial Reporting Standards', *Socio-Economic Review*, 5(4): 725–54.

Streeck, Wolfgang. 2017. *Buying Time: The Delayed Crisis of Democratic Capitalism*. London, New York: Verso.

Tamm Hallström, Kristina. 2004. *Organizing International Standardization: ISO and the IASC in Quest of Authority*. Cheltenham: Edward Elgar.

PART II

Coping and casualties: labour and the social

3

A fragile triangle: collective bargaining systems, trade unions and the state in the EU

Steffen Lehndorff

The situation of the trade unions in Europe is complicated. Unemployment, precarious employment, the increase in social inequalities and the rise of right-wing nationalist parties pose serious challenges for them in most countries. It is true that their possible courses of action at national level have evolved very differently in the wake of the crisis management policies adopted within the EU since 2008, so that many of them must have gained the impression that they are battling in different worlds. However, in this increasingly disjointed European trade union landscape, there are at the same time some very striking transnational challenges. One of the most important concerns collective bargaining systems which in a number of European countries have more and more been exposed to similar threats. This crucial basis of trade unions' institutional power is at increasing risk of being hollowed out and being driven into a precarious state of dependency on changes of policy approaches of governments.

In principle, from a labour point of view it would be desirable if the trade unions were in a position to increase the rate of unionization to such an extent that they could increase the rate of coverage by collective agreements through their own autonomous bargaining strength. However, overall trends in union density over past decades demonstrate that, for the time being, this is more than unlikely to happen. Deep and rapid structural changes on the labour markets have undermined the traditional bastions of trade union power.

Against this background it used to be a widely shared view in many EU countries that the functioning of independent collective bargaining systems must to some extent be guaranteed by additional support from the state. This support can take a number of very different forms and is by no means identical with direct interventions in the wage-setting process. On the contrary, even in countries like Sweden with strong trade unions it is the state that establishes strong protective and participative labour standards, thus providing for a 'shadow of the law' which protects autonomous bargaining.[1] However, it also follows from this that under certain circumstances, the reduction or withdrawal of this state support can cause serious damage to the whole bargaining system and wage-setting process. Once labour market deregulation changes an 'enabling' into a 'disabling state' (Bosch and Lehndorff 2017), the institutional triangle of collective bargaining, trade unions and the state is under pressure.

Just how fragile this triangle has become in many EU member states can be shown by a comparison of trade union density with the share of employees working in an establishment covered by a collective agreement (Figure 3.1).

This comparison reveals a possibly surprising discrepancy in a number of countries. The relative stability of the collective bargaining systems compared with the rate of union density, which has fallen considerably in most countries, is linked to a large extent to the design of the collective bargaining systems. The entire structure is attached to just a few anchor points. One of them is the so-called favourability principle: employers bound by collective agreements do not have the right to enter into agreements with workforce representatives in which the conditions for employees are less favourable than those laid down in the relevant national or industry-level agreement. If the favourability principle is abolished in labour law, the rate of coverage by collective agreements may initially remain unchanged but the collective bargaining system may erode from within. The second anchor point in many countries is the practice of declaring collective agreements generally binding (extension mechanism); this may be done either by the government or virtually automatically through labour legislation. The starkest example of the importance of this anchor point is France, where the rate of union density is one of the lowest in the EU but the rate of coverage by collective agreements is one of the highest (see Pernot 2018).

This discrepancy makes two things clear. On the one hand, it shows how fundamentally important the state guarantees for the collective

---

[1] Following the distinction made by Sengenberger (1994), protective standards, such as minimum wages or maximum working times, directly establish norms governing employment conditions. Participative standards confer consultation or codetermination rights on employees or their representatives and organizations. For country-specific examples see also Bosch and Lehndorff (2017).

Figure 3.1: Coverage by collective agreement and trade union density in selected EU member states*

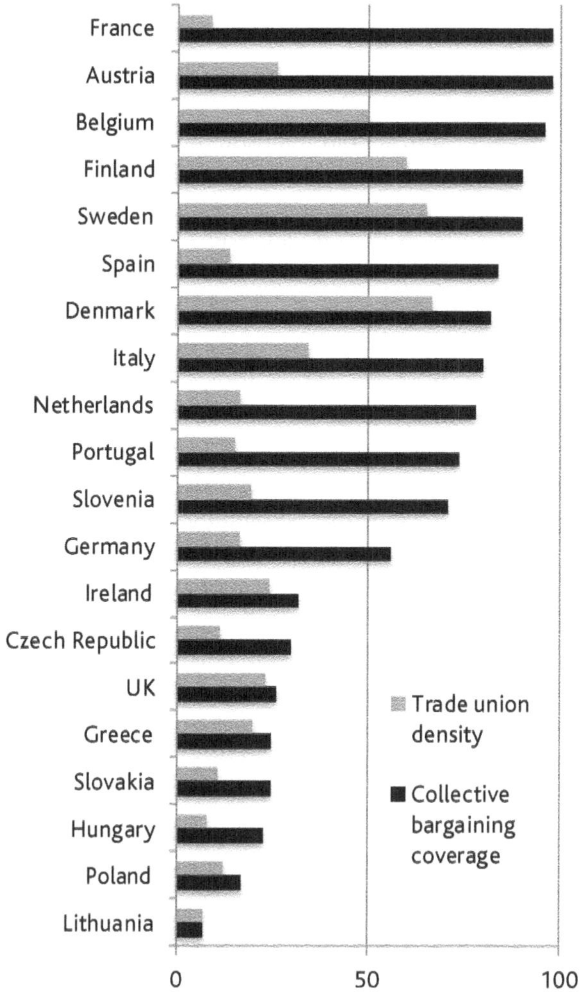

Notes: * As a % of all dependent employees in companies covered by general or industry-level collective agreements. Data on coverage by collective agreement from 2015 to 2017 except for Ireland (2014); data on trade union density from 2016 to 2018 except for Greece (2015).
Source: OECD.Stat

bargaining systems are, particularly the practice of extending collective agreements. On the other hand, however, it indicates how dependent the unions' institutional influence can be on the benevolence of governments when it is not underpinned by other power resources, such as their organizational power, their leverage in the labour market (due to low unemployment or certain occupational groups' potential for exerting targeted pressure) and, last but not least, the political power generated by their capacity for extra-parliamentary mobilization and the weight they carry in the political sphere.[2] It is this vulnerability that became glaringly obvious in the past decade especially in Southern European countries.

It is in the so-called European 'periphery' where the 'disabling state' approach has been taken furthest since the beginning of the euro crisis (which only seemingly has been resolved for a couple of years and is popping up as a menace again in the wake of the COVID-19 crisis), geared to deprive the trade unions of the legally guaranteed 'institutional anchors' (Grimshaw and Lehndorff 2010) that underpin their negotiating power in the collective bargaining system. This is why in what follows, I draw on the examples of Greece, Spain and Italy to give, firstly, a summary of three of the particularly extensive attacks on the collective bargaining systems and to show the different effects they have had in each of these countries. This summary shows the possibilities the trade unions have exploited in order to defend their institutional power resources as well as how contradictory the effects of such efforts can be. The experiences presented in what follows highlight the need to underpin the unions' institutional power by intensifying efforts to strengthen their organizational and societal power in order to stabilize the triad of trade unions, collective bargaining system and state specific to each country. On this basis I conclude by putting forward some proposals for strengthening collective bargaining systems from the EU level which, in view of the startling uncertainty and disunity among the EU elites, may be easier to push through than was the case just a few years ago.

An attack on the collective bargaining systems ...

When in 2010 the GFC of 2008–09 turned into a crisis of the European Monetary Union, the dominant actors at EU level launched a 'silent

[2] On the concept of trade union power resources see, among others, Gumbrell-McCormick and Hyman (2013), Lehndorff et al (2018) and Schmalz et al (2018).

revolution' that aimed for, as former Commission President Barroso put it, 'a quantum leap of economic surveillance in Europe' (EUobserver 2011). In a series of decisions the EU established a 'new economic governance' within the framework of the so-called 'European Semester' – an institutionalized annual process in which the European Commission elaborates analyses and gives 'recommendations' for the individual EU member states. The latter may be binding or non-binding, and if a country needs assistance in case of speculative attacks against its sovereign bonds, binding 'recommendations' may be enforced by rigid diktats, most prominently implemented in some countries by the 'Troika' of the EU Commission, European Central Bank (ECB) and the IMF.[3]

Austerity policy in combination with so-called 'internal devaluation' has been the hard core of this policy approach.[4] As to austerity policy, the alleged 'consolidation of public finances' had to be accomplished until very recently with the help of spending cuts focused on pensions, infrastructural investment, health care and social services (the impacts of the latter two have become a major issue in the course of the COVID-19 crisis – thus giving rise to the debate indicated in footnote 4). Internal devaluation as the second pillar, in turn, has been focused on what is usually called 'structural reforms for more competitiveness'. Labour costs have been regarded as the decisive factor here, and the main road to strengthen international competitiveness by low labour costs are more 'flexible' labour standards.

This is where collective bargaining systems come into play. The details of their 'flexibilisation' were spelled out by the Directorate-General for Economic and Financial Affairs (European Commission 2012). Its strategy of 'adjusting wages more closely to the economic conditions at establishment level' was explicitly geared to 'an overall reduction of the wage-setting power of trade unions'. To that end, the following so-called 'structural reforms' of collective bargaining systems were declared to be urgent: reduction of coverage by collective agreements, reduction in the practice of (automatically) extending

[3] For overviews and country-specific analyses regarding the European Economic Governance see, among others, the contributions of Lehndorff (2015), Van Gyes and Schulten (2015), Myant el al (2016) and Marcuzzo et al (2020).

[4] The use of the past tense would not be appropriate here even though at the beginning of the COVID-19 crisis the European Commission suspended the binding character of the 'rules' of the Stability and Growth Pact. This has triggered the (at the time of writing: ongoing) conflict within the EU about whether or not, and if so, when and to what extent, these rules shall come into effect again.

collective agreements, decentralization of the collective bargaining system, for example by abolishing or restricting the favourability principle, introduction or extension of the possibilities for diverging at company level from industry-wide collective agreements and/or for negotiating company agreements, and cuts of statutory or collectively agreed minimum wages (European Commission 2012, iii, 51, 103). This approach was adopted with particular emphasis in those countries under the diktat of the EC-ECB-IMF Troika or subjected to closer supervision by the EU Commission and the ECB as they attempted to weaken or even virtually destroy their collective bargaining systems.

That we are indeed dealing with a blueprint here is shown by the spotlight turned on the legal so-called 'reforms' of collective bargaining systems introduced between 2010 and 2012 in the analyses of three Mediterranean countries contained in Lehndorff et al (2018) and Müller et al (2019). In Greece, the favourability principle was abolished and the possibility created of concluding agreements with non-union workforce representatives in small firms. Once the term of a collective agreement has expired the agreement itself becomes null and void after three months. The previous widespread practice of extending collective agreements was made legally more difficult and virtually stopped. The national minimum wage was no longer to be set through collective bargaining but by the government (whereupon it was reduced by 22 per cent). In Italy, company agreements can undercut the labour standards agreed at industry level if they have been signed by a majority of the representative trade unions in the company (which would indirectly terminate the practice of automatically extending collective agreements, hitherto guaranteed by judgments establishing a principle in labour law). In Spain, employers have been given the option of withdrawing from a collective agreement for economic reasons. Collective agreements that are not renewed become null and void after a year. Company agreements take precedence over industry-level agreements and can undercut them (here too the 'erga omnes' principle of almost automatically extending collective agreements is quashed).

Even though deregulation policy everywhere adhered to the same blueprint, its immediate effects were very diverse.

... with differing effects

The differences leap to the eye when the evolution of coverage by collective agreements is considered (Figure 3.2). In Italy, the share of employees working in companies bound by collective agreements was

Figure 3.2: Coverage by collective agreements before and after deregulation*

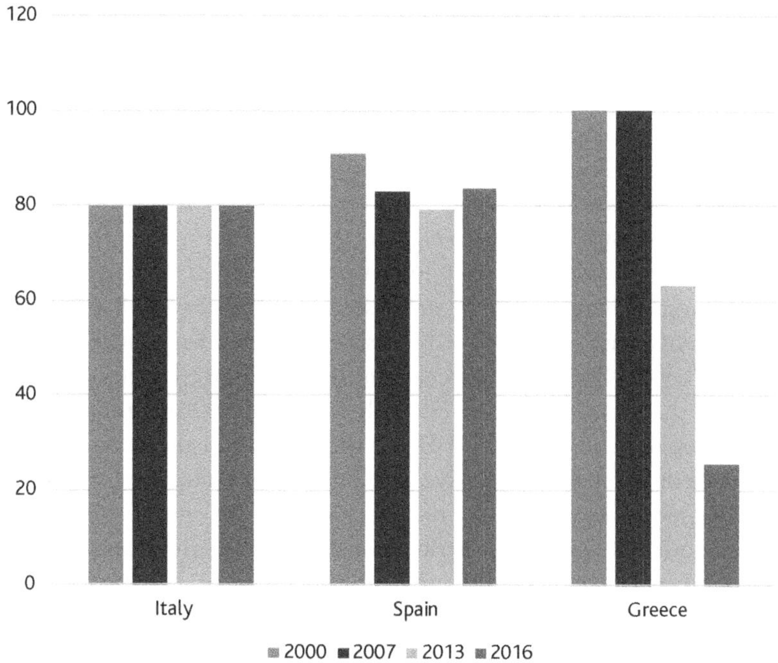

Note: * As a % of all dependent employees in companies covered by general or industry-level collective agreements
Source: OECD.Stat

just as high following deregulation as it had been prior to the crisis, and in Spain there was only a slight decrease, while in Greece the drop was dramatic. How are these contrasts to be explained?

Let us turn first to Greece. Major elements of the breakdown of the collective bargaining system, as Katsaroumpas and Koukiadaki (2019, 287) claim, 'did not emerge from the crisis; rather their seeds were planted in periods of stability'. Since the 1990s, the country's collective bargaining system had been resting on a small number of pillars (see Karamessini 2015), namely trade union membership and bargaining power in a very small number of sectors (public utilities in particular), the practice of extending collective agreements and the setting of minimum standards through the negotiation of a national minimum wage, which the government then turned into the statutory minimum wage. The leadership of the trade union umbrella association for the private sector was firmly ensconced in this setting and relied on the system continuing to function in the usual manner, not least because of its close ties with the conservative and social democratic parties.

Unlike in other countries, trade union revitalization initiatives were not regarded as necessary and young members were rare birds indeed. What then happened is summarized by Koukiadaki et al (2016, 79) as follows: 'when state support in the form of extension mechanisms and the favourability principle was withdrawn, unions were not able to draw on other resources to rebalance the structure of bargaining'. And Vogiatzoglou (2018, 129) encapsulates the situation pithily as follows: 'employers no longer need trade unions to secure labour peace'. As a result, 2013 saw a regular upsurge of company agreements below sector level, most of which were concluded with non-trade union representatives, while the system of industry-level collective agreements practically collapsed (Katsaroumpas and Koukiadaki 2019). Only after the Syriza-led government had announced in the summer of 2018 that it intended to re-establish the collective bargaining system following the end of the third Troika memorandum and to restore the practice of extending collective agreements did collective bargaining recover somewhat. The more recently elected right-wing government has announced that it will restrict the favourability principle again and allow firms in financial difficulties to withdraw from industry-level collective agreements.

In Spain, on the other hand, both of the parties to collective bargaining demonstrated a pronounced capacity for inertia or resilience.[5] At first sight, the consequences of the increasingly harsh austerity and deregulation approach of the Spanish government were not so different to the ones in Greece. Next to the institutional weakening of the collective bargaining system, the marginalization of tripartite concertation was particularly painful for the unions who, too, had failed to develop revitalization initiatives in the years before the crisis (Köhler and Calleja Jiménez 2018). Nevertheless, what happened next differed from the downturn in Greece. To some extent, this was due to a specific hierarchy of agreements in Spain, where industry-level agreements have served to set modest minimum standards which used to be exceeded, not undercut, by company-level agreements particularly in larger firms (Banyuls and Recio 2017). Thus, the deregulation of the collective bargaining system by the Rajoy government in 2012 did little to change the character of sector-level agreements. In some cases, bargaining was even revived as part of deliberate bilateral efforts to preserve the architecture of the collective bargaining system, while in the manufacturing sector at least, company agreements undercutting

[5] For a similar development in Portugal see Campos Lima (2019).

the collectively agreed minimum standards tended to remain the exception. Most employers had no interest in opening the gates to wage dumping below the sector's already low minimum standards. Koukiadaki et al (2016, 111) describe the approach adopted by the parties to negotiations at both industry and company level as 'process-focused concession bargaining'. The objective of the trade unions in particular is said to have been 'to maintain and conclude collective agreements wherever possible, even if the general conditions for doing so had deteriorated'. As a result of this process, both collectively agreed and actual incomes declined, it is true, and average bargaining coverage dropped, if moderately as compared to Greece, but the structure of the collective bargaining system remained largely intact in practice despite the legal deregulations. It has been eroded by concession bargaining, but in principle it can be reactivated if economic conditions improve.

The current left-wing coalition minority government, whose socialist predecessor already increased the minimum wage and revitalized tripartite agreements at national level, has declared its intention of reversing the legal dismantling of the collective bargaining system. Against this background, trade unions' strategies are not totally clear. While following the deregulation attacks against the collective bargaining system some sections of the unions had started to develop important revitalization initiatives, it cannot be excluded that at least parts of the unions might once again shift their attention primarily to hope for improvements initiated by the present government to materialize.

Developments in Italy were particularly unusual and instructive (see Leonardi 2018). As early as 2009, the second- and third-largest trade unions had already concluded a framework agreement with the employers' association – to the acclaim of the Berlusconi government – that was intended to facilitate the decentralization of collective bargaining and, under certain conditions, to open the gate to firm-level derogations from the regional collective agreements (abolition of the favourability principle). The largest union (CGIL) was to be isolated but it did not cave in. It launched a campaign against this agreement and brought a number of actions before the labour courts. This led two years later to a new agreement that restored the favourability principle with less significant restrictions and fewer detailed definitions. After some internal debates and arguments, it was signed by the CGIL. This prompted the Berlusconi government, now in its dying days, to enact legislation shortly afterwards denying explicitly the favourability principle – completely in accordance with the admonitory letter that it had received in August 2011 from the ECB (see Simonazzi 2015). As Pedersini (2019, 351) summarizes, the present legal regulation has 'jeopardised the traditional hierarchy between industrial and decentralised deals by establishing equal regulatory power of all bargaining levels, thereby confirming the lack of any favourability principle, but reversing formerly well-established practises'. In response, however, the employers' associations and all three major trade unions strengthened the agreement they had reached earlier, thus confirming the 'well-established practises'. Leonardi (2018, 103) quotes a leading CGIL official as saying: "I've spent my life negotiating the enforcement of the law and now I find myself having to negotiate against the law, or act as if it didn't exist".

For all their differences, these three Southern European cases show how rickety the supports on which the widespread impact of the collective bargaining systems rests can be. The problem is that the state certainly bears a great responsibility for 'strengthening the negotiating position of the weaker side of the labour market, i.e. employees and their trade unions' (Bosch 2019). Yet in a number of countries, the trade unions now lack the strength to force the state into assuming this responsibility if it wishes to shirk it. Consequently, more and more bargaining systems are becoming dependent on government decisions and political circumstances. How might trade unions deal with this dependency?

Collective bargaining: dependent on the government or should the state be forced into assuming responsibility?

The collective bargaining systems' dependency on the state has been reinforced by the euro crisis and the neoliberal policies that have further aggravated it. This has left the unions vulnerable to falling headlong into a precarious situation. If they rely primarily on their traditional political allies in the government, as they did in Greece, they are exposed – virtually without defence – to a change of political direction. True, there were initially many strikes and massive demonstrations; understandably, however, exhaustion soon set in and where the struggle continued, in workplaces and social initiatives, the trade union leaders were often regarded as part of the establishment. There was no discernable interest on the part of the trade union umbrella association in preparing jointly with the Syriza-led government for the time after the end of the Troika diktat; rather, it adopted a wait-and-see approach that distanced it very much from the government but made no detectable effort to tackle the structural weaknesses in its own organization that had become evident long before the crisis. As a result, the trade union leadership has also been ill-prepared to meet future challenges which may pop up under the present right-wing government.

In Spain too, the unions had 'neglected to maintain and develop independent sources of union power' in the years before the crisis, while being 'overconfident about their growing institutional power' (Köhler and Calleja Jiménez 2018, 70). And they too initially protested against government policy with general strikes and mass demonstrations and then had to face up to the fact that such tactics soon reach their limits. And as far as the simultaneously burgeoning Occupy movement was concerned, most of the trade unions were regarded as part of the establishment. What then emerged was a balancing act – which certainly gave rise to disputes within the union movement – between, on the one hand, concession bargaining with the aim of maintaining wage structures and, on the other, attempts to revitalize the unions.

One of the most important innovations was the public service unions' contribution to the partially successful citizens' movements against privatization and cutbacks in the social services, which were sustained by a broad network of civil society organizations. The unions' collaboration with the women's movement took a similar course on the occasion of the national days of action on 8 March 2018 and 2019: 'the increased presence of women in the trade unions is a valid asset for establishing solid cooperation with feminist groups in terms of broadening the social base and political reputation of trade unions' (Köhler and Calleja Jiménez 2018, 81). At the same time, a number of grass-roots strike movements emerged at local level, some with the active involvement of plant-level union branches, others independently of the large trade union federations, which tended to be regarded as 'toothless'. Fernández Rodríguez et al (2019, 579) consider these contradictory trends as a 'curious form of historical irony in which industrial relations finds itself between the vestiges of a coordinated model, on one hand, and a more social or mobilising model, on the other', which has 'to some extent politicised collective bargaining'.

Last but not least, the Italian example best highlights the possibilities for active trade union resistance. The mobilization led by the CGIL was crucial to the survival of the collective bargaining system. The CGIL is still one of the strongest trade unions in Europe, and the density rate for all Italian trade unions taken together has remained more or less unchanged over the last 20 years at almost one third of all dependent employees.[6] Furthermore, the CGIL has been involved in various aspects of trade union revitalization for years, from recruitment drives among young, precarious employees to a major campaign for a thoroughgoing reform of Italian labour law. All this meant that the existing collective bargaining system could be defended against attacks by the state.

And yet what it has been possible ultimately to achieve in practical terms with this collective bargaining system is limited.

Socio-political autonomy

To stay with the case of Italy, Leonardi (2018, 111) comes to the conclusion that trade unionism in this country has been 'resilient' and 'capable of resisting the onslaught of the crisis', but he also points to the 'gap between the power resources Italian trade unions can still formally rely on – members, financial resources, bargaining coverage, ability to mobilize – and the results they have been able to achieve over the past 25 years. Results have been poor in the key areas of wage dynamics, employment rate, workers' participation, universalism in social protection, lifelong learning, gender issues and work-life balance, all indicators in respect of which the Italian workforce is at the bottom in Europe'.

It stands to reason that, in the light of such limited 'structural', that is, labour market-based power resources, the practical opportunities for realizing their policy objectives are also limited, even for relatively strong trade unions. This is reflected, for example, in the evolution of real wages since 2010, which were only very slightly higher in Italy than in Spain, which suffered significantly higher unemployment and even greater neoliberal pressures (Figure 3.3). The stagnation of real wages in Italy has to be regarded as one aspect of the overall economic stagnation which has become a key feature in this country long before the crisis of 2008–09 (Simonazzi 2015).

In such circumstances, trade unions obviously have to extend their sphere of action and concern themselves with the entire labour market far beyond their core clientele and with the future of the economy as a whole. They must become independently active without continuing

[6] The reference here is to the so-called net union density rate, in which the unemployed and pensioners, a particularly high share of whom are trade union members in Italy, are not counted. The net union density rate in Italy is almost twice as high as in Germany and is to date one of the highest and most stable in Europe.

Figure 3.3: Evolution of average real wages 2010–19* (Italy, Spain, Greece and Eurozone)

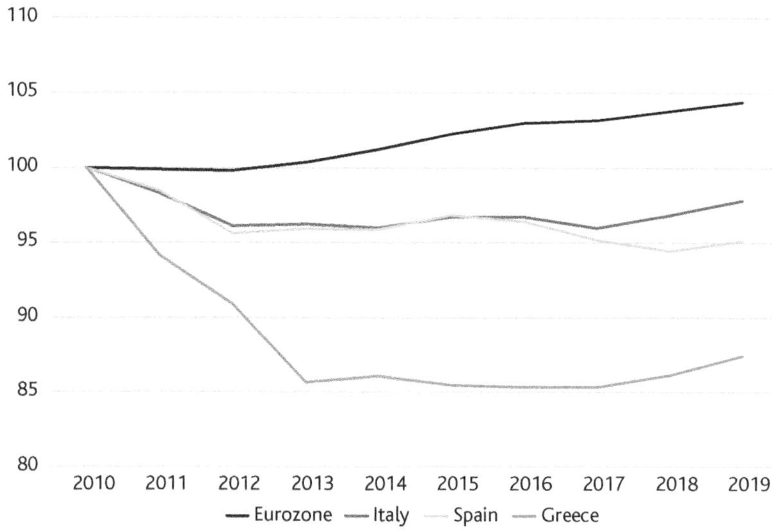

Note: * 2010=100; private consumption deflator
Source: Ameco

to place their trust in parties they have traditionally befriended but have become increasingly weak. In Italy, the decline of the left and – at least until recently – of the social democrats as well has created a political vacuum that is forcing the trade unions to act autonomously.

For Leonardi (2018, 98), the Italian trade unions are largely without partners in the party system and are suffering from 'progressive marginalisation by the political system'. This is becoming a particularly pressing problem in Italy and other countries, where this political vacuum is being filled by the nationalist right. This is demonstrated by, among other things, the examples of Poland and Hungary (see Bernaciak 2018; Neumann and Tóth 2018). A representative survey is telling here in which participants in large-scale social protests of recent years were asked which party they inclined towards. In Portugal and Spain a clear majority indicated they would vote for left-leaning parties, while in Poland and Hungary the majority declared their sympathy for right-wing parties (Campos Lima and Martín Artiles 2018).

As a consequence, it is fair to assume the trade unions' traditional core activities and even more broadly based social protest will not be sufficient to lessen the threats posed by the nationalist right. In short: the trade unions have no other option than to make considerably greater efforts to become independent socio-political actors.

Of course, socio-political independence does not mean that trade unions could or should replace political parties (Deppe 2012). However, it is becoming increasingly essential for them to be able to set the socio-political agenda if they are to be able to conduct routine union business, such as the defence and improvement of working and employment conditions, with any prospect of success.

The implications for collective bargaining systems are twofold. On the one hand, the unions need to strengthen their own capabilities in order to be able to exert greater societal pressure on the state and force it to assume its responsibility to protect and strengthen inclusive collective bargaining systems with the broadest possible impact. On the other hand, they need to take advantage of the leeway thus obtained in order to adopt a more aggressive policy approach in collective bargaining. This could also be regarded as an attempt to establish a win-win situation that would significantly stabilize the triad of trade unions, collective bargaining system and state.

A mutual strengthening of this kind could also be promoted at EU level to good effect, particularly because many of the destructive forays against collective bargaining have emanated from or been supported by the EU Commission. This would create an opportunity to establish toeholds for a countervailing social power within the hitherto dominant EU economic policy, which has virtually acquired constitutional status.

Planting a social foreign body in the economic governance of the EU

In the debate on wages policy within the EU's economic governance framework, Schulten and Müller (2017, 48) have highlighted the significance of two reform projects that could strengthen national wages policies and the collective bargaining institutions through which they are implemented. They are, firstly, a European minimum wage policy (on the respective levels of national living wages) and, secondly, a political strengthening of collective bargaining systems through the setting of EU-wide targets for a high rate of coverage by collective agreement, to be achieved in particular through the greater use of extension mechanisms. As they suggest, the so-called 'European Semester', with its analyses and recommendations for the individual EU member states could constitute the political framework for the implementation of both projects.

Now of course there is, as the authors point out, 'thoroughly justified scepticism about any reorientation of European economic governance'. And indeed any thought of pushing through fundamental progressive reforms in the foreseeable future must be regarded as unrealistic (Seikel and Truger 2019). This is why there are good reasons to regard proposals for selectively 'extending' the European Semester, such as those highlighted by Schulten and Müller, as all the more interesting. There are two reasons for this.

Firstly, there are issues around which campaigns can be organized. For all their difficulties, the European trade unions – frequently prompted by their industry associations at EU level – have been able to acquire significant experience with relatively effective Europe-wide campaigns (such as that against the so-called Bolkestein Directive on the 'liberalization' of services, the mass movement against the neoliberal free trade agreement TTIP, the European Citizens' Initiative against water privatization and, finally, the transnational series of strikes at Ryanair that were also effective as good publicity). In some cases, a broad spectrum of social actors in a number of countries were encouraged to mobilize jointly with the trade unions. This could be further encouraged by linking up with other initiatives. Thus incorporating binding targets for reducing the gender pay gap into the European Semester would impart additional momentum to the drive for a high level of coverage by collective agreements. The same applies to the proposal to make compliance with collectively agreed standards a condition for public procurement at EU level (Müller et al 2019, 664). This proposal also raises an issue around which a campaign could be organized. Implementation of it would give the authorities at regional and municipal level greater scope to take action. It would constitute a significant shift of emphasis in the unclear and contradictory case law at EU level and make an important contribution to strengthening the collective bargaining systems (Jaehrling et al 2018).

And secondly, these proposals are in effect intended to plant a foreign body in the European Semester. Even relatively small shifts of emphasis within EU economic policy in favour of the protection or strengthening of social standards are not likely to be achievable unless more and more cause for conflict is built into the process itself. Basic workers' rights, such as a gender-equitable collective bargaining system covering a broad spectrum of employees that is supported by a minimum wage on which one can live, are obvious pegs on which such conflicts could be hung. This could become germane to our purpose provided that such elements do not simply remain non-binding add-ons in the European Semester, as is the case with the 'social pillar' proposed by the previous EU Commission (and is also evident in the fact that country-specific recommendations continue to press for deregulation of the collective bargaining systems; see Müller et al 2019). They would have to be made equally as binding as the core elements of the annual monitoring process. In view of the uncertainty and disunity among the EU elites, which has become even more evident since the COVID-19 crisis, this is something that is perhaps more feasible than it was a few years ago.

If this is made a matter for trade union cooperation at EU level, then the outcome might be similar to what happened in the trade union campaigns in Italy and Spain mentioned earlier. It is the linking of members' interests with broader societal concerns, the combination of core trade union activities with socio-political agenda setting and the mobilization of unions' own powers in combination with those of other societal actors that are the core elements of trade union revitalization. Depending on how successful trade unions acting independently to set the socio-political agenda at both European and member state levels are in forcing the state to take its social responsibilities more seriously, they will be able to take advantage of the room for manoeuvre they create at both levels in order to pursue a more aggressive collective bargaining policy.

References

Banyuls, Josep and Albert Recio. 2017. 'Labour Segmentation and Precariousness in Spain: Theories and Evidence', in D. Grimshaw, C. Fagan, G. Hebson and I. Tavora (eds) *Making Work More Equal. A New Labour Market Segmentation Approach*. Manchester: Manchester University Press, pp 129–49.

Bernaciak, Magdalena. 2018. 'Coming Full Circle? Contestation, Social Dialogue and Trade Union Politics in Poland', in S. Lehndorff, H. Dribbusch and T. Schulten (eds) *Rough Waters. European Trade Unions in a Time of Crises*. Brussels: ETUI, pp 161–84.

Bosch, Gerhard. 2019. 'Strengthening and Re-Building Collective Bargaining'. Paper presented at the 6th Regulating for Decent Work Conference, ILO, Geneva, 8–10 July 2019 (Ms.).

Bosch, Gerhard and Steffen Lehndorff. 2017. 'Autonomous Bargaining in the Shadow of the Law: From an Enabling Towards a Disabling State?', in D. Grimshaw, C. Fagan, G. Hebson and I. Tavora (eds) *Making Work More Equal. A New Labour Market Segmentation Approach*. Manchester: Manchester University Press, pp 35–51.

Campos Lima, Maria da Paz. 2019. 'Portugal: Reforms and the Turn to Neoliberal Austerity', in T. Müller, K. Vandaele and J. Waddington (eds) *Collective Bargaining in Europe: Towards an Endgame*. Brussels: ETUI, pp 483–504.

Campos Lima, Maria da Paz and Antonio Martín Artiles. 2018. 'Social Protests, Discontent and Politics in Southern and Eastern Europe: Trends, Patterns and Polarization', *Transfer: European Review of Labour and Research*, 24(2): 195–215.

Deppe, Frank. 2012. *Gewerkschaften in der großen Transformation: von den 1970er Jahren bis heute*. Köln: Papyrossa.

EUobserver. 2011. 'EU Ushers in "Silent Revolution" in Control of National Economic Policies'. http://euobserver.com/institutional/31993

European Commission. 2012. 'Labour Market Developments in Europe 2012', *European Economy* 5. Brussels: European Commission.

Fernández Rodríguez, Carlos J., Rafael Ibáñez Rojo and Miguel Martínez Lucio. 2019. 'Spain: Challenges to Legitimacy and Representation in a Context of Fragmentation and Neoliberal Reform', in T. Müller, K. Vandaele and J. Waddington (eds) *Collective Bargaining in Europe: Towards an Endgame*. Brussels: ETUI, pp 563–82.

Grimshaw, Damian and Steffen Lehndorff. 2010. 'Anchors for Job Quality: Sectoral Systems of Employment in the European Context', *Work Organisation, Labour and Globalisation*, 4(1): 24–40.

Gumbrell-McCormick, Rebecca and Richard Hyman. 2013. *Trade Unions in Western Europe: Hard Times, Hard Choices*. Oxford: Oxford University Press.

Jaehrling, Karen, Mathew Johnson, Trine P. Larsen, Bjarke Refslund and Damian Grimshaw. 2018. 'Tackling Precarious Work in Public Supply Chains: A Comparison of Local Government Procurement Policies in Denmark, Germany and the UK', *Work, Employment and Society*, 32(3): 546–63.

Karamessini, Maria. 2015. 'Greece as an International Test-Case. Economic Adjustment Through a Troika/State-Induced Depression and Social Catastrophe', in S. Lehndorff (ed) *Divisive Integration: The Triumph of Failed Ideas in Europe – Revisited*. Brussels: ETUI, pp 95–126.

Katsaroumpas, Ioannis and Aristea Koukiadaki. 2019. 'Greece: "Contesting" Collective Bargaining', in T. Müller, K. Vandaele and J. Waddington (eds) *Collective Bargaining in Europe: Towards an Endgame*. Brussels: ETUI, pp 267–93.

Köhler, Holm-Detlev and José Pablo Calleja Jiménez. 2018. 'Spain: A Peripheral Economy and a Vulnerable Trade Union Movement', in S. Lehndorff, H. Dribbusch and T. Schulten (eds) *Rough Waters. European Trade Unions in a Time of Crises*. Brussels: ETUI, pp 65–86.

Koukiadaki, Aristea, Isabel Távora and Miguel Martínez Lucio. 2016. 'Joint Regulation and Labour Market Policy in Europe during the Crisis: A Seven-Country Comparison', in A. Koukiadaki, I. Távora and M. Martínez Lucio (eds) *Joint Regulation and Labour Market Policy in Europe during the Crisis*. Brussels: ETUI, pp 7–134.

Lehndorff, Steffen (ed). 2015. *Divisive Integration: The Triumph of Failed Ideas in Europe – Revisited*. Brussels: ETUI.

Lehndorff, Steffen, Heiner Dribbusch and Thorsten Schulten (eds). 2018. *Rough Waters. European Trade Unions in a Time of Crises*. Brussels: ETUI.

Leonardi, Salvo. 2018. 'Trade Unions and Collective Bargaining in Italy during the Crisis', in S. Lehndorff, H. Dribbusch and T. Schulten (eds) *Rough Waters. European Trade Unions in a Time of Crises*. Brussels: ETUI, pp 87–116.

Marcuzzo, Maria Cristina, Antonella Palumbo and Paola Villa (eds). 2020. Economic Policy, Crisis and Innovation. Beyond Austerity in Europe. London and New York: Routledge.

Müller, Torsten, Kurt Vandaele and Jeremy Waddington (eds). 2019. *Collective Bargaining in Europe: Towards an Endgame*. Brussels: ETUI.

Myant, Martin, Sotiria Theodoropoulou and Agnieszka Piasna (eds). 2016. *Unemployment, Internal Devaluation and Labour Market Deregulation in Europe*. Brussels: ETUI.

Neumann, László and András Tóth. 2018. 'Hungarian Unions under Political and Economic Pressure', in S. Lehndorff, H. Dribbusch and T. Schulten (eds) *Rough Waters. European Trade Unions in a Time of Crises*. Brussels: ETUI, pp 135–60.

Pedersini, Roberto. 2019. 'Italy: Institutionalisation and Resilience in a Changing Economic and Political Environment', in T. Müller, K. Vandaele and J. Waddington (eds) *Collective Bargaining in Europe: Towards an Endgame*. Brussels: ETUI pp 337–59.

Pernot, Jean-Marie. 2018. 'France's Trade Unions in the Aftermath of the Crisis', in S. Lehndorff, H. Dribbusch and T. Schulten (eds) *Rough Waters. European Trade Unions in a Time of Crises*. Brussels: ETUI, pp 39–64.

Schmalz, Stefan, Carmen Ludwig and Edward Webster. 2018. 'The Power Resources Approach: Developments and Challenges', *Global Labour Journal*, 9(2): 113–34.

Schulten, Thorsten and Torsten Müller. 2017. 'Stärkere Lohnkoordination in Europa?', *Sozialismus*, 10: 45–8.

Seikel, Daniel and Achim Truger. 2019. 'Die blockierte Vollendung der Europäischen Währungsunion: Plädoyer für eine pragmatische Nutzung von fiskalischen Handlungsspielräumen', *Wirtschaft und Gesellschaft*, 1: 43–65.

Sengenberger, Werner. 1994. 'Protection – Participation – Promotion: The Systemic Nature and Effects of Labour Standards', in W. Sengenberger and D. Campbell (eds) *Creating Economic Opportunities: The Role of Labour Standards in Industrial Restructuring*. Geneva: ILO, pp 45–60.

Simonazzi, Annamaria. 2015. 'Italy's Long Stagnation', in S. Lehndorff (ed) *Divisive Integration: The Triumph of Failed Ideas in Europe – Revisited*. Brussels: ETUI, pp 69–94.

Van Gyes, Guy and Thorsten Schulten (eds). 2015. *Wage Bargaining under the New European Economic Governance. Alternative Strategies for Inclusive Growth*. Brussels: ETUI.

Vogiatzoglou, Markos. 2018. 'Re-Paving the Path to Hell? Greek Trade Unions Amid Crisis and Austerity', in S. Lehndorff, H. Dribbusch and T. Schulten (eds) *Rough Waters. European Trade Unions in a Time of Crises*. Brussels: ETUI, pp 117–34.

4

Privatizing the sacrifice: individualized funding, austerity and precarity in the voluntary sector in Australia and Scotland

Donna Baines, Ian Cunningham, Philip James and Chandrima Roy

Stanford (2020) argues that post-pandemic recovery requires a modern Marshall Plan, similar to the far-reaching, government-funded programme that rebuilt Western Europe after WWII. Rather than viewing the COVID-19 crisis and its accruing public debt as debilitating and responding with predictable and ineffective austerity policies, this pandemic should be viewed as an example of what governments can do when they put the well-being of their citizens ahead of the best interests of the private market. Stanford (2020) argues further that in order to rebuild the economy, governments should increase the debt in order to finance all-round reconstruction, massive fiscal injections and a Marshall Plan-like 'willingness to use tools of direct economic management and regulation – including public service, public ownership and planning'. This includes building a fair and sustainable economy that protects groups that have been made vulnerable by government policies claiming to expand human rights and social inclusion.

Two such policies in Scotland and Australia, namely the NDIS and the Personalisation Self-Direct Care (PSDC), claimed to promote human rights and 'consumer choice' for people with disabilities and others requiring social care. Seen as some of the most important social policy since the National Health Service in the UK and Medicare in Australia, these policies actively restructured social care labour markets, promoted the expansion of precarious employment and precarious service organizations, and placed support and care options for service users in serious jeopardy (Howard et al 2015; Baines and Young 2020).

In effect these policies pitted the rights of workers against the rights of people with disabilities in a downward sloping, zero-sum game (Baines et al 2020).

The COVID-19 pandemic seems to have exacerbated the fault lines in these pro-market social programmes with informal evidence from the first few months of the pandemic showing that vulnerable service users experienced a serious reduction in supports and services, and little or no choice in service options or workers, and many workers experienced a sharp drop in working hours and wages. Of serious concern was the increased social isolation of vulnerable service users, which expanded exponentially. In Australia, informal evidence suggests that many service users who usually received daily support found themselves with only one worker able to come in once or twice per week. This was partly because service agencies lacked PPE and pandemic protocols, hence their default plan to protect workers and service users was to reduce possible transmission by restricting the number of workers in contact with service users, often limiting contact to one senior worker or supervisor. Obviously, the one supervisor or senior worker could not provide anything close to the support required by many service users. Service gaps sprung up immediately and dramatically during a time of high need and anxiety, while workers found their hours and income seriously reduced.

Though formal evidence needs to be collected to analyze the extent and impacts in the context of COVID-19, increased instability comes as no surprise given the turmoil experienced in the disability and social care sectors in both countries following the introduction of these marketized social policies. As Macdonald and Charlesworth (2016) argue, if an agenda of funding cuts underlies this kind of policy they will be unable to realize their human rights intentions, and both service users and workers will be negatively impacted. The balance of this chapter will draw on qualitative interview data collected in Scotland and previously published and original data collected in Australia to argue that austerity saturates these policies and the experience of those working and living within them. These policies introduced significant instability to social service organizations, service users and workers, including the emergence of gig work in Australia (Baines et al 2020) and increasing worker insecurity and service organization insolvency in Scotland (Cunningham 2016). The chapter starts with a brief review of the contexts and policies, before moving on to a description of the research studies, and an analysis of findings. The chapter closes with discussion and conclusions.

Contexts

Austerity

Austerity policies stem from neoclassic economic assertions that, during times of economic downturn, cutting public budgets and reducing government debt will generate market 'confidence' and a return to growth and prosperity (Blyth 2013, 3). Austerity and neoclassic economics are closely associated with neoliberalism, a hegemonic set of economic and social policies that seek to curtail social solidarity and to reduce public services and entitlements, replacing them with market and individual solutions to macro and micro social issues (Harvey, 2007; Evans and McBride 2017). Using the GFC of 2007–08 as its jettison point, the current manifestation of austerity followed close on the heels of the initial government fiscal stimulus packages. These packages increased government debt and, for as long as they lasted, slowed the recession's worst effects, however, austerity policies were soon introduced in most countries. According to McBride (2018) austerity involved three interlinked processes: 1) fiscal consolidation through balanced budgets (generally spending cuts rather than revenue increases); 2) restructuring of the public sector (devolution, downsizing, marketization, privatization and PPPs) and structural reform of social policy programmes (changes to disability, elder care and health care programmes, the erosion of pensions and elimination of early retirement policies, and the reduction of employment benefits and other social welfare supports); and 3) the flexibilization of labour markets and lowering production costs through wage caps and cuts (McBride 2018, 4). The NDIS and the PSDC were introduced in the post-GFC era of austerity and though the policies had laudatory goals in terms of respecting human rights and expanding choices for service users, they simultaneously advanced all three of the processes noted by McBride, particularly spending cuts, marketizing and privatizing the public sector and the flexibilization and degradation of social care labour markets.

Hitchen (2019) argues that austerity also operates at an ideological level, justifying sacrifice from average people and acceptance of service reductions and deferred benefits. Evans and McBride (2017) argue similarly that austerity involves transferring blame 'from the private sector that caused the crisis to the public sector, and from the public sector to the populace' (2017, 13). Clarke and Newman (2012) refer to the alchemy of austerity, an ideological process in which governments secure consent to austerity and lowered expectations, through unfounded claims that austerity revives struggling economies and prosperity will return at some undetermined point in the future.

The National Disability Insurance Scheme

The NDIS was piloted in Australia during the austerity years, starting in 2013 and rolled out nationwide in 2016. It was intended to provide 'choice' in services for people with permanent disabilities through a cash-for-care system of funding that replaced the earlier organization-based system of funding (Howard et al 2015). Like Scotland's PSCD, the NDIS appeared to respond to activists' demand for substantive equality and empowerment of people with disabilities. However, as Backhouse (2017) asserts, these goals have been 'compromised by a political discourse of privatization and marketisation' (2017, 2).

Instead, they argue that 'structural barriers continue to hinder full actualisation of citizenship rights' and warn that 'some groups of people with disability may be left behind in a user-led system' (Backhouse 2017, 2). Ferguson (2012) argues likewise that individualized funding programmes are more consistent with attempts to reduce welfare dependency than with the promotion of social justice (2012, 60).

Cortis et al (2017) have studied the NDIS extensively in order to identify the mechanisms through which underfunding operates. These mechanisms include: 1) underfunding services in relation to the needs of people; and 2) underfunding of contracted services (see also, Productivity Commission 2017). In Australia, the terms and conditions for disability workers are set by the federal administrative body, Fair Works Commission, in an agreement known as the Social, Community, Home Care and Disability Services Award. However, as Cortis et al (2017) argue, pricing within the NDIS has been set too low to meet Award wage minimums, let alone to cover the costs of those employers committed to paying above the Award. This means that better employers risk insolvency, leaving the market open to those willing to pay lower wages.

Indeed, in order to fill the shortfall generated by the two mechanisms noted earlier, service users and service organizations tend to pay lower wages and to shorten shifts (Williams 2014; Cortis et al 2017). This adds to the churn and turnover in the sector as low wages fail to retain or attract workers. Minimum shifts are also differentiated with the Award, with home care workers having a minimum engagement period of one hour compared to two hours for a disability support worker. This provides an additional incentive for cash-strapped service users and employers to call for shorter shifts for disability workers and to cut costs by hiring home care workers for shockingly short shifts of one hour (Macdonald and Charlesworth 2016).

These factors mean that workers face a government-instigated labour market characterized by short notice shifts, multiple employers, multiple job holding, dispersed work sites, no travel pay and short-term work assignments (Macdonald et al 2018). This work is increasingly privatized, fragmented, and gig-like, including operating through digital platforms in which the employers do little more than provide an electronic interface between workers and service users (Macdonald nd; van Doorn, 2017). This type of labour market, precipitated by government policies, reflects neoliberal themes of privatization and individualization that are undergirded by ideological narratives expecting workers to sacrifice wages, time and conditions to ostensibly empower services users (Baines et al 2020). As the following discussion will confirm, these same policies have introduced increased precarity and insecurity and, in the case of the recent pandemic, reduced service options and increased service user isolation and exclusion.

Personalization of self-directed care in Scotland

The approach to individualization or personalization of social care services in Scotland under the legislative framework of Self-Directed Support (SDS) is different to the policy in England which predates it. The Self-Directed Support Act (Scotland) 2013 sought to realign social care along the principles of delivering 'personalized, reflexive and flexible' services, giving greater choice and control to individuals over their support (Hunter et al 2012). The Scottish approach is less target-focused than England's and offers, via the four options that underpin SDS policy, a more flexible – for both service users and agencies – set of possibilities for implementation. SDS is a vehicle for personalization, with Direct Payments (DPs) as one of four options as defined in the Self-Directed Support Act (Section 13, p 4, 2013). In the case of DPs, individuals who have been assessed as needing services are provided cash payments by the local authority, and the person can then use the payment to arrange his/her support. The second option is to have an Individual Budget (IB), which is managed by a third party, or where the service user directs to arrange support from the local authority or from a commissioned provider through the IB. The third choice is the status quo, that is, local authority managed provision. The fourth is a combination of the aforementioned three.

There are a number of implementation issues and workforce implications from the introduction of SDS. As in Australia, user-led choice leads to uncertainty in the market. The devolution of purchasing responsibility to service users means providers need to reduce their reliance on block contracts with local authorities. Under the new framework, agreements are set up by the councils under SDS. Providers are to provide services but are not guaranteed business, as decisions on whether to use them rests with the service users. This has obvious implications for worker security as demand for services from users becomes more intangible (Fair Work Convention 2019).

Adding austerity to such insecurity is obviously a problem for the workforce. Even prior to austerity it was feared that personalization was inadequately resourced (West 2013). Personalization and austerity are intertwined as individual forms of funding can help shrink expenditure (Cunningham 2016). Cash-strapped local authorities have used SDS as a vehicle to cut costs further (Cunningham 2016) by increasing the onus on users to do more for themselves by cutting hours of service. Local authorities were also likely to play an important role in controlling cost and quality of care by introducing lower hourly rates to pay for care, which can have a negative impact on resources to adequately pay the workforce, or cover costs over and above essential service user needs (Rummery et al 2012; Beresford 2014).

There have been concerns that the empowerment of service users can be used as an alternative to adequately resourcing public services (Hickey 2012). Cunningham and Nickson (2010), in their study of voluntary services, expressed concerns that pressures arising from local authorities' drive to cut costs in the face of austerity would likely impact on services and overall terms and conditions of work. The SDS strategy is thus seen as one of vehicles pushing workforce insecurity in public services (Cunningham 2016), as well as another step towards the commodification of care work, where services are bought and sold in a market and 'users' are re-classified as 'customers' (Needham 2011).

Tying the personalization agenda to public service cuts has led to tensions within the workforce. Specifically, starting from a reduced public expenditure resource base, the allocation of money to users through DPs has been seen to bring about various forms of insecurity to front line voluntary sector workers (Cunningham and Nickson 2013). In organizations that recruit people based on skills, personal values and commitment to a particular service group, serious tensions among the workforce can also emerge when the move to personalization leads to reductions in service quality (Cunningham and Nickson 2013). There is also evidence to suggest that some workers see personalization as a commodification of care (Needham 2011), which leads to a degree of dissonance among those committed to traditional social entitlement approaches to care and relationships with users (Cunningham and Nickson 2013).

The studies

The data for the Scottish section of the chapter has been drawn from a qualitative study funded by a public service union (UNISON). The study involved semi-structured interviews with front line staff (21), some of their managers (14) and union representatives (4) in four case study organizations representative of a range of different types of service providers in the non-profit voluntary sector. Front line staff were asked about their thoughts on personalized approaches to service delivery and their experiences of work in this context. They were broadly representative of the overall gender profile (female) of the sector, and included workers on multiple forms of contract, including full-time permanent, and more casualized forms of employment, such as temporary, part-time and zero-hours. Most of them were pursuing or acquiring either Scottish or national vocational qualifications (SVQ or NVQ) at different levels, had experience in health care or a certificate in complementary care work. The length of employment varied from five to 35 years, with a majority having more than ten years' experience.

The Australian section of the chapter draws on previously published (Baines et al 2019; Baines et al 2020) and original unpublished data from a qualitative study involving 19 in-depth, semi-structured interviews, using an interview guide with disability sector workers in one of the early roll-out regions (this roll-out started in July 2016). Research participants were recruited through an open call distributed by unions in the sector and took place in a central location. Interviewees were asked questions regarding changes in their work under the NDIS, challenges, successes and where they saw themselves in the future. The sample was 70 per cent female which is slightly lower than the sector (Cortis and van Toorn 2020), and all participants had higher education and/or training. They ranged in length of employment from 1.5 to 30 years, with a majority having more than eight years' experience. The interviews were audiotaped, transcribed and analyzed for patterns and themes (Fram 2013).

Ethics approval was received at the universities involved. Limitations of the studies include their relatively small sample size, possible bias in recruitment strategies and the qualitative method itself which generates rich insights that may be applicable in other contexts and is not aimed at generalization.

Findings

Drawing on the strongest themes in the data and exemplar quotes, this section analyzes some of the ways that the ideology and policies of austerity are lived/experienced in the everyday work life of those employed in the sector. These are discussed for each country and then compared in the next section of this chapter. In Australia, themes include: the privatization and individualization of workers, including the work, risk and cost (travel, meals, training, work in private homes (multiple short shifts)) which overlapped and interwove with the second theme of expectations of ongoing sacrifice. In Scotland, themes include: multiple rounds of cuts and greater organizational insecurity, deterioration in services; struggling to provide decent pay and conditions, work intensification, multiple forms of employee insecurity, and worker sacrifice.

Consistent with the literature that notes that austerity and neoliberalism advance privatization of services and risk (Blyth, 2013; McBride, 2018), the Australian data show that the experience of work under the NDIS is privatized in a number of ways. In particular, rather than working as part of a team based in an agency setting, the individualized, cash-for-care aspects of the NDIS takes the work out of an agency setting and sets it largely in private homes, splintering the work and isolating both worker and service user. In effect, by shifting the work from the public sphere of community non-profit organizations to the private sphere of home and individual activities, this requires workers and service users to sacrifice consistent, (often) long-term, agency-based workplace relationships.

The main way this shift to the private realm operates is through underpricing and underfunded care packages. These austere care packages mean that service users do not have the funds to pay for longer shifts or better wages, and quickly run out of funds for transportation and activities, leaving them isolated in their own homes. For workers, this means that they are frequently required to work multiple, short shifts in private homes as the service users do not have the funds to pay for longer shifts. In addition, the workers absorb the costs of travel between very short shifts with low pay, often very little advance notice and frequent last-minute cancellations or changes. As one worker noted, "It's all over the shop … some of the shifts are two hours. Some of these people drive 60+k for two hours a day." This amplifies the austerity theme of sacrifice from workers and the public, as workers sacrifice wages, stability and continuity for a system that aims to produce human rights and inclusion for service users in some possible point in the future. Service users, similarly, sacrifice quality care and fulsome participation in community activities as their individual funding packages fail to cover their needs and interests.

Reflecting a further aspect of privatization in terms of the dynamics of the private family, workers noted a lack of clarity from some families regarding rules for safe workplaces (now private homes), as well as a lack of commitment to respecting the start and end of shifts and a tendency to overestimate the capacities of their family member to remain alone when shifts end and workers have to leave. In the private home, workers do not have colleagues or supervisors to call on for coverage or advice. Instead, they individually shouldered the risk and the increased unpaid work. As one worker observed, 'Families don't always acknowledge when a shift is finished and don't let the staff person leave. Or don't come home on time to take over … In some cases, clients are very afraid to be left alone or too unstable to be left alone and so we can't leave' (Baines et al 2019). This can represent a significant form of unpaid work for the largely female labour force. Unpaid work also extended to shift preparation and reading client files, as one long-time worker told us:

> The only way I get information on the clients is if I go into the head office on my own time and read the files. There is no paid time for it. The NDIS only pays for face-to-face time, no prep time. With short notice and new clients, I usually can't manage to get to the office before my shift. (Baines et al 2019)

Macdonald et al (2018) studied the work time of NDIS workers over a three-day period and found that if 'unpaid overtime and time spent travelling directly between clients had been paid, workers would have received between 2% and 27% more for their three-days' work' (2018, 91). This represents a substantial wage subsidy to employers and a substantial loss to low-wage, precarious workers. Moreover, this dynamic exacerbates the sacrifices expected of workers in this female majority sector, where unpaid work is endemic and often viewed as a natural extension of the unpaid care work expected of women in the home and community (Charlesworth and Malone 2017). In a classic article, Land and Rose (1985) coined the term 'compulsory altruism' to capture the gendered, taken-for-granted expectation of uncomplaining, unrecognized and mandatory unpaid work.

Service user transportation was also privatized. In the past, employers frequently provided vehicles for service user transport but workers are now required to use and bear the cost of insuring their own private vehicles for service user transport with no exceptions: 'If you don't use [y]our own vehicle, you won't be working. They're not playing ball, they're not being nice about it, they're not even hiding it anymore.' Privatization also extended to other aspects of work, as articulated by this worker: 'Now we're expected to provide our own phones, our own cars, our own resources, our own supervision and pretty much pay if there's things that participants that we're working with would like to go to, we're expected to pay, too, ourselves' (Baines et al 2019).

In Scotland all types of respondents indicated significant problems with the way that personalization had become connected with local authority cuts to public spending, and forms of privatization. Most of the case study organizations securing contracts through individual budgets received financial resources that were smaller than offered through conventional block contracts. There were concerns that the finances of the sector were reaching the crisis point and that one or more of the big providers could 'go under' (UNISON official). Some providers were reportedly drawing from their own financial reserves.

There were also various manifestations of privatization occurring in the personalized market. The first aspect of privatization was the increased presence of private sector organizations in the newly configured SDS markets. These organizations were seen as offering much cheaper provision than the voluntary sector with accompanying concerns around quality. In terms of services, privatization and public expenditure cuts occurred through the closure of Day Centres (activity centres for people with disabilities). Closures meant the removal of opportunities for service users to socialize with friends. Services were further privatized by focusing on the individual, with one-to-one provision based in the community. At the same time, service user activities were constrained because of limited time and funds to fully cover the support staff to accompany them. Staff further commented that a lack of resources meant there were few opportunities to properly engage people with the community – "there's only so many times a week you can take somebody bowling before it gets boring … it can be hard for it not get samey for them." Another respondent observed: "A lot of the time is spent on buses to keep out of the rain, or going into buildings and buying coffee because it's too cold outside for customers … My working life is just about keeping people safe and dry and warm basically."

Cuts in hours in these community services meant that previously there was round-the-clock support; now there could be gaps from after an early morning call by a worker and up to an evening call, or no cover overnight beyond electronic alarms. Care managers in local authorities reportedly argued that these gaps in provision represented times when a user was being independent in the community. In contrast, workers reported significant unease with regard to service user well-being, especially among extremely vulnerable individuals, where they felt the risk of accidents was present. One union official reported:

> 'She's got a letter from the councilor and the fire officer that came down and done their check, and said she shouldn't be left alone at all. But she's still got breaks, like three hours. What's it, we leave her at 9 o'clock, we're back in at 12, sometimes 1.00pm. And we're there 'til half past four or 5 o'clock and then we're back in again at 7 to 10 sleepover. So, she's got blocks of maybe two or three hours with a break. So, what happens if, in that time, something happens to her and you walk back in and there's something wrong? You've left her, she's not buzzed or contacted anybody because she's scared of it.'

Interviewees drew repeated attention to the steady corrosive impact of successive waves of austerity-driven cuts on their service users. Each of these organizations felt they were prepared to see and manage reductions in resources to accompany personalization's implementation, but reported the steady degradation of services as rolling cuts took their toll:

> 'We understood there would be a certain amount of cuts. We understood that it could be a way of people becoming more independent, which is what personalisation is.

> However, you then saw that the cuts they made were more brutal than we had first thought they would be ... but there are situations where people's budgets are being cut all the time and it's becoming ... or getting to such a point where they aren't having a good life. So that bit is not right and it's not working and that's not giving people the independence they want.'

Purchasing services above and beyond basic care for users was also becoming more difficult. The rhetoric of the personalization agenda from local authorities emphasized its aim was to enhance lives by providing choices and opportunities rather than basic care. Here, community integration included not only support to allow people to live in their own homes, it was also supposed to involve, where appropriate, personalized outcomes such as the ability to improve educational and job opportunities, pursue hobbies and interests, travel and form new social ties, bonds and friendships. However, respondents reported that successive cuts meant that these forms of community integration were increasingly difficult to resource:

> 'Tight local authority funding is, it's reducing people's options and choices ... their funding is going to provide basic care and not much more than that ... there's no support left over for activities. So, people are having to choose. For me, proper personalisation, and choice and control, you wouldn't have to choose one or the other. Even in some packages of care, we're actually struggling to meet basic needs because of funding ... the last six months, it used to be that there would be lots of bespoke purchasers factored into people's budgets, but that's now getting pulled out. My issue is when you're having to choose between actually having a life, and your basic needs, you know there's a difference.'

This financial environment had significant implications for workers. In terms of pay and conditions, when SDS was first introduced, cuts in expenditure meant workers in two support service units suffered pay reductions. As the policy developed, one of the organizations studied bid for services under its local authority's framework. The organization was committed to paying all its staff a 'living wage', that is, several pounds above the UK statutory national minimum wage. The trade-off for this commitment to a living wage was that these workers would have to be employed on zero-hour contracts, and receive no sick pay.

As a consequence of two rounds of restructuring, workers experienced cuts in hours, sick pay and holidays. In relation to the cuts in holidays, one line manager noted the adverse implications this had for older staff in particular: "[They] took six days, basically, from everybody, six days in an organization 'with an ageing population' in a staff team in which 'there's lots of kind of, you know, health and well-being problems with staff, which are starting to kind of come in.'"

New shift patterns also brought their own forms of work intensity. One worker described a new pattern of shifts to meet the demands of service user that he found exhausting:

> 'I'm starting at half past one, working through the evening to half past ten, then it's a sleepover. Then the following morning, well, the following day, I'm working until ten o'clock at night straight through. If I was younger it wouldn't bother me, but it starts to affect me now … I was really exhausted at the end of the week.'

Workforce insecurity came from a mixture of intangibility in demand from service users and austerity. In one example, a combination of reduced care packages and individualized services led to the increased likelihood of staff having gaps between 'care sessions', therefore raising the question of when this was of a length sufficient to create a split shift and hence an unpaid period of work. Relatedly, a growing use of split shifts was also apparent among the other organizations as the priority accorded to individual service user needs increased in a context of declining funding. Such changes to staff work rotas to support the more user-focused delivery of services was serving to reduce the ability for them to accommodate the needs of staff regarding their demands for flexibility, as the following quote from one senior manager illustrates:

> 'To be able to grant flexible working it's more difficult … There is an increase in need for staff flexibility whereas maybe three, four years ago it wouldn't be an issue if a staff said I only want to work a Tuesday, Thursday. I only want to do an early shift. I don't want to do sleepovers – now it is difficult. The contracts are quite explicit that we need

> flexibility built-in with that we may not be able to give you notice when we need to change rotas …'

Some workers across case studies felt insecure in their jobs because of personalization and austerity. A small number of workers reported how the constant restructuring undertaken by their employers in the face of demands for greater individualized services had, alongside cuts, unsettled them:

> 'It's always a worry because there's been that many cuts. I mean that twice we've had voluntary redundancies. You just wonder is this going to come up again. So, there's always that worry about my employment … am I safe because what would I do if I lost my job? I've got a mortgage like most people so of course I worry about my employment, I do worry.'

The growth in 'hours poverty' was evident. In one organization, workers had their hours cut directly as a consequence of their funder's austerity-driven personalization programme. Some employees quit as a consequence of these cuts, and those remaining on the job experienced increased difficulties:

> 'I started off at 38 hours, I'm down to 36 now. [The organization] is in the process of cutting people's hours, trying to cut their wages, which we are all dead against. The excuse was that it was the local government. It affects them, so inadvertently, it's affecting us. I stay in xxx, so I'm roughly travelling about 39 miles a day. So, if they cut my wages, it's gonna be financially impossible for me to carry this job on … it would still be quite a drastic amount off my salary. I don't want to lose my job … if financially it doesn't work out for me, then I will have to leave.'

Elsewhere uncertainty over the number of hours' work available to employees was common:

> 'We can't say to people you've got guaranteed 35-hour contracts. We've got a lot of staff that's on 16 and below … but in actual fact the additional hours they're getting offered because of the short staffed they're getting their 35 hours but it's not guaranteed.'

Despite the austerity-driven impact on working conditions, there was evidence of workers self-sacrificing to deliver services. This included 'presenteeism' among some workers who, conscious of people paying for services through individual budgets, were reluctant to go sick:

> 'Sometimes, even if you are feeling a bit unwell you wouldn't want to call in sick because you know your diary is full and that would mess all the diary up … you do push sometimes when you are not well because you don't want to let people down because … I'm loaded with cold this morning, I felt really sick and weak, but I was like, no come on, you can do it … I try and never phone in sick unless it was really like I couldn't move out of bed.'

The worker added that although there was never any direct pressure from management to attend when sick, every worker knew the rotas, schedules and diaries of the team and how difficult it was to cover if they phoned in sick:

> 'I was off for a wee while and was really ill. I landed in hospital and was made to feel really very guilty. Again, if you've got gastric, anything like that, you can't work … I stayed with my uncle for three years who was in his 80s. Anytime he took ill near the end and you know, "No, you can't have time off." I says, "But he's dying. I need time off. I'm taking it off." I said, "I'm not going to work in [a] caring profession and I can't care for my family." You're made to feel guilty, very guilty.'

Comparing NDIS and SDS

Comparative research on austerity-driven forms of individualized care is rare so the aforementioned studies provide some useful points of comparison. Each of the policies reveal forms of privatization. In the Scottish case, this begins with private providers entering the market offering cheaper service provision. There are also common forms of approach as organizations in Australia and Scotland were forced to close in-agency provision in favour of individualized services in private homes or the community.

Service provision has also deteriorated across the two countries as the system moved to individual funding, not matching the former provision under block services in the case of Scotland, and divided across many service users with little or no capacity for economies of scale in Australia. As a consequence, user interests and needs have been curtailed or have not been met beyond basic personal services, that is, hygiene, shopping and so on. In Scotland, cuts in support in the name of service user self-reliance and 'independence in the community' also bring safety fears for those requiring greater support.

With regard to workforce issues, common problems are apparent with regard to increased demands for worker flexibility, with limited reciprocity to meet their own needs. Impacts on pay and income for workers show similar effects. In Australia, employees subsidize wages through not being paid for travel or down time. In Scotland, these issues are also apparent, but further include direct cuts to salaries and forms of 'hours poverty'. Indeed, hours poverty is apparent in the care sector in both countries. In Scotland, perceptions of job insecurity resulting from changes in preferences of users and waves of austerity are also common, and workers further experience work intensification.

Forms of self-sacrifice are common among workers across the two forms of individualized care system, with slight differences. In Australia, workers sacrifice through extending shifts and engaging in forms of unpaid work. Again, this is not uncommon in Scotland, but self-sacrifice was manifesting through 'presenteeism' during bouts of sickness, although there was some suggestion of 'compulsory altruism' as some workers were unable to claim any sick pay.

Conclusion

At the beginning of this chapter we noted that the COVID-19 pandemic has further exposed the deep fault lines in the NDIS and the PSDC. These fault lines include the ways that austerity saturates these social policies, fracturing and privatizing the experience of workers and service users, while simultaneously demanding greater sacrifice from them today in order to achieve much-needed human rights goals sometime further down the road. Characteristic of austerity, the promises of benefit for all at a distant unstated point in time undergirds the operation and experience of these two major pieces of social policy (Hitchen 2019). Workers in the sector forgo job permanence and security in the name of the new policies and meeting the 'consumer' needs of services uses, while service organizations are required to operate with reduced funds, as well as increased overall precarity and exposure to business collapse. The earlier analysis suggests that in the operation and everyday experience of these austere policies, even sacrifice has been privatized with individual, largely female workers undertaking unpaid work to fill the gaps in individualized funding packages.

Sacrifices have continued to be expected of care workers and other essential workers during the COVID-19 pandemic, including the sacrifice of health and even life. Recognizing this sacrifice and inequities in wages during the pandemic, some governments raised the wages of care workers, particularly those working in long-term care with older people and other essential workers, and required that they only work in one site so as to limit the transmission of the virus (Wadhwani 2020; Zussman 2020). These measures were significant and very symbolic and, on the surface, further recognition of the importance of these highly gendered jobs to the well-being of society. Increased pay is also an acknowledgement that these jobs cannot be done well and safely if they are fragmented, awarded low pay and are precarious. Caution needs to be applied to seeing government pronouncements on wages as symbolic recognition of a new importance attached to social care workers. In relation to our Scottish case, for example, early in the pandemic the government proclaimed all workers were to receive an increase to meet the level of the 'real living wage' as reward for their contribution to controlling the pandemic. The reality was that this pay rise was already scheduled as part of a long-term government policy. The key difference was that the award was immediate rather than backdated (Scottish Government 2020). Moreover, recent UK government pronouncements of negotiated above-inflation pay rises for essential public service workers has excluded much of the social care workforce on the grounds these pay awards are outside its scope given the workforce is fragmented because of much of it being privatized (Trades Union Congress (TUC) 2020).

Though governments have largely received strong support from the public for their leadership and intervention during the pandemic, particularly in terms of direct payments, income supports, health care funding and economic stimulus, many governments are warning of austerity measures in the post-pandemic period. In contrast, Stanford (2020) argues that deficits will need to soar in order to pull economies out of what will otherwise be the worst depression in the last two centuries. To do so, there needs to be a reappraisal and debunking of the 'deficit myth' that equates the economy as a household that can go bust because of excessive government spending, and that this justifies the current and any future austerity measures. Once such myths are debunked, policy makers can then take advantage of the greater fiscal space afforded to them from deficit spending (Kelton 2020). Perhaps alongside the social solidarity witnessed in the self-quarantines and the nightly cheers and banging of pots and pans for essential workers, policy changes can build alternatives to austerity and, in the process, address the environmental, social justice and equity questions that continue to plague our planet and disrupt the advancement of human rights for the most vulnerable and marginal.

References

Backhouse, Stephanie. 2017. *Who loses out in the NDIS? An analysis of the early rollout of the National Disability Insurance Scheme in Australia.* Unpublished Doctoral dissertation, Murdoch University, Perth.

Baines, Donna and Douglas Young. 2020. 'Austerity, Personalised Funding and the Degradation of Care Work: Comparing Scotland's Self-Directed Support Policy and Australia's National Disability Insurance Scheme', in Donna Baines and Ian Cunningham (eds) *Working in the Context of Austerity and Work. Challenges and Struggles.* Bristol: Bristol University Press.

Baines, Donna, Fiona Macdonald and Jim Stanford. 2020. 'Zero-Sum Social Policy: Going Gig and the Australian National Disability Insurance Scheme', *Studies in Political Economy*, 101(1): 17–34.

Baines, Donna, Fiona Macdonald, Jim Stanford and Jessie Moore. 2019. *Precarity and Job Instability on the Frontlines of NDIS Support Work.* Canberra, ACT: The Centre for Future Work at the Australia Institute.

Beresford, Peter. 2014. *Personalisation.* Bristol. Policy Press.

Blyth, Mark. 2013. *Austerity: The History of a Dangerous Idea.* Oxford: Oxford University Press.Charlesworth, Sara and Jenny Malone. 2017. 'Re-Imagining Decent Work for Home Care Workers in Australia', *Labour & Industry*, 27(4): 284–301.

Clarke, John and Janet Newman. 2012. 'The Alchemy of Austerity', *Critical Social Policy*, 32(3): 299–319.

Cortis, Natasha and Georgia van Toorn. 2020. *Working in New Disability Markets: A Survey of Australia's Disability Workforce.* Sydney: UNSW.

Cortis, Natasha, Fiona Macdonald, Bob Davidson and Eleanor Bentham. 2017. *Reasonable, Necessary and Valued: Pricing Disability Services for Quality Support and Decent Jobs.* Sydney: Social Policy Research Centre, University of New South Wales.

Cunningham, Ian. 2016. 'Non-Profits and the "Hollowed Out" State: The Transformation of Working Conditions Through Personalising Social Care Services during an Era of Austerity. Special Section, States of Work', *Work, Employment and Society*, 30(4): 649–68.

Cunningham, Ian and Dennis Nickson. 2010. *Personalisation and Its Implications for Work and Employment in the Voluntary Sector*. A Report to the Voluntary Sector Social Services Workforce Unit, Edinburgh, Scotland.

Cunningham, Ian and Dennis Nickson. 2013. *Public Sector Austerity, Personalisation and the Implications for the Voluntary Sector Workforce*. Report for Community Care Providers Scotland, Edinburgh.

Evans, Brian and Stephen McBride. 2017. 'Austerity. The Lived Experience', in Brian Evans and Stephen McBride (eds) *Austerity: The Lived Experience*. Toronto: University of Toronto Press, pp 3–16.

Fair Work Convention. 2019. Fair Work in Scotland's Social Care Sector 2019. www.fairworkconvention.scot/our-report-on-fair-work-in-social-care/. Last accessed 24 February 2020.

Ferguson, Iain. 2012. 'Personalisation, Social Justice and Social Work: A Reply to Simon Duffy', *Journal of Social Work Practice*, 26(1): 55–73.

Fram, Shiela.M. 2013. 'The Constant Comparative Analysis Method Outside of Grounded Theory', *Qualitative Report*, 18(1).

Harvey, David. 2007. *A Brief History of Neoliberalism*. Oxford University Press, Oxford.

Hickey, Robert. 2012 'End-users, Public Services, and Industrial Relations: The Restructuring of Social Services in Ontario', *Relations Industriellles*, 67(4): 590–611.

Hitchen, Esther. 2019. 'The Affective Life of Austerity: Uncanny Atmospheres and Paranoid Temporalities', *Social & Cultural Geography*, 22(2): 1–24.

Howard Amanda, Tamara Blakemore, Lou Johnston, Darleen Taylor and Rani Dibley. 2015. '"I'm Not Really Sure But I Hope It's Better": Early Thoughts of Parents and Carers in a Regional Trial Site for the Australian National Disability Insurance Scheme', *Disability & Society*, 30(9): 1365–81.

Hunter, Susan, Charlotte Pearson and Sally Witcher. 2012. *Self-directed Support (SDS): Preparing for Delivery*. Glasgow: Institute for Research and Innovation in Social Services.

Kelton, Stephanie. 2020. *The Deficit Myth: Modern Monetary Theory and How to Build a Better Economy*. London: John Murray.

Land, Hilary and Hilary Rose. 1985. 'Compulsory Altruism for Some or an Altruistic Society for All?', in P. Bean, J. Ferris and D. Whynes (eds) *In Defence of Welfare*. London: Tavistock.

Macdonald, Fiona. nd. *'Personalised Risk' in Paid Care Work and the Impacts of 'Gig Economy' Care Platforms and other Market-Based Organisations*. Manuscript submitted for publication.

Macdonald, Fiona and Sara Charlesworth. 2016. 'Cash for Care under the NDIS: Shaping Care Workers' Working Conditions?' *Journal of Industrial Relations*, 58(5): 627–46.

Macdonald, Fiona., Eleanor Bentham and Jenny Malone. 2018. 'Wage, Theft, Underpaymephenent and Unpaid Work in Marketised Social Care', *Economic and Labour Relations Review*, 29(1): 80–96.

McBride, Stephen. 2018. 'Eight Things the Crisis Taught Us about Austerity', *The Monitor*. Ottawa: Canadian Centre for Policy Alternatives. www.policyalternatives.ca/publications/monitor/eight-things-crisis-taught-us-about-austerity. Last accessed 10 July 2020.

Needham, Caroline. 2011. *Personalising Public Services: Understanding the Personalisation Narrative*. University of Bristol, Bristol: Policy Press.

Productivity Commission. 2017. *National Disability Insurance Scheme (NDIS) – Costs*. www.pc.gov.au/inquiries/completed/ndis-costs/report. Last accessed 10 July 2020.

Rummery, Kirstein., David Bell, Alison Bowes, Alison Dawson and J. Elizabeth Roberts. 2012. *Counting the Cost of Choice and Control: Evidence for the Costs of Self-directed Support in Scotland*. Edinburgh: Scottish Government.

Scottish Government. 2020. *Pay Rise for Social Care Staff*. www.gov.scot/news/pay-rise-for-social-care-staff/. Last accessed 12 August 2020.

Stanford, Jim. 2020. 'We Are Going to Need a Marshal Plan to Rebuild After COVID'. *Policy Options/Options Politique*. https://policyoptions.irpp.org/magazines/april-2020/were-going-to-need-a-marshall-plan-to-rebuild-after-covid-19/. Last accessed 10 July 2020.

TUC. 2020. *The Public Sector Pay Rise is Long Overdue – But Many Workers Are Still Left Out*. www.tuc.org.uk/blogs/public-sector-pay-rise-long-overdue-many-workers-are-still-left-out. Last accessed 12 August 2020.

van Doorn, Neils. 2017. 'Platform Labor: On the Gendered and Racialized Exploitation of Low-Income Service Work in the "On-Demand" Economy', *Information, Communication & Society*, 20(6): 898–914.

Wadhwani, Ashley. 2020. '"Pandemic Pay" to Give Temporary Wage Top-Up to 250,000 B.C. Front-Line Workers'. *Victoria News*. www.vicnews.com/news/pandemic-pay-to-give-250000-eligible-b-c-front-line-workers-temporary-wage-top-up/. Last accessed 14 July 2020.

West, Karen. 2013. 'The Grip of Personalization in Adult Social Care: Between Managerial Domination and Fantasy', *Critical Social Policy*, 33(3): 638–57.

Williams, Tony. 2014. 'The NDIS: What Can Australia Learn from Other Countries', *New Paradigm*, 1(12): 30–3.

Zussman, Richard. 2020. 'B.C. Front-Line Health Workers to Receive Pandemic Pay Top-Up'. *Global News*. https://globalnews.ca/news/6960819/pandemic-pay-b-c/. Last accessed 14 July 2020.

5

Austerity and the social innovation agenda

Meghan Joy, John Shields, Sharon Broughton and Siu Mee Cheng

Social innovation has come to be widely embraced as a fresh problem-solving approach to address what are framed as stubborn and costly social policy challenges. Paradoxically, despite claims to newness, SI is often cast as a neutral path to identify 'what works' to solve problems. This apolitical positioning fails to contextualize the socio-economic and political dynamics in which problems and SI have arisen. This chapter engages in such a contextualization and re-politicization of the SI agenda.

The SI agenda jumped into prominence in the wake of the 2008 'Great Recession' and must be understood as tightly tied to neoliberal projects of austerity. In this chapter, we argue that SI helps us to understand the ways in which the neoliberal project has proven to be 'an adaptive creature of crisis', embracing policy ideas and reforms needed to drive forward its agenda. Its engagement in a 'permanent revolution' of experimentation and policy shapeshifting has been necessary, ironically, because so much of its market-based reforms have been failures (Peck et al 2012). We argue that the movement from 'roll back' ('greed-is-good') to 'roll out' ('markets-with-morals') neoliberalism has been facilitated through SI (Peck nd) and warn that this current phase of 'neoliberalism with a smile' remains centred in austerity. Neoliberalism's adaptive abilities enables it to co-opt many seemingly alternative ideas, stripping them of more progressive political projects that might be at their root. For instance, the *Stanford Social Innovation Review* has accepted the austerity argument that there is just not enough state fiscal capacity to deal with meaningful social policy reform. It endorses a non-statist 'realist position' of employing the use of the non-profit sector, charity and venture-based philanthrocapitalism as a way to harness private initiative and capital for public good. Yet, this was not always the case as SI has roots in radical, restorative and transformative movements. In this chapter, we explore the lineage of SI, including its amorphous definition, seemingly conflicting idea-sets, and associated tools and techniques to understand how it has been used to extend the neoliberal project through austerity and to identify internal conflicts that might be exploited to challenge austerity politics. We use Wendy Brown's (2015) understanding of neoliberal rationality to help us identify and analyze the ways in which SI has been captured by this dominant political project.

As we write this chapter, the world is facing another crisis. The COVID-19 pandemic challenges neoliberal austerity and demonstrates that markets and the retreat of public provision are not the solution to growing social problems. The pandemic has brought into focus the deep-seated structural inequalities of the neoliberal capitalist order, intersected with systems of oppression such as racism, patriarchy and ageism. Only state responses have been able to provide income and health supports and stabilize the economy. SI responses focused on the non-profit sector, voluntarism and philanthrocaptalism as social shock absorbers have proven woefully inadequate to the impacts of the pandemic. The service providing non-profit sector, for example, has been hard hit by the threats of 'revenue loss, office closures and service cancellations, and human resource challenges' (Philanthropist 2020). The capacities of a strained non-profit sector are incapable of addressing rapidly expanding need. Financial stress is seeing a significant shrinkage of the sector as many non-profits fail. Venture philanthropy is also in retreat with deep economic recession. The pandemic has opened a policy window with a contest as to whether the future will be shaped by another round of neoliberal austerity or a pathway to a more progressive opening (Shields and Abu Alrob 2020). We warn against the dominant version of SI as a solution and encourage an exploration of how to harness more radical orientations of SI to move forward.

The social innovation agenda

SI eludes succinct characterization. It is understood at once as a noun, referring to specific types of policy approaches, tools and actors; a verb, used to characterize certain policymaking processes; and an adjective, used to distinguish something as new or different from what came before. SI may thus be best characterized as an orientation to policy and policymaking rooted in change, making it highly ambiguous, amorphous and porous to various political projects. SI can thus only be understood in context, making a genealogical analysis of the approach particularly helpful.

Ayob et al (2016) conduct a longitudinal analysis of SI's definitional discourse from 1989 to 2013. While only recently emergent in government policy spheres, SI has a long legacy within a radical tradition where social movements were situated as important actors; new forms of social relations were envisioned as key to SI processes and outputs; and reshaping power relations were understood as central values and outcomes (Ayob et al 2016). In the criminal justice sector, for example, the 1970s' restorative justice movement, whose SI approach to the carceral state was first ridiculed and opposed, proved transformative and led to the modern community justice practices of 'restorative justice; prevention and early intervention; and community strengthening and self-determination', all of which involve engaging citizens and cross-sector collaboration (Fox and Grimm 2015, 68).

Ayob et al (2016) note a creeping utilitarian/management approach entering into the discourse of SI from 2004 to 2008, which placed emphasis on locating novel solutions to social challenges that are '*more effective, efficient, sustainable or just*' (2016, 644). We begin to see a melding of neoliberal reason, and especially notions of SI for cost savings, with seemingly progressive concepts of sustainability *or* justice as secondary. These projects are aligned through the notion of social value creation, which understands social change produced through SI as a product that can be measured with respect to money saved. The 'old ways' of public service provision are considered costly and inefficient at solving social problems. Different actors in the field may emphasize different dimensions of this radical/utilitarian distinction in their definitions and conceptualizations of SI. Van der Have and Rualcaba (2016) illustrate how more sociological SI definitions seem to place emphasis on the 'satisfaction of human needs', 'changes in social relations' and 'an empowerment dimension in the form of increasing socio-political capability and access to resources', while economic definitions privilege outcomes, 'ideas, services or new systemic transformations and associated social impacts' (1924–1925). Both traditions share an emphasis on (1) new forms of social relations (collaboration); (2) innovation (new ideas); and (3) social impact (change) but differ significantly on power and process dimensions (Ayob et al 2016, 649). The radical stream emphasizes new forms of power relations while utilitarian streams focus on social value creation foremost (Ayob et al 2016). Montgomery notes 'social innovation is never neutral but always political and socially constructed', with two emergent paradigms dominating: (1) a technocratic, neoliberal school emphasizing public sector efficiencies, new markets, expert entrepreneurs, innovative finance and measurement; and (2) a democratic school aspiring to transform power structures, emancipate those marginalized and privilege social justice in production and distribution (Nicholls and Murdock 2012, 1–30).

The SI agenda has taken off post-2008. Ayob et al (2016) note that this most recent period of SI development is characterized by a merging of the radical and utilitarian streams, which they understand as progressive. The SI definitional discourse used by governments today places overwhelming emphasis on social value creation. The EU characterizes SI as 'new ideas (products, services and models) that simultaneously meet social needs (more effectively than alternatives) and create new social relationships or collaborations' (Fougère et al 2017, 831). The United States defines SI as 'new ways to solve old problems that are faster, cost-effective, data-driven and lead to better results for the public good' (Corporation for National and Community Service 2020). The Canadian state understands SI as 'a response to a social or environmental problem (including everything from a program or a service to different ways of structuring organizations) which, once adopted, results in better outcomes than existing approaches' (Employment and Social Development Canada (ESDC) 2018, 11). There is an understanding that SI differs from commercial and technological innovations in that it results in value creation that is social, not strictly commercial (ESDC 2018). In this way, SI is often presented as both a growth engine like business innovation and as a way to address social challenges; as Fougère et al (2017) note, it is an ideological win-win-win, 'social challenges are systematically transformed into social and economic opportunities ... thanks to innovative thinking and technology' (2017, 835).

A 2018 global mapping identified 1,005 SI initiatives spanning five continents (Howaldt et al 2018). SI has emerged within multiple disciplines (Rana et al 2014) and is directed to numerous policy fields, with poverty alleviation, education, employment, health and the environment as dominant practice areas (Cukier and Gagnon 2017). SI often involves design thinking, experimentation, collaboration across sectors, non-linear processes and transformation targeting complex wicked problems necessitating significant social change (Svensson et al 2018; Shields et al 2020). To facilitate this transformation, governments have been constructing enabling frameworks, structures and programmes through which the SI ecosystem can thrive. This includes the following:

- Enabling Social Entrepreneurs[1] (legislation allowing for profit-making, training and capacity building as well as alternative funding access);

---

[1] Includes private social ventures, colleges and universities, governments, the private sector, non-profit organizations and social capital philanthropists (Cukier and Gagnon 2017, 21).

- Developing a Social Finance[2] Infrastructure (establishing and/or supporting social investment wholesalers and promoting the creation of social finance intermediaries within and outside of government);
- Driving Social Finance Investor Demand (regulatory and tax incentives as well as public service commissioning via new social finance vehicles such as Social Impact Bonds (SIBs), which enable private investment and profit-making based on the social value created through SI interventions);
- Supporting Collaboration through Social Innovation Labs (enabling networks and collaboration through the creation of distinct government 'problem-solving' SI labs (SILs) and working with SILs in other sectors);
- New Governance Structures, Measurement and Networks (administrative bodies for data collection, evidence, evaluation and best practices and the identification of social priorities); and
- Market Access/Public Procurement Initiatives (new legislation and institution-building privileging social entrepreneurs in government procurement processes) (ESDC 2018; Howaldt et al 2018, 98–100).

This enabling framework strongly suggests that the post-2008 SI agenda has been captured by a technocratic ideal that serves to economize social services. We argue that rather than being progressive, this economization of SI risks invisibilizing what was once a more radical civil society tradition rooted in transformative justice. Is there hope for these more radical elements of SI to re-emerge? We argue that this requires a distinctly anti-neoliberal SI agenda, the development of which necessitates a thorough analysis and identification of the intricate ways in which the SI agenda has been used to facilitate the austerity project. Wendy Brown (2015) conceptualizes neoliberalism as a governing rationality whereby a state's legitimacy is constituted in its ability to advance markets and facilitate economic growth. The state itself comes to operate like a firm, economizing its tools, institutions and procedures, part of which is governing citizens to act as self-investing human capital who make no demands on the collective. The state works to economize all aspects of life through the discursive and material practices of benchmarking, governance, devolution and

[2] Social Finance describes diverse classes of investments, from private debt and equity, to bond-like instruments (for example community bonds) to outcomes-based vehicles (for example Social Impact Bonds), with the common objective of delivering measurable social and environmental impact in addition to financial returns (ESDC 2018).

responsibilization (Brown 2015). We apply these practices to SI to help us understand the ways in which the neoliberal project works through the agenda, coopting and transforming more radical understandings and actors. This analysis serves to identify tensions and inconsistencies in the current SI agenda that we hope can be used to combat austerity and serve the ends of transformative justice in a post-pandemic era.

Benchmarking

Benchmarking is an administrative process through which firms research and work to replicate the best practices of market leaders (for example cost structures, customer experience frameworks and so on) both within and across sectors. Benchmarking, now widely applied across private, public and non-profit domains, has been operationalized within neoliberalism as a technique that privileges economic valuation and backgrounds expressive, mission centred pursuits and normative concerns such as equity and social justice (Brown 2015). Despite their framing as neutral and simply emphasizing 'what works', best practices are utilized to further economize the social by equating all aims to those of the market (for example cost savings, profit-making) (Brown 2015).

SI is presented as a best practices approach for government that embraces various innovative, effective processes and tools from other public, private and non-profit organizations to tackle complex public policy problems. Advocates of the SI agenda submit that there are no alternatives: issues such as housing insecurity and poverty '*threaten individual and collective wellbeing*', impeding economic growth and increasing the demand for '*expensive public services*'; government grants are ill-equipped to support social purpose organizations (that is, non-profit organizations, charities, social enterprises, cooperatives) in confronting these long-term, complex challenges; and, increased pressure on government budgets make innovation and cross-sector collaboration requisite (ESDC 2018, 1, 7, 24). This dominant logic that we need SI to solve problems and save money in the present and future prevails across contexts; from SI's appropriation in pursuit of the UK's aggressive austerity agenda of devolution, reduced social programme budgets and a 50 per cent decline in grants to charitable organizations, to Germany's efforts to mitigate projected welfare expenditure growth (Dowling 2017; UK Parliament 2017, 41). In this way, the best practices element of SI is associated with the movement to 'fast policy' (Peck and Theodore 2015). The recession, which demanded public action in a plethora of policy domains, occurred in a pre-existing neoliberal policy environment characterized by a retreating welfare state, weakened government policy capacity and a dominant value orientation that state action cannot solve problems. Fast policy serves as a response to this conundrum: appear to address problematic issues on the ground by engaging in policy learning on solutions 'that work' in other jurisdictions and by other private and non-profit sector actors. Not surprisingly given the dominant neoliberal context, these policies tend to favour entrepreneurial, behavioural-oriented and market-based solutions to policy problems (Peck and Theodore 2015).

Government SI offices and their associated networks and labs collect and disseminate data, analytics and evidence of best practices that create social value; funding, deploying and sharing those proven to work (Obama Whitehouse Archives 2016; ESDC 2018). This new problem-solving process can constitute a turn to a kind of rationalist policymaking that is centred in the idea that social solutions can be found in 'objective', technical and scientific approaches to problem-solving that have universal application (Torgerson 1986). So-called rationalist approaches are an attempt to move beyond ideological and politically based divisions in seeking technical solutions to problems. The idea is that technical problems can be solved through the use of experts utilizing practical knowledge and experience as applied to social issues. However, this can divorce social problems from the deeper socio-economic and political context in which they have been formed and sustained. This approach neglects what Peck (nd) calls 'the redistribution problem': there is an abject failure to address the fundamental issue of wealth redistribution, placing the ability to engage in meaningful social reform into question. This is especially the case where fast policy solutions are sought because investment and profit making are on the line with the turn to social finance.

SIBs represent a shift from the funding of public services to funding policy outcomes and doing so by tapping into private financing. Markets are presented as a neutral force that can be used for social good. Private capital can be channelled into ethical social investments where private investors and entrepreneurs can employ innovative approaches to solving social problems. One of the advantages of SIBs is their supposed ability to innovate and bypass the problem of government's aversion to risk-taking. The success of these social interventions would then be awarded with a healthy return on their investment (TVO 2019). However, these privately financed social programmes are delivered by non-profit providers with a proven track record of effective delivery. Consistently, SIBs have been awarded to large service providers deemed 'investment ready' (OECD 2016; Edmiston and Nicholls 2018); this in part relates to the requisite scale to justify both the investment and significant transactional costs involved (Smith 2018). In reality, the types of projects that SIBs are developed around have a proven record of success as private investors are strongly motivated to get a safe return on their money. This was illustrated in a study concerning the London Homelessness SIB, where an interview respondent explained a bid had been unsuccessful 'because of its innovation' (Cooper et al 2016, 76). Furthermore, despite claims to support new approaches, a 2015 analysis of the Obama administration's Social Innovation Fund showed that evidence (that is, proven outcomes, cost-effectiveness) superseded innovation in determining funding allocations (Cohen 2015).

The dominance of social finance in the SI landscape demands exacting quantitative and/or financial indicators, regardless of whether such metrics are appropriate. SIBs, for example, begin with research to investigate the issue and identify an established best practice response (Davidson Knight et al 2017); which can occur without consideration to the nature of the problem (Joy and Shields 2020). SIBs are then pursued where the best practice proposed leads to 'quantified savings to the government: The savings associated with the outcome (e.g. reduction in the number of persons re-incarcerated) must be higher than the cost of delivering the outcome (e.g. reduction in recidivism)' (Deloitte 2020). Thus, all aspects of the issue, solution and evaluation are economized (Joy and Shields 2020). This continues to occur despite public sector research demonstrating outcomes-based contracting has been shown to deliver improvements only in narrow silos and that it is unsuitable for complex environments (Davidson Knight et al 2017). This is an agenda that narrowly defines best practices and outcomes, with greater reverence to the market than to those in need. Whereas SI research demonstrates that participatory, flexible evaluation methods are more appropriate (Svensson et al 2018), the Global Impact Investment Rating System (GIIRS) seeks more traditional economic impact ratings, allowing investors to compare SIB initiatives and transform impact investment into a recognized asset class (Deloitte 2020). Additionally, the expectation of investor profit level is high (8 to 12 per cent). Government is able to defer payment into the future, but ultimately it is the public purse that pays for the programming plus the profit dividend; hardly a real cost saving for social initiatives that are lacking in innovation (TVO 2019).

Despite these limitations, supporters continue to advocate for continued SIB market expansion. SIBs have attracted considerable attention; however, 107 implementations between 2010 and 2017 (42 per cent of which are in the US and UK), represents only modest growth, and the lack of participation by institutional investors has been cited as a barrier (Del Giudice and Migliavacca 2018, 56–9). Del Giudice and Migliavacca's (2018) research identified three factors to attract institutional investors – fewer SIB investors per project, a local public administrator and the use of a special purpose vehicle – all factors that mitigate innovation and grant greater investor control.

Governance

Governance under neoliberalism involves the consolidation of business and political practices; a downsizing of the state (supported by devolution and privatization); and the supplanting of hierarchical command-and-control modes of public administration with networked, horizontal governance whereby the boundaries between the government, third sector and private corporations dissolve as they all come to operate as firms (Brown 2015; Evans and Shields 2018). Far from an egalitarian, collaborative cross-sector model, governance imposed through neoliberalism's New Public Management (NPM) has emphasized cost efficiencies, marketization and uneven power relations through the competitive contracting of social services (Evans and Shields 2018). Reductions in state capacity are celebrated as the government's role is minimized to 'steering'. For neoliberalism, governance becomes 'the political modality through which it creates environments, structures, constraints and incentives and hence conducts subjects' (Brown 2015, 122).

Governance as a political modality is clearly articulated throughout the SI agenda. The SI required to solve complex problems is understood to be no longer within the remit of governments. Rather, governments construct an enabling economic, legal and administrative environment to support an SI ecosystem outside of traditional processes and actors. This environment has been most significantly enacted through the creation of social finance structures, the enablement of new entrepreneurial actors and through the establishment of collaborative policy environments such as Social Innovation Labs (SILs).

SILs are said to promote independent problem-solving away from state-centric processes. SILs are designed to tackle complex and hard to solve social problems by bringing together a diverse team of experts from many fields focusing on a 'doing what works' approach to problem-solving. In this regard, SILs are cast as pushing policymaking from government hands to society. While it is claimed that SILs help to democratize policymaking by bringing societal interests into the policymaking process, this is occurring in a context where non-profit service providers are being pressured to refrain from exercising their voice function by government funders; the problem of 'advocacy chill' (Evans and Shields 2018). SILs are said to embrace 'change thinking' designed to break with the 'government think' mould, which can push entrepreneurial and business centred ideas into the problem-solving process. SILs can be understood as an innovation to NPM as they work to create a 'knowledge market for policy' outside of government, providing an expanded role for consultancies like KPMG and Deloitte. Neoliberalism's shrinking of the state has also meant that the government's policy capacity has been greatly reduced and disabled (Baskoy et al 2011). There is an anti-statist orientation to these developments. The state is presented as inherently risk adverse and unable to embrace the innovation necessary to address wicked policy challenges. Complex social problems are thus cast as beyond the state's sole capacities to solve and, consequently, they must be met through the use of a 'social policymaking market'. By design, this moves policy decision-making beyond the supposed constraints of overly bureaucratic and siloed state-based processes.

SIBs claim to be about building partnerships between government, private investors and non-profit providers and might best be thought of as a public-private partnership applied to social policy. The limited research to date, however, challenges the legitimacy of the 'partnership' claim and suggests efficiencies may be to the detriment of non-profit service providers and their employees. A study of four SIBs in the UK, for example, found micro-management, reduced flexibility, onerous reporting and pressure to act in ways that contradicted the non-profit's social mission in order to satisfy investors (Edmiston and Nicholls 2018). Competitive bidding can also result in heavy and unreasonable discounting (Smedley 2015; OECD 2016). It is therefore not surprising that SIBs have been associated with an increased use of volunteers, which critics argue 'could lead to self-exploitation of altruistic volunteers who enable SIBs to be successful and receive nothing when investors are paid out' (Dowling 2017; Berndt and Wirth 2018, 10). Investors often stagger payments, structure the contracts to allow for the replacement of non-profit service providers and retain the option to cancel amid uncertain returns (Dowling 2017), thus placing non-profit 'partners' in a precarious state.

While governments may set the SI agenda and identify costly 'problems' to be solved, these new entrepreneurial actors are expected to operationalize and increasingly fund and even profit from this vision. In this way, the state's steering role is further reduced (Joy and Shields 2020). With SIBs, for instance, private funders may select service delivery agents, often through competitive bidding processes and investors have a significant influence in the establishment of outcome metrics and programme design (TVO 2019).

> Commissioning of public services is now becoming a very fluid concept. We have been asked as a function to become a commissioner for services and we've absolutely said that is not our place, we're not democratically accountable. That goes back to almost Victorian times, when you had the rich factory owner determining what good outcomes were for the people who lived there. We should have moved a long way from that. (Caroline Mason, Esmée Fairbairn Foundation (Pequeneza 2018: 46:36 min))

In this environment, non-profit organizations are expected to become more entrepreneurial and like firms, market their programmes to attract social finance. As the drivers and deliverers of SI, third sector organizations are recast as 'social purpose organizations' or 'social entrepreneurs' aided by innovative finance and working in conjunction with private sector experts and other collaborators. Government funded, third party executed Investment Readiness Programs[3] facilitate this transition, building the capacities of these social entrepreneurs to access social finance by improving their business acumen, organizational and marketing capabilities; formalizing social impact measurement systems; strengthening their innovation programmes; and, helping them demonstrate revenue model sustainability (Jervs 2012; OECD/EU 2017; ESDC 2019).

Regulatory amendments have created new organizational forms for social enterprises (such as Charitable Incorporated Organizations and incorporated Community Interest Companies in the UK), thus removing trustee personal liability as a barrier to leveraging social finance and debt and additionally, allowing social entrepreneurs to raise equity capital (James et al 2016; UK Government 2020b). To provide for their sustainability, charities are expected to charge fees, launch unrelated businesses and reinvest new revenue proceeds in the pursuit of their missions (ESDC 2018). In this new world of SI governance, 'management' can supplant advocacy and social justice

[3] The UK government funded the Investment and Contract Readiness Fund and later the Big Potential Investment Readiness Program (Jervs 2012; OECD/EU 2017). Canada's Investment Readiness Program launched in 2019 (ESDC 2019).

pursuits which cannot be quantified within a return-on-investment framework (Berry 2016).

With social finance, the government further exerts its steering capacity to enable market actors through regulatory amendments to investment and charitable legislation, incentives via impact investment tax credits and significant investments in social finance wholesalers to incentivize and provide seed capital to new market intermediaries. This appears to be without consideration of cost-effectiveness or appropriateness of enacting capital markets as a funding source for social innovation or for civil society organizations. It is a strategy in service of government legitimization in the guise of economic and market growth, thus demonstrating the neoliberal preference for marketization. Social finance is said to challenge the logic of traditional investment and provide inventive private capital funding (Moore et al 2012), where fiscally constrained governments cannot. As Canada's Task Force on Social Innovation and Social Finance states:

> Social finance has the potential to put billions of dollars in private and philanthropic capital to work on social and environmental issues and, in doing so, to create new sources of revenue for organizations to develop and scale projects that improve community well-being. Social finance is itself a social innovation, as it can reshape financial markets to harness the power of capital to deliver social outcomes, and also acts as a key source of financial support for developing and scaling social innovation in Canada. (ESDC 2018, 16)

While an emerging and thus difficult to quantify market segment, a 2019 Global Impact Investment Network (GIIN) report estimated the global impact investment market at USD 502 billion assets under management (AUM) (GIIN 2019, 3). Signifying the potential, the broader Environmental, Social and Governance segment of which impact investment is part, is now valued at USD 30.7 trillion (Global Sustainable Investment Alliance (GSIA) 2018). The UK social impact investment market, recognized as the world's most advanced, was estimated at £3.6 billion in 2018, an increase of 30 per cent from 2017 (Big Society Capital 2020). Dowling (2017) details the City of London's expressed social finance aspiration: 'the aim is for Britain to achieve a further competitive advantage in financial services by encouraging the use of social investment in the UK, promoting London as a leading global hub connecting social enterprise to capital markets' (2017, 297). In 2016, the Responsible Investors Association surveyed

87 intermediaries and investors active in Canada's social finance market and found 67 per cent target at or above market returns (ESDC 2018, 87). As Deloitte notes in its guidance to hedge fund managers, 'the biggest value proposition for this strategy is that a growing class of investors wants to see these types of products within their suite of investment options … Competition is fierce and any opportunity to show responsiveness to investor demands while being first in an untapped market is key' (DeWitt 2016, 6).

Devolution

Devolution operates as a neoliberal technique to minimize the state's policymaking role by downloading responsibility for often large, complex policy areas to smaller operational units such as local governments (Brown 2015) or social purpose organizations. While this tactic engages actors who are closer to the local community and its needs, these organizations lack the resources, funding and political power to both address systemic root causes and appropriately deal with the growing need for services on the ground.

Through devolution, the SI agenda transfers the nation's most complex social issues for solutioning to expert entrepreneurs, the private sector and social purpose organizations acting as both convenors and delivery agents. Here, complex social issues requiring integrated policy solutions are restated as discrete, tactical projects that can be 'solved'. This can divorce social problems from the broader socio-economic and political contexts in which they have been formed and sustained. Further, the stated benefits of devolution are questionable since social finance has been inaccessible for smaller social purpose organizations who might best understand the challenges of the most vulnerable citizens. In the UK, where the SI project is furthest along, non-profit grants have fallen from an estimated £6.1 billion to £2.8 billion (UK Parliament 2017, 41). Social finance has been accessible only to large social purpose organizations and as a result, from 2008–09 to 2012–13, spending among small and medium-sized UK charities has declined (UK Parliament, 2017). Charities in the £100k to £500k revenue range have reduced expenditures on staff costs by 50 per cent, leading to further precarity, and presumably either reduced service delivery or a substitution of volunteer hours for what was previously paid employment (National Council for Voluntary Organisations (NCVO) 2016, 3, 35).

SIBs are a clear illustration of devolution as they are directed to localized social issues related to prevention and early intervention. To date, SIBs have been targeted at issues such as recidivism, early childhood education, homelessness, employment and supports for people with mental health challenges. Social value is produced through savings that flow from such things as the reduction in criminal reoffending and transforming those that are unemployed into 'working taxpayers'. The realized social value should be able to offset the cost of the social intervention and the profit paid on the private investment. 'The claim is that the interests and needs of all SIB partners can be aligned: targeted individuals are reformed; taxpayers save money; private investors gain a new asset class; intermediaries profit by advancing a new market; and service agencies are supported and recognized for their creation of "social value"' (Joy and Shields 2018a, 682). There are significant issues with this logic: (1) essential benefits (for example social inclusion) may not be monetizable, thus rendering them secondary to economic concerns; (2) SIB metrics are reductive, ascribing basic measures to represent the root causes of complex social issues and the long-term needs of vulnerable populations (for example counting the number of rough sleepers placed in housing to address the issue of chronic homelessness); and (3) the calculations rely on assumed future savings after investors have been paid, which may or may not materialize once the SIB supports are removed (Nicholls and Ziegler, 2019). Investor needs are satisfied when the SIB pays out but in the absence of systemic change, such as in the housing market, sustained positive outcomes for the targeted individuals are less certain.

Responsibilization

Responsiblization under neoliberalism aims to reconfigure citizens as human capital; worthy citizens are independent and contribute to production whereas persons who are vulnerable, dependent or unable to conform risk being blamed for their lack of self-investment (Brown 2015). Within this framework, public services are conceived as a burden to society, as are the recipients of such services who have failed to operationalize as human capital. It is a logic that seeks to justify welfare reductions and reorient policy towards inciting behaviour change, leaving responsibilized citizens to provide for themselves even where austerity measures have frustrated their ability to do so (Brown 2015). Responsibilization shifts risk that was previously assumed collectively through the state and places it on individuals, in effect de-socializing citizenship (Joy and Shields 2017 & 2018a).

The SI agenda recasts the collective risk and responsibility essential to social citizenship as a burden to society. Issues such as poverty are portrayed as a threat to economic growth and accelerated pressures on government budgets necessitate creative solutions (ESDC 2018); solutions that preclude a collective state response. Vulnerable individuals, the recipients of expensive public services, become targets for behavioural change through SIL or SIB interventions to enhance job skills, provide health education, offer cognitive behavioural therapy for at-risk-youth and so on. (Joy and Shields 2018a, 2018b) SIB investors speculate on subjects' ability to be made responsible, thus triggering a payout. Where structural barriers and inequities remain unaddressed, SI can offer targeted individuals 'success' only at the margins. Inequality can perpetuate as those with capital receive returns regardless of whether individual outcomes are sustainable once SIB supports dissolve.

SIBs work to extend the market deeply into the welfare state and as such, pass important elements of social policy construction into private hands. Such developments in social policy have a transformative impact at the level of the citizen. The idea of the citizen under neoliberalism is shaped by an individual and market lens. As Joy and Shields (2018a) note: '… the definition of a worthy citizen under the neoliberal project becomes the self-reliant, responsible, ever resilient, pro-active lean citizen; those who fail to conform to these norms are failed citizens subject to policies aimed at behaviour modification and state sanctioned discipline' (2018a, 688). With SIBs, however, responsibilization is imposed without participation as research has demonstrated that within the SIB structure, service users are often not granted agency in decisions affecting their lives (Dowling 2017; Ziegler et al 2019).

While SILs may offer new opportunities to include citizens into policy decision-making, they can also be used to bypass value conflicts with the claim that overly politicized government policymaking processes have kept the state from learning from citizen experiences and from the more applied and practical experiences offered by the private sector and civil society. This orientation risks viewing social problems as being rooted in population and community behaviours, with solutions to be found in targeted, place-based programming that can ignore the need for more systemic change such as fair wages, affordable housing, free childcare and transit, and an end to racialized police violence.

Conclusion

This chapter warns that by design, the current SI agenda is being captured by neoliberalism as it has sought to economize social policy and advance markets through the techniques of benchmarking, governance, devolution and responsibilization. The SI agenda can be understood as an extension of NPM, where the government steers while unequal power relations, competitive contracting, cost efficiencies and marketization dominate. Social purpose organizations must become investment ready social enterprises while those with capital become the commissioners of public services. Complex social issues requiring integrated policy solutions are restated as discrete, tactical, local projects that can be packaged as impact investments, generating market returns regardless of whether the long-term prospects of the recipients of such services improve.

To date, the SI agenda has failed to deliver on its aspirations. Globally, social innovation has been associated with small-scale, fragmented programs ill-equipped to address the urgent, systemic and immense scale of need (Cukier and Gagnon 2017; Howaldt et al 2018). SIBs remain controversial, have demonstrated questionable efficacy (based on available evaluations) (Nicholls and Edmiston 2019), and have been associated with aggressive competitive bidding processes (Smedley 2015), in which only large, established, less innovative non-profit service providers prevail (OECD 2016; Edmiston and Nicholls 2018; Smith 2018). While 'investment ready' non-profits are theoretically 'empowered' as social entrepreneurs, the social finance power dynamic and competitive contracting approach has in many instances led to further precarity.

Debate persists as to whether the social enterprise model is desirable or whether contradictory for-profit goals and social mission tensions will in fact undermine critical social outcomes (Smith et al 2013). Supply-demand models are inadequate when the client cannot pay or is unable to seek help; the salience of a social need is mediated by government priorities, media attention and other factors (Antadze and Westley 2010). The complexities and outcomes related to tacking marginalization are not marketizable; the reductive nature of social finance conflicts with the broader social goals needed to support our most vulnerable citizens (Nicholls and Ziegler 2019). Social investors do not understand the 'absolute fabric of the social sector' and the unique contexts in which social purpose organizations operate (UK Parliament 2017, 83); investor efforts to exert control, quantify and standardize outcomes are antithetical to the true drivers of social change. Overall, SI's breadth, scale and rate of adoption have been remarkable given the lack of proof of concept, and the many issues to date. This agenda is not about driving transformative and meaningful social change. This is a project to continue neoliberal change that serves to further entrench structural inequalities in society, a project to responsibilize those who are most vulnerable and privilege capital accumulation over democratic rights.

The pandemic has called into question the neoliberal austerity project that has dominated policy for the last four decades. This has opened up possibilities for progressive manifestations of SI as a fundamentally anti-oppression approach to take hold. Here, there is a need to go back to the origin of the SI concept and process, rooted in transformative justice; the application of critical thinking and learning to the cultural and material roots of intersecting social oppressions; healing and reconciliation on the complex individual and intergenerational lived traumas of these intersecting social oppressions; and collaborative and equitable processes of policy decision-making and design that tackle the interscalar nature of problems and create opportunities for all living things to thrive. These critical, creative and innovative concepts and approaches that imagine and work to create a new world rooted in care, justice, freedom and transformation remain part of our communities. Academics interested in social policy and social innovation should turn to study these transformative movements and approaches to decipher how they can be supported and scaled up while remaining rooted in everyday experience and immanently critical.

References

Antadze, Nino and Frances Westley. 2010. 'Funding Social Innovation: How Do We Know What to Grow?', *The Philanthropist*, 23(3): 343–56.

Ayob, Nooresha, Simon Teasdale and Kylie Fagan. 2016. 'How Social Innovation "Came to Be": Tracing the Evolution of a Contested Concept', *Journal of Social Policy*, 45(4): 635–53.

Baskoy, Tuna, Bryan Evans and John Shields. 2011. 'Assessing Policy Capacity in Canada's Public Services: Perspectives of Deputy and Assistant Deputy Ministers', *Canadian Public Administration*, 54(2): 217–234.

Berndt, Christian and Manuell Wirth. 2018. 'Markets, Metrics and Morals: The SIB as an Emerging Public Policy Instrument', *Geoforum*, 90(March): 27–35.

Berry, Jeffrey M. 2016. 'Negative Returns: The Impact of Impact Investing on Empowerment and Advocacy', *PS: Political Science and Politics*, 49(3): 437–41.

Big Society Capital. 2020. *UK Social Impact Investment Market Now Worth More Than £5 Billion*, 28 October. https://bigsocietycapital.com/latest/uk-social-impact-investment-market-now-worth-more-than-5-billion/

Brown, Wendy. 2015. *Undoing the Demos: Neoliberalism's Stealth Revolution*. Brooklyn: Zone Books.

Cohen, Rick. 2015. 'Social Impact Fund Report Finds Less Than Overwhelming Results', *Nonprofit Quarterly*. https://nonprofitquarterly.org/social-impact-fund-report-finds-less-than-overwhelming-results/

Cooper, Christine, Cameron Graham and Darlene Himick. 2016. 'Social Impact Bonds: The Securitization of The Homeless', *Accounting, Organizations & Society*, 55:63–82.

Corporation for National and Community Service. 2020. *Social Innovation Fund*. United States Federal Government. www.nationalservice.gov/programs/social-innovation-fund.

Cukier, Wendy and Suzanne Gagnon. 2017. *Social Innovation: Shaping Canada's Future*. Diversity Institute, Ryerson University. www.ryerson.ca/content/dam/diversity/reports/social-innovation-shaping-canadas-future.pdf

Davidson Knight, Annabel, Toby Lowe, Marion Brossard and Julie Wilson. 2017 (May). *A Whole New World: Funding and Commissioning in Complexity*. Joint Report by Collaborate, Newcastle University, Big Lottery Fund. http://wordpress.collaboratei.com/wp-content/uploads/A-Whole-New-World-Funding-Commissioning-in-Complexity.pdf

Del Giudice, Alfonso and Milena Migliavacca. 2018. 'Social Impact Bonds and Institutional Investors: An Empirical Analysis of a Complicated Relationship', *Nonprofit and Voluntary Sector Quarterly*, 48(1): 50–70.

Deloitte. 2020. 'Paying for Outcomes. Solving Complex Societal Issues Through Social Impact Bonds'. www2.deloitte.com/ca/en/pages/insights-and-issues/articles/paying-for-outcomes-social-impact-bonds.html

DeWitt, J. Lynette. 2016. *Impact Investing: A Sustainable Strategy for Hedgefunds*. Deloitte Centre for Financial Services. www2.deloitte.com/content/dam/Deloitte/us/Documents/financial-services/us-fsi-hedge-fund-impact-investing.pdf

Dowling, Emma. 2017. 'In the Wake of Austerity: Social Impact Bonds and the Financialisation of the Welfare State in Britain', *New Political Economy*, 22(3): 294–310.

Edmiston, Daniel and Alex Nicholls. 2018. 'Social Impact Bonds: The Role of Private Capital in Outcome-Based Commissioning', *Journal of Social Policy*, 47(1): 57–76.

ESDC (Employment and Social Development Canada). 2018. *Inclusive Innovation – New Ideas and New Partnerships for Stronger Communities*. Recommendations of the Social Innovation and Social Finance Strategy Co-Creation Steering Group. www.canada.ca/en/employment-social-development/programs/social-innovation-social-finance/reports/recommendations-what-we-heard.html

ESDC. 2019. *Investment Readiness Program*. www.canada.ca/en/employment-social-development/programs/social-innovation-social-finance/investment-readiness.html

Evans, Bryan and John Shields. 2018. 'The Third Sector, the Neoliberal State and Beyond: Reshaping Contracting and Policy Advocacy', in Christopher Dunn (ed) *The Handbook of Canadian Public Administration*. Don Mills, ON: Oxford University Press, pp 489–500.

Fougère, Martin, Beata Segercrantz and Hannele Seek. 2017. 'A Critical Reading of the European Union's Social Innovation Policy Discourse: (Re) Legitimizing Neoliberalism', *Organization*, 24(6): 819–43.

Fox, Chris and Robert Grimm. 2015. 'The Role of Social Innovation in Social Criminal Justice Reform and the Risk Posed by Proposed Reforms in England and Wales', *Criminology & Criminal Justice*, 15(1): 62–83.

GIIN (Global Impact Investment Network). 2019. *Sizing the Impact Investing Market*. https://thegiin.org/assets/Sizing%20the%20Impact%20Investing%20Market_webfile.pdf

GSIA (Global Sustainable Investment Alliance). 2018. *2018 Global Sustainable Investment Review*. www.gsi-alliance.org/wp-content/uploads/2019/03/GSIR_Review2018.3.28.pdf

Howaldt, Jürgen, Christop Kaletka, Antonius Schröder and Marthe Zirngiebl. (eds). 2018. Atlas of Social Innovation. 2nd Volume – A World of New Practices. Munich: *oekom Verlag GmbH*. www.socialinnovationatlas.net/articles/

James, Deb, David Kane and Charlotte Ravenscroft. 2016. *Understanding the Capacity and Need to Take on Investment Within the Social Sector: Summary Report. NCVO*. www.ncvo.org.uk/images/documents/policy_and_research/funding/investment-within-the-social-sector-2016-summary.pdf

Jervs, Joe 2012 (18 May). 'Best Bits: Advice from Our Experts on "Investment Readiness"'. *The Guardian*. www.theguardian.com/social-enterprise-network/2012/may/18/best-bits-investment-ready-live-qanda#maincontent

Joy, Meghan and John Shields. 2017. 'Austerity and the Non-profit Sector: The Case of Social Impact Bonds', in Stephen McBride and Bryan Evans (eds) *The Austerity State*. Toronto: University of Toronto Press, pp 309–29.

Joy, Meghan and John Shields. 2018a. 'Austerity in the Making: Reconfiguring Social Policy Through Social Impact Bonds', *Policy & Politics*, 46(4): 681–95.

Joy, Meghan and John Shields. 2018b (21 March). 'Profiting from Pain: Social Impact Bonds and Social Policy', *Policy & Politics: Journal Blog*. https://policyandpoliticsblog.com/2018/03/21/profiting-from-pain-social-impact-bonds-and-social-policy/

Joy, Meghan and John Shields. 2020. 'Debate: How Do Social Impact Bonds Economize Social Policy', *Public Money & Management*, 40(3): 1–3.

Montgomery, Tom 2016. 'Are Social Innovation Paradigms Incommensurable?', *Voluntas*, 27: 1979–2000.

Moore, Michele-Lee, Frances R. Westley and Alex Nicholls. 2012. 'The Social Finance and Social Innovation Nexus', *Journal of Social Entrepreneurship*, 3(2): 115–32. https://uwaterloo.ca/waterloo-institute-for-social-innovation-and-resilience/sites/ca.waterloo-institute-for-social-innovation-and-resilience/files/uploads/files/social_finance_and_si_nexus.pdf

NCVO (National Council for Voluntary Organisations). 2016. *Navigating Change: An Analysis of the Financial Trends for Small and Medium Sized Charities*. www.ncvo.org.uk/images/documents/policy_and_research/funding/financial-trends-for-small-and-medium-sized-charities-ncvo-lloyds-bank-foundation-2016.pdf

Nicholls, Alex and Daniel Edmiston. 2019. 'Public Policy as Social Innovation: Social Impact Bonds', in Alex Nicholls and Rafael Ziegler (eds) *Creating Economic Space for Social Innovation*. United Kingdom: Oxford University Press, pp 300–37.

Nicholls, Alex and Alex Murdock. 2012. 'The Nature of Social Innovation', in Alex Nicholls and Alex Murdock (eds) *Social Innovation: Blurring Boundaries to Reconfigure Markets*. Basingstoke: Palgrave Macmillan.

Nicholls, Alex and Rafael Ziegler (eds). 2019. *Creating Economic Space for Social Innovation*. United Kingdom: Oxford University Press.

Obama Whitehouse Archives. 2016. 'Social Innovation Funds Future New Grant Competition'. https://obamawhitehouse.archives.gov/blog/2016/04/05/forum-social-innovation-funds-future-and-new-grant-competition-0

OECD. 2016. *Social Impact Bonds: State of Play and Lessons Learnt*. www.oecd.org/cfe/leed/SIBs-State-Play-Lessons-Final.pdf

OECD/EU. 2017. 'Big Potential: An Investment Readiness Programme'. www.oecd-ilibrary.org/docserver/9789264268500-20-en.pdf?expires=1586575975&id=id&accname=guest&checksum=0277F87F06C298178B8A7A627223BB56

Peck, Jamie. nd. 'Social Innovation … At the Limits of Neoliberalism'. https://crises.uqam.ca/wp-content/uploads/2018/10/J_Peck_CRISES_2011.pdf

Peck, Jamie and Nik Theodore. 2015. *Fast Policy: Experimental Statecraft at the Threshold of Neoliberalism*. Minneapolis, MN: University of Minnesota Press.

Peck, Jamie, Nik Theodore and Neil Brenner. 2012. 'Neoliberalism Resurgent? Market Rule After the Great Recession', *The South Atlantic Quarterly*, 111: 2.

Pequeneza, Nadine 2018. The Invisible Heart. www.theinvisibleheart.ca/

Philanthropist, The. 2020 (21 April). 'How Crisis Breeds Innovation and Making the Case for Policy Overhauls', *Sector News Digest*.

Rana, Nripendra P., Vishanth Weerakkody, Yogesh K. Dwivedi and Niall C. Piercy. 2014. 'Profiling Existing Research on Social Innovation in the Public Sector', *Information Systems Management*, 31: 259–73.

Shields, John and Zainab Abu Alrob. 2020 (July). 'COVID-19, Migration and the Canadian Immigration System: Dimensions, Impact and Resilience'. Research Paper of the Building Migrant Resilience in Cities (BMRC) Project. Toronto: York University.

Shields, John, Meghan Joy and Siu Mee Cheng. 2020. 'Austerity and Social Innovation: The Case of Social Innovation Labs and Social Impact Bonds', *Austerity and its Alternatives*, McMaster University, February. https://altausterity.mcmaster.ca/documents/shields-and-joy-berlin-2019-paper-to-post.pdf

Smedley, Tim. 2015 (10 December). 'Do Social Impact Bonds Really Work for Charities?', *The Guardian*. www.theguardian.com/voluntary-sector-network/2015/dec/10/do-social-impact-bonds-really-work-for-charities

Smith, Steven Rathgeb. 2018. 'The Future of Nonprofit Human Services', *Nonprof Pol Forum*, 8(4): 369–89.

Smith, Wendy K., Michael Gonin and Marya L. Bescharov. 2013. 'Managing Social-Business Tensions: A Review and Research Agenda for Social Enterprise', *Business Ethics Quarterly*, 23(3).

Social Finance. 2018 (30 January). 'Social Impact Bonds Reach Global Mass: 108 Projects Launched in 24 Countries'. https://globenewswire.com/news-release/2018/01/30/1314226/0/en/Social-Impact-Bonds-reach-global-mass-108-projects-launched-in-24-countries.html

Social Finance. 2020. 'Social Finance: Impact Bond Database'. https://sibdatabase.socialfinance.org.uk/

Svensson, Kate, Barbara Szijarto, Peter Milley and J. Bradley Cousins. 2018. 'Evaluating Social Innovations: Implications for Evaluation Design', *American Journal of Evaluation*, 39(4): 459–77.

Torgerson, Douglas. 1986. 'Between Knowledge and Politics: Three Faces of Policy Analysis', *Policy Sciences*, 19(1): 33–59.

TVO. 2019 (22 January). 'Social Impact Bonds Examined', *The Agenda*. www.tvo.org/video/programs/the-agenda-with-steve-paikin/social-impact-bonds-examined

UK Government. 2020a. *Guidance: Use SITR to Raise Money for Your Social Enterprise*. www.gov.uk/guidance/venture-capital-schemes-apply-to-use-social-investment-tax-relief

UK Government. 2020b. *Setting Up a Social Enterprise*. www.gov.uk/set-up-a-social-enterprise

UK Parliament. 2017. *Select Committee on Charities Report of Session 2016–17 – Stronger Charities for a Stronger Society*. https://publications.parliament.uk/pa/ld201617/ldselect/ldchar/133/133.pdf

Van der Have, Robert P. and Luis Rubalcaba. 2016. 'Social Innovation Research: An Emerging Area of Innovation Studies?', *Research Policy*, 45: 1923–35.

Ziegler, Rafael, Alex Nicholls, Jari Aro, Cees van Beers, Enrica Chiappero-Martinetti, Daniel Edmiston, Attila Havas, Risto Heiskala, Nadia von Jacobi, Klaus Kubeczko, Martijn Jeroen van der Linden, Lara Maestripieri, Georg Mildenberger, Gyorgy Molnár and Gudrun-Christine Schimpf. 2019. 'The Extended Social Grid Model Revisited', in Alex Nicholls and Rafael Ziegler (eds) *Creating Economic Space for Social Innovation*. Oxford: Oxford University Press, pp 341–62.

PART III

Beyond coping: protest, pathologies and the development of real alternatives

6

Politics as an alternative to constitutionalization

Stephen McBride and Joy Schnittker

In the long period of neoliberal hegemony there have been marked and overlapping transfers of political authority: from the national to international levels; from institutions where popular sovereignty might be exercised, to opaque technocratic, expert bodies where complex networks of public and private actors arrive at decisions; and, from public authorities to private ones. These processes have often been termed 'depoliticization', a term that connotes the removal of issue areas from the scope of normal politics and their transfer to geographically, or institutionally remote and unaccountable decision-making bodies. Despite the label, such processes are, of course, highly political, and the type of 'depoliticization' achieved is only with respect to democratic and popular impact (McBride and Schnittker 2021). The periodic crises experienced in the neoliberal era have provided opportunities to intensify these trends or, potentially at least, reverse them.

Austerity, defined as fiscal consolidation, public sector structural reforms and flexibilization of labour markets, presents a common thread among capitalist states in the neoliberal era and received particular prominence as a, slightly delayed, response to the economic crisis following 2007–08. It had long been a central component of neoliberal ideology, and its associated policies considered as a capital accumulation strategy (Harvey 2005). Viewed as a policy response to the 2007–08 financial crisis austerity has a number of dimensions extending to fiscal matters of budget balances and debt ceilings, repurposing and privatizing, or marketizing as much of the public sector as possible, and restructuring social and labour market policies. The language of balanced budgets and debt limits is presented as a contribution to sustainable public finance, restructuring the public service on market lines is seen as a means of enhancing efficiency, and labour market reform as a means to competitiveness (see Whiteside et al 2021).

The defects of austerity received much attention (Gough 2011; Guajardo et al 2011; Blyth 2013; Herndon et al 2013) yet the critics made little progress in reversing the priorities of states or international organizations. Indeed, the needed policy debate was partially stifled by institutional measures intended to 'depoliticize' debates on economic policy and render a variety of policies subject to the application of permanent and fixed rules. In the process democracy was diminished and a prerequisite of good policy undermined.

Until a subsequent 2020 crisis, the COVID-19 pandemic and the associated deep contraction of economic activity, the democratic malaise was noted but mostly framed in terms of the rise of right-wing populism and 'illiberal democracies' (Zakaria 2007). Less commented upon was undemocratic (neo)liberalism in which the structured atrophy of democratic governance takes the form of depoliticization through institutionalizing and 'constitutionalizing' matters that were formerly dealt with by democratic processes (see Bruff 2014, 115). As a result of the recent crisis, although outcomes are highly uncertain, the relentless mantra of an inefficient and dysfunctional public sector seems in retreat, and, to stave off complete economic collapse, money has been pumped into economies on a scale that neoliberal and particularly austerity-driven analyses would have found unimaginable. Echoing the early 'Keynesian' response to the 2008 crisis, this has raised hopes that structures and policies established to sustain neoliberalism might be permanently reformed to achieve a more just society. Whether the current turn proves, like its 'Keynesian' predecessor in 2008–10, a temporary interregnum in neoliberal orthodoxy, or the occasion for a permanent departure from it, is one of the great issues of our time. One thing that will clearly be tested is the efficacy of neoliberal attempts to depoliticize and constitutionalize particular outcomes.

Analysis of depoliticization and the decline of democratic input has been conducted at three levels. First, there is the national/international intersection in which international entities (remote from any form of democratic control) dictate, reinforce or are used by national elites to legitimate priorities. Second, at both national and international scales, there is the conflict between democratic accountability and technocratic rule application in which institutions lacking popular accountability (such as executives, bureaucracies, central banks and judiciaries), are seen as gaining strength compared to those more amenable to democratic input (such as legislatures). Third, class relations need to be integrated into the discussion as the neoliberal content of institutionalized policies and practices is designed to advantage capital over labour.

One vehicle of depoliticization can be observed in efforts to constitutionalize austerity. These measures hollow out democratic decision-making and lock in place policy options that reflect asymmetrical relations between social classes. Policy areas significantly insulated from democratic pressures or control include monetary policy, trade and investment policy, and fiscal policy, with others like labour relations and labour market policies close behind (McBride 2016; McBride and Mitrea 2017; Whiteside et al 2021). Significant components of these policies are embedded in pre-arranged and, by design at least, permanent rules, and are rendered remote and unaccountable from the public and from democratic processes. We begin by reviewing the architecture of neoliberal constitutionalization, then turn to consider an earlier effort to incorporate a progressive alternative within those structures. Our focus is on developments within the European Union which is presented as a case or illustration of trends that are also apparent elsewhere.

Constitutionalization as an alternative to politics

We use the term constitution broadly to apply to identifying a variety of instruments – some formal and 'hard'; others and informal and legally 'softer' – that separate particular policy areas from normal politics and establish high thresholds for contravening the rules or outcomes established. Using the term this way, several varieties of constitutionalization are identifiable.

Internationally, constitutionalizing various economic policy areas is associated with the concept of integration. As authority is internationalized, the more integrated states become into an international, global or regional order. Yet integration itself comes in various forms. Writing of the European Union, Claus Offe (2003) argued that the process of European integration could be either positive or negative. Positive integration was a framework for cooperation and regulation, and a regime of fair and peaceful competition among member states. Negative integration was a strategy for institution building, market enlargement and triumph of market liberalism on the European continent.

Neoliberal constitutionalism at the international level has comprised negative integration. Nation-states have committed to observe specified rules as part of binding and enforceable international treaties or membership in international organizations. Examples include the institutions of global economic governance, such as the IMF, World Bank, and World Trade Organization, regional pacts such as NAFTA and its successor, and much more integrated entities such as the EU. Second, some have embedded obligations and rules into their own national or subnational constitutions.[1] Third, ordinary legislation or regulations can normalize certain outcomes. Fourth, international consultations serve to internalize norms and practices. The first two types are the 'hardest', and have stronger enforcement, but the 'softer' third and fourth modes also affect decision-making. Such measures create expectations with which there is general compliance.

Constitutionalization captures two important dynamics. First, democracy is diminished by locating key powers in venues where accountability is poorly realized. Second, the rules embodied in them are designed to 'lock-in' neoliberal outcomes. Their effectiveness in doing this seemed proven by the turn to austerity after the 2008 financial meltdown but is undergoing a major test because of the enormity of the COVID-19 crisis.

A number of examples can illustrate the lock-in motive. In monetary policy, central banks have been made more independent of governments[2] and hence of the public. Autonomous central banks tend to favour austerity and financial orthodoxy over policies of stimulus (Kurzer 1988). In Europe central bank independence was accomplished by international agreements or treaties. Within the Eurozone, the ECB has the primary goal in normal times of maintaining price stability.[3] Its independence has quasi-constitutional status in the European System of Central Banks statute, and in the European Community Treaty itself.[4] Its other effect is its conversion of monetary policy into technical issues beyond the scope of public scrutiny (Hay 2007: 116–17).

Fiscal rules covered 96 countries by 2015 (IMF Fiscal Affairs Department 2017). In Europe, thresholds have been imposed that, if exceeded, result automatically in austerity measures. The intention has been to establish rules beyond politics and thereby constrain the state and insulate it from democratic pressures that tend towards expansion.

[1] Mexico, for example, made 30 amendments to its constitution to ensure compatibility with NAFTA; and Spain in 2011 entrenched the concept of 'budget stability' while introducing the absolute priority of debt and interest repayment.

[2] Over the 1989–2010 period there was a steady movement towards central bank independence (CBI) (Polillo and Guillén 2005; Dincer and Eichengreen 2014).

[3] The focus on anti-inflationary policy fits the interests of finance capital in an era of deregulated financial markets and capital mobility, and the credibility of states in this area is enhanced by deflationary policies of fiscal austerity (Burnham 1999; 2014).

[4] The ECB's own account shows its independence to be extremely robust and its accountability to consist of little more that transparency and explaining its actions (see www.ecb.europa.eu/pub/pdf/infobr/ecbbren.pdf).

Examples include the Maastricht Treaty (see Buti and Giudice 2002), the Stability and Growth Pact (Balassone and Franco 2000; Buti et al 1998; De Haan et al 2004; Heipertz and Verdun 2004; Schuknecht 2005) and the Fiscal Compact, 2012.

This rules out the stimulative use of budget deficits. Within the Eurozone, the single currency rules out external devaluation through currency adjustments. That means that any imbalances must be dealt with through internal devaluation, essentially by compressed wages and unemployment. The new procedures may not be watertight (Burret and Schnellenbach 2014: 12); however, the intention behind the Fiscal Compact was to tighten controls.

Part of a 'new European Interventionism' model in the EU governance system extends to areas such as wages and collective bargaining (despite the EU having no formal competences in this). Downward wage flexibility or internal devaluation is seen as the main adjustment mechanism for macroeconomic imbalances (Degryse 2012; Cacciatore et al 2015; Leschke et al 2015, 295; Schulten and Mueller 2015, 331; European Commission 2016).

The Euro Plus Pact, adopted in March 2011, made the constitutionalization of labour market and labour relations policies more explicit than previously. Wages were defined as 'the main economic adjustment variable for overcoming economic imbalances and fostering competitiveness' (ETUI 2014; Schulten and Mueller 2015, 334). By 2015, 19 out of 28 EU member states had been affected (see Schulten and Mueller 2015) via two main mechanisms which vary in disciplinary power: either country-specific recommendations issued through the European Semester, or 'quid pro quo of reforms for financial support' under Memoranda of Understanding between the Troika or IMF and states (ETUI 2014, 74; Schulten and Mueller 2015, 337). The areas covered include: decentralization of collective bargaining, reform or abolition of wage indexation, moderation of minimum wage development, linking wages to productivity growth, restrictions on extension of collective bargaining agreements, reduction or freezing of minimum wages and/or public sector wages, and wage freezes in the private sector.

The content of the 'constitutional' provisions reviewed earlier (and under other treaties and regimes which are not analyzed here – but see McBride 2010) are unmistakably neoliberal. One view is that this type of integration by constitution has been driven by crises, with successive crises from the 1970s stagflation, to the recessions of the 1980s and 1990s, to the GFC of 2007–08, leading to 'doubling down' on the certainties of neoliberal doctrines.

Integration through crisis

The notion that economic crises and European integration occur simultaneously is central to both historical institutionalism (Pierson 1996) and neo-neofunctionalism (Schmitter 2002). Neo-functionalists believe that crises create a functional need towards integration in order to re-establish the efficacy of policies and institutions that have been rendered ineffective.

Following the logic of path-dependency (Torfing 2009; Rixen and Viola 2015), this frequently results in doubling-down on previous neoliberal approaches. However, this has often been accompanied by measures such as European Social Model (ESM), designed to legitimate the notion of Europeanism. Post-pandemic spending by the EU may play a similar role in legitimating further integration, including transferring more fiscal authority to the supranational level. On the centre-left, enthusiasts of the European ideal hope that post-pandemic spending may be a game changer promoting fiscal flexibility in the EU, and undermining the fiscal and monetary neoliberalism that has characterized it. Whether the pandemic will trigger such a result or, like the ESM, pave the way to a re-assertion of neoliberalism through integration-through-crisis (ITC), remains unclear.

ITC involves a series of characteristics. It has been described as ends-driven (aimed at preserving the monetary union without the departure of any member); technically extra-constitutional (and uses novel legal and political instruments to avoid treaty change), though with constitutional effect; re-enforcing technocratic governance by concentrating power in the executive and non-majoritarian bodies; emphasizing coercive enforcement of the 'rules', justified through emergency rhetoric (Scicluna 2019). ITC thus allows executives and technocratic experts to decide on fundamentally political questions, and operates according to emergency rationality (urgent, discretionary, sensitive to market forces). Functional pressures continue to push governments towards more integration (through bailout mechanisms, banking union, fiscal surveillance). Popular resistance to 'more Europe' has made it nearly impossible to adopt and embed crisis initiatives into the existing formal framework of EU constitutionalism via treaty change. Thus, 'emergency politics' is made extra constitutional, further undermining EU legitimacy (Scicluna 2019).

Historically, in moving to neoliberal integration, there have been attempts to address issues of social cohesion through mechanisms such as the ESM. Despite the varieties of European welfare systems at the national level, they shared common features including a universalist approach, and an active state role in the provision of the necessary means of reproduction. This had a rather decommodifying effect, allowing citizens to be less dependent on market forces (Hermann and Hofbauer 2007). The welfare state and its institutions acted as a vehicle for identity formation in a split society post-war, and was strongly related to social justice and social peace (Mahnkopf 2009).

Rather paradoxically, the term European Social Model was introduced into the public discourse during a time when the distinctive features of western European social models were beginning to fade. This period was experiencing the liberalization of international trade, abolition of capital controls, the introduction of market mechanisms into social provisions, and the subjugation of new spheres to capital accumulation (Hermann and Mahnkopf 2010). The term itself is often traced to Jacques Delors, former president of the European Commission in the 1980s and 1990s, in order to create an alternative to (the United States') unregulated, pure-market capitalism. Delors and fellow social democrats envisaged that Europe should be more than an economic association, and economic and social progress should go hand in hand. An economically successful union must therefore take the 'high road' and have an explicit social policy agenda and strong social and labour standards (Hermann and Hofbauer 2007). The origin of the ESM has been considered a political intervention to strengthen a fragile European identity through differentiating Europe from the US's ultra-liberal capitalism and British imprinting to promote further European integration (Hermann 2017). Internally, the ESM and by extension the European Employment Strategy was intended to be a counterweight to the European Economic and Monetary Union, in order to balance economic (negative) and social (positive) integration (Tsarouhas 2016).

If European integration is understood as a hegemonic project (Jessop 2005), it then requires a hegemonic bloc that delivers the required support to keep the integration progress going. In Europe, because of the relative strength of labour organizations and centre-left political parties this initially required that a class and social compromise be built into it. The ESM (which unions associated with social progress and high labour standards) helped pacify left-wing opposition and maintain trade union support for what became a predominantly neoliberal integration project. Because ESM remained ill-defined both theoretically and empirically, it only helped this process (Hermann and Hofbauer, 2007; Ray, 2016). Essentially, in order for negative (economic) integration of the EU to progress forward, it needed to use positive (social) integration as an incentive. While the two go hand in hand, they are not equal in terms of application. Social provisions are not constitutionalized into the model in the way that neoliberal economic provisions are. On balance, as we shall see, the ESM appears to have played a legitimation role in the construction of a neoliberal Europe, rather than incorporating an alternative into it.

In the early 2000s ESM was deployed in the argument for the radical restructuring and restriction of existing European welfare systems. Faced with growing issues surrounding globalization and an ageing population, it was proposed that Europe must increase its competitiveness internationally through using ESM as a productive factor in Europe's success. Modernizing the ESM was represented as necessary to ensure intergenerational justice and sustainability through neoliberal flexibilization and deregulation. Social policy became identified with a focus on sufficiently high employment rates, and as a mechanism to help people adjust to the market. Modernizing the social model and investing in people was promoted as integral to retaining the European social values of solidarity and justice, while improving economic performance (Hermann and Hofbauer 2007). Thus, 'Social Europe' was neoliberalized.

The GFC and resulting fiscal consolidation packages accelerated the process (Vaughan-Whitehead 2014; Hermann 2017). Post-crisis analyses identified lack of structural reforms as a major cause, and as a barrier to renewed growth. Consequently, austerity measures and their associated structural reforms tackled areas such as collective bargaining and flexibilization of the labour market, social benefits and pensions. Essentially, the crisis further eroded elements of the ESM which had intended to protect citizens from the harms of the free market. Not surprisingly, this was followed by increased poverty and economic deprivation, alongside wealth and income inequality (Hermann 2017).

The crisis increased European institutions' influence in national employment and social models. Tighter economic integration, macroeconomic surveillance and disciplinary mechanisms further reduced member states' capacity to use traditional national economic policy instruments, such as exchange rates, deficit spending and monetary policy, to achieve social policy goals (Tsarouhas 2016). The crisis response and pressure towards consolidating national budgets, flexibilizing labour markets and ensuring financial sustainability of social security systems therefore created an 'economic reading of social policy goals', and reinforced the one-sidedness of the European Semester (Hacker 2019). The crisis allowed for an extension of economic integration, while utilizing the previous 'modernization' argument to further restructure welfare states in the name of EU progress.

The (further) neoliberalization of the ESM post-crisis has exacerbated inequalities and arguably has contributed to the de-legitimization of the whole European integration project. The crisis increased the asymmetry between the North and South. Member states receiving 'rescue' packages have been transformed into 'zero choice democracies', unable to control their own vulnerabilities (Joerges et al 2019).

To mitigate the disparities of the economic crisis and decaying social cohesion, the European Pillar of Social Rights (EPSR) was introduced in 2017 and was proclaimed by the Commissioner for Employment, Social Affairs, Skills and Labour Mobility as a 'milestone' and 'upgrade' of the Social Model (Hacker 2019). The EPSR (re)states how economic and social progress are intertwined, and EPSR must be a part of wider efforts to build a more inclusive and sustainable growth model by improving Europe's competitiveness and making it a better place to invest, create jobs and foster social cohesion (EPSR 2017). The EPSR remains as more of a promise than a legally binding pledge, as it does not have the same legal footing as other treaties. It also included rather contradictory language, including 'necessary flexibility for employers to adapt swiftly to changes in the economic context', applying to areas such as wages, minimum income and unemployment benefits. Others have critiqued EPSR for not strengthening social policies, and for remaining focused on a 'growth-friendly' reading of social policy, reflecting the predominance of business-oriented players in the EU governance process. The EPSR 'Social Scoreboard' indicator is also to be used within the context of the European Semester. Because EPSR exists within a constitutionally asymmetric framework (which prioritizes negative integration over positive integration) (Hacker 2019), it is hard to discern a shift towards any de-commodifying policies.

The European Union's pandemic response

The current pandemic has revealed the price of the turn to austerity. The erosion of ESM aspirations and national welfare state capacity over decades of neoliberalism exacerbated the impact of the pandemic. In response the Commission proposed EU funding to protect jobs and support a green, digital, inclusive society and economy. The European Social Fund Plus (a pre-existing cohesion policy fund) will be used as the main instrument to implement the EPSR in order to 'ensure a socially fair recovery'. Other areas of social funding include the Recovery and Resilience Facility, as well as InvestEU, which budgets €32 billion to support social infrastructure and microfinance to entrepreneurs (European Commission 2020a). Building on the EPSR,

'Building a fair and Social Europe' post-pandemic aims to tackle issues regarding digitalization and demographic change, while focusing on building a labour market that can adapt to changes in the economy (that is, automation, AI) alongside reskilling and educating workers (Council of the European Union 2020).

The current European Council agreement follows the lines of the Commission's original plans, with five amendments: an increase in the amount of loans to the detriment of grants; a strengthening of socio-economic conditionality to ensure far-reaching reforms; a diminished degree of 'rule of law' conditionality; a slightly smaller size of the Multiannual Financial Framework (that is, long-term budget); and the grant of lump sum compensation to several countries (Special Meeting of the EC 2020; Utrilla 2020).

The European Commission activated the general escape clause of the SGP to respond to the pandemic. This allows for member states to deal adequately with the crisis, while departing from the budgetary requirements which normally apply under the European fiscal framework (while remaining within the rules-based framework of the SGP). This so-called 'flexibility' is applied to both fiscal and state-aid frameworks (European Commission 2020b). Importantly, the general escape clause stipulates that its application must not endanger fiscal sustainability, and deviation from the requirements will be temporary in nature (European Commission 2020c).

Similarly, the Recovery and Resilience Facility is firmly embedded in the European Semester and thus in the EU's budgetary management and control systems (European Commission 2020d). Member states must create recovery and resilience plans[5] which will be assessed by the Commission. The criteria include consistency with country-specific recommendations, as well as strengthening national growth potential, job creation and economic and social resilience. Grants and loans will be paid in instalments, and as such, the positive assessment of payment requests will be subject to satisfactory fulfillment of relevant milestones and targets, based on the opinion of the Economic and Financial Committee. If one or more member states consider that there has been serious deviation from this, they may request the President of the European Commission to refer the matter to the next European

[5] The Structural Reform Support Programme (also referred to as the Technical Support Instrument, I believe) helps support reform efforts and helps member states design, prepare and implement reforms (see Structural Reform Support Programme, 2020 for more details).

Council (in line with Article 17 TEU and Article 317 TFEU) (Special Meeting of the EC 2020).

In order to set funding priorities to achieve the set goals and control their implementation, the Commission will follow the model of the Budgetary Instrument for Convergence and Competitiveness (BICC), applied to all member states within the Multiannual Financial Framework (Valero 2020a). The BICC will set the priorities for investment and reforms in the euro area, building on the European Semester. Because fiscal policy is decided by national authorities, the BICC establishes a new budgetary tool which aims at bringing euro-area economies into greater conformity. This aims at increasing the effectiveness of monetary policy, and to ease concerns of the need for permanent fiscal transfers (or risk-sharing).

Overall, post-COVID-19 recovery plans remain focused on unlocking the 'full potential of the Single Market', complementing the Single Market with an 'ambitious social agenda', improving EU competitiveness and supporting access to the labour market (European Economic and Social Committee (EESC) 2020). The response presents social policy as a productive factor in restabilizing the economy and the Single Market, while neglecting pre-existing asymmetries. In these respects the pandemic response does not seem like a departure from past 'social' agendas and may once again be overshadowed by economic competitiveness and eventually financial sustainability considerations.

Reversal of neoliberal constitutionalism? Politics as an alternative to constitutionalization

The EU's response to the pandemic indicates the new constitutional rules intended to protect economically orthodox prescriptions did not entirely hold. And 'depoliticization' proved to have its limits in the sense that the process of deciding on COVID-19 support in the European Union was intensely political. One aspect of political contention was about conditionalities related to accessing money. Hard-hit countries such as Italy and Spain want minimum conditionality, while the 'Frugal Four' (Netherlands, Austria, Sweden and Denmark) want stricter adjustments and reforms to unlock funds (Valero 2020b). Chancellor Angela Merkel and French President Emmanuel Macron appeared to be the moderators between the frugal north on the one hand and the southern nations on the other. They supported making more aid available as grants in order to shield the public finances of hard-hit countries such as Italy (Seputyte et al 2020). Eventually the grant-to-loan ratio was reduced prior to the mid-July negotiations, with loans now exceeding grants. This may represent the strength of northern countries vis-à-vis the south within the negotiation process. ESM Financial Assistance versus Eurobonds[6] (aka coronabonds) also prompted heated debate. Eurobonds were proposed by France, Italy, Spain and six other EU member states as a form of long-term common debt instrument to mutualize Eurozone debt. Germany, Finland, Austria and the Netherlands, however, prefer the existing ESM toolkit which is already available and has an unused lending capacity (Heuer et al 2020). Comparatively wealthier Northern European countries have cited fear of irresponsible governments using Eurobonds to go on a 'spending spree' to further discredit the idea. The Netherlands and Germany consider this may result in countries 'living beyond their means' or avoiding making painful adjustments post-pandemic. They resisted calls to grant Italy and Spain additional borrowing power without some guarantees that this money would not result in financially unsound behaviour (Jones 2020).

Clearly, at one level the jostling between groups of nation-states about the design of the rescue packages in Europe is anything but depoliticized. However, in terms of democratic participation it largely remains so.[7] The type of politics on offer at the EU serves as a support to neoliberal constitutionalization rather than an alternative to it. Extending the EU role in fiscal policy may be a type of integration through crisis, but there is no reason to believe that the short term is an indicator of a more progressive fiscal stance emerging in the long run.

Fiscal rules in the EU have only been *temporarily* suspended. The monetary and fiscal rules have not been revised and could return in the future. In terms of the ESM Pandemic Crisis Support, ex-ante conditionality (except in the allocation of funds) may be minimal, however it includes ex-poste surveillance by Eurozone authorities regarding the macroeconomic outlook and budgetary policy of debtor countries. Similarly, crisis support is embedded in the regulatory framework of Euro Treaties and therefore existing fiscal rules, once temporary suspensions are uplifted. Although there have been declarations in favour of 'no conditionality', enhanced surveillance is an inescapable feature, meaning a closer investigation of finances, with the obligation to provide at the EU level the same information as under the excessive deficit procedure. It also includes 'regular review missions' of the Commission, the ECB and 'where appropriate the

---

[6] On the Eurobonds controversy following the financial crisis see Plehwe 2017.

[7] See the descriptions of EU political processes in Gillingham 2016.

IMF' (with the same actors but different roles as the Troika). Then, the EU Council may recommend to the State 'corrective measures' or a 'macroeconomic adjustment programme', a weighty 'recommendation' especially when combined with a fear of negative market reaction (Strati 2020).

If politics is to be an alternative to constitutionalization it is important to specify what kind of politics and at what spatial level. We have seen that through 'depoliticizing' crucial spheres of policymaking that used to be – however imperfectly – responsive to the public, the scope for the exercise of democratic politics has been diminished, as the technical application of rules replaces debate and choice between alternatives, and the overall health of democracy is limited (Hay 2007; Schafer and Streeck 2013, 1).[8] Indeed, the constitutionalization of neoliberal economic policy in terms of austerity and internal devaluation is highly authoritarian and reinforces the power of capitalist elites at the expense of labour (Koukiadaki et al 2016; Myant et al 2016). Structural reforms increase inequality and precarity, weaken unions and decrease wages (Heyes and Lewis 2014). These shifts increase the power of capital in relation to workers as the latter have fewer resources for survival beyond accepting market conditions. However, removing these issues behind a depoliticized wall of rule application is not necessarily a sign of strength. It may reflect a fragility which apparent institutional rigidity tries to disguise.

Logically, if constitutionalization and other measures have depoliticized democratic decision-making then the solution is to repoliticize it. Theoretically this could be accomplished at either international or national scales, or by rebalancing the relations between the two. But it cannot be accomplished if important areas of decision-making are simply removed and replaced by automatically or technocratically applied rules.

Based on the experience of the two crises we have touched upon, the options are posed in terms either of democratizing or reforming international institutions to serve social ends rather than narrow economic orthodoxy as represented by the austerity response to economic crisis, versus the populist demand to return control to the nation-state level. Would solutions to the ongoing crisis of neoliberal globalization be found through further internationalization, or through

[8] These trends are exacerbated by 'network governance' in which lines of responsibility and accountability are quite blurred.

attempting to rebalance the international system by returning greater power or autonomy to nation-states?

Posing the issue in this way actually may not be the most helpful entry into the debate. Rather, it might be posed as a choice between popular sovereignty and the rule of capital; or between democratic accountability and bureaucratic and technocratic governance by 'experts' (see Lapavitsas 2019, especially Chapter 6).

If left as national versus international choice, then most liberals and the centre-left would prefer an internationalist solution. More international decision-making and coordination is seen as necessary to steer the global economy. Partly this is driven by the argument that international capital can no longer be controlled by any nation-state (though many of the people making this argument do not, in truth, favour controlling international capital anyway).

But most on the internationalist side of the debate, not to mention the (neo)liberal elites of all political affiliations, fail to comprehend the reasons behind increasing popular rejection of globalization and internationally integrated institutions. In recent years large numbers of people have indicated their alienation from the existing economic and political system. At some level they consider, correctly, that they have been left behind economically and their views and opinions are ignored politically. Many attribute this situation to globalization and the remote and cosmopolitan elites in charge.

For those seeking 'more Europe' or 'more Global' solutions to crises there is the awkward fact that international institutions show little inclination to control capital. Rather, the purpose of most actually existing international institutions has been to liberate capital from controls and confer greater rights upon it. As income and wealth inequality statistics show, the result has been the further enrichment of the already rich. Democratic accountability through national governments has been sacrificed and there are virtually no supranational accountability mechanisms.

So the issue of at which spatial level challenges to the prevailing orthodoxy are likely to emerge or be successful cannot be avoided, even if efforts to produce a more equal and democratic society can and should continue at multiple levels. Neither the evolution of the global economic governance architecture, nor the post-crisis posture of the European Union, with its ongoing efforts to constitutionalize neoliberal principles in its institutions (McBride 2016) offer any reason for optimism about further internationalization. The established elites – economic, political or media – may have some internal differences but for the most part consider the characteristics of the global order as natural, valid and beyond dispute. For those favouring greater equality, and greater security, the international reform option seems hardly promising.

That leaves either the national level, or an international system that leaves more scope for national-level political preferences to emerge and be implemented. Of course, the same criticisms made of international elites can be levelled at national elites – they are as firmly committed to the prevailing economic, social and political order as their international counterparts. But the prospects of counter hegemonic mobilization, so remote at the international level, may be higher at the national level.

References

Balassone, Fabrizio and Daniele Franco. 2000. 'Public Investment, the Stability Pact and the "Golden Rule"', *Fiscal Studies*, 21(2): 207–29.

Blyth, Mark. 2013. *Austerity: The History of a Dangerous Idea*. Oxford: Oxford University Press.

Bruff, Ian. 2014. 'The Rise of Authoritarian Neoliberalism', *Rethinking Marxism*. 26(1): 113–29.

Burnham, Peter. 1999. 'The Politics of Economic Management in the 1990s', *New Political Economy*, 4(1): 37–54.

Burnham, Peter. 2014. 'Depoliticisation: Economc Crisis and Political Management', *Policy and Politics*, 42(2): 189–206.

Burret, Heiko T. and Jan Schnellenbach. 2014. *Implementation of the Fiscal Compact in the Euro Area Member States: Expertise on Behalf of the German Council of Economic Experts* (No. 08/2013e). Working Paper, German Council of Economic Experts.

Buti, Marco and Gabriele Giudice. 2002. 'Maastricht's Fiscal Rules at Ten: An Assessment', *JCMS: Journal of Common Market Studies*, 40(5): 823–48.

Buti, Marco, Daniele Franco and Hedwig Ongena. 1998. 'Fiscal Discipline and Flexibility in EMU: The Implementation of the Stability and Growth Pact', *Oxford Review of Economic Policy*, 14(3): 81–97.Cacciatore, Federica, Alessandro Natalini and Claudius Wagemann. 2015. 'Clustered Europeanization and National Reform Programmes: A Qualitative Comparative Analysis', *Journal of European Public Policy*, 22(8): 1186–211.

Council of the European Union. 2020. *Taking Forward the Strategic Agenda*. European Council. www.eu2020.de/blob/2354332/d2f4bc33ade0af634ae79552060d6332/pdf-trioprogramme-en-data.pdf

Degryse, Christophe. 2012. *The New European Economic Governance*. Report. Brussels: ETUI.

De Haan, Jakob, Helge Berger and David-Jan Jansen. 2004. 'Why Has the Stability and Growth Pact Failed?', *International Finance*, 7(2): 235–60.

Dincer, N. Nergiz and Barry Eichengreen. 2014. 'Central Bank Transparency and Independence: Updates and New Measures', *International Journal of Central Banking*, 10(1): 189–253.

EESC (European Economic and Social Committee). 2020. *EESC Proposal for post-COVID-19 crisis Reconstruction and Recovery*. European Economic and Social Committee. www.eesc.europa.eu/en/documents/resolution/eesc-proposals-post-covid-19-crisis-reconstruction-and-recovery-eu-must-be-guided-principle-being-considered-community

EPSR. 2017. *European Pillar of Social Rights*. European Commission. https://ec.europa.eu/commission/sites/beta-political/files/social-summit-european-pillar-social-rights-booklet_en.pdf

ETUI. 2014. *Benchmarking Working Europe*. Report. Brussels: ETUI.

European Commission. 2016. *EU Economic Governance. European Commission*. http://ec.europa.eu/economy_finance/economic_governance/index_en.htm

European Commission. 2020a. *Recovering from the Crisis: EU Funding to Protect Jobs and Support Green, Digital, Inclusive Society and Economy*. European Commission. https://ec.europa.eu/social/main.jsp?langId=en&catId=89&newsId=9686&furtherNews=yes

European Commission. 2020b. *Coronavirus: Commission Proposes to Activate Fiscal Framework's General Escape Clause to Respond to Pandemic*. European Commission. https://ec.europa.eu/commission/presscorner/detail/en/ip_20_499

European Commission. 2020c. *Questions and Answers: Commission Proposes Activating Fiscal Framework's General Escape Clause to Response to Coronavirus Pandemic*. European Commission. https://ec.europa.eu/commission/presscorner/detail/en/qanda_20_500

European Commission. 2020d. *Questions and Answers on the EU Budget for Recovery: Recovery and Resilience Facility*. European Commission. https://ec.europa.eu/commission/presscorner/detail/en/QANDA_20_949

Gillingham, John R. 2016. *The EU: An Obituary*. London: Verso.

Gough, Ian. 2011. 'From Financial Crisis to Fiscal Crisis', in Kevin Farnsworth and Zöe Irving (eds) *Social Policy in Challenging Times: Economic Crisis and Welfare Systems*. Bristol: Policy Press.

Guajardo, Jaime, Daniel Leigh and Andrea Pescatori. 2011. *Expansionary Austerity: New International Evidence*. IMF Working Paper. July. www.imf.org/external/pubs/ft/wp/2011/wp11158.pdf

Hacker, Björn. 2019. *A European Social Semester? The European Pillar of Social Rights in Practice*. Working Paper 2019.05 ETUI. www.etui.org/publications/working-papers/a-european-social-semester

Harvey, David. 2005. *A Brief History of Neoliberalism*. Oxford: Oxford University Press.

Hay, Colin. 2007. *Why We Hate Politics*. Cambridge: Polity.

Heipertz, Martin and Amy Verdun. 2004. 'The Dog That Would Never Bite? What We Can Learn from the Origins of the Stability and Growth Pact', *Journal of European Public Policy*, 11(5): 765–80.

Hermann, Cristoph. 2017. 'From Austerity to Structural Reform: The Erosion of the European Social Model(s)', in B.M. Evans and S. McBride (eds) *Austerity: The Lived Experience*. Toronto: University of Toronto Press, pp 251–77.

Hermann, Christoph and Ines Hofbauer. 2007. 'The European Social Model: Between Competitive Modernisation and Neoliberal Resistance', *Capital and Class*, 31(3): 125–39.

Hermann, Christoph and Birgit Mahnkopf. 2010. *The Past and Future of the European Social Model*. Working Paper No 05/2010 Berlin School of Economics and Law. www.econstor.eu/bitstream/10419/59306/1/718083032.pdf

Herndon, Thomas, Michael Ash and Robert Pollin. 2013. *Does High Public Debt Consistently Stifle Economic Growth: A Critique of Reinhart and Rogoff*. Working Paper 322. Amherst: University of Massachusetts, Political Economy Research Institute.

Heuer, Dennis, Henning M. Berger, Carsten Losing, Martin Weber, Claire-Marie Mallad and Alexander Kreibich. 2020. 'ESM Financial Assistance vs. Eurobonds – A Dilemma and the Pandemic Crisis Support', *White & Case*, 15 April. www.whitecase.com/publications/alert/esm-financial-assistance-vs-eurobonds-dilemma-and-pandemic-crisis-support

Heyes, Jason and Paul Lewis. 2014. 'Employment Protection under Fire: Labour Market Deregulation and Employment in the European Union', *Economic and Industrial Democracy*, 35(4): 587–607.

IMF Fiscal Affairs Department. 2017. *Fiscal Rules Dataset 1985–2015*. International Monetary Fund. www.imf.org/external/datamapper/fiscalrules/matrix/matrix.htm

Jessop, Bob. 2005. 'The European Union and Recent Transformations in Statehood', in S.P. Riekmann, M. Mokre and M. Latzer (eds) *The State of Europe: Transformations of Statehood from a European Perspective*. New York: Campus Verlag.

Joerges, Christian, Vladimir Bogoeski and Lukas Nuse. 2019. 'Economic Constitutionalism and the European Social Model', in Herwig C.H. Hoffman, Katerina Pantazatou and Giovanni Zaccaroni (eds) *The Metamorphosis of the European Economic Constitution*. Northampton MA: Edward Elgar Publishing Limited.

Jones, Erik. 2020. 'Old Divisions Threaten Europe's Economic Response to the Coronavirus'. *Foreign Affaris*, 6 April. www.foreignaffairs.com/articles/europe/2020-04-06/old-divisions-threaten-europes-economic-response-coronavirus

Koukiadaki, Aristea, Isabel Távora and Miguel Martínez Lucio. (eds). 2016. *Joint Regulation and Labour Market Policy in Europe during the Crisis*. Report. Brussels: ETUI.

Kurzer, Paulette. 1988. 'The Politics of Central Banks: Austerity and Unemployment in Europe', *Journal of Public Policy*, 8: 21–47.

Lapavitsas, Costas. 2019. *The Left Against the EU*. Cambridge: Polity.

Leschke, Janine, Sotiria Theodoropoulou and Andrew Watt. 2015. 'Towards "Europe 2020"? Austerity and New Economic Governance in the EU', in Steffen Lehndorff (ed) *Divisive Integration: The Triumph of Failed Ideas in Europe – Revisited*. Burssels: ETUI, pp 295–331.

Mahnkopf, Birgit. 2009. 'The Impact of Privatization and Liberalisation of Public Services on the European Social Model', in Marcia Frangakis, Christoph Hermann, and Karoly Lorand (eds) *Privatization Against the European Social Model: A Critique of European Policies and Proposal for Alternatives*. New York: Palgrave Macmillan.

McBride, Stephen. 2010. 'The New Constitutionalism: International and Private Rule in the New Global Order', in Gary Teeple and Stephen McBride (eds) *Relations of Global Power: Neoliberal Order and Disorder*. Toronto: University of Toronto Higher Education, pp 19–40.

McBride, Stephen. 2016. 'Constitutionalizing Austerity: Taking the Public out of Public Policy', *Global Policy*, 7(1): 5–14.

McBride, Stephen and Sorin Mitrea. 2017. 'Austerity and Constitutionalizing Structural Reform of Labour in the European Union', *Studies in Political Economy*. DOI: 10.1080/07078552.2017.1297011

McBride, Stephen and Joy Schnittker. 2021. 'Taking Institutions Seriously: Alternatives for a New Public Purpose', *Alternate Routes*.

Myant, Martin., Sotiria Theodoropoulos and Agnieszka Piasna (eds). 2016. *Unemployment, Internal Devaluation and Labour Market Deregulation in Europe*. Report. Brussels: ETUI.

Offe, Claus. 2003. 'The European Model of "Social" Capitalism: Can It Survive European Integration?' *The Journal of Political Philosophy*, 11(4): 437–69.

Pierson, Paul. 1996. 'The Path to European Integration', *Comparative Political Science*, 26(2): 123–63.

Plehwe, Dieter. 2017. 'Fighting the Financial Crisis or Consolidating Austerity? The Eurobond Battle Reconsidered', in Stephen McBride and Bryan Evans (eds) *The Austerity State*. Toronto: University of Toronto Press, pp 189–218.

Polillo, Simone and Mauro F. Guillén. 2005. 'Globalization Pressures and the State: The Worldwide Spread of Central Bank Independence', *American Journal of Sociology*, 110: 1754–802.

Ray M. 2016. 'The European Social Model, Social Partnership and the ETUC', *rs21*, 2 December. www.rs21.org.uk/2016/12/02/revolutionary-reflections-for-another-europe-part-2-the-european-social-model-esm-social-partnership-and-the-etuc/

Rixen, Thomas and Lora Anne Viola. 2015. 'Putting Path Dependence in Its Place: Toward a Taxonomy of Institutional Change', *Journal of Theoretical Politics*, 27(2): 301–23.

Schäfer, Armin and Wolfgang Streeck. (eds). 2013. *Politics in an Age of Austerity*. Cambridge: Polity.

Schmitter, P. 2002. *Neo-neo Functionalism*. Working Paper for the Publication in Antje Wiener and T. Dies (eds) (2009) *Theories of European Integration*. Oxford University Press.Schuknecht, Ludger. 2005. 'Stability and Growth Pact: Issues and Lessons from Political Economy', *International Economics and Economic Policy*, 2(1): 65–89.

Schulten, Thorsten and Torsten Mueller. 2015. 'European Economic Governance and Its Intervention in National Wage Development and Collective Bargaining', in Steffen Lehndorff (ed) *Divisive Integration: The Triumph of Failed Ideas in Europe – Revisited*. Brussels: ETUI.

Scicluna, Nicole. 2019. 'Integration-through-Crisis: The Triumph of Expediency over Democratic Legitimacy?' *EU Visions*, 17 April. www.euvisions.eu/integration-through-crisis-expediency-or-democratic-legitimacy/

Seputyte, Milda, Boris Groendahl and John Follian. 2020. 'Europe's Recovery Plan Comes under Fire from Budget Hardliners', *Bloomberg*, 18 July. www.bloomberg.com/news/articles/2020-07-18/europe-s-recovery-plan-comes-under-fire-from-budget-hardliners

Special Meeting of the European Council. 2020. *Conclusions*. 21 July 2020. European Council. www.consilium.europa.eu//media/45109/210720-euco-final-conclusions-en.pdf

Strati, Antonella. 2020. 'Europe's Fateful Choices for Recovery – An Italian Perspective', *Institute for New Economic Thinking*, 13 July. www.ineteconomics.org/perspectives/blog/europes-fateful-choices-for-recovery-an-italian-perspective

Torfing, Jacob. 2009. 'Rethinking Path Dependence in Public Policy Research', *Critical Policy Studies*, 3(1): 70–83.

Tsarouhas, Dimitris. 2016. 'Rethinking the European Social Model', in A. Gusenbauer et al (eds) *Delivering Empowered Welfare Societies*. Foundation for European Progressive Studies.

Utrilla, Dolores. 2020. 'The European Deal for Post-Pandemic Economic Recovery: Content and Meaning', *EU Law Live*, 21 July. https://eulawlive.com/the-european-deal-for-post-pandemic-economic-recovery-content-and-meaning/

Valero, Jorge. 2020a. 'EU Recovery Funds Will Come with Strings Attached', *Euractiv*, 20 May. www.euractiv.com/section/economy-jobs/news/eu-recovery-funds-with-strings-attached/

Valero, Jorge. 2020b. 'Fiscal Adjustment Needed to Unlock Recovery Funds, EU Official Warns', *Euractiv*, 19 June. www.euractiv.com/section/economy-jobs/news/fiscal-adjustment-needed-to-unlock-recovery-funds-eu-official-warns/

Vaughan-Whitehead, Daniel. 2014. 'The European Social Model in Times of Crisis: An Overview', in Daniel Vaughan-Whitehead (ed) *European Social Model in Crisis: Is Europe Losing its Soul?* Northampton, MA: Edward Elgar Publishing.

Whiteside, Heather, Stephen McBride and Bryan Evans. 2021. *Varieties of Austerity*. Bristol: Bristol University Press.

Zakaria, Fareed. 2007. *The Future of Freedom: Illiberal Democracy at Home and Abroad*. New York: W.W. Norton & Company.

7

There could be alternatives! German economic advisory councils and the institutional reproduction of austerity economics

Dieter Plehwe and Moritz Neujeffski

Austerity-related expertise and mainstream economics in particular have been widely blamed for locking in austerity regimes and reproducing austerity policies in European countries and in the EU. Austerity is here understood in the broader sense of social reforms to reduce private sector charges beyond the narrower 'technocratic' concern with balanced budgets and 'sound' public finance or the reduction of public debt. Austerity politics are designed to reverse the historic development of the expansion of the public sector in general and in the area of social policy and welfare provision in particular. Reducing welfare state benefits would qualify much like cutting public services, for example, because the aim is to overall reduce the level of taxes and social security contributions in spite of clear evidence of fundamental flaws, pathologies and counterproductive impacts of such welfare state retrenchment and resulting redistribution from the bottom to the top (Blyth 2013).

Although a range of economists in the field of social (in)equality, (modern) monetary theory and Post-Keynesianism like Thomas Piketty (2015), Stephanie Kelton (2020) or Steve Keen (2001) have long worked to debunk claims made by neoliberal and neoclassical economists of various schools (supply side economics, public choice, monetarism, ordoliberalism and so on), heterodox positions have been marginal in many countries. German economics has been found to constitute a particularly problematic case due to a strong conservative-neoclassical and neoliberal bias in the German profession (Heise and Thieme 2015; Grimm et al 2018). Botzem and Hesselmann (2018) document the close proximity of neoliberal think tanks and the German Council of Economic Experts (compare also Pühringer 2020).

Fricke (2016) observed a reversal of this long-term development following the GFC. But it remains to be seen if this will lead to a change in the institutional sphere of policy consulting. In one way or another, the argument about the German economic field emphasizes asymmetry and bias in favour of austerity.

Opposing claims can be found in the literature on German economic expertise under the labels of corporatism and pluralism. Campbell and Pedersen (2014) introduce the German system of expertise as a classical model of inclusion. Different groups in society in general and capital and labour in particular are considered well represented in policy-related knowledge production. The country has well-funded think tanks and research foundations associated with the different political parties, employer organizations and trade unions as well as the major religious denominations, for example. Some of the high-ranking economists and government advisors concur pointing to another academic dimension of institutional diversity: 'In Germany, there is no need to worry about plurality in policy advice, since in addition to the *German Council of Economic Experts* … there are six major state-supported economic research institutes as well as the scientific councils at the various ministries' (Wagner and Wiegard 2002, 11; italics in original). Wagner and Wiegard thus seem to regard the diversity of the advisory councils of the ministries differently than Fricke (2016). Schwarzbauer et al (2019) examine consecutive surveys of ministry staff and members of the German parliament. These surveys probe their views and assessment of relevant economists. Their results confirm the existence of two major camps of experts in Germany. A 'team Fuest' (market liberal head of the ifo-Institute) and a 'team Fratzscher' (social liberal head of the German Institute for Economic Research (DIW)). The two clusters are found to be rather stable and are predominantly made up by economists that can be considered influential in conservative and market liberal political environments and in Social Democrat and Green environments, respectively. Members of the profession outside these clusters on the other hand are suggested not to enjoy much weight as consulting experts.

The two perspectives presented here are not easy to reconcile. Can the German economics profession in general and the relevant group of experts at the science policy interface have a market liberal bias and belong to normatively and politically opposing camps? Are they both, nevertheless, supportive of austerity politics, broadly speaking? If only one camp supports austerity politics, can the whole group of economists nevertheless be blamed for the lock-in of austerity regimes?

We focus on the particular group of economists in high-level advisory bodies relevant to public finance and wider austerity subjects, namely in the field of economic and social policy between 1998 and 2017. This enables coverage of different government and policy coalitions: Social Democrats (Schröder I and II, SPD-Green coalition), and three governments led by the Christian Democrat Angela Merkel (CDU/CSU – Free Democrats, and twice the so-called grand coalition of conservatives and Social Democrats, CDU/CSU – SPD). Looking more closely at institutionalized advisory bodies, firstly, allows us to empirically and comparatively examine a concrete sample of relevant experts, their professional background, normative orientation and capacity beyond the academic sphere. While the composition of the advisory bodies has been relatively stable throughout this period of time, the demand side has changed frequently both at the level of government in general and at the level of ministry leadership in particular. Secondly, examining major reforms of the German welfare system, such as labour market and public finance reforms allows us to track and trace the positions produced by the councils as well as their opinions and those of individual members on the controversial welfare state reforms.

We thus look closely at the members of four advisory bodies, namely the German Council of Economic Experts, two Federal Ministry councils (Economic Affairs and Energy and Finance) and one council on pensions attached to the Federal Ministry of Labour and Social Affairs, called the Social Advisory Council in charge of the public pension system. The four advisory councils are comprised of 141 individuals. We scrutinize information on the individual members of these councils, and draw on additional sources from the policy processes and on expert interviews in ministries and councils, related studies and a survey of relevant news media.

Considering major austerity-related reforms in our time period – the so-called 'Hartz' labour market/social insurance reforms, pension reforms, 'debt brake'/fiscal federalism reform and minimum wage legislation – in which the advisory groups were involved, a perhaps surprising and paradoxical synthesis of the two arguments presented earlier will be advanced. The four institutionalized advisory bodies under examination were frequently complemented – if not sidelined – by alternative sources such as special commissions (Hartz-Commission, Rürup Commission, Federalism Commission) in addition to sourcing from economic and other academic research institutes (Siefken 2007; Patzwaldt 2008). As a result, it is fair to state that the official councils have not been very influential with regard to concrete pieces of legislation, although individual members like Bert Rürup (pensions), Lars Feld (debt brake mechanism) and Peter Bofinger (minimum wages) clearly left a mark. At the same time, the major thrust of reforms in the labour market, pension and federalism/public finance domains between 1998 and 2017 was market liberal in spite of alternative sourcing opportunities postulated by the pluralism argument. The minimum wage legislation provides for a lonely counter-case in need of further discussion in particular because it has been passed by the coalition government led by Christian Democrats. Still, while there exist two major competing normative and political camps of social liberal and neoliberal/conservative neoclassical economists in Germany (center-left and center-right), there seems to have been a market-liberal spell over major parts of the discipline including the nominally left-leaning group of social liberal economists with regard to labour market, pension and public finance reforms in the 2000s. We argue that this constitutes a case of neoliberal hegemony in the Gramscian sense of mainstream compromise,[1] which has been supported and secured by the asymmetrical professional and public influence of the dominant conservative neoclassical and neoliberal economists. While there are alternative voices in the profession, and even in the advisory institutions, in order for them to matter significant changes have to occur in a number of realms.

In the first section we will introduce the four advisory bodies in greater detail (1.1) not least because they operate in in different ways and perform somewhat different functions that are important to understand the picture at large. We will next provide brief information on the methods employed (1.2) and offer the results of our survey (1.3) regarding the composition of the four expert bodies, highlight startling asymmetries with regard to gender compounded by the differences in tenure, strong hierarchies in terms of the home institutions of council members, highly unbalanced relations to think tanks and, a staggering bias in favour of austerity perspectives. Section two will briefly discuss the four major reform efforts and look at council policy input. This section helps to obtain a more realistic perspective with regard to the council dimensions of the science-policy interface, and of the limits of the austerity-minded experts.

[1] Antonio Gramsci recognized the role and relevance of intellectuals in public policy, namely their ability to bring relevant perspectives to the table in order to secure consent. A viable compromise would typically integrate even subaltern strata of society to a certain extent (Bates 1975).

We will revisit the theoretical and political controversy on German economics in the conclusion and reflect on changes required to move beyond coping with austerity.

Independent advisory bodies in the field of German economic and social policy

Scientific policy advice in general and dedicated advisory bodies were highly valued in the Federal Republic following WWII. Ministry councils were introduced with the establishment of the Council of the Ministry of Economics. In light of the country's experience during National Socialism, institutional precautions were taken to shield academics from political influence. The Council of Economic Experts (GCEE) instead was introduced later in the 1960s following the US example of the Council of Economic Advisers to a certain extent. In line with the German corporatist model, employers and trade unions were given an informal role in the allocation of GCEE members, though the government officially appoints new members. The Social Advisory Council instead is a fully fledged corporatist body with tripartite membership in addition to academic experts. It advises on public pension matters only and has the largest number of non-academic functionaries. Let us look at the four bodies that are home to our sample of 141 individual members between 1998 and 2017 in somewhat greater detail.

German advisory bodies in economic and social policy areas

The German Council of Economic Experts (GCEE)

The GCEE is the most prominent of the four advisory councils. The institution was established in 1963 to assess German macroeconomic development once a year. Only in 1968 with the arrival of economics minister Karl Schiller (SPD), however, the GCEE matched the new policy design of advanced macroeconomic coordination (Globalsteuerung). Its work is supposed to strive for a stable price level, low unemployment and inflation levels as well as a balanced trade account (the 'magic square'). The GCEE always consists of five economists. Members are appointed by the government for a period of five years, with the possibility of an extension. Unofficially, both employer associations and trade unions are given the right to recommend one member for the GCEE, which have been consistently appointed after the nomination. The five members have a working staff assisting the major report issued once a year to which the government has to respond. The GCEE hearing certainly constitutes a major public and media event even if the government is not forced to heed the advice of the experts.

The academic advisory councils of the Ministries of Economics (FMEAE) and Finance (FMFA)

Mostly composed of economists and to a much lesser extent of members of law faculties, the government appoints (and rarely rejects) members based on the recommendation of the advisory board itself. The government has limited power of appointment, and the composition of the board cannot be controlled by any incoming government. Scholars have to rise within the profession before they have a chance of being considered (Schanetzky 2007, 60), which means that highly ranked economists working on economic policy-related subject matters are appointed – pure theory academics do not enter the picture. This is obviously important with regard to the normative orientation of ministry council members to be discussed later. The advisory councils are considered independent, which allows them to pick topics and decide on timing, but they are of course also expected to be responsive to calls for advice from the government.

The Social Advisory Council (SAC)

The SAC, established in 1958, was set up to advise the government and the labour ministry in particular on pension issues. It is assigned to examine and comment on the annual pension report of the Federal Ministry of Labour. Upon request the council might also provide expert opinion on specific policy issues in relation to the pension system and provides 'ad hoc advice' on current challenges (SAC 2017). In total the SAC has 12 members representing stakeholder groups of the German pension system in addition to experts. These include: insured persons, employers, the Deutsche Bundesbank, and economic and social science faculties.

These members are nominated by the different groups they represent. The council's membership structure resembles the corporatist or stakeholder model of coordinated research organizations described in the literature as typical for Germany (Campbell and Pedersen 2014).

Individual level survey data, document analysis and news media analysis

In order to assess the composition of the councils and the position of the 141 council members on austerity politics, we employ a mixed method design. This consisted of data sets on educational background, gender, employment history, their links to additional organizations and networks relevant to austerity-related public policy discourse. In order to determine the policy positions towards austerity measures of the members of the four academic councils, we profile each council member to identify a pro or con austerity point of view. This involved screening publicly available statements on the four major reforms (Hartz 4, pension reform, reform of federalism/debt brake, minimum wage). Support for the first three reforms and opposition to minimum wages broadly correspond with a pro-austerity perspective and vice versa. In addition, we retrieved publications and statements on the financial crisis and the development of the European sovereign debt crisis in Southern Europe. We also collected information on support for prominent public appeals in favour of austerity such as the Hamburger Appeal.[2] We distinguish between moderate and strong pro- or anti-austerity perspectives (see Table 7.8 later in this chapter). In order to triangulate our results, we invited experts of and on the German economics profession and our interview partners (at councils and ministries) to assess our findings of attitudes on austerity politics. We were able to locate about two thirds of the sample on our pro- and contra-austerity scale.

In order to examine the assessment and policy evaluations of the four major welfare state reforms we have also collected the relevant documents from the individual council websites. Last but not least we have examined the media presence of councils and council members in the German media between 1998 and 2017.[3]

We start the presentation of our results with a table on the academic background of our council members, which shows the dominance of economists in the four councils under investigation (see Table 7.1).

---

[2] The Hamburger Appeal dismissed anti-cyclical fiscal policy interventions in principle. It was released shortly before the general elections in 2005 and was signed by more than 200 academics.

[3] These comprise the following daily newspapers: *Handelsblatt*, *Financial Times Deutschland*, *FAZ*, *Die Welt*, *SZ*, *Der Tagesspiegel*, *Frankfurter Rundschau*, *Taz*, *Neues Deutschland*; and the following weekly papers: *Die Zeit*, *Der Spiegel*, *Wirtschaftswoche*, *Fokus*.

Table 7.1: Distribution of members of the four councils according to academic disciplines

Discipline	Members
Economics	104
Law	15
Social science	6
No information	16
Total	**141**

Note: Eight council members held positions in two respective advisory councils within the time period of our sample (1998–2018). Thus, 141 individuals held 149 positions within the four advisory councils.

Source: Author

While it might seem logical that expert councils in the fields of economic and finance are predominantly selected from the economics discipline it is interesting to note that legal scholars are given some attention in the council circles whereas social scientists play a role only in the SAC's deliberations on public pensions. A first case might be made for the introduction of some disciplinary diversity in the mainstay of economic policy advice considering the relevance of economics and finance for social policy issues.

In order to adjudicate between pluralism and hierarchy claims we look at a number of demographics, educational and ideational criteria next. The following figure presents our results of the gender distribution in the four different advisory bodies.

The key economic advisory councils are mainly populated by male economists (see Figure 7.1). Only in the corporatist SCA do women traditionally hold a larger share, followed by the GCEE. Only two women at the SCA are delegates of employers or trade unions. Seven women are academics from various disciplines (two economists, two sociologists, two political science and one law). The lack of female representatives from the social groups represented in the SAC is the responsibility of the groups themselves. In terms of academic experts, seven women out of 17 people is a much higher share than the share of women in the other councils under consideration. Given the distribution of members across disciplines there appears to be a greater sensibility to gender balance in councils in relation to social sciences compared to economics.

The share of women in the two federal ministry councils does not even make up ten per cent. Quite independent from educational background and normative perspectives the numbers suggest that the economic and

Figure 7.1: Gender distributions within the four advisory councils

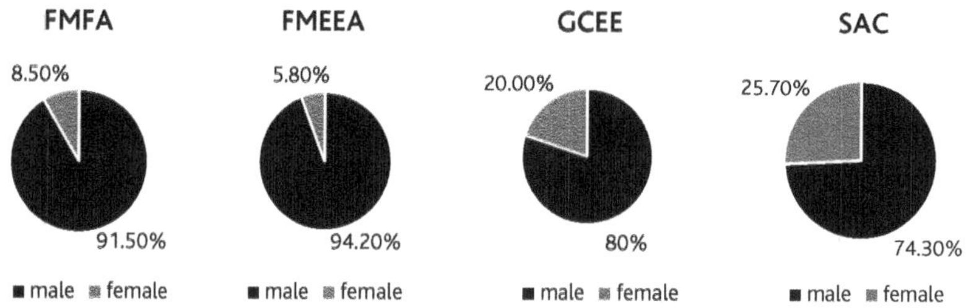

Source: Author

Table 7.2: Duration of tenure of council members

Advisory body	Average duration (years)	Longest membership duration (years)
German Council of Economic Experts (GCEE)	8	15
Social Advisory Council (SAC)	9	21
Adv. Council (FMFA)	24	51
Adv. Council (FMEEA)	24	48

Source: Author

social policy advice mainly provided by economists that matters in the advisory institutions is advice from a male perspective. In recognition of the lopsided composition of the GCEE and the increasing gender sensitivity of German politics, finance minister Scholz has recently nominated two women to replace the next departing Council members, Veronika Grimm and Monika Schnitzer. In contrast to the three other councils, the government itself can take charge of the composition of the Council of Economic Experts, which also has the highest turnover among the advisory bodies. The results can be seen in Table 7.2.

The results obtained reflect the different rules on membership duration in the statutes of the four advisory councils. Given the gender asymmetry, for example, institutional self-regulation and independence helped to marginalize women in the ministry councils. Unsurprisingly, few women held leadership positions in the councils.

Next, we looked at the main employers of the council members. Germany's academic research landscape has a large number of high-level research institutes, 120 public universities and a handful of private schools, and 300 universities of applied science. Where do members of the ministry councils and the other council members come from?

Institutional affiliation of board members

Only a small group of academic institutions account for the bulk of the members of the four advisory bodies. The two advisory bodies of the economics and finance ministries furthermore display a fairly similar pattern, which suggests a strong hierarchy in economic departments and research institutes in particular.

As Table 7.3 shows, the 13 home institutions represented most frequently account for 43 per cent main employment positions held by the 141 council members. The top six account for 26 per cent. Just 11 universities (of 120 in Germany) and just two research institutes (the Centre for European Economic Research in Mannheim and the Munich-based Ifo institute) thus show a strong concentration of sourcing economic experts in advisory institutions.

As a result of the analysis of home institutions it can be noted that members of the four councils come from strong clusters. If you are an economist and would like to serve on an advisory council, clearly

Table 7.3: Top main employers of the council members (main employer for at least five council members)

Organization	Number of council members
LMU Munich	13
University of Cologne	12
Goethe University Frankfurt	10
University of Mannheim	9
ZEW – Leibniz Centre for European Economic Research	7
University of Bonn	7
Kiel University (CAU)	6
Albert Ludwig University of Freiburg	6
Ifo Institute	5
Johannes Gutenberg University Mainz	5
FAU Erlangen-Nürnberg	5
TU Berlin	5
Humboldt University of Berlin	5
Total	**95 positions**

Source: Author

it is beneficial to be employed by a rather small group of academic institutions in addition to being male.

Survey results: austerity perspectives, think tank relations

Turning our attention to the normative and political perspectives of council members on the large theme of austerity we now enter the realm of social constructivism. We measured the individuals in our sample based on our assessment of their writing (academic and media publications) and additional expert judgement. It is clear that the findings we present then need to be put into perspective because individuals can and do change perspectives over time. In the case of Carl Christian von Weizsäcker, for example, we took note of a more critical attitude towards fiscal consolidation policies after the GFC (compare his 2013 interview).[4] We therefore do not want to overplay our presentation here, yet we think the assessment is relevant in terms of the pronounced asymmetry in favour of (strong) support of austerity politics.

We managed to obtain results for 90 individuals in the sample. We were unable to find adequate information needed to assess 51 individuals.[5] The vast majority did have a preference (23), or even strong preference (56) for austerity politics. A maximum of 12 individuals only expressed strong opposition to austerity ideas, and eight of those are members of the SAC. The SAC thus is the only high-level advisory body of the four that features a balance of pro- and anti-austerity forces within its ranks. This is due to the corporatist institutional set-up through which union representatives have a continuous representation in the SAC.

The small minority opposed to austerity in the GCEE is easy to explain as one member is informally chosen at the request of the German trade unions. There are a few moderate Keynesian voices in the councils of the economics and finance ministries, but they are by far outnumbered by the share of pro-austerity voices. Except for the corporatist SAC, there has been a staggering bias in favour of austerity in Germany's three most important advisory councils. While it should be acknowledged that some rethinking of the issue

---

[4] www.spiegel.de/spiegel/print/d-124097507.html

[5] Again because eight of the 141 advisors hold a membership in two councils, Table 7.4 lists 149 council positions.

Table 7.4: Support and opposition among council members for austerity policies

Opposition/support of austerity policies	FMEEA	FMFA	GCEE	SAC	Total
Strongly opposing austerity politics	1	2	1	8	**12**
Opposing austerity politics	2	0	1	3	**6**
Supporting austerity politics	15	6	2	0	**23**
Strongly supporting austerity politics	18	19	11	8	**56**
Unknown	16	20	0	16	**52**
Total	52	47	15	35	149

Source: Author

of public debt has taken place after the GFC even among strong supporters of 'order economics'[6] (see Holtfrerich et al 2015 on public debt), centre-right economists make a case for a certain amount of pragmatism and flexibility in the face of extraordinary crises rather than against the principles of austerity as their continuing support for the debt brake mechanism shows (for example Lars Feld at the finance ministry council).

In addition to the bias in favour of austerity, the distribution of pro- and con voices within the council on austerity across academic institutions is highly uneven. We found concentrations of up to seven pro-austerity professors in Mannheim and six in Munich and Cologne.

The hierarchy of the academic institutions employing council members is very close to the concentration of pro-austerity voices. Mannheim and Munich stand out because of the presence of a high concentration at major universities and research institutes (the ZEW and the Ifo institute respectively). Only the Berlin universities in conjunction with the DIW suggest a comparable concentration of anti-austerity perspectives. Apart from the wide range of universities employing a single member of the anti-austerity community, Tables 7.5a and 7.5b show the trade unions and pension-related associations as employers of austerity critical members of the one council in which such stakeholder knowledge matters, the SAC and the one GCEE member (Peter Bofinger in Würzburg succeeded by Achim Truger at

[6] Since traditional ordoliberalism has been significantly transformed under the influence of both Austrian economics and public choice, the contemporary Freiburg school version of neoliberalism has been named order economics (Biebricher and Ptak 2020).

Table 7.5a: Main employer organization of members supporting austerity politics*

Organization	No. of positions
University of Mannheim	7
LMU Munich	6
University of Cologne	6
ZEW – Leibniz Centre for European Economic Research	6
FAU Erlangen-Nürnberg	5
Goethe University Frankfurt	4
University of Bonn	4
Johannes Gutenberg University Mainz	4
Kiel University	4
Ifo Institute	4
University of Konstanz	4
Humboldt University of Berlin	3
Saarland University	3
University of Tübingen	3
Albert Ludwig University of Freiburg	3
Hamburg University	2
Free University of Berlin	2
Ruhr University Bochum	2
Marburg University	2
University of Zurich	2
Heidelberg University	2
University of Hanover	2
Kiel Institute for the World Economy	2
University of Münster	2
German Central Bank	2
Total	**86**

Note: *Institutions with only one membership are not displayed in this table

University Duisburg). German economic elite universities seem to help reproducing the pro-austerity bias represented at the expert councils.

The pronounced bias in favour of austerity is aggravated by the distribution of think tank relationships across the pro- and con austerity camps. Compared to a small group of (Keynesian/progressive) think

Table 7.5b: Main employer organization of members opposing austerity politics

Organization	No. of positions
Technical University of Berlin	2
German Institute for Economic Research (DIW)	2
Free University of Berlin	2
Humboldt University of Berlin	2
Saarland University	2
Giessen University	1
University of Würzburg	1
University of Hannover	1
LMU Munich	1
Albert Ludwig University of Freiburg	1
University of Bremen	1
Goethe University Frankfurt	1
London School of Economics	1
Massachusetts Institute of Technology (MIT)	1
Max-Planck-Institute for Human Development	1
German Salaried Employees' Union (DAG)	1
ver.di	1
Trade Union for Building-Agriculture-Environment (IG BAU)	1
German Trade Union Confederation (DGB)	1
Fund for Salaried Employees Germany (BfA)	1
Association of German Pension Schemes (VDR)	1
Total	**26**

Source: Author

tanks and academic networks we find a large number of links to neoliberal think tanks and academic networks. The two camps are clearly divided.

In addition to the distinctly neoliberal/conservative and social-liberal/progressive think tanks we note a few think tanks and networks that appear to be open to different normative perspectives at least with regard to the presence of both pro- and contra austerity council members, such as the Center for Economic Policy Research (CEPR) in Washington, DC, the World Economic Forum (WEF), the IZA in Bonn and the Brussels-based think tank Bruegel.

If we focus on partisan think tanks which support or oppose austerity politics, we can see that council members had links to 21 groups that diffuse pro-austerity messages in the country (see Table 7.6). Vice versa, some of these groups even enjoy the presence of members of different expert councils and thus have privileged access to important information flows.

On the contra side, few council members maintain links to civil society think tanks committed to anti-austerity agendas. Vice versa, only the Keynes society and the quite recent Institute for New Economic Thinking (INET) count multiple council members (two each).

Media presence of members of the four academic councils

So far, we have established that individuals supporting austerity politics dominate the four academic councils in terms of numbers, hold key positions in well-established universities and economic research institutes and have close links to a large number of neoliberal and conservative think tanks committed to austerity. The strength of the pro-austerity cluster is reflected in the frequency of media representations. We have examined 555 newspaper articles between 1998 and 2017 dealing with the four major welfare state reforms in one way or the other. Of these, 420 articles refer to individual council members either as authors, interview partners or mention them as sources of expertise. The following figure shows the articles across time.

Articles on labour market reforms (22 per cent) and minimum wages (17 per cent) outnumber pension (13 per cent) and federalism reform (13 per cent). The remaining articles dealt with economic policy in general, policy advice and finance subjects.

Table 7.7 displays the dominance of council members supporting austerity positions within the newspaper publications. In total, four out of five articles identified express support for austerity.

Concentrating on the leadership of the ministry councils and the SAC along with the members of the GCEE also demonstrates that the official council voices in the public rarely, if ever, oppose austerity measures. While the frequent minority position opposed to austerity of Peter Bofinger in the GCEE is documented in the report, it is not mentioned in the summary that reflects the position of the majority only.

Table 7.6: Think tank landscape: neoliberal and social-liberal (pro-/contra austerity)

Think tanks	**No. of council members**	**Positions in 1–4 councils**
Think tanks supporting austerity politics		
Stiftung Marktwirtschaft/Kronberger Kreis	13	3
Mont Pèlerin Society	7	3
Aktionsgemeinschaft Soziale Marktwirtschaft	4	3
New Social Market Initiative (INSM)	4	3
Ludwig Erhard Foundation	4	3
Economics and Social Philosophy Network (NOUS)	2	3
ECONWATCH	2	2
German Economic Institute (IW) Cologne	2	2
Economic Council of the CDU	1	2
Herbert Giersch Foundation	1	2
Wilhelm-Röpke-Institute	1	2
Bund der Steuerzahler	1	1
Center for Economic Studies (ces)	1	1
European Center for Public Choice	1	1
Foundation Familienunternehmen	1	1
Friedrich a. von Hayek Foundation	1	1
Friedrich a. von Hayek Society	5	1
Institute for Free Entreprise Berlin	1	1
Institute of Economic Affairs (iea)	1	1
Open Europe Berlin	1	1
Roman Herzog Institute	1	1
Total number of think tanks: 29	**29 individuals***	**4 (all councils)**
Think tanks opposing austerity politics		
German Keynes Society	3	2
Institute for New Economic Thinking (INET)	2	2
Progressive Economy	1	1
Total number of think tanks: 3	**4 individuals****	**3 of the 4 councils**

Notes: * 29 individuals hold a total of 55 positions in pro-austerity think tanks

** 4 individuals hold a total of 6 positions in think tanks opposed to austerity

Source: Author

Table 7.7: Media occurrences of members of the four advisory councils

	Type of media occurrence			
Austerity position	**Author**	**Interviewed**	**Mentioned**	**Total**
Supporting austerity	38 (90%)	36 (77%)	261 (79%)	335 (80%)
Opposing austerity	4 (10%)	10 (21%)	62 (19%)	76 (18%)
No clear opinion on austerity	0 (0%)	1 (2%)	8 (2%)	9 (2%)
Total	**42**	**47**	**331**	**420**

Source: Author

The councils and the policy process

The strong bias in favour of austerity politics suggests a certain amount of influence by the austerity-minded council members and the councils as such in the labour market, pension and federalism reforms. While this is certainly true for individual council members like Bert Rürup (pension reform) Lars Feld (debt brake), most of the council members and the councils as advisory bodies did not play a major role in the reform process. The governments and ministries in charge chose or had to rely instead on dedicated commissions like the Hartz commission (labour market reforms), the Rürup commission (pension reform), and the federalism commission (Patzwaldt 2008; Wehlau 2009; Eicker-Wolf and Himpele 2011; Pautz 2012; Bosch 2015). Peter Bofinger of the GCEE was a lonely dissenter in the advisory bodies in support of the minimum wage law eventually introduced in 2017. Since the relevant ministries additionally rely on contract research to prepare and to assess reform legislation,[7] the role of the councils with regard to the concrete policy process should not be exaggerated. But the key role of individual members in neoliberal pension and labour market reforms stipulating partial privatization and workfare solutions, the introduction of the debt brake and the long delay of minimum wage legislation suggests to nevertheless consider the role of the austerity bloc in the realm of

[7] We counted 73 reports ordered by the FMEAE alone related to the fields of the labour market (22), minimum wages (20), pensions (11) and federalism (20) (Bundesregierung 2018; 2019).

economic policy expertise. We will very briefly summarize the reforms and take a look at the council position to see in which ways they tried to influence the direction of the policy.

The pension reforms of 2001 and 2004

In 2001 the coalition of Social Democrats and the Green Party agreed to lower the overall pension level in order to reduce the non-wage labour costs in support of international competitiveness. In order to compensate for the reduced pension levels, the coalition decided to restructure the statutory pension insurance system in a fundamental way and introduced subsidized complementary private pension plans, paving the way for partial privatization. The reform of 2004 based on the GCEE member Bert Rürup-led Commission (started in 2002) increased the retirement age and changed the pension formula according to which pensions are adjusted in relation to wage increases to continuously reduce the pressure to wage-related contributions ('sustainability factor').

The reforms were hotly debated and met strong opposition from the German trade unions. The advisory councils presented different opinions on the reforms with Rürup at the GCEE generating support for the government consolidation plans. In this case, the SAC took centre stage as its main function is to comment on pension reforms. Resistance to the pension reforms from the labour group were muted to a certain extent by the replacement of strong opponents with moderates who were open to reforms (Wehlau 2009, 156). The government thus managed to marginalize the opposition by way of securing a favourable composition of experts even in the more diversified SAC.

Federalism/debt brake

The federal system in Germany involves both policy cooperation and joint fiscal responsibilities of the federal government and the 16 state governments (*Länder*). Two inter-state fiscal adjustment mechanisms (*Länderfinanzausgleich*) are designed to reduce regional inequality, vertical funding of disadvantaged regions and horizontal redistribution from rich states to poorer states. *Länder* with below-average tax revenues are thereby eligible for significant amounts of financial compensation. The federalism reforms of 2006 and especially the second federalism reform in 2009 restructured the inter-state fiscal adjustment mechanisms and introduced the German debt brake mechanism, a blueprint for the European fiscal compact.

Table 7.8: Categories for examining austerity positions of advisory council members

Category	Supporting austerity policies	Strongly supporting austerity policies	Opposing austerity policies	Strongly opposing austerity policies
Explanation	A moderate-pragmatic view on austerity. Principal support of fiscal consolidation, which aims at a restrictive fiscal policy to reduce the public spending ratio. Specific ideas about structural, institutional or political austerity measures are – at this point – not given.	The moderate, pragmatic idea of austerity is combined with distributional concerns. Beyond the ideal of household consolidation, market liberal ideals, such as social welfare cuts, are promoted.	The household consolidation view is being dismissed whereas a demand-oriented Keynesian-fiscal approach is favoured.	Dismissed household consolidation policies plus opposition to structural reform of the welfare state such as the privatization of the public pension system or the flexibilization of the labour market.
Examples	Market-oriented views; anti-Keynesian debt/stimulus statements; opposition to fiscal burden; pro fiscal consolidation; opposition to (Greek) debt cut.	Pro flexibilization of the labour market; pro privatization (pension reforms); in favour of tax reforms (tax cuts for rich in particular); contra ECB cheap money policies; pro structural welfare state reforms such as Hartz IV [...] Signatory Hamburger Appell.	Contra the priority given to household consolidation, but not outspoken against structural reforms.	Contra household consolidation in a wide sense; contra structural reforms; pro increasing taxes for the wealthy (property tax, inheritance tax).

Source: Author

The report of the GCEE in 2002–03 summarizes the position of the advisory councils well: 'The German cooperative federalism must be replaced through a competitive federalism. Federalism without competition is actually no federalism' (GCEE 2002–03, 235). Concomitantly, they see the need for a 'limited tax-autonomy for the federal states' (GCEE 2002–03, 305), which could reduce the 'totally excessive redistribution [between the federal states]' (GCEE

2002–03, 305). No board member expressed a minority opinion in this case. The pressure from austerity-minded experts to reduce the level of fiscal solidarity and to move towards competitive federalism apparently had been too strong. The policy recommendations are expressed again in 2005, with an appeal not to forget reforming the fiscal adjustment mechanisms (GCEE 2005–06 18–20). In 2006 the council calls for the introduction of a 'debt brake' and describes the Swiss debt brake as a possible blueprint (GCEE 2006–07, 312–15). The two ministry councils commented on the reforms as well. The advisory council of the FMEEA explains the disciplinary character of the reform: 'the current financial constitution makes it less urgent for financially weak federal states to consolidate their household. It is tempting to exploit the loophole of indebtedness. The federal government can be expected to step in in the case of an emergency'. (FMEAE Council 2005, Documentation Nr. 551 p 14). In their 2005 paper 'household crisis within the federal state' the advisory board of the Federal Ministry of Financial Affairs (FMFA) reveals similar ideas on reforming the inter-state fiscal adjustment regime. The council identifies household consolidation as a main target, calls for an 'expert-commission' to evaluate the financial situation of the German states and to take countermeasures in case of a financial crisis. The policy should aim at 'restricting expenses'. In case of noncompliance 'financial aid should be denied and previous payments should be reclaimed' (FMFA Council 2005, 47). Both advisory boards clearly promoted restrictive public finance and austerity politics. Both favour tight fiscal rules, which makes it much harder to deviate from a pro-cyclical fiscal policy. Compared to the actual reforms, the councils demand an even stronger enforcement of competitive federalism.

Hartz labour market reform

The committee on reforms to the German labour market headed by former VW senior executive Peter Hartz produced several recommendations for restructuring the German labour market system as well as the unemployment security in particular. Four Measures – Hartz I–Hartz IV – were introduced by the coalition of the Social Democrats and the Green party between 2003 and 2005. The Hartz IV reform fused the system of unemployment benefits (*Arbeitslosenhilfe*) with the welfare benefit system (*Sozialhilfe*). Previously German citizens could claim unemployment benefits (60–67 per cent of their net income) for a period of 12 to 36 months. This was lowered to 12 months in general. Afterwards, citizens could claim the so-called Hartz IV benefit (*Arbeitslosengeld II*), which is usually low compared to the previous level of unemployment benefits. The Hartz reforms sparked an extension of the German low-wage sector by way of demanding recipients to accept jobs below previous standards or risk cuts in benefits. Proposals of the Commission to significantly increase the support for further education and other provisions aiding the unemployed were not implemented, which led to strong criticism of the law from some experts including Peter Hartz. The trade unions mobilized against the law, but the German trade union federation demobilized following a concession from the government with regard to the protected level of savings of Hartz IV recipients. The law effectively introduced a German workfare regime (Pautz 2012).

The advisory council of the Federal Ministry for Economic Affairs and Energy (FMEAE) addressed the Hartz reforms in supportive policy briefs focusing on 'administrative efficiency' (FMEAE Council 2003, 19), the need to restructure the social security system (the Council stated: 'The Council had already previously criticized the role of unions in the German collective bargaining system, demanding lower wage arrangements to increase the number of jobs for low qualified workers' (2003, 11)), the potential budgetary burden due to the institutional set-up of the 'job-centers' – the newly introduced administration focusing on labour market re-integration, and the need 'to reform the duration of unemployment benefit I in such a way that the incentives to seek work are promoted in the best possible way' (2003, 19). These imply support for a minimalistic framework for the unemployment benefits.

The recommendations of the GCEE point to a similar direction in several assessments: 'The Council of Experts renews its proposal for a fundamental reform of social assistance/unemployment benefit II, so that more employment is created in the low-wage sector' (GCEE 2003–04, 361, already 2002–03, 216–17). It also supported the Hartz reform ideas in terms of reducing the duration of the first level unemployment benefits. The SAC and the advisory council of the FMFA did not address the Hartz reforms in their assessments.

Minimum wage

The introduction of the minimum wage in 2015 is an exception to the three other welfare state reforms. Minimum wages were long considered incompatible with the German system of collective bargaining autonomy by both employer organizations and trade unions in the Federal Republic before unification. Since trade unions opposed state mandated wages the Social Democratic Party did not advocate minimum wages. The constellation changed when trade unions recognized that they were unable to effectively organize widening segments of low-wage labour following unification of the country. Research support and campaigns in favour of minimum wages were developed by trade union researchers at the Institute of Social and Economic Research (WSI) among others. The united service sector union Ver.Di and the food and restaurant union NGO started to endorse minimum wages. Following the Hartz reforms the German low-wage sector was deliberately grown even faster, which led to a complete realignment. Henceforth trade unions, the Left Party, the Green party and eventually the Social Democrats demanded minimum wages which were opposed by employer organizations, the Christian Democrats and the Liberals. When the Social Democrats joined the coalition government led by Angela Merkel, again following the financial crisis, the Social Democrats started to press for minimum wages in an effort to recover from the negative image the party had attained during the Schröder years due to the Hartz reforms. In the face of sluggish demand and a slow recovery from the deep recession, the Christian Democrats in 2014 finally compromised on the introduction of minimum wages regulated by a tripartite minimum wage commission. The law stopped downward wage pressure at the bottom of the wage scale and translated into double-digit increases in a few low-wage segments. Overall the wage increase across the low-wage spectrum was modest, however, which probably explains why fears about significant job losses were unfounded.

Minimum wage proposals met fierce opposition of the economic advisory councils (FMEAE and GCEE) and campaigns from neoliberal think tanks and employer associations.

The experts of the FMEAE council claimed that the minimum wage is an example of protectionist tendencies which negatively affect Germany's global competitiveness and strongly advised against the introduction of minimum wage legislation by the state (FMEAE Council 2006, 11).[8] Similar arguments were made by the GCEE. The Expert group suggested that basic unemployment benefits introduced by Hartz IV are an employment-friendly alternative to

[8] Within their 2006 assessment, the authors state for example that 'minimum wages are not only economically ineffective, they are also out of place given the current legal situation' (p 29). Translated from German: 'Mindestlöhne sind nicht nur wirtschaftlich unwirksam, sie sind auch angesichts der gegenwärtigen rechtlichen Lage fehl am Platz' (p 26).

minimum wages, referring to the negative income tax, low wage supplementing income (GCEE 2004–05, 3). The arguments made by the two Councils display the general supply side bias of the advisory bodies. The argument effectively returns to dated neoclassical ideas of labour markets as just another market that will return to equilibrium provided there are no obstacles resulting from external intervention.

The position of the austerity-minded experts in the councils was backed up by studies conducted at the major economic research institutes, DIW and RWI for example, which claimed that the introduction of minimum wages would lead to up to 1.2 million job losses and have additional negative fiscal effects (Müller et al 2008, Bachmann et al 2008). The findings of these studies were circulated widely by employer organizations and neoliberal think tanks. Unsurprisingly, counter-expertise and relevant studies were conducted in research centres close to the trade unions (Bispinck and Schulten 2008; Bosch et al 2009).

While the opposition from the conservative-liberal coalition government and the economics ministry headed by Rösler has certainly been reinforced by the council experts and the research in the economic institutes, the limits of the hierarchical interrelation between decision makers and privileged experts became evident during the next coalition of Christian Democrats and Social Democrats. Now the marginal expertise supplied by research institutes of the trade unions or by researchers with greater proximity to the trade unions became the go-to science instead of its lack of representation in the advisory councils with the exception of the minority voice on the GCEE.

Lessons from the policy process

Evidence from the reform processes suggests a limited role of the advisory councils. Although council advice and the dominant austerity-minded experts supported the direction of the labour market, pension and federalism reforms, the advisory institutions did not matter much compared to the role played by individual council members in dedicated commissions created to guide the governments. The opinions voiced by the councils typically marked a more radical position than the market liberal-minded reform commissions and helped to push the reform process, which gained a more centrist character due to the critical voices on both the progressive and conservative-neoliberal spectrum of the science. In the case of minimum wages, the pro-austerity/supply side majority on the councils helped delay the reforms, but proved unable to prevent the introduction of minimum wages when the government coalition changed. The public media impact of council members was much stronger in the case of labour market and minimum wage reforms (see Figure 7.2), but in the case of minimum wages the mobilization of conservative-neoliberal opposition in councils and civil society think tanks did still not prove sufficient to block the reforms. German trade unions and their allies among progressive economists and social scientists recovered some ground lost in the earlier labour market, pension and federalism reforms. This demonstrates that there are alternatives to the dominant austerity and supply side wisdom, and also sheds light on the conditions under which alternative voices come to matter in the policy process.

Conclusion

This chapter has detailed the asymmetrical distribution of experts in four high-level economic advisory bodies in Germany. Predominantly male economists from a handful of leading economics departments and research institutes constitute a solid pro-austerity bloc in the academic advisory councils of the Economics and Finance ministries, in the GCEE and to a lesser degree in the SAC in charge of the public pension system. Corporatist concerns and stakeholder inclusion appear to limit the overpowering share of conservative-neoclassical and neoliberal academics in the economics profession in the case of the SAC, but those who emphasize stakeholder inclusion (for example Campbell and Pederson 2014) seem to underestimate government influence in expert

Figure 7.2: Media hits related to council members 1998–2017, four reform projects

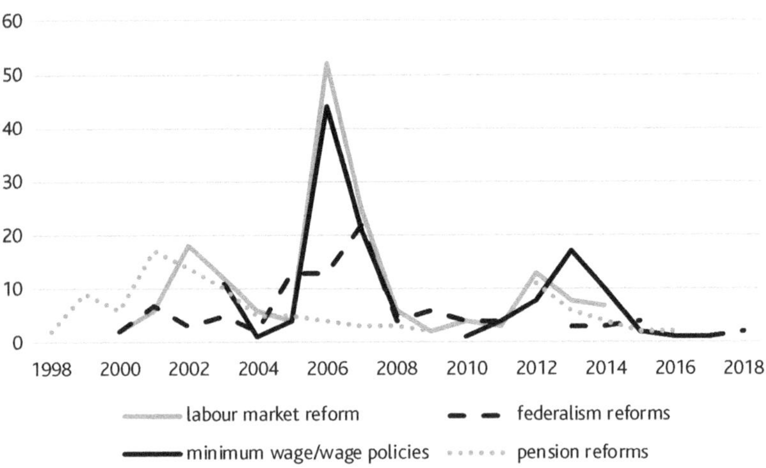

Source: Author

circles. In light of the bias in favour of male economists and in favour of pro-austerity positions it nevertheless appears to be necessary to rethink the question of 'independent' policy advice in Germany, or rather the hierarchical self-regulation of the academic nomination system. The resulting advice from members of the ministry councils appears to be overdependent on a rather narrow spectrum of the academic discipline when it comes to economic and social policy questions. The share of women and heterodox economists in the ministry councils cannot be easily increased if the present mode of self-selection is to be maintained.

In order to bring women and heterodox economic voices to bear in academic and economic policy debates there appears to be a need for three major changes in the country. Firstly, the economics profession appears to be in a strong need to change the composition of the leading departments. A dedicated effort needs to be made to increase the number of social economists and of researchers with a broader spectrum of epistemological and normative inclinations. Secondly, the rules that govern the ministry councils should be changed to encourage greater diversity. It should be mandatory to increase the number of female economists and of economists who are not in the mainstream of the German profession. A rethinking has been taking place with regard to the GCEE as there are now two women on this council for the first time, for example. Thirdly, the various stakeholders in economic and social policy questions should take a closer look at their own capacities in the field of civil society think tanks and social networks. If the introduction of minimum wages against the forceful opposition of the corporate sector and conservative-neoclassical and neoliberal economists provides some guidance, the research and mobilization capacities of the trade unions show that heterodox economists and social scientists can work successfully to obtain a strong position in legislative reforms. It might be interesting for other social groups to invest in stronger research and consulting capacities, which might be possible if different groups are willing to pool resources. It will nevertheless be necessary to move alternative voices into the mainstream of economics, because otherwise progressive economists of networks like the Memorandum group (founded in opposition to the GCEE back in the 1970s) will continue to shout from the outside rather than being part of the politically relevant conversation.

Although the pro-austerity bloc was not found to matter as much as might be expected in the policy reforms, the link between the hierarchy in the economic profession and the pro-austerity bias in the advisory councils certainly presents an obstacle for progressive reforms. Even more moderate academics on the more relevant reform commissions were broadly supportive of the market liberal character of three of the four reforms we discussed. Hierarchical interrelations between science, policy and stakeholder clusters helped to silence and sideline the opposition to neoliberal reforms. The weight of the German conservative-neoclassical and ordoliberal economists presents a challenge both for academic pluralism and societal debate. Asymmetrical power of neoliberal think tanks adds to fortification of austerity in the country. Minimum wages can be considered cutting against the grain, but may also be considered a necessary effort to stabilize the German path of neoliberal transformation. Not only can low-wage workers now make a somewhat better living, but higher minimum wages also reduce the need for public spending and thereby stabilize austerity politics in the sphere of public finance.

If and to what extent the COVID-19 pandemic and related economic crisis opens up new academic, discursive and political space remains to be seen. There are cracks in the ceiling of the ordo economic and conservative neoclassical fortress and there is some learning going on within the centre-right circles. There is a new discussion on the limits imposed by the debt brake and recognition for increasing fiscal capacity and cross-country transfers in the EU. But a lot remains to be done for pluralism to become a meaningful term in German economics.

References

Bachmann, Ronald, Thomas K. Bauer, Jochen Kluve, Sandra Schaffner and Christoph M. Schmidt. 2008. 'Mindestlöhne in Deutschland. Beschäftigungswirkungen und fiskalische Effekte'. *Essen RWI* , 43.

Bates, Thomas R. 1975. 'Gramsci and the Theory of Hegemony', *Journal of the History of Ideas*, 36(2, April–June 1975): 351–66.

Biebricher, Thomas and Ralf Ptak. 2020. *Soziale Marktwirtschaft und Ordoliberalismus zur Einführung*. Hamburg: Junius Verlag.

Bispinck, Reinhard and Thorsten Schulten. 2008. 'Aktuelle Mindestlohndebatte: Branchenlösungen oder gesetzlicher Mindestlohn?' *WSI-Mitteilungen*, 61(3): 151–8.

Blyth, Mark. 2013. *Austerity: The History of a Dangerous Idea*. New York: Oxford University Press.

Bosch, Gerhard. 2015. 'Der holprige Weg zum gesetzlichen Mindestlohn in Deutschland', *Sozialer Fortschritt*, 64(7, July 2015): 173–81.

Bosch, Gerhard, Claudia Weinkopf and Thorsten Kalina. 2009. *Mindestlöhne in Deutschland. Abteilung Wirtschafts- und Sozialpolitik der Friedrich-Ebert-Stiftung*. Bonn. http://library.fes.de/pdf-files/wiso/06866.pdf

Botzem, Sebastian and Judith Hesselmann. 2018. 'Gralshüter des Ordoliberalismus? Der Sachverständigenrat zur Begutachtung der gesamtwirtschaftlichen Entwicklung als ordnungspolitischer Fluchtpunkt bundesrepublikanischer Politikberatung', *Leviathan*, 46(3): 402–32.

Bundesregierung. 2018. *Antwort der auf die Kleine Anfrage des Abgeordneten Stephan Brandner und der Fraktion der AfD*. Drucksache 19/2448.

Bundesregierung. 2019. *Antwort der Bundesregierung auf die Kleine Anfrage der Abgeordneten Katharina Willkomm, Stephan Thomae, Michael Theurer, weiterer Abgeordneter und der Fraktion der FDP*. Drucksache 19/7823.

Campbell, John L. and Ove K. Pedersen. 2014. The National Origins of Policy Ideas: Knowledge Regimes in the United States, France, Germany, and Denmark. Princeton, NJ: Princeton University Press.

Eicker-Wolf, Kai and Klemens Himpele. 2011. 'Die Schuldenbremse als politisches Projekt', *PROKLA. Zeitschrift für Kritische Sozialwissenschaft*, 41(163, June 2011): 195–212. https://doi.org/10.32387/prokla.v41i163.349

FMEAE Council. 2003. *Gutachten des Wissenschaftlichen Beirates beim Bundesministerium für Wirtschaft und Arbeit. 2003. Forschungsbericht Nr. 518. Die Hartz-Reformen – ein Beitrag zur Lösung des Beschäftigungsproblems?* Berlin.

FMEAE Council. 2005. *Gutachten des Wissenschaftlichen Beirates beim Bundesministerium für Wirtschaft und Energie. 2005. Forschungsbericht Nr. 551, Zur finanziellen Stabilität des deutschen Föderalstaates*. Berlin.

FMEAE Council. 2006. *Gutachten des Wissenschaftlichen Beirates beim Bundesministerium für Wirtschaft und Energie. 2006. Forschungsbericht Nr. 554, Mai 2006: Der Deutsche Arbeitsmarkt in Zeiten globalisierter Märkte*. Berlin.

FMFA Council. 2005. *Gutachten des Wissenschaftlichen Beirates beim Bundesministerium der Finanzen. Haushaltskrisen im Bundesstaat*. Berlin

Fricke, Thomas. 2016. *Wenn Wirtschaftsweise den Erkenntnisfortschritt Bremsen*. FGW-Impuls (Neues ökonomisches Denken 03). www.fgw-nrw.de/fileadmin/user_upload/FGW_Impuls-NOED-03-Fricke-A4-Web.pdf. Last accessed 2 July 2017.

GCEE. 2002–03. *Sachverständigenrat zur Begutachtung der gesamtwirtschaftlichen Entwicklung. 2002/3. Zwanzig Punkte für Beschäftigung und Wachstum. Jahresgutachten 2002/3*. Stuttgart: Metzler-Poeschel.

GCEE. 2003–04. *Sachverständigenrat zur Begutachtung der gesamtwirtschaftlichen Entwicklung. 2003/4. Staatsfinanzen konsolidieren – Steuersystem reformieren*. Berlin.

GCEE. 2005–06. *Sachverständigenrat zur Begutachtung der gesamtwirtschaftlichen Entwicklung. Jahresgutachten 2005/6. Die Chance nutzen – Reformen mutig voranbringen*. Berlin

GCEE. 2006–07. *Sachverständigenrat zur Begutachtung der gesamtwirtschaftlichen Entwicklung. Jahresgutachten 2006/7. Widerstreitende Interessen – Ungenutzte Chancen*. Berlin

Grimm, Christian, Stephan Pühringer and Jakob Kapeller. 2018. *Paradigms and Policies: The State of Economics in the German-Speaking Countries*. Linz: ICAE Working Paper Series – No. 77 – March 2018.

Heise, Arne and Sebastian Thieme. 2015. *What Happened to Heterodox Economics in Germany after the 1970s?* Discussion Papers, Zentrum für Ökonomische und Soziologische Studien, No. 49.

Holtfrerich, Carl-Ludwig, Lars P. Feld, Werner Heun et al. 2015. *Staatsschulden: Ursachen, Wirkungen und Grenzen*. Berlin.

Keen, Steve. 2001. *Debunking Economics the Naked Emperor for the Social Science*. Sydney: Pluto Press.

Kelton, Stephanie. 2020. *The Deficit Myth: Modern Monetary theory and How to Build a Better Economy*. New York: Public Affairs.

Müller, Kai-Uwe and Viktor Steiner. 2008. 'Mindestlöhne kosten Arbeitsplätze: Jobverluste vor allem bei Geringverdienern', DIW Wochenbericht, ISSN 1860-8787, *Deutsches Institut für Wirtschaftsforschung (DIW)*, Berlin, 75(30): 418–23.

Patzwaldt, Katja. 2008. *Die sanfte Macht. Die Rolle der wissenschaftlichen Politikberatung bei den rot-grünen Arbeitsmarktreformen*. Bielefeld: Transcript.

Pautz, Hartwig. 2012. *Think-Tanks, Social Democracy and Social Policy*. London: Palgrave.

Piketty, Thomas. 2015. 'Austerity Has Failed: An Open Letter from Thomas Piketty to Angela Merkel', *The Nation*. www.thenation.com/article/archive/austerity-has-failed-an-open-letter-from-thomas-piketty-to-angela-merkel/. Last accessed 24 September 2020.

Pühringer, Stephan. 2020. 'Think Tank Networks of German Neoliberalism: Power Structures in Economics and Economic Policies in Postwar Germany', in D. Plehwe, Q. Slobodian and P. Mirowski (eds) *Nine Lives of Neoliberalism*. London: Verso.

SAC (Social Advisory Council). 2017. *Assignment and Task*. www.sozialbeirat.de/en/assignment+task/. Last accessed: 2 July 2017.

Schanetzky, Tim. 2007. *Die große Ernüchterung: Wirtschaftspolitik, Expertise und Gesellschaft in der Bundesrepublik 1966 bis 1982*. De Gruyter.

Schwarzbauer, Wolfgang, Tobias Thomas and Gert G. Wagner. 2019. 'Gleich und gleich gesellt sich gern? Eine Netzwerkanalyse von politikberatenden Wissenschaftlern', *Wissenschaftsdienst*, 4: 278–85. DOI: 10.1007/s10273-019-2444-6

Siefken, Sven. 2007. Expertenkommissionen im politischen Prozess Eine Bilanz zur rot-grünen Bundesregierung 1998–2005. Wiesbaden, Germany: Springer VS.

Wagner, Gert G. and Wolfgang Wiegard. 2002. 'Economic Research and Policy Advice – Also a Note on Immanuel Kant's "Actus der Urteilskraft"'. *DIW Berlin Research Notes*. www.diw.de/documents/publikationen/73/diw_01.c.38829.de/diw_rn02-01-10.pdf. Last accessed 15 February 2019.

Wehlau, Diana. 2009. *Lobbyismus und Rentenreform: Der Einfluss der Finanzdienstleistungsbranche auf die Teil-Privatisierung der Alterssicherung*. VS Verlag für Sozialwissenschaften.

8

Negotiated austerity? A comparative survey of social concertation in Canada, Denmark, Ireland and Spain

Bryan Evans, Stephen McBride and James Watson

This chapter deals with the impact of austerity and, more broadly, neoliberalism on one of the mechanisms used by labour to shape or modify the political-economic environment that it encounters in its dealings with capital. We refer here to social concertation as an umbrella term encapsulating processes and institutions of social partnership/social dialogue/social concertation/and neo-corporatism. Labour has other instruments. These include political action – either through endorsement or participation in political parties representing its interests, or through lobbying or otherwise seeking to influence political decision makers; direct action of various types – general strikes, boycotts, civil disobedience, use of legal processes and the courts; and various forms of industrial action. Here we focus on one aspect of labour's representative role. Through unions, or trade union federations at various geographic scales, labour has engaged in joint negotiations or discussions with employers' federations and the state in processes and institutions designed to promote cooperation on various policy issues through partnership and dialogue.

As Guy Standing noted (1999, 43) regarding voice regulation of labour markets, these arrangements will work best where there is a relatively even balance between the social actors. Without such balance capital will see little need to participate (arguably this is the Canadian case); or the structure will simply be an exercise in which the weaker party (labour) receives symbolic recognition but whose participation functions mostly to legitimate decisions over which it has little control. One of the ingredients for the success of this type of regulation is the 'shadow of the future' – the realization by all sides that they have to deal with each other on a continuing basis, and hence that the maximization of some short-term advantages may not be desirable. Absent that, little meaningful dialogue or partnership can occur, though top-down concertation remains a possibility.

Various forms of social concertation between trade unions, capital and the state emerged in much of Europe in the process of post-war reconstruction. Over time, a variety of terms have been applied to the practices of social concertation including corporatism, neo-corporatism, tripartism, social dialogue and social partnership. These are, in essence, an institutionalized process of social dialogue expressed through 'institutional arrangements ... that directly involves major interest groups in policy development and implementation' (Bradford and Stevens 1996, 146). More precisely, this phenomenon is understood as a 'system of economic governance and policymaking which combines a certain type of structure of organized interests in society (corporatism) with a certain type of process of policy-making (concertation)' (Alfonso 2013, 26). The end product of the negotiations taking place within this tripartite space consists of negotiated formal or informal agreements arrived at by the participants (Pochet and Natali 2010, 17).

Panitch defined corporatism as 'a political structure within advanced capitalism which integrates organized socioeconomic producer groups through a system of representation and cooperative mutual interaction at the leadership level and mobilization and social control at the mass level. Seen in this way, corporatism is understood as an actual political structure, not an ideology' (Panitch 1980, 173). It was a means of expressing labour's voice but, at the same time, the political role of neo-corporatist structures was the containment of the political and economic capacities of the working class in the post-World War II period. Specifically, neo-corporatist structures provided a forum for trade union perspectives with respect to economic planning and incomes policy. In exchange, the requirement was that trade unions would integrate 'capitalist growth criteria in union wage policy and their administration of wage restraint to their members' (Panitch 1980, 174).

The social concertation model was neither a single template nor universally adopted. There were distinct national differences in its design and in the degree to which it operated. One of the purposes of our chapter is to track the impact of austerity policies on these institutional variations – did they prove resilient and manage to defend or deflect attacks on the living standards and political opportunities of working-class people, or were all affected by the common thread of austerity?

Where they were adopted social concertation models went through a number of stages. By the late 1960s, and certainly into the 1970s, the economic foundations of the original model were under serious stress. A host of developments including increased international competition, 'stagflation', and rising support for free-market fundamentalism, resulted in a capital offensive against the working class of the Global North and its principal organizations the trade unions. The ensuing reorganization of global capitalism, enabled by state policies of trade and investment liberalization, labour market flexibilization and more aggressive industrial relations practices by both private and public sector employers resulted in declining union density, a growing number of workers employed outside of traditional employment relationships, the effect of new technologies, the weakening of nationally based legal frameworks in the face of deepening globalization of trade and production, and, but not least, the dominance of neoliberal policy perspectives which, at their base, seek greater self-regulation of markets and labour (Rychly 2013, 22).

International competition intensified through the 1980s and consequently 'corporatist bargains were subjected to the pressures of maintaining profitability' (Albo and Roberts 1998, 169). Negotiations within neo-corporatist structures had transformed from a process where workers' incomes were restrained in exchange for an expansion of the 'social wage', into a mechanism for negotiating the implementation of neoliberalism. This transformation was one where the state coordinated the compromises necessary between employer and union organizations to establish the conditions facilitating sustained capital accumulation (Teague and Donaghey 2009, 56). The processes thus became the vehicle through which governments would negotiate the implementation of competitiveness strategies.

In the post-2008 crisis period, social concertation processes shifted further towards 'negotiated flexibility' as a means of containing job loss but were also the site for manufacturing austerity policies (Anxo 2015, 263). Trade union participation in neoliberal corporatist structures has been characterized as a 'policy of powerless social dialogue' (Wahl 2004, 46).

Like austerity, neo-corporatism has a long history (see Schmitter 1974). In some cases it can be seen as incompatible with austerity, there being nothing much on the table in austere conditions for the partners to negotiate about. And there is evidence that in some countries these arrangements were among the first casualties of the post-2008 drive to austerity. In other places they have proven to be more tenacious, even though subject to dilution of various kinds.

In this chapter we deal with four national cases, in which social concertation ranged from highly developed (Denmark) to (almost) non-existent (Canada). The selection was influenced by the comparative political economy of welfare states and varieties of capitalism literatures. The most famous welfare state typology (Esping-Andersen 1990) identified three types – liberal, social democratic and conservative/corporatist – and advanced explanations for their development and characteristics). The varieties of capitalism schema (Hall and Soskice 2001) identified two main models – liberal market economies and coordinated market economies (Iversen and Soskice 2015). Both typologies have been extended to fit non-conforming systems – for example Southern European or Mediterranean systems (MEs), and frequently countries are identified as 'hybrids' exhibiting some combination of characteristics. Canada provides an example of a liberal welfare state/liberal market economy; Denmark of a social democratic welfare state and coordinated market economy. Spain is typically classified as a Mediterranean or Southern European type and Ireland is best seen as a hybrid which mostly conforms to the liberal model but has aspects of corporatism through social partnership institutions and the lingering influence of Catholic social doctrines.

During the neoliberal period generally, more flexible labour markets empowered employers. In Europe, integration placed constraints on national-level discretion in the formulation of economic policy. As neoliberalism progressed, for labour, there were few remaining incentives to deliver wage restraint in return for improvements to the social wage and employment security. Both state and employer partners held fewer bargaining chips to offer and had their own diminished incentives to compromise with labour (Streeck and Schmitter 1991). Social bargaining was undermined by market forces which became capable of imposing discipline on labour (Gobeyn 1993, 20). Financialization and, particularly in the European Union, economic and political integration required governments to dismantle or restructure institutions and political arrangements which were not acceptable to capital (Kurzer 1993, 244–5). And the transformation of employment relations more generally and the marked decline in working-class political capacities spelled the end of one form of social concertation (Grahl and Teague 1997). As neoliberalism ascended, other goals would emerge to achieve objectives reflecting the profound shift in class power and economic structure.

Impact of austerity on social concertation

Having emphasized thus far the common thread of austerity measures we now turn to explore the issue of how much variety there has been within this common framework.

Through and following the 2008 Financial Crisis, as aggressive fiscal consolidation followed the short-lived pragmatic 'Keynesian' revival, social partnerships and social pacts sometimes functioned as important mechanisms in negotiating the terms of austerity. Social dialogue in several European countries enabled a negotiated response to the crisis where trade unions often agreed to 'cuts in working time, wage moderation measures and flexibilisation of remuneration contracts' (Urban 2015, 269–70). This defensive strategy of some trade unions reflected the weakening of working-class organizations to resist the profound shift in power relations which had taken place since the 1980s. European trade unions through their participation in social pacts demonstrated a willingness 'to acquiesce to wage moderation, more flexible working conditions or privatised social services in exchange for maintaining employment' (Bieling and Lux 2014, 154).

In other countries (see further on), where deep fiscal retrenchment and labour market disciplinary policies were implemented, such structures dissolved. Where they continued to exist, austerity social partnerships were mechanisms through which to bargain wage restraint, more flexible working hours, and welfare reforms in exchange for tax cuts and employment security. In addition, the social pacts sought to fulfil the requirements of the Economic and Monetary Union (EMU), since the negotiated outcomes contributed to lowering state budget deficits. The consequence of this type of austerity corporatism has been to reinforce the declining share of wages as a proportion of GDP and this is 'despite the formal commitment of European unions to a wage policy intended to reverse or at least halt this decline' (Hyman 2010, 8).

The lived experience of social concertation both before and after the 2008 crisis is one where 'the institutions of social partnership … by integrating labour's interest representatives in policy-making … also turned out to be conducive to implementing austerity measures after the crisis' (Hermann and Flecker 2012, 134). That these mechanisms have proven so effective in implementing austerity speaks to the weakness of the organized working class. This bargaining requires concessions (Urban 2015, 273). Austerity social concertation thus is significantly different from previous variants. The power resources of each of the actors have changed where the class compromises have moved from symmetrical during the post-war phase to one characterized as an alliance of the weak (labour, state and industrial capital) facing the demands of financial capital. The role of trade unions in this context was to stabilize the economy and thus protect employers in the 'real' economy from disaster (Urban 2015, 278).

The following are brief, and necessarily incomplete, snapshots of social concertation developments in our selected four countries, and at the supranational level where applicable. The general picture is as follows: in Denmark there has been erosion of social concertation arrangements at the national level and greater difficulty in reaching agreements at the sectoral level; in Spain, government unilateralism in the immediate post-crisis period undermined national level arrangements. Sectoral social concertation is increasingly bipartite rather than tripartite; in Ireland, national level social concertation collapsed and only limited bipartite (government-public sector agreements) continue. At the supranational level, arguably EU institutions have gained power and importance, but the extension of social concertation to that level has been very limited and ineffective; and in Canada faint traces remain, confined principally to Quebec, but have been weakened.

Denmark

Supranational: EU

In 2001 Denmark established the Contact Committee for the Europe 2020 Strategy to encourage social tripartite dialogue between the social partners within the European Semester process. However, a study on the role of the social partners in the European Semester process (Eurofound 2017) revealed that although Danish social partner consultation was 'regular and predictable', its involvement was 'not relevant' to policy outcomes. Such limited influence as occurred came from tripartite meetings held outside the framework of the European Semester.

National

Danish policy concertation was built upon consensus between labour and capital and involved highly centralized collective bargaining characterized by unified representation of labour and employer interests. State involvement was limited. However, through the 1980s and 1990s, the trend was one of 'centralized decentralization' and this posed problems for the sustainability of Danish social concertation. Decentralization meant that decision-making competencies and wage-setting increasingly being devolved to the sectoral and enterprise levels, rendering traditional peak organizations based on labour and capital less significant. Geographically, there was a shift from the national to county and municipal levels of representation. Simultaneously, shifts in the make-up of the Danish economy and labour market have made other peak organizations which represent a range of professionals, more powerful. These problems of representation have likely affected the state's willingness to engage in policy concertation given that the latter has been dependent on the assumption that credible compromises can be attained across the board by the respective social partners.

The side-lining of the trade unions arrived at a significant milestone in the mid-1990s when the Social Democrats severed the formal organizational links they had with the labour central (LO). However, as Mailand (2002; 2011) has noted, despite the dearth of tripartite policy concertation in the 1990s and 2000s, tripartite cooperation on established committees and councils continued on a number of specific policy issues.

Further marginalization of the social partners' involvement in policy concertation by the 2001–09 liberal-conservative coalition and the overt hostility directed towards the labour movement at the end of the coalition's reign, when unemployment benefits and early retirement retrenchment was unilaterally implemented, marked a nadir in Danish social concertation. The liberal-conservatives pursued policies that significantly weakened the trade unions by attempting to further decentralize collective bargaining to the sectoral level (as demanded by employers) and breaking the central role of unions in the provision of unemployment benefits, which had fallen under their administration and offered significant incentives for union membership. This undoubtedly contributed to a decline in trade union density, which accelerated during the 2000s before levelling off after the crisis.

Organized resistance to the post-crisis austerity measures was tepid. Hansen and Mailand (2013) have suggested that the seemingly muted response by the trade unions might have been caused by a shift in the terrain of struggle to the sectoral rather than national level, the relative moderation of austerity measures in comparison to the rest of the EU, and the rarity of large-scale strike actions or labour disruptions in Denmark. But in general, they concede that there has been a shift in power towards employers, which was clearly manifested in the post-crisis collective bargaining rounds that saw a real decline in wages.

After the Social Democrats returned to power in 2011, there was some effort by the government to court the social partners in developing stimulus packages that were aimed at reviving the Danish economy and also restoring the role of tripartite policy concertation, with negotiations starting in May 2012. Mailand (2012; 2016) suggests that this was the first real broad-based policy concertation effort in Denmark's recent history, going against the trend of narrow policy scopes and superficial tripartite cooperation that was the order of the day during the 1990s and 2000s. The talks broke down, however, mainly because the LO found it difficult to justify increased work hours during times of relatively high unemployment (which had climbed from 2.5 per cent in 2007 to 6.9 per cent in 2012).

The economic crisis of 2008 strained social partnership in Denmark as the tradition of compromise has been increasingly replaced by concessionary bargaining. Despite these concessions, reflecting the balance of power shifting even further in favour of business, industrial action has dropped and remained low since 2009. And there was evidence of significant pressure on the processes of social dialogue, as 'win-win' scenarios gave way to concession bargaining (Eurofound 2013).

The GFC put a great deal of pressure on the highly institutionalized Danish social partnership model which has various bipartite, tripartite and multipartite bodies at different jurisdictional levels. This led to varying levels of cooperation among the social partners. Austerity measures targeting unemployment benefits, early retirement regulations, public sector budgets, and the continued use of flexicurity were all implemented in the post-GFC years. These measures have led to a growth in inequality, higher-than-average unemployment and a mild erosion of the Danish welfare state and tripartite corporatist arrangements.

Spain

Supranational: EU

Until 2014, the Spanish authorities actively attempted to keep social consultation to a minimum using only written consultations. Since 2014 there have only been ad hoc tripartite meetings. In a 2014 report, the Spanish trade union UGT argued in favour of a greater involvement on the part of national social partners in the shaping and implementation of the national responses. Despite the EC explicitly recommending that Spain consult with its social partners, the national government actively chose not to comply. The Spanish trade union CCOO has criticized the European Semester for being limited to applying 'austerity measures and structural reforms aiming to decentralize collective bargaining, make labour law more flexible and making employment more precarious'.

National

During the transition to democracy, an extensive system of social dialogue and bargaining was built. The main tripartite body is the Spanish Social and Economic Council (Consejo Económico y Social), a consultative body created in 1991 that submits reports to the government before laws and royal decrees are enacted and analyzes various issues under its own initiative. There are equivalents at the Autonomous Community (AC) level, and other tripartite bodies operate at the sectoral level in various industry sectors and in the construction sector.

In this context, the first attempt at designing economic and labour policies conducted through and by political parties without the direct participation of non-governmental actors. The resulting agreement – *Pactos de la Moncloa* (Moncloa Pacts) – prioritized democratic and macroeconomic stability, wage moderation and moved towards the legal recognition and regulation of trade unions (Cabrera 2011). Within the framework of *the Pacts* a series of laws were adopted which established the policy bases for social concertation. This included the following elements: 1) participation of the 'most representative unions' in collective bargaining defined by support on works council elections rather than by membership; 2) 'statutory extension' which stipulated that collective agreements applied to all companies and workers of the geographical and/or sector constituency, regardless of whether or not they form part of the organizations engaged in the bargaining process; and 3) 'ultra-activity', which defined that collective agreements remained valid beyond their formal expiration date until they were renewed or renegotiated (Fernández et al 2016). Trade union revitalization in Spain was largely based on participation in social dialogue institutions with the aim of widening the bargaining agenda beyond immediate items of wages and working conditions, and thus enhancing union legitimacy.

The initial labour market reforms in Spain were pushed through in 2010 and 2011 without the consent of the social partners after tripartite negotiations failed. The 2010 reforms were a mixed bag which saw restrictions on the use of temporary work, increases in severance pay, the creation of a 'redundancy fund' for workers, but also a redefinition of 'fair dismissal' to include economic losses, and increased employer powers to change employees' work hours, working time and location. The 2011 reforms targeted collective bargaining resulting in an intense decentralization from sectoral to firm level agreements, and a marked decreased (4.5 per cent) in the number of workers covered by collective agreements. Between February 2012 and September 2014, an additional six labour market reform packages were imposed with no social dialogue consultation with the social partners.

The idea of adjustment to the broad political and economic conditions is crucial for understanding social partnership in Spain. Thus, periods that have seen pacts include the economically stagnant years of the late 1970s to early 1980s as well as the late 1990s that saw rapid growth, while collective bargaining structures have remained relatively stable across the past four decades. Social pacts reappeared after Spain's accession to the EU and the onset of neoliberal restructuring. Social concertation in democratic Spain has mostly constituted a strategic response by the two dominant political parties to particular historical conjunctures where consensus-building was necessary in order to minimize and mitigate the potential for social and political conflict and to legitimize the institutions of liberal democracy (Martínez Lucio 2002).

Significant reforms to the structure of collective bargaining implemented by the PSOE in 2011 increased pressure towards a decentralized system of bargaining, expanded opt-out clauses and reduced the regulatory reach of sectoral agreements (Molina and Miguélez 2013), introducing enterprise-based micro-corporatism (Hamann and Martinez Lucio 2003).

With the PP's victory in 2012, the government of Mariano Rajoy imposed a new labour reform designed to alter the structure of social concertation and further weaken unions. Although the unions and business organizations had renegotiated the Agreement on Employment and Collective Bargaining for 2012, the PP dismissed this agreement and limited the conditions by which expired agreements would be automatically renewed (Pérez 2014). Without the automatic renewal that 'ultra-activity' provided, unions lost a recurrent entry point for negotiations (Pérez Infante 2017).

An immediate effect of the crisis was that social dialogue institutions were weakened and bypassed. Tripartite policy concertation was abandoned as a response to the crisis, and the period following 2008–09 has seen the normalization of unilateral government legislation and efforts to weaken collective bargaining through decentralization, with a concomitant increase in the power of both employers and the state to circumvent tripartite negotiations. Out of the decline of Spanish social concertation, new social movements and radical parties on the left emerged, challenging the institutional status quo within the labour movement and rejecting the politics of social partnership in austerity.

The slight economic recovery of 2014 somewhat reactivated social dialogue. The government, unions and employers signed an Agreement on Proposals for the tripartite bargaining to promote economic growth and employment. (Consejo Económico y Social, 2015). Yet, neither labour reforms nor changes in social dialogue were reversed (Bacaria et al 2015). In general, social dialogue and collective bargaining deteriorated during the crisis due to unilateralism by the state, at both national and regional levels. As a result, there has been significant conflict and strikes (Molina and Godino 2020, 318).

Confirming this general picture, an ILO report from Molina and Miguélez (2017) found that of the ten major labour market reforms in Spain between 2008 and 2015, only one was delivered through a tripartite agreement. While the first two reforms were unilateral actions after tripartite negotiations had failed (in 2010 and 2011), six major reforms were unilaterally passed between 2012 and 2014 without negotiations or consultations from social partners (Molina and Miguélez 2016) However, despite the breakdown of tripartite relations, bipartism in the private sector has remained relatively strong, though collective bargaining at this level has increasingly been disaggregated to the company level.

Ireland

Supranational: EU

Ireland was exempt from the European Semester's monitoring and assessment procedure while it was a part of the Troika's macroeconomic adjustment programme. Rather than receiving country-specific recommendations (CSRs) the country was bound by Memorandums of Understanding. Ireland's restructuring under the Troika's 'Macroeconomic Adjustment Programme' made social dialogue irrelevant. Under the Troika Memoranda, the terms and conditions of bailout packages had strict policy conditions that had to be followed. Despite Ireland later exiting the Troika programme, social concertation has not been revived.

National

Following the economic collapse, Ireland's long tradition of social partnership and centralized collective bargaining became the targets of reform. The form and content of social dialogue in Ireland was consistently undermined by a concentration of power in the executive and judicial branches. Although a number of bipartite agreements were signed in the early stages of the crisis, neither the ICTU or the Irish

Business and Employers Confederation (IBEC) were directly involved in labour market policy from 2011 to 2016. These policies were run by the Department of Jobs, Enterprise and Innovation under the oversite of the Minister of Jobs.

The final national programme negotiated by the social partners prior to the financial crisis was the *Towards 2016* (T16). This was a ten-year agreement running from 2006 to 2016 (O'Kelly 2010). As part of its response, the government attempted to renegotiate the pay agreement with a view to cutting wages, particularly in the public sector, while the IBEC argued that the agreement should simply be annulled. The ICTU rejected both options and countered with a ten-point recovery plan in February 2009. This plan reiterated the unions' commitment to social partnership and offered a broad-based set of proposals to address the crisis in ways other than recourse to cuts in public expenditures and wages. Despite widespread opposition to the government's austerity proposals and the largest anti-government demonstrations in decades, the government unilaterally withdrew from negotiations in March 2009 and introduced an emergency budget that included across the board pay cuts and increased pension levies for public sector workers (Doherty 2011).

The IBEC had signaled its intention of withdrawing from the previously agreed national wage agreement if compromises on private sector pay increases could not be reached, and it formally withdrew on 23 December 2010 citing the need for a return to economic competitiveness (Sheehan 2010). IBEC's withdrawal effectively decentralized pay negotiations to the enterprise level and marked the first time since the 1981–87 period that Ireland did not have a functioning national wage agreement, the central pillar of Irish social partnership.

While the ICTU had resisted employers' attempts to renegotiate the *Toward 2016* pay increases and opposed the government's unilateral imposition of public sector pay cuts, its leadership nevertheless attempted to salvage what was left of social partnership by imposing a unilateral moratorium on industrial action and seeking a return to the negotiating table with the government in the latter's plans to reform the public sector. These actions effectively put an end to the mobilizations that had occurred in early 2010 in response to public sector pay cuts. Bilateral (state to union) negotiations resulted in the Croke Park Agreement, concluded in March 2010 and ratified by the ICTU on 6 June 2010. The agreement traded further public sector pay cuts and compulsory redundancies in exchange for greater redeployment flexibility. But it also committed to increased work hours and finding service efficiencies, limits on industrial action and a reduction in staff levels of between 18,000 to 21,000 positions by 2014 through attrition and early retirement. Teachers also saw the introduction of a two-tier pay scale, with new hires entering after January 2011 earning a fraction of what their more senior colleagues were paid, and the imposition of the 'Croke Park hours' which forced teachers to spend an additional 33 unpaid hours per annum on school meetings and other administrative duties.

Deteriorating economic conditions in 2013 led the government to seek an additional €1bn in savings over three years by renegotiating the parameters of the original Croke Park deal through pay cuts of between 5.5 and 10 per cent on public sector employees earning over €65,000, a reduction in overtime pay and an increase in the allowable distance of job redeployment (from 45km to 100km).

This evolved into the Haddington Road Agreement, which maintained the central pay cut provisions of Croke Park II, backed by amended financial emergency legislation (FEMPI) that would impose harsher measures on those unions which rejected the deal, including unilateral pay cuts. Almost all public sector unions accepted the deal as recommended by most of the leadership, with the notable exception of the Association of Secondary Teachers' Ireland (ASTI), which rejected the terms and voted to respond with industrial action (ASTI 2013).

The austerity measures unilaterally introduced by the Fianna Fáil coalition government in 2009 combined with the withdrawal of the employers' association from the national wage agreement effectively ended Irish social partnership (Walshe 2015).

Canada

When the crisis struck in 2008, Canada had long fitted the decentralized model being recommended by international organizations. Neo-corporatist institutions of social dialogue or social partnership have left traces, but have played a very limited role in comparison to our three other cases (McBride 1995). Over the course of the 1980s and into the 1990s, a number of quasi-neo-corporatist institutions were established but were limited to a purely advisory role on labour and labour market policy. As such these were fora to enable social dialogue rather than structures to arrive at agreed upon decisions through social concertation.

Quebec has provided a rather different space for insitutions and processes for social dialogue. Haddow has argued that Quebec's political economy is more centralized, interventionist and redistributive than

Ontario's as a result of four major 'causal mechanisms', among which is 'the extent of policy collaboration among economic and social actors' (Haddow 2015, 4). Studying fiscal and budgetary policies, social assistance, childcare systems and economic development, Haddow came to the conclusion that at the root of the 'Quebec model' – which he describes as a 'hybrid' between coordinated and liberal market economies (2015, 45) – is the fact that the 'intermediation of social and economic interests' in the province relies in good part on structures of 'concertation' which ensure efficient representation of 'non-business' actors such as community organizations and, most importantly, labour unions (2015, 10). As opposed to Ontario and the rest of Canada, where 'pluralist' structures of representation dominate and tilt the 'balance of power' and policy influence in favour of business interests, policymaking in Quebec is a lot more of a collaborative process, where a broader range of powerful actors can have a significant influence.

Quebec thus constitutes a partial exception to the absence of social concertation within Canada. But, even there, there is the view that the model has become less robust in the face of neoliberalism (Graefe 2012).

Conclusion

Social dialogue or partnership has not fared well during or since the crisis. It has been bypassed, effectively abolished or, where it remains, reduced in scope and significance. Whatever its limitations in the past, this avenue for expressing labour's voice on policy issues is even less effective than formerly.

Historically, the concepts of Coordinated Market Economy and Liberal Market Economy provide a useful categorization, but only up to a point. Why some, such as Denmark, become 'coordinated' and others, such as Canada and Ireland, liberal, and Spain, indeterminate as a Mediterranean example, is a function of class formation and organization, the electoral fortunes of social democratic parties at different points in history, democratic stability (in the case of Spain) and, of course, the cycle of crises endemic to capitalist economies and how these are responded to by the state and other social actors, specifically labour and business.

Social concertation arrangements reflected the uneven distribution of the power resources available to the social partners. That distribution changed over time: 'the balance between the negotiating partners has shifted substantially as compared with the situation prevailing when the pacts of the 1960s and 1970s were signed' (Pochet et al 2010, 22). The Golden Age trade-offs where employment wage restraint was purchased with an expansion of the social wage and industrial democracy gave way in the Insecure Age of neoliberal era to bargains where wage restraint endured but to this was added an agenda to 'lower social charges and greater flexibility of work conditions' (Rhodes 2001, 180). This is particularly evident in European cases presented here. In Canada the highly decentralized federation, relatively modest success of labour-friendly political parties and limited success of labour in achieving a larger role in the policy process meant there had, in any case, been limited use of social concertation. In all cases the continued erosion of working-class strength has rendered this route to labour influence less effective than in the past.

References

Albo, Gregory and Chris Roberts. 1998. 'European Industrial Relations: Impasse or Model?', in E.M. Wood et al (eds) *New York Monthly Review Press*, pp 164–79.

Alfonso, Alexandre. 2013. *Social Concertation in Times of Austerity*. Amsterdam: Amsterdam University Press.

Anxo, Dominique. 2015. 'The Swedish Model in Times of Crisis: Decline or Resilience?', in S. Lehndorff (ed) *Divisive Integration: The Triumph of Failed Ideas in Europe, Revisited*. ETUI, pp 253–68.

ASTI. 2013. 'ASTI Members Reject Haddington Road Agreement and Vote for Industrial Action'. *ASTI News*. 20 September 2013. www.thejournal.ie/asti-haddington-road-1092876-Sep2013/

Bacaria, Jordi, Elena Sánchez-Montijano and Joseph M. Coll. 2015. 'The Labour Market in Spain: Problems, Challenges and Future Trends: Policy Brief'. *SIM Europe: Bertelsmann Stiftung*.

Bieling, Hans-Jürgen and Julia Lux. 2014. 'Crisis-Induced Social Conflicts in the European Union – Trade Union Perspectives: The Emergence of "Crisis Corporatism" or the Failure of Corporatist Arrangements?', *Global Labour Journal*, 5(2): 153–75. doi:10.15173/glj.v5i2.1156

Bradford, Neil, and Mark Stevens. 1996. 'Whither Corporatism? Political Struggles and Policy Formation in the Ontario Training and Adjustment Board', in Thomas Dunk et al (eds) *The Training Trap: Ideology, Training and the Labour Market*. Winnipeg: Fernwood Publishing, pp 145–66.

Cabrera, Mercedes. 2011. *TheMoncloa Pacts: Political Agreements in the Face of the Crisis*. Dissertation, Historia y Política.

Consejo Económico y Social. 2015. *Contribuciones a la gobernanza de la FAO*. Engelberg, Switzerland: United Nations Digital Library.

Doherty, Michael. 2011. 'It Must Have Been Love … But It's Over Now: The Crisis and Collapse of Social Partnership in Ireland', *Transfer: European Review of Labour and Research*, 17(3): 371–85. https://doi.org/10.1177/1024258911410803

Esping-Andersen, Gøsta. 1990. *The Three Worlds of Welfare Capitalism*. Princeton: Princeton University Press.

Eurofound. 2013. *Report on Impact of the Crisis on Social Dialogue*. www.eurofound.europa.eu/publications/article/2013/report-on-impact-of-the-crisis-on-social-dialogue.

Eurofound. 2017. *Involvement of the Social Partners in the European Semester: 2016 Update*. Luxembourg: Publications Office of the European Union.

Fernández Rodríguez, Carlos J., Rafael Ibáñez Rojo and Miguel Martínez Lucio. 2016. 'Austerity and Collective Bargaining in Spain: The Political and Dysfunctional Nature of Neoliberal Deregulation', *European Journal of Industrial Relations*, 22(3): 267–80. doi:10.1177/0959680116643433

Gobeyn, Mark James. 1993. 'Explaining the Decline of Macro-Corporatist Political Bargaining Structures in Advanced Capitalist Societies', *Governance*, 6(1–3): 3–22. doi:10.1111/j.1468-0491.1993.tb00134.x

Graefe, Peter. 2012. 'Whither the Quebec Model? Boom, Bust and Quebec Labour'. Essay, in J. Peters (ed) *Boom, Bust and Crisis: Labour, Corporate Power and Politics in Canada*. Halifax: Fernwood Pub.

Grahl, John and Paul Teague. 1997. 'Is the European Social Model Fragmenting?', *New Political Economy*, 2(3): 405–26.doi:10.1080/13563469708406315

Haddow, Rodney. 2015. *Comparing Quebec and Ontario: Political Economy and Public Policy at the Turn of the Millennium*. University of Toronto Press.

Hall, P. and D. Soskice. (eds). 2001. *Varieties of Capitalism: The Institutional Foundations of Comparative Advantage*. Oxford: Oxford University Press.

Hamann, Kerstin and Lucio Miguel Martinez. 2003. 'Strategies of Union Revitalization in Spain: Negotiating Change and Fragmentation', *European Journal of Industrial Relations*, 9(1): 61–78. doi:10.1177/0959680103009001451

Hansen, Nana Wesley and Mikkel Mailand. 2013. 'Public Service Employment Relations in an Era of Austerity: The Case of Denmark', *European Journal of Industrial Relations*, 19(4): 375–89. https://doi.org/10.1177/0959680113505038

Hermann, Christoph and Jörg Flecker. 2012. 'The Austrian Model and the Financial and Economic Crisis', in S. Lehndorff (ed) *A Triumph of Failed Ideas: European Models of Capitalism in the Crisis*. European Trade Union Institute, pp 121–36.

Hyman, Richard. 2010. *Social Dialogue and Industrial Relations During the Economic Crisis: Innovative Practices or Business as Usual?* Working Paper No. 11. Geneva: International Labour Organization.

Iversen, Torben and David Soskice. 2015. 'Politics for Market', *Journal of European Social Policy*, 25(1): 76–93.

Kurzer, Paulette. 1993. *Business and Banking: Political Change and Economic Integration in Western Europe*. Ithaca: Cornell University Press.

Mailand, Mikkel. 2002. 'Denmark in the 1990s: Status Quo or a More Self-Confident State?', in S. Berger and H. Compston (eds) *Policy Concertation and Social Partnership in Western Europe: Lessons for the 21st Century*. Berghahn Books, pp 83–96.

Mailand, Mikkel. 2012. FAOS Website. *National Report Denmark – Social Dialogue and the Public Services Aftermath of the Economic Crisis.* https://faos.ku.dk/english/news/national-report-denmark---social-dialogue-and-the-public-services-in-the-aftermath-of-the-economic-crisis/

Mailand, Mikkel. 2011. 'Trepartssamarbejdet gennem tiderne – hvordan, hvorna°r og hvilke udfordringer', FAOS, Sociologisk Institut, University of Copenhagen.

Mailand, Mikkel. 2012. 'Overenskomstfornyelsen 2011 – den kommunale sektor perspektiveret. Forskningsnotat', no. 122. FAOS, Sociologisk Institut, University of Copenhagen.Mailand, Mikkel. 2016. 'Active Employers and Teachers Working Time Regulation – Public Sector Industrial Conflicts in Denmark and Norway', *Economic and Industrial Democracy*, 1–18.

Mailand, Mikkel and Nana Wesley Hansen. 2016. 'Denmark and Sweden: The Consequences of Public Service Reform and Economic Crisis for Public Service Employment Relations', in S. Bach and L. Bodogna (eds) *Public Service Management and Employment Relations in Europe*. New York: Routledge.

Martínez Lucio, Miguel. 2002. 'Spain in the 1990s: Strategic Concertation', in S. Berger and H. Compston (eds) *Policy Concertation and Social Partnership in Western Europe: Lessons for the 21st Century*. New York: Berghahn Books, pp 265–77.

McBride, Stephen. 1995. 'Coercion and Consent: The Recurring Corporatist Temptation in Canadian Labour Relations'. Essay, in C. Gonick, P. Phillips and J. Vorst (eds) *Labour Gains, Labour Pains: Fifty Years of PC 1003*. Winnipeg: Society for Socialist Studies, pp 79–96.

Molina Romo, Oscar and A. Godino. 2020. 'Industrial Relations in Deep Water: The Spanish Public Sector During the Crisis'. Essay, in M. Keune, N.E.R Martin and M. Mailand (eds). *Working under Pressure: Employment, Job Quality and Labour Relations in Europe's Public Sector since the Crisis.*Brussels: ETUI.

Molina Romo, Oscar and Fausto Miguélez. 2013. *From Negotiation to Imposition: Social Dialogue in Austerity Times in Spain.* Geneva: International Labour Organization.

Molina Romo, Oscar and Fausto Miguélez. 2016. *Post-Crisis Social Dialogue in Spain: The Calm After the Storm.* Geneva: International Labour Office.

Molina Romo, Oscar and Fausto Miguélez. 2017. 'Post-Crisis Social Dialogue in Spain: The Calm after the Storm'. Essay, in I. Guardiancich and O. Molina (eds) *Talking Through the Crisis: Social Dialogue and Industrial Relations Trends in Selected EU Countries.* Geneva: International Labour Organization.

O'Kelly, Kevin P. 2010. 'The End of Social Partnership in Ireland?', *Transfer: European Review of Labour and Research*, 16(3): 425–9.

Panitch, Leo. 1980. 'Recent Theorizations of Corporatism: Reflections on a Growth Industry', *The British Journal of Sociology*, 31(2): 159–74. doi: 10.2307/589686

Pérez Amorós, Francisco. 2014. 'Concertación Social Para El Empleo En España', *Anuario Del Trabajo y Relaciones Laborales*, 2: 95–108.

Pérez Infante, José Ignacio. 2017. 'La Crisis Económica, Las Reformas Laborales y La Negociación Colectiva', *Revista De Economía Laboral*, 13(2): 92–134. doi: 10.21114/rel.2016.02.05

Pochet, Philippe and David Natali. 2010. 'The Last Wave of Social Pacts in Europe: Problems, Actors and Institutions', in P. Pochet et al (eds) *After the Euro and Enlargement: Social Pacts in the EU.* Brussels: European Trade Union Institute and OSE, pp 13–44.

Rhodes, Martin. 2001. 'The Political Economy of Social Pacts: Competitive Corporatism'. Essay, in P. Pierson (ed) *The New Politics of the Welfare State.* Oxford: Oxford University Press, pp 165–96.

Rychly, Ludek. 2013. 'The Changing Fortunes of Labour Administration', in J. Heyes and L. Rychly (eds) *Labour Administration in Uncertain Times: Policy, Practice and Institutions*. Cheltenham: Edward Elgar, pp 18–45.

Schmitter, Philippe C. 1974. 'Still the Century of Corporatism?', *The Review of Politics*, 36(1): 85–131. doi: 10.1017/s0034670500022178

Sheehan, Brian. 2010. 'Employer Body Withdraws from National Pay Deal', *EurWORK*. www.eurofound.europa.eu/observatories/eurwork/articles/industrial-relations/employer-body-withdraws-from-national-pay-deal.

Standing, Guy. 1999. *Global Labour Flexibility: Seeking Distributive Justice*. Basingstoke: Macmillan.

Streeck, Wolfgang and Philippe C. Schmitter. 1991. 'Community, Market, State – and Associations? The Prospective Contribution of Interest Governance to Social Order', in G. Thompson et al (eds) *Markets, Hierarchies and Networks: The Coordination of Social Life*. London: Sage, pp 227–42.

Teague, Paul and Jimmy Donaghey. 2009. 'Why Has Irish Social Partnership Survived?', *British Journal of Industrial Relations*, 47(1): 55–78. doi:10.1111/j.1467-8543.2008.00706.x

Urban, Hans-Jurgen. 2015. 'Between Crisis Corporatism and Revitalization: Trade Union Policy in the Era of European Financial Market Capitalism', in S. Lehndorff (ed) *Divisive Integration: The Triumph of Failed Ideas in Europe, Revisited*. ETUI, pp 269–94.

Wahl, Asbjørn. 2004. 'European Labor: The Ideological Legacy of the Social Pact', *New York Monthly Review*, 55(8): 37–49. doi:10.14452/mr-055-08-2004-01_4

Walshe, Mark. 2015. 'Lansdowne Road – Another Straightjacket for Workers', *Socialist Worker*.

9

Market populism, its right-wing offspring and left alternatives

Ingo Schmidt

No spending cuts, privatizations and lowering of social standards without left criticism (for an equally prominent and comprehensive example see Blyth 2013). These criticisms fit nicely into a broader stream of left-leaning scholarship that portrays neoliberalism as a political project, as a class struggle from above, that includes austerity, along with the reorganization and relocation of production processes, aiming to shift the balance of power, income and wealth distribution from the popular to the propertied classes (Saad-Filho and Johnston 2005; Harvey 2007).

No election of populist governments without liberal criticism (Mudde 2017; Müller 2017). Without much differentiation between left- and right-wing populism on the one hand and between economic, that is, free market, liberalism and liberal democracy on the other hand, populism and liberalism are portrayed as antitheses in these criticisms. By mobilizing 'the people' against presumptuous elites, populists deny individuals their rights of free expression and exchange. Populism, liberal critics conclude, lead to the decay of democracy and markets (for a critical view see Streeck 2017).

Left critics of austerity and neoliberalism and liberal critics of populism have one thing in common: they see the individuals belonging to the popular class or 'the people' as rather passive, easy prey for corporate media or populist agitators. Left critics don't spend much time asking why so many workers have voted, over and over again, for parties advocating for the rollback of unions and the welfare state. They either claim or imply that workers just don't understand their interests as a class. Liberal critics are usually more open in denouncing 'the people' as a bunch of stupids who don't recognize the virtues of open societies and markets. They rarely ask whether markets allow the advancement of a few at the expense of the many who are left behind. They are even less concerned with the question of whether the subjugation of liberal democracy to the profit imperatives of neoliberal globalization produces its own discontents who are then ready to be picked up by various brands of populism.

Left and liberal critics adopt a model in which the supply of neoliberal or populist ideas, respectively, create their own demand. This chapter shifts the focus to the demand side. It seeks to explain why ideas gain popularity, why they remain popular even if the practical application of these ideas doesn't yield the expected results and, if this is not the case, whether disappointment about one set of ideas paves the way for other ideas to gain traction. The chapter starts with a few theoretical arguments about the reasons why individuals adopt, or don't adopt, ideas. The next sections try to substantiate those arguments: first by explaining the rising and declining popularity of neoliberal ideas from the 1980s into the 2000s, then by looking at the shift from neoliberalism to right-wing populism or even fascism (Panitch and Albo 2015; Gandesha 2020). The last section of the chapter takes up the question of why the right benefits much more from the crisis of legitimation of neoliberal capitalism than the left.

What should become clear is that liberalism and populism are by no means polar opposites (Finchelstein 2017, Chapter 3; Revelli 2019, Chapter 1). In fact, one kind of populism, market populism (Frank 2000), created the legitimacy that allowed governments and corporate elites to pursue austerity and other neoliberal policies without much opposition. Right-wing and, on a much smaller scale, left-wing populism didn't gain traction until market populism lost its persuasiveness (Schmidt 2019). The new right, though ideologically posturing as a radical alternative to market populism, actually brings some hidden traits of neoliberalism to the fore – this is particularly true for the racialized and gendered divisions of labour brought about by neoliberal globalization. The left, on the other hand, aims at defending democracy and civil liberties against neoliberal economic policies and right-wing identity politics and authoritarianism.

Theory: what makes you think that?

What makes ideas persuasive? Following the history of ideas back to the places and contexts in which they were produced and distributed offers clues about the agendas of the social forces with which the producers of ideas, 'conceptive ideologists' as Marx and Engels (1846, Part 1) dubbed them, align themselves. Struggles between the advocates of different ideas serve as keys to understanding the relations between different factions of the ruling class and the making of ruling class ideologies, each of them articulating a specific balance of forces between different class factions and strategies to pursue ruling class interests under given circumstances. It might well be that 'the ideas of the ruling class are in every epoch the ruling ideas, i.e. the class which is the ruling material force of society, is at the same time its ruling intellectual force'. However, having 'the means of mental production at their disposal' does not give the ruling class automatic control over the consciousness of the popular classes. Paraphrasing Marx and Engels one might say that, even short of being revolutionary, the 'existence of oppositional ideas [...] presupposes the existence of an oppositional class (Marx and Engels 1846, Part 1)'. This oppositional, antagonistic or even revolutionary class may possess its own 'conceptive ideologists' whose ideas, if adopted by individuals identifying as members of this class, would challenge ruling class rule. If that, even if only as a possibility, is the case, the ruling class needs to persuade the popular class that its rule is legitimate. To sustain its rule, the ruling class needs consent from the subordinate classes. Ruling class efforts at 'Manufacturing Consent' (Herman and Chomsky 1988) may be plenty, but success is still not guaranteed.

With respect to sustaining ruling class rule, the key question is: what makes ruling class ideas popular or legitimate among the subordinate classes? For this to happen, I will argue, ruling class ideas need to answer three questions simultaneously: what's the problem? How to tell? Who's gonna fix it?

The what's-the-problem question needs to pick up the concerns that individuals have about current or expected working and living conditions. The answer to this question needs to point at causes and possible solutions for these concerns. To do this, this question has to be answered in a language that the people having these concerns can understand. Answering the how-to-tell question in a commonly used language faces a problem, though. Such a language is tied to the very ideas and conditions that produce the concerns the individuals are grappling with. Using the same language to articulate the concerns produced by the ideas and conditions that gave rise to these very concerns requires the redefinition or recontextualization of familiar concepts. Redefinition attaches new meanings, recontextualization applies a concept with its established meaning in a new context. Particularly important in both respects is the appropriation of alternative languages and ideas that, without being dominant, have been around for a while. Such languages usually developed as part of the formation of subordinate classes as collective agents. Integrating them into ruling class discourse leaves the subordinate classes speechless and allows the expression of ruling class ideas in a popular tone that resonates with individuals belonging to the subordinate classes. Rendering oppositional movements speechless and articulating widespread concerns in a common and popular language may give individuals the feeling that their concerns are heard, or even that they have a voice, but is still not sufficient to make the ideas articulated this way legitimate. This requires the step from theory to practice, an answer to the who's-gonna-fix-it question. Closely related to the identification of problems and possible solutions, such answers identify a culprit, some agent who is charged with causing the concerns, and a rescuer, an agent presented as capable of fixing the problems by overcoming the culprits' power.

Answers to these three questions don't come from masterminds sitting in their study, pondering the issues at hand, consulting other masterminds' ideas about them and finally handing out their own ideas. Answers are given by conceptive intellectuals collaborating in networks of production and distribution of ideas. Some in these networks specialize in systematizing and synthesizing an array of ideas. Their work, presented in seminal books or keynote speeches, may appear as the product of the lone mastermind. But, in fact, it relies a great deal on the ideas that are already swirling around and on the intermediaries who, as journalists, researchers and educators, collect them among the groups of people they communicate with. These intermediaries are also important in distributing a synthesized set of ideas. Often expressed in a rather obscure and abstract language, such ideas need translation into popular language and application to myriads of concrete issues. In the process of producing and distributing ideas, intermediaries are just as important as 'synthesizers' and 'systematisers'. Historically, networks of the production and distribution of ideas have taken different forms, from bourgeois public spheres in early capitalism to the mass universities of welfare capitalism to the spread of neoliberal think tanks and consultancies.

The simultaneous articulation of problems' causes and solutions and of culprits and rescuers in a language that appropriates, redefines and recontextualizes oppositional languages starts with a 'populist moment', in which a 'thin ideology' demarcates a corrupt and presumptuous elite from the honest and hard-working people (Stanley 2008; Mudde 2017). Starting with the 'thin' juxtaposition between 'elite' and 'people', populism can be 'thickened' in various ways, leaning towards Marxist conceptions of capital against labour, the neoliberal juxtaposition between states and markets, or xenophobic distinctions between superior and inferior races or nations. This thickening process can lead to the emergence of a historical bloc in which the specific interests of the ruling classes, most notably its dominant factions, are perceived as common interests by individuals from all classes. For this to happen, a sufficiently large number of individuals has to adopt a specific set of ideas while others, who do not agree with those ideas, remain largely speechless. When one set of ideas gains traction and a historical bloc coalesces around them, other ideas appear increasingly out of touch with reality, elitist or become unthinkable altogether.

However, each set of ideas, to become hegemonic, must correspond somehow with everyday experiences and the divisions of labour within and between firms, households and countries within which individuals lead and experience their lives. In other words, each set of hegemonic ideas articulates, one way or the other, the divisions of class, race and gender that, long before they may become signifiers for individual or collective identities, determine everyone's position in the social divisions of labour (Wallerstein 1991). Ideas offer frameworks through which individuals, or groups of individuals, make sense of their experiences and articulate individual or collective aspirations. If the policies derived from, or conducted in the name of, a certain set of ideas don't yield expected results, these ideas and policies will lose persuasiveness, trigger a crisis of legitimacy and possibly the downfall of the historical bloc that was built around this set of ideas and policies. A new historical bloc can emerge, though there is no guarantee that this will happen, out of the crisis and the intensified struggles between and within classes that come with the falling apart of an existing historical bloc.

Market populism: I ain't gonna work for the taxman no more

This section draws on the earlier considerations about the way ideas gain traction and serve as rallying points for the emergence of historical blocs to understand the rise of neoliberalism. The ideas around which a neoliberal bloc would eventually coalesce were developed starting in the 1920s, when a young generation of economists who charged their liberal ancestry with losing its grip on politics and public opinion in the face of rising state intervention. However, neoliberalism's populist moment didn't come until the 1970s when welfare capitalism, the kind of state interventionism that came to shape Western countries in the post-World War II period, entered a period of economic and legitimation crises. From the 1920s to the 1970s, neoliberal intellectuals developed their policies, built their networks, even scored some bestselling books (Hayek 1944; Friedman 1962), but were either ignored or seen as cranks by most fellow economists, policy makers and the broader public. During the 1970s crises, though, it was neoliberals, not old or new leftists or a neo-Nazi right, that seized the moment. They successfully translated the combination of abstract economic models, empirical data sets and ingroup-lingo that marked the elaborations inside their own networks into a market-populism that had more mass appeal than the class-against-class language of the left, let alone the Nazi-nostalgia coming from the right.

This success relied in part on the answers market-populists gave to the what's-the-problem question. Keynesian-inspired adherents of welfare capitalism had great difficulties admitting to economic crises as they thought their demand-management techniques had put the spectre of crises to rest. Marxists offered lengthy explanations of the internal contradictions of the capitalist mode of production. The hard right had nothing to say about economics even though economic issues were high on everybody's agenda after decades in which economic growth and high levels of employment had seemingly overcome the age of capitalist crises, class struggles and mass poverty.

Market-populists had a lot to say about economics (Chernomas and Hudson 2017). More precisely, they offered a moral critique of the welfare state from which they concluded that markets needed to be liberated so that individuals would be free to truck, barter and exchange without being hampered by state regulations and taxes. This critique turned the Keynesian argument that state intervention was needed to counteract capitalism's tendency towards crisis and stagnation. For the market-populists, state intervention was not a cure for but the cause of economic crisis. States, they charged, invite laziness, cause inflation and deficits, all of which, they concluded, weaken the 'national economy' in the face of increasing foreign competition and oil-price shocks. More to the point, emboldened by labour law, unions turned the wage-price-spiral to increase their members' wages beyond the productivity of their work, all at the expense of everybody else whose income wasn't indexed to inflation. Market-populists added that welfare cheques invited people to avoid work while the taxes needed to pay those cheques punished those who do work or, more importantly, invest.

The stories explaining crises are told in a morally charged language. They presented greedy union bosses, lazy welfare mothers, Japanese competitors not playing by the rules and sneaky oil-sheiks jacking up oil prices to sustain oriental luxuries. Touching on issues from inflation and competitiveness to taxes and deficits, these stories had one punchline: democracy had gone too far (Crozier et al 1975). It had invited an unholy alliance of tax-collectors and lazy-butts whose wrongdoings produced economic crises and unemployment and thereby weakened the national economy vis-à-vis other economies (Olson 1982). Clearly, democracy that had captured the state and strangled the economy was the culprit in the market-populist master-narrative. Individuals were called to the rescue of the market economy which, once liberated from red tape and taxes, would allow everyone's self-realization.

Earlier efforts to mobilize the moral or silent majority against new left protestors didn't get very far as most state actors and even the then leading factions of capital, far from being friends of the left, were still committed to the class compromise around which the welfare state was built. The success of market populism relied very much on its ability to appropriate new left ideas of liberation and turn them against the welfare state. Doing so allowed market populism to destroy new left self-presentations as the vanguard of bottom-up activities and denounce them as self-appointed elite instead. It also allowed market populism to turn the manifold discontents that the welfare state had produced in different segments of the popular classes away from the idea of improving and expanding the welfare state to actually rolling it back. For its success, this early phase of market liberation relied greatly on its embeddedness in conservative morals (Hancock 2016). A blend of market liberation, family and fatherland was most prominently represented by Margaret Thatcher and Ronald Reagan, both of whom attracted considerable electoral support from the working classes.

However, it soon turned out that belt-tightening, according to the market populists a necessary antidote to inflation and public deficits that would pave the way to prosperity for all, was, in fact, a means of redistribution from the bottom to the top. Moreover, conservative family values didn't fit a world in which labour market participation of women was one of the few means to sustain living standards under belt-tightening pressures. But the growing contrast between market populist narrative and neoliberal reality didn't lead to a return of more welfare state-oriented policies; it led to a radicalization of policies and a transformation of narrative instead.

A key factor behind the changes in pro-market theory and practice was the collapse of the Soviet Union that, even before Eastern markets were reintegrated into the capitalist world-market, rendered the great power posturing of the Reagan-Thatcher era outdated, if it didn't signal the end of history altogether (Fukuyama 1989). As if market populists had never denied the existence of classes before, they were now quick to announce the end of class struggle. The end of history also included the end of the nation state, at least if this was understood as states having regulatory capacities that could potentially be used to rebuild the welfare state. Conservatives saw the state giving way to a clash of civilizations (Huntington 1993) while market populists heralded a borderless world (Ohmae 1991).

After the Cold War, the market populist promise that globalization would render conflicts between nations, classes or, for that matter, civilizations obsolete had more appeal than the conservative call to defend Western civilization against other civilizations, notably Islam. However, this call became a rallying point from centre-right to far-right once financial crises and permanent warfare belied globalist promises.

Throughout the 1990s, an assemblage of neoliberals, converted leftists and computer freaks used the tailwinds blowing from post-communist Moscow and world-market-integrating Beijing to sail into a cosmopolitan and networked world (Boltanski and Chiapello 2005; Slobodian 2018; Frank 2000, Chapter 8). Liberated from state borders, conservative morals, fiscal austerity or company hierarchies, the new world allowed everyone to self-realize according to their individual preferences. Computers would facilitate such efforts technically. Global finance would transcend the budget constraints of the old economy. The sky was the limit.

The globalcentrics (Coronil 2000) were busy distancing themselves from the conservative-market-populist blend that was so persuasive in the 1980s but appeared hopelessly outdated in the 1990s. Yet, neoliberal globalization during that decade very much followed the trajectories of technological developments, going back to state-sponsored computer labs in the Cold War days (Mazzucato 2018), and the outsourcing and relocation efforts corporations used to bypass unions and tax-collectors since the days of Reagan and Thatcher (Harvey 2007). New was the proliferation of global governance structures that shielded private investments from interference by democratically elected governments. Also new was the globalcentrics' abandonment of the silent majority that had rallied behind market populism wrapped in conservative morals. Branded as symbol analysts (Reich 1992), new middle-class layers took its place.

Many self-styled symbol analysts truly believed that corporate power had withered away in the global networks of information and financial exchanges. Most of them were blind to their dependence on the work of a fast-growing service proletariat. Once financial crises revealed and reinforced the power of corporations and big money, many a symbol analyst, feeling betrayed for their dreams, turned against this service proletariat. As it was largely female and immigrant, a substantial share of the new middle-class resentment took the form of racism and sexism. Faced with severe crises that undermined the persuasiveness of the globalcentric narrative, the middle class turned out to be as susceptible to racism and sexism as many in the working class after losing faith in the welfare state.

The new right: we like livin' right and bein' free

This section will show how a new right used deepening cracks in the neoliberal bloc to attract a following that, at this time, isn't large and coherent enough to form its own historical bloc but is large enough to impede the formation of any conceivable alternative bloc. A first generation of market populists appropriated the libertarian language of the new left, in which a lot of the discontent and disappointment with the welfare state had been expressed first, to sell market liberation blended with conservative morals. However, after a few years it turned out that austerity policies were not, as first-generation market populists had argued, unavoidable measures that would hurt anyone but allow prosperity for all once the deficit-and-inflation-hangover from the welfare state would have been overcome. Instead, it became clear that these policies enriched the happy few at the expense of everybody else. At that point it was a second generation of market populists that saved the neoliberal project.

This second generation of market populists identified the conservative morals and policies that their predecessors had added to the market populist programme as the reason prosperity for all hadn't come forth. By shedding those morals and radicalizing the neoliberal policy package of privatizations and the lowering of legal standards, they managed to remake the neoliberal bloc, dropping commitments to conservative layers of the working class and embracing aspiring, cosmopolitan and computerphile layers of the middle class.

The expectations that second-generation market populists roused around notions of globalization and a new economy were much higher than earlier appeals to family values, fatherland and thriftiness. The economic crises that belied the prosperity promises given by first-generation market populists were light breezes compared to the 2001 dot-com crash, the 2008–09 Great Recession and the current COVID-19 crises that tore to pieces the idea of a borderless world of unlimited potential for self-realization. During the Great Recession, the state, rendered a relic of the past bound to wither away in the world market according to the globalcentrics, revealed itself as a generous bailout machine for corporate capital and an austerity enforcer for everybody else. The COVID-19 lockdown went hand in hand with massive spending programmes, the former invited the new right to charge a globalist conspiracy with taking ordinary people hostage, the latter provoked market populist die-hards to call for austerity no matter what. Yet neither the new right nor the market populists can garner sufficient support to construct a new historic bloc (Strikwerda and Schmidt 2020). This stalemate is the outcome of, on the one hand, the crisis of legitimacy that has lingered since the dot-com crash and came to the fore during the Great Recession, and on the other hand the rise of the new right with roots in 1970s neo-Nazism (Kriesi and Takis 2015; Guiso et al 2018; Renton 2019, Chapter 2).

In the 1970s, the far right was too much affiliated with Nazism to attract significant parts of those who were discontent but not attracted by anything the left had to offer as an alternative to the Keynesian welfare state. For some, who didn't care about, or even approved of, the Nazi atrocities, the idea of bringing Nazism back might have been attractive but also unrealistic. Others sought right-wing policies but without the atrocities. The far-right's inability to deliver such policies helped to get the merger between conservatism and neoliberalism on track (Hall 1979). Since then, a new right has developed. Taking a culturalist turn, it replaced much of the biological racism the Nazis had advanced with notions of a culturally constructed ethno-pluralism that assigns different spaces to different ethnicities and warns that mingling between ethnicities would lead to cultural and social decay (Jacobson 2018). Ironically, the culturalist turn of the right was similar to the same turn much of the left had taken. Where the right abandoned biologism, the left abandoned much of its former discourse on economics and class (Wood 1986). It was exactly this left, focused on the discursive construction of identities around the issues of race and gender, that the new right identified as self-appointed cosmopolitan elite allegedly working towards the destruction of local communities and their traditional cultures (Wagner 2017). The new right's construction of these communities also included the white working class that second-generation market populists had abandoned (Pied 2018).

At the same time, the new right portrayed left protestors from the World Social Forum to Occupy Wall Street, as part of the global and footloose elite. It lumps together left protestors and the very institutions these left-wing movements are protesting against: corporate capital, the WTO, the IMF and others. Neoliberal globalists and their left critics all appear as part of the same footloose elite, which also includes feminists, LGBTQ-activists and environmentalists – all united in their hatred of hard-working people enjoying their authentic, that is, untainted by globalism, culture. The new right, then, emerges as self-defence against globalist efforts to impose all kinds of politically correct behaviours. The new right replaced the positive utopia of the market populists and the liberation of markets from red tape and taxes so that they can serve individuals as platforms for self-realization, with the dystopian threat of the subordination of authentic communities and cultures to the levelling forces of cosmopolitanism. However, the programme the new right offers to ward off this threat doesn't include much beyond transforming discontent into hate against allegedly lesser races, nations and seemingly foreign cultures. One of the reasons this hate propaganda resonates is that it picks up discontent produced by the remaking of racialized and gendered divisions of labour brought about by neoliberal globalization (Revelli 2019, Chapter 3).

In their efforts to bypass bastions of organized labour and the welfare state, neoliberal globalists integrated workers of all colours and sexual orientations into new divisions of labour within and between firms, households and countries. While a handful of women and people of colour made careers, managed to express their views publicly or even joined ruling class ranks, the vast majority were integrated into the lower rungs of the labour market, employed to underbid existing wage rates and legal standards. To mobilize workers, students or retirees who actually suffer from this underbidding, or fear to do so in the future, the far right points at the handful of social climbers to prove that women and people of colour are taking over the world but never mention the new racialized and gendered proletariat working at the bottom. What the new right really appeals to are the suppressed fears of losing the race to the bottom and ending up working, or looking for work, alongside the already existing racialized and gendered proletariat. Such fears are further fuelled by neo-Malthusian propaganda pointing at too many 'undeserving' stealing not only decent jobs and social protections from the 'deserving', but also the natural resources needed to sustain such jobs and protections. This neo-Malthusianism is linked to charges against a cosmopolitan elite not only telling ordinary people how to behave but also to restrict the use of natural resources (Forchtner and Kølvraa 2015). The new right is mostly silent about economic austerity and deflects the fear of social downgrading caused by austerity measures into the fierce rejection of any notion of cutting back the use of natural resources. It is an organizing hub for fossil counter-revolution.

The new right uses the discontent, insecurities and anxieties that neoliberal globalization produced across the popular classes to denounce global elites whom they charge with promoting feminists, anti-racists and environmentalists at the detriment of local communities and cultures. References to the White working class as the backbone of these communities doesn't signal a right-wing turn to class-politics but turns the idea of working class into another signifier for right-wing identity formation. The working class that can't constitute itself without demarcation from its significant other, the capitalist class, remains absent from right-wing discourse because the capitalist class is substituted by global elites. Instead of antagonistic class-relations, the new right presents a dichotomy between global elite and local community. No matter how much hate they mobilize against elites and how much violence they propagate or even organize against immigrant and non-White communities and against activists identified as part of the elites – they don't have an alternative economic and social project to offer that really could, or could be suspected to, solve the problems of the communities they claim to speak for.

This distinguishes them sharply from the neoliberals whose promises eventually turned out to be wrong, the expected trickle-down never came, but was attractive enough to be supported by significant layers of the popular classes and worked well for the ruling classes even through recurrent crises. It also distinguishes the new right from their Nazi-ancestry who embraced forms of state-intervention at a time when ruling elites clung to the policy prescriptions of classical liberalism, prescriptions that only aggravated economic and political crises of the interwar period (Garvy 1975). To be sure, by now the same is true for ruling elites clinging to neoliberal policies. With the new right venting without offering actual alternatives, and the market populists trying to sell policies that have fallen out of favour and produce ever more crises, one might expect the left to fill the void. Yet recurrent mobilizations and even some electoral successes notwithstanding, this hasn't happened. At least not yet. The final section of this chapter will explore the reasons for the failure of the left to take advantage of a situation very much resembling left prognoses of capitalist crises and class struggles from below emanating from these crises.

The left: where do you think you're going?

The weakness of today's left goes back all the way to the 1960s when much of the old left was integrated into the Keynesian welfare state, its adherents either thinking that capitalist exploitation and crises had been overcome by negotiating a class compromise that allowed endless prosperity, or hoping that this prosperity would allow continuous expansion of the welfare state and its ultimate transformation into some kind of democratic socialism. There was a rift between this old left and a new left that forcefully articulated discontent that had been simmering in various segments of society. This discontent revolved mostly around the exclusion of certain demographics, notably women, minority ethnic and immigrants, from some or all welfare state gratifications, its technocratic management and the ecological destruction caused by economic growth. This discontent, sharpened by capital's increasing hostility to the welfare state in the face of combative social movements and economic crises in the 1970s, turned the rift between old and new left into a three-way split between a hard core committed to sustain class compromise and the Keynesian welfare state, a socialist left, itself divided between revolutionaries and reformists, and the new social movements, each focusing on a particular issue but all of them committed to the horizontalism that was already popular in parts of the new left.

Efforts to build coalitions around a Keynesian core amended by the new social movement agenda were defeated by the first generation of market populists who adopted the libertarian agenda from the new left and new social movements, dropped old left commitments to redistribution and social equality and replaced them with the promise that markets, freed from red tape and taxes, would create equal opportunities for everybody. Blending market libertarianism with conservative morals, the market populists could attract layers of the working class that had never been fond of unions and welfare state managers, without turning down the material benefits that were negotiated by those bureaucrats, and were hostile to new left and new social movement types. On the other hand, old and new left cultures were so far apart that finding common ground was next to impossible. The old left, sometimes overlapping with the moral majority successfully courted by the market populists, had no appetite for new left culture, the latter considered much of the former as hopelessly backward. The welfare state bloc fragmented; a neoliberal bloc could take its place (Schmidt 2011).

First cracks in the neoliberal bloc, caused by the realization that the hoped for trickle-down may never come, offered the left chances to reinvent itself. This actually happened on two planes. One was the movement against corporate globalization, a coming together of all kinds of concerns and tactics, more an articulation of discontent than a movement towards an at least vaguely defined alternative (Mertes 2003). Considering the history of left certainties, failures and defeats, the vagueness of the alterglobalistas was not only understandable but probably a necessary starting point before reinventing more clearly defined left politics and strategies. However, it was also its weakness.

The turn to permanent war following the invasion of Iraq met the movement unprepared and finished it off after an intense but brief period of anti-war protests.

More lasting was Third Way Social Democracy – not because it invented a viable left but because it helped to reinvent market populism. If Reagan and Thatcher represent market populism mark I, Bill Clinton, Tony Blair and Gerhard Schröder came to symbolize mark II (Evans and Schmidt 2012, Schmidt 2016). Embracing the free trade agenda, most notoriously the WTO, they were eager to institutionalize the subjugation of welfare states and democracy to global finance, a subjugation that had already begun with increasing capital mobility and industrial restructuring during the Reagan-Thatcher era and that many social democratic strategists saw as an insurmountable barrier to Keynesian demand management and policies of redistribution (Scharpf 1991).

The social democratic turn from Keynes to Hayek went hand in hand with the adoption of the libertarian agenda of the new social movements. Unlike most of their 1970s predecessors who felt threatened by these movements, 1990s social democrats embraced them as part of an ideological realignment that allowed them to distance themselves both from their own 1970s predecessors and 1980s conservatives. Retaining the latter's commitment to Hayek and blending it with the libertarian heritage of the new social movements allowed them to present themselves as something new, a progressive neoliberalism that was allegedly up to the challenges of globalization in a post-Cold-War-world (Fraser 2017). The Third Way-turn was a, possibly naïve, possibly helpless, attempt to make a virtue out of necessity. Many in the old industrial working classes might have been more committed to the Keynesian welfare state after the first doses of neoliberal welfare-state rollback than they had been during the heyday of welfare state expansion in the 1970s. Yet, the industrial restructuring that was part of this rollback had also diminished their numbers. The emerging service proletariat was far from having its own voice while new layers of the middle class, centered in IT and finance but also in consultancies and NGOs, were extremely vocal about their aspirations. Third Way social democrats heeded their call but overestimated their numbers and cosmopolitan commitments. Faced with repeated crises, many of the erstwhile supporters of Third Wayism turned to the new right, just like many malcontents in the old industrial and new service working classes.

The irony of market populism, mark I and II, and right-wing populism on the ideological plane, and neoliberal government and management practices is that class, no matter how exactly one defines it, became ever more visible since the 1970s crisis of the Keynesian welfare state, but also became ever more unmentionable under the hegemony of market populism and remains so in new right narratives. Neoliberal ideologists developed a counter-narrative to left class-narratives that had developed alongside, if not been a key part of, the making of working classes from the 19th century onwards. This counter-narrative transposed the notion of consumer choice into a universal programme for individual freedom of choice. The fact that the interplay of income and property, and institutionalized racism and sexism allows very different choices from accepting lousy jobs or starving to buying these or those assets was ignored, or presented as the outcome of individual choices, counterfactually portraying those doing the hardest and lowest-paid work as unwilling to save enough to become investors. At least, as second-generation market populists would have it, even individuals who weren't born into riches could choose to invest in their human capital and become symbol analysts instead of service workers.

Fully aware that market populists added insult to injury, the new right recovered the notion of working class but restricted access to White-skins. Cosmopolitan lifestyle choices were replaced by culturally, if not ethnically, determined belongings. The White working class which the new right calls to action fights against non-Whites, replacing the left idea of class struggle and ultimately the liberation of humans from all forms of exploitation and suppression with dystopian visions of an endless struggle between culturally determined ethnicities if not biologically defined races.

However, as more and more people who can be seen as belonging to the popular classes realized that neoliberal promises of choice were wrong and trickle-down was delayed indefinitely, members of the popular classes flocking to the new right these days may also come to understand that they have more in common with people of other colours also struggling to get by than with like-coloured well-to-dos. If that happens, they may see that their problems can't be solved by beating up members of allegedly inferior cultures or races. Some of them, a 'collective of conceptive ideologists', may find a language of workers versus capitalists that is open for the reality of working-class diversity in terms of skin complexion, gender, skill levels and maybe some other regards. Such a language could help to forge ties, build unity in diversity and form a historical bloc able to push for alternatives to neoliberal capitalism and its new-right outgrowth (Schmidt 2015). Protest movements like Occupy Wall Street and against austerity in the aftermath of the Euro-crisis along with electoral successes of Syriza, Podemos, and Bernie Sanders' and Jeremy Corbyn's campaigns could turn out to be steps towards a new left bloc. Although, the fact that they were short-lived and didn't leave tangible results also shows that it will be a long way to such a bloc, and its coming shouldn't be taken for granted.

References

Blyth, Mark. 2013. *Austerity: The History of a Dangerous Idea*. Oxford: Oxford University Press.

Boltanski, Luc and Eve Chiapello. 2005. *The New Spirit of Capitalism*. London, New York: Verso.

Chernomas, Robert and Ian Hudson. 2017. *The Profit Doctrine: Economists of the Neoliberal Era*. London: Pluto Press.

Coronil, Fernando. 2000. 'Towards a Critique of Globalcentrism: Speculations on Capitalism's Nature', *Public Culture*, 12(2): 351–74.

Crozier, Michel, Samuel Huntington and Joji Watanuki. 1975. *The Crisis of Democracy – Report on the Governability of Democracies to the Trilateral Commission*. New York University Press.

Evans, Bryan and Ingo Schmidt (eds). 2012. *Social Democracy After the Cold War*. Athabasca: Athabasca University Press.

Finchelstein, Federico. 2017. *From Fascism to Populism in History*. Oakland: University of California Press.

Forchtner, Bernhard and Christoffer Kølvraa. 2015. 'The Nature of Nationalism: Populist Radical Right Parties on Countryside and Climate', *Nature and Culture*, 10(2): 199–224.

Frank, Thomas. 2000. *One Market Under God: Extreme Capitalism, Market Populism, and the End of Economic Democracy*. New York: Anchor Books.

Fraser, Nancy. 2017. 'From Progressive Neoliberalism to Trump – And Beyond', *American Affairs*, 20 November, 1(4). https://americanaffairsjournal.org/2017/11/progressive-neoliberalism-trump-beyond/

Friedman, Milton. 1962. *Capitalism and Freedom*. Chicago: University of Chicago Press 2002.

Fukuyama, Francis. 1989. 'The End of History?', *The National Interest*, 16(3): 3–18.

Gandesha, Samir (ed). 2020. *Spectres of Fascism: Historical, Theoretical, and International Perspectives*. London: Pluto Press.

Garvy, George. 1975. 'Keynes and the Economic Activists of Pre-Hitler Germany', *Journal of Political Economy*, 83(2): 391–405.

Guiso, Luigi et al. 2018. 'The Populism Backlash: An Economically Driven Backlash', *VOX CEPR Policy Portal*, 18 May. https://voxeu.org/article/populism-backlash-economically-driven-backlash

Hall, Stuart. 1979. 'The Great Moving Right Show', *Marxism Today* (January): 14–20.

Hancock, David. 2016. 'Neoconservatism, Bohemia and the Moral Economy of Neoliberalism', *Journal for Cultural Research*, 20(2): 101–21.

Harvey, David. 2007. *A Brief History of Neoliberalism*. Oxford: Oxford University Press.

Hayek, Friedrich A. 1944. *The Road to Serfdom*. Chicago: Chicago University Press.

Herman, Edward S. and Noam Chomsky. 1988. *Manufacturing Consent*. New York: Pantheon Books.

Huntington, Samuel P. 1993. 'The Clash of Civilizations?', *Foreign Affairs*, 72(3): 22–49.

Jacobson, Gavin. 2018. 'The Complex Roots of Populism', *New Statesman*, 28 November 2018.

Kriesi, Hanspeter and Pappas Takis (eds). 2015. *European Populism in the Shadow of the Great Recession*. Colchester: ECPR Press.

Marx, Karl and Friedrich Engels. 1846. *The German Ideology*. Moscow: Progress Publishers 1968. www.marxists.org/archive/marx/works/1845/german-ideology/

Mazzucato, Mariana. 2018. *The Entrepreneurial State: Debunking Public vs. Private Sector Myths*. London: Penguin Books.

Mertes, Tom (ed). 2003. *A Movement of Movements: Is Another World Really Possible?* London, New York: Verso.

Mudde, Cas. 2017. *Populism: A Very Short Introduction*. Oxford: Oxford University Press.

Müller, Jan-Werner. 2017. *What Is Populism?* London: Penguin.

Ohmae, Kenichi. 1991. *The Borderless World: Power and Strategy in the Interlinked World*. New York: Harper & Collins.

Olson, Mancur. 1982. *The Rise and Decline of Nations: Economic Growth, Stagflation and Social Rigidities*. New Haven: Yale University Press.

Panitch, Leo and Greg Albo (eds). 2015. *The Politics of the New Right*. London: Merlin Press.

Pied, Claudine M. 2018. 'Conservative Populist Politics and the Remaking of the "White Working Class" in the USA', *Dialectical Anthropology*, 42(2): 193–206.

Reich, Robert. 1992. *The Work of Nations: Preparing Ourselves for 21st Century Capitalism*. New York: Vintage.

Renton, David. 2019. *The New Authoritarians: Convergence on the Right*. London: Pluto Press.

Revelli, Marco. 2019. *The New Populism: Democracy Stares into the Abyss*. London: Pluto Press.

Saad-Filho, Alfredo and Deborah Johnston. 2005. *Neoliberalism: A Critical Reader*. London: Pluto Press.

Scharpf, Fritz W. 1991. *Crisis and Choice in European Social Democracy*. Ithaca: Cornell University Press.

Schmidt, Ingo. 2011. 'There Were Alternatives: Lessons from Efforts to Advance Beyond Keynesian and Economic Policies in the 1970s', *Working USA: The Journal of Labor and Society*, 14(2): 473–98.

Schmidt, Ingo. 2015. 'Counteracting Factors: The Unmaking and Remaking of Working Classes in Europe', *Perspectives on Global Development and Technology*, 14(1–2): 129–45.

Schmidt, Ingo (ed). 2016. *The Three Worlds of Social Democracy: A Global View*. London: Pluto Press.

Schmidt, Ingo. 2019. 'The Populist Race: Neoliberalism Falling Behind, New Right Forging Ahead, the Left Stumbling Along', *Perspectives on Global Development and Technology*, 18(1–2): 61–78.

Slobodian, Quinn. 2018. *Globalists: The End of Empire and the Birth of Neoliberalism*. Cambridge: Harvard University Press.

Stanley, Ben. 2008. 'The Thin Ideology of Populism', *Journal of Political Ideologies*, 13(1): 95–110.

Streeck, Wolfgang. 2017. 'The Return of the Repressed', *New Left Review*, 104 (May–April): 5–18.

Strikwerda, Eric and Ingo Schmidt. 2020. 'COVID-19: A View from the Great Depression of the 1930s', *Socialist Project Bullet*, 21 June. https://socialistproject.ca/2020/06/covid19-view-from-great-depression-of-1930s/

Wagner, Thomas. 2017. *Die Angstmacher – 1968 und die Neuen Rechten*. Berlin: Aufbau Verlag.

Wallerstein, Immanuel. 1991. 'The Ideological Tensions of Capitalism: Universalism versus Racism and Sexism', in E. Balibar and I. Wallerstein (eds) *Race, Nation, Class: Ambiguous Identities*. London, New York: Verso, pp 29–36.

Wood, Ellen Meiksins. 1986. *The Retreat from Class: A New 'True' Socialism*. London, New York: Verso.

10

Austerity-induced populism: the rise and transformation of the new right

Hans-Jürgen Bieling

Public and academic discussions in the European Union often relate to two processes, the interaction of which requires some clarification. One is the rise and mode of operation of neoliberalism, particularly, the establishment and implementation of an austerity agenda, that is, efforts to consolidate public budgets through spending cuts (Hermann 2007). This process started in the late 1970s and became more pervasive in most member states since then. Consequently, the austerity policy guidelines were enshrined as an important component of the European treaties. Furthermore, they were made even stricter in the transition from the financial to the so-called sovereign debt crisis. The second process is the strengthening of right-wing populism in the member states of the European Union (Kriesi 2014). This process also began in the 1970s with the foundation of Progress Parties in Scandinavia, the Vlaams Belang in Belgium, the Swiss People's Party and the Front National (FN) in France, all, more or less, with an ethno-nationalist orientation and a critical attitude to the comprehensive, centralized welfare state. This policy stance, extended by a critique of European integration, was also adopted by a second group of parties founded since the late 1980s: the Lega Nord in Italy, the United Kingdom Independence Party (UKIP) in Britain, the Sweden Democrats, the True Fins, or the newly oriented Freiheitliche Partei Österreichs (FPÖ) in Austria. Finally, the 2000s saw a third foundation wave – the Partij voor de Vrijheid (PVV) in the Netherlands, the Polish Party Prawo I Sprawiedliwosc (PiS), or Alternative für Deutschland (AfD) in Germany – all further hostile to immigration and Islam, but less determined in terms of economic and welfare policies.

This chapter aims to clarify the relationship between these two processes. It is assumed that they have not developed independently of each other. While the impact of right-wing populism on the austerity agenda seems to be rather weak or modest at best – only few of them have been in power, so far – there are good reasons to assume that austerity has contributed to the rise of right-wing populist parties. At least partly, this argument challenges all those explanations which interpret the success of right-wing populism primarily or even solely as a socio-cultural phenomenon, that is, as the expression of nationalism, xenophobia, anti-migration and anti-Islam discourses and so on. In this sense, it is maintained that socio- and political-economic developments matter as well. The chapter lines up with more recent contributions to an explicitly political economy perspective (Manow 2018; Rodrik 2018). However, instead of following an either/or logic, this chapter takes both the relative autonomy of the struggles in the political arena serious and the particular articulation of socio-cultural and socio-economic developments into account.

More concrete, the chapter is structured as follows. The first section will clarify the meaning of populism conceptually and explain how the rise and development of the new right can be captured with the help of a political-economic approach. The chapter then turns to the significance of austerity programmes and the specific interaction patterns of austerity and right-wing populism. These are primarily discussed in relation to the strategic orientations, political party programmes and concrete activities of parties in different groups of countries specifically affected by austerity politics. The focus is above all on the political supply-side. However, the demand-side, that is, the reception – support and/or questioning – by party members and voters cannot be ignored. Ultimately, it is decisive to understand the nature and the political handling of the contradictions inscribed into right-wing populism.

Aspects of a political economy perspective on populism in the European Union

In the academic discussion, populism is mostly understood as a content wise unspecific and in this sense 'thin-centered' ideology (Freeden 1996; Taggart 2000). This 'thin-centered' ideology is characterized by some general features: by a positive appraisal of the true people, which in the case of right-wing populism is often constructed as ethnically homogeneous; by the reference to the common sense of ordinary citizens; by a profound critique of ruling elites in the economy, the state, academia and media, all out of touch to given realities; by a dismissal and rejection of intermediary organizations – established parties and most associations in civil society –; and by a moralizing and personalized style of discussion and policymaking. Apart from these rather formal and procedural features, populism can connect itself with different host ideologies, that is, substantially defined worldviews (Priester 2012; Müller 2016). Accordingly, it is hardly surprising that the term populism includes very different, programmatically sometimes contradictory movements and parties. The left-wing populist or popular positions are characterized by the fact that they do not regard the 'people' as an (ethnically) homogeneous entity, but as a general reference point which is internally divided – along the axes of class, gender and ethnicity – and suffers from manifold problems of marginalization and exclusion. In contrast to this, the right-wing populist programmatic is itself exclusionary and discriminates against all those groups that do not fit into the self-image of propagated nationalism.

In order to explain the ascent of populism, especially of right-wing populism, in Europe, most observers primarily refer to cultural factors, for example a value-oriented, often essentialized production of meaning or identity-political attributions and classifications such as race, ethnicity, nation, femininity and masculinity and so on (Mudde 2010). Only more recently has there been an increase of efforts to take greater account of political economic factors. In a first, rather general political-economic approximation, populism can be seen not only but also as a reaction to the accelerated globalization of recent decades, not least to the social inequalities, uncertainties and distortions stimulated by it (Rodrik 2018, 23). The negative effects of globalization are specific to different social groups in the individual countries and are interpreted differently in political terms. Dani Rodrik (2018) distinguishes between two forms or patterns of politicization: the left-wing populist or popular politicization – for example, in Latin America or Southern Europe – can be seen as the outcome or the concomitant phenomenon of the critique of the far-reaching liberalization of trade and capital. It articulates the social claim of bringing the unleashed world markets back under political control. In contrast to this, right-wing populism is less directed against trade and capital market liberalization than against the liberalization of labour markets and migration. Furthermore, this kind of politicization does not amount to propagating trans- or supranational but national answers. Rodrik (2018, 17) himself explains the predominant consent in Europe to trade and capital market liberalization as follows:

> One difference with the US that may account for this contrast is that Europe has long had strong social protections and a generous welfare state. Most countries of Europe, being smaller than the US, are much more open to trade.

> But openness to trade has been accompanied by much greater redistribution and social insurance. A number of empirical analyses have shown that there is a direct link between exposure to trade and expansion of public transfers … It is not an exaggeration to say that the European welfare state is the flip side of the open economy.

At the same time, Rodrik suggests, however, that under conditions of accelerated globalization the mode of operation of the welfare state – particularly, its capacity to compensate for detrimental globalization effects – becomes more and more precarious. Welfare state services no longer appear to be guaranteed to relevant social groups and classes in society. Increasingly, these groups and classes are inclined to defend endangered welfare state services by resorting to a welfare-chauvinistic orientation and strategy, that is, a policy view which is based on a 'nativist agenda' turning against migrants and religious minorities or minority ethnic who are often perceived as the embodiment of an unfettered and much too far-reaching globalization. In general, this conceptualization of causal relations is not inappropriate. On closer inspection, however, Rodrik's political economy framework needs some further conceptional differentiation. Though it captures important differences between the politicization of globalization by left- and right-wing populist forces, it remains unclear why the politicization within the EU differs from one region to another and changes over time.

In terms of the regional differentiation – particularly between Northern and Southern Europe – Philip Manow (2018, 61–9) has found the answer in the specific design of given welfare state regimes. For him, these regimes are rather rudimentary in Southern Europe. Hence, they cannot offer effective protection against the risks of social decline or marginalization. As a consequence, the fairly powerful group of labour market insiders rejects comprehensive labour market liberalization, but also fears no immigration into the systems of social security provision. According to Manow, the constellation is quite different in Nordic European countries. In most of these countries, the liberalization of trade and the financial markets is not problematized, since the strong export orientation and productivity in turn enable high wages and a relatively comprehensive welfare state, which should not be further jeopardized. However, as social security is relatively comprehensive, labour market insiders fear that refugees place an additional financial – and cultural – burden on them. At least subjectively perceived, they feel confronted with a loss of social status.

The conceptual refinement concerning the size and mode of operation of national welfare regimes is certainly promising. Eventually, however, the analysis has to go one step further. This implies that the welfare state should not only be seen as an institution which mitigates the contradictions between capitalism and democracy (Offe 1984) by dealing with the negative effects – income losses, unemployment – of globalization, but also as an arena of struggles over the general political economic development. In this sense, it needs to be emphasized that the welfare state is not only, as suggested by many political economy scholars (Manow 2018; Rodrik 2018; Foster and Frieden 2019), an institution of redistribution and compensation. Other components and instruments, for example the provision and management of the material and public infrastructure (Collective Foundational Economy 2018) – including areas such as education, training, research – that have an economic steering function, belong to an effective welfare state as well. So, if one tries to conceptualize the relationship between the reorganization of the welfare state and the rise of right-wing populism, infrastructure policies should also be taken into account. At least indirectly, such policies co-determine the mode of integration of capitalist models into the globalized economy. Besides, they show that national governments still have quite a few policy options to address the so-called challenges of globalization.

The still available domestic resources and policy options are the rational core of populist claims to regain national sovereignty. They highlight that the outside-in perspective of most political economic explanations, which discuss right-wing populism as a consequence of a globalization-induced shrinkage of the welfare state is too narrowly conceptualized. A more comprehensive political economy perspective has to highlight additional domestic aspects and dimensions. This is particularly the case if one aims to understand the thrust of populist mobilization in relation to governmental austerity programmes.

Two conceptual extensions may illustrate this. The first one suggests taking into account the specific mode of operation of individual welfare states, as austerity programmes have not only a strong impact on the schemes of redistributive compensation but also on the instruments and resources of economic steering. The latter dimension is strongly linked to the politics of productivity and the pattern by which national models of capitalism are integrated into the international division of labor (Jäger and Springler 2015; Hopkin and Blyth 2019). This concerns the sectoral structure, the relevance of the export industries, the size and dynamics of the domestic market as well as the trade and current account balance and the associated international creditor or debtor position. Countries with a positive current account, that is, a strong creditor position, are much more inclined to plea for a general European austerity agenda, while countries with a negative current account, that is, debtor economies, tend to reject austerity policies with a view to economic and social development.

The second suggestion is to regard the strategic and programmatic orientation of populist forces not only as the outcome of material conditions, but also influenced by the prevailing political culture, especially the economic and financial culture. The public discourses and the norms, meanings, practices, memories and identities mobilized in them do certainly have an impact on social and economic policymaking. They show that there is no immediate relationship between material structures and interests on the one and politics on the other hand. Instead, political activities represent the result of the articulation of socio-economic and socio-cultural processes: an articulation which takes place in the field of public policy, in social milieus and within the subjectivity of individuals (Gidron and Hall 2017; Bieling 2019). For the positioning of populist actors, this is quite significant. Irrespective of the imagined rebellion against the 'elites', they take a nationalist stance which links traditional, often ethnic narratives and concrete economic and social policies. More or less, imbued with nationalist attitudes, the latter become practically relevant in traditionalist-conservative or welfare-chauvinist discursive settings (Fenger 2018).

These two factors, that is, the specific profile of the respective models of capitalism and the social constructivist accentuation, do ensure that some of the outlined political-economic interrelationships are also contingent and less clear-cut than expected. The image of populism generated in this way may thus become more confusing, but at the same time also more realistic insofar as it takes the discursive struggles over the goals and effects of austerity programmes as relatively autonomous components into consideration.[1]

Austerity and right-wing populism

Like many concepts, the concept of austerity is by no means clearly defined. In the academic and political debate, the way in which it is

[1] This claim is above all theoretically grounded. An empirical substantiation would require an in-depth process analysis which is beyond the aim of this chapter to provide a general overview of the development of the economic and social policy orientation of populist actors.

used sometimes differs considerably. Simplified, a narrow and broad understanding of austerity can be identified and distinguished from each other. The narrow understanding of austerity refers to a specific strategy of budgetary consolidation. In contrast to expansionary variants of consolidation, which aim to increase government revenues and reduce the public debt burden in relation to the increased gross domestic product by reviving the economy, this strategy is contractionary and concentrates entirely on the output side. The main objective is therefore to establish a regime of fiscal discipline, that is, to reduce public debt by means of austerity measures, that is, spending cuts in terms of public investment, personnel expenditures or social benefits.

This narrow understanding marks the core of the meaning of austerity. It has been inscribed in the European economic constitution in the wake of accelerated market and currency integration (McNamara 1998). Then, in the course of the 2000s, the austerity policy guidelines were somewhat weakened, and after the outbreak of the transatlantic financial crisis they were even temporarily pushed into the background, before they were reactivated in the transition to the euro and sovereign debt crisis. In this context, the meaning of austerity has become somewhat extended, not least in critical historical retrospective accounts (Blyth 2014). The extended meaning of austerity generally refers to the way in which transnational financial market capitalism operates – economically, institutionally and discursively – according to the interests of transnational creditors and financial investors (Peet 2011). It also refers to the embedding of fiscal austerity in corresponding regimes of ideological, political and social organization (Hayes 2017). This is evident not least in the connection with the concept of competitiveness. In the European political reform discourses on the so-called 'Six Pack' and 'Fiscal Compact' (Bieling and Guntrum 2019) it was repeatedly pointed out that not only a consistent monetary policy, but also fiscal discipline, has the effect of curbing inflation, sometimes even generating an 'internal devaluation' via deflationary developments, in order to increase the competitiveness of the national economy within the eurozone.[2]

[2] The concept of 'competitiveness' is very controversial. Here, it may be sufficient to point out that competitiveness is a relational concept. This means, an improvement in one's own performance only really takes effect if the competitors do not also improve to the same extent. Improved competitiveness can be generated in two ways: firstly by increasing productivity, that is, output per hour worked, which is based on improved skills, infrastructure, research and so on – all factors that require additional public investment and are opposed to austerity; and secondly by reducing

In general, austerity politics have a clear socio-economic or even class component. They are beneficial to creditors, asset holders and real estate owners, but detrimental to all those dependent on public services and social transfer payments. These groups certainly suffer from budget cuts and were confronted with increasingly precarious living conditions. However, not only the recipients of social transfers but also large parts of the workforce suffer from the fiscal contraction as well, particularly if they are employed in the public sector or if they feel the adjustment pressure on wages and employment due to a depressive business climate. In view of such socio-economic effects – loss of income and increased social insecurity – it is no surprise that the emergence and institutionalization of a common austerity agenda has stimulated the rise of populist movements and parties across Europe.

Some of the left-wing populist or popular forces – this applies above all to the Southern European periphery, for example Syriza (Greece), Podemos (Spain) or the Bloco de Esquerda (Portugal), but also to the Momentum campaign by Jeremy Corbyn or La France Insoumise by Jean-Luc Mélenchon – have made their mark in explicit criticism of the austerity policy introduced in the transition to the sovereign debt crisis (della Porta 2015). For other left-wing populist or popular organizations, such as the Socialist Party (SP) in the Netherlands or the Left Party in Germany, the austerity bias of the European Economic and Monetary Union (EMU) has been a fundamental problem of European integration for some time now, preventing a growth- and employment-oriented policy. At least partially and for a period, the growing public criticism of austerity proved to be beneficial for the left parties, particularly, if they proved to be able to address the social effects on the ground.

Compared to the plain rejection by left-wing parties, the political stance of the right-wing populists on questions of austerity is less obvious. They often adopt a rather ambivalent position. The reason for this is that most of the new right parties – irrespective on the populist policy style – were founded and regarded themselves as parties within the bourgeois camp. However, at the same time they were increasingly confronted with the fact that large parts of their electorate do not only belong to the – upper – middle classes but to other groups and milieus – rural and/or working class-based – which see themselves as losers of capitalist modernization, globalization and austerity. In the

---

wage and non-wage costs (taxes and social security contributions) – a strategy that is more short term and corresponds to the strategy of fiscal discipline.

aftermath of the financial crisis from 2008 to 2010 and the orchestration of a fairly comprehensive austerity agenda (Bieling 2012; McBride and Mitrea 2017) this trend has become more apparent. Particularly in those countries in which austerity programmes have been implemented very sharply or over a longer time period and in which the criticism levelled at them by large social groups was pervasive, right-wing populists showed increasingly responsive.

One example is the UK. According to Thiemo Fetzer (2019, 3850) the Conservative government brought about a substantial fiscal contraction since 2010: 'aggregate real government spending on welfare and social protection decreased by around 16 percent per capita. At the district level, the level at which most administration of welfare spending takes place, welfare spending per person fell by 23.4 percent in real terms between 2010 and 2015.'

A closer look at these aggregate data reveals that austerity affected particularly health care and education, including salaries of public employees, while the individual costs for pensions increased. As a consequence of these developments, the support for UKIP and Brexit swelled. The populist sentiment was not only nourished by upcoming nationalist Euroscepticism among the more affluent middle-class people, but also by the alienation of parts of the working class – low-skilled workers in services and manufacturing, often with precarious legal protection – from the Labour Party.

Even more substantial and far-reaching was the critique of the European austerity agenda in France. Originally, an unmistakably neoliberal party, the FN went through a phase of political reorientation when Marine Le Pen took over the party chairmanship in 2011. The reorientation concerned not only moderating racist and antisemitic positions, but also a different social and economic policy (Ivaldi 2015). Against the background of a deep economic crisis and the acceptance of austerity by the Holland government, Marine Le Pen criticized capitalism and globalization again and again; and the FN – meanwhile renamed as Rassemblement National (RN) – put forward a fundamental critique of the Euro and the related austerity agenda and instead pleaded for higher public debt in order to stimulate purchasing power, investment and jobs, but also to keep comprehensive pensions (Le Pen 2016, 5). At least temporary, the anti-austerity stance was insofar successful as in the presidential elections Le Pen made it into the final round with an impressive approval from the 'ordinary people' – workers, small businesspeople and pensioners – in the rural and deindustrialized areas.

The transformation of the former 'Lega Nord' in Italy took a similar direction. As a coalition party in the Berlusconi government between 2008 and 2011, it has been in favour of austerity. Then, in opposition to the Monti cabinet it changed its economic strategy. Like the Movimento 5 Stelle (M5S), the Lega 'became the voice of those who complained that Italy's government had not been elected by its people but had been imposed by the EU' (D'Alimonte 2019, 118). The quite sharp criticism of austerity policies (Dolcini 2018, 40–1) was programmatically promoted, after Matteo Salvini took the chairmanship of the party in 2013. It was part of a double transformation from a regionalist to a nationalist party – the 'Lega Nord' became the 'Lega' – and from a neoliberal to an anti-globalist, protectionist party. Daniele Albertazzi et al (2018, 662) characterized this transformation as follows: 'The "internal enemies" (the Italian state, the corrupted elite in Rome, and southern Italians) have been replaced by "external ones" (the EU and the corrupted elites in Brussels), which are now portrayed as the culprits of the country's major ills – from sluggish economic growth, to austerity and 'uncontrolled' migration.'

The more far-reaching programmatic reorientations in France and Italy are remarkable. In contrast, developments in Central and Eastern Europe, that is, in Poland and Hungary, are less conspicuous. Nevertheless, they are substantial as in both countries right-wing populist parties – Fidecz in Hungary and PiS in Poland – are in power for a while; and both pursue a fairly similar economic and social policy-agenda (Becker 2018, 73–119). This agenda is characterized by a general acceptance of the rules of the European internal market, however, also by an adherence to the national currency as a prerequisite to a broadened room for manoeuvre in economic policymaking. In this sense, both governments launched initiatives to strengthen domestic capital – particularly in the banking sector, in services, the media or construction – in order to develop the material and infrastructural basis of their authoritarian rule. Obviously, they are primarily concerned about fostering industrial development through a particular mix of investment incentives: lower taxation, technological and infrastructural modernization and so on. In general, they are disposed to politically intervene in the economy; and, in terms of the public budget, they show a greater willingness to turn away from a strict austerity agenda.

The selective economic nationalism, based on elements of protectionist state-intervention, corresponds with a propensity to address problems of social disintegration through a national-conservative social policy (Stubbs and Lendvai-Bainton 2020). This is more evident in Poland, where the PiS – still partially linked with the trade union Solidarność – remarkably enhanced childcare allowance, reversed the raise of the pensionable age, supplied additional one-time pension payments, improved the minimum wage and also the employment situation for workers with temporary contracts. In comparison, the Fidecz government, oriented more towards the middle classes, pursued a less distinctive social policy agenda. The reversal of the privatization of pensions and only few social improvements in family and childcare provision remained in the shadow of a clear workfare strategy (Szikra 2018). However, when large parts of homeowners with mortgages denominated in Swiss Franc were highly burdened by the revaluation of the foreign currency, the government stepped in and offered a loan rescheduling programme financed through bailout fees on foreign companies and foreign banks.

The programmatic and strategic orientation of right-wing populist parties in other European countries with neo-corporatist systems of interest mediation is different from the outlined cases again (Erben and Bieling 2020). If we take the cases of Austria and Germany, we can see that both parties, the FPÖ (Freiheitliche Partei Österreichs) and the AfD (Alternative für Deutschland) – originally (re)founded as neoliberal organizations with strong roots in small businesses and the upper middle classes – had difficulties to adjust to the socio-economic claims of large parts of their rural and/or working class-based electorate. In Germany, the party is split over a more social orientation. The western parts still stand for a primarily ordo-liberal view, while the eastern parts are more open for a socially flanked nationalist agenda. In Austria, the situation is slightly different. Here, after Heinz-Christian Strache became chairman, the FPÖ stylized itself as a 'soziale Heimatpartei'. However, though it proclaimed to be representing the interest of workers and the ordinary people, in practice – from 2017 to 2019, again as junior partner in a coalition with the ÖVP – the FPÖ eventually agreed on a series of neoliberal labour and social policy reforms.

Comparatively more attentive to the social issues were the Dutch PVV and the Sweden Democrats. The PVV was first fairly neoliberal and tolerated the minority government of Rutten (2010–12), before the toleration was cancelled in opposition to the austerity packages after the financial crisis (van Kessel 2015). In this context, the focus was on defense of social security provision, above all in the fields of pensions and health care. In addition, social compensation and regulation in the field of labour market policies played only a minor role. Nevertheless, this turn seemed to be too far-reaching for large parts of the middle classes who are much more in favour of a nationalist strategy in line with neoliberal economic and social policy reforms. The discontent with Geert Wilders, chairman and single member of the PVV, allowed for the emergence of the FvD (Forum voor Democratie), as a second, however, unambiguously neoliberal right-wing populist party in the Netherlands.

Slightly different was the development in Sweden. The Sweden Democrats (SD) had never seen themselves as a neoliberal party, but rather one which – irrespective of its neo-fascist ties – has strong links to the middle classes. In this sense, the SD was programmatically supportive of a business-friendly economic agenda as a precondition for a well-functioning welfare state. At the same time, the SD argues for a nationalist reform of the welfare state, which needs to guarantee sufficient social security provision in terms of health care and pensions, flanked by a stronger role of the police (Nordensvard and Ketola 2015). This indicates that the SD – as other right-wing populist parties in continental Europe – would like to establish a more authoritarian and centralized mode of governance. The welfare state should be preserved by 'nativist' reforms, while the institutions and practices of neo-corporatist involvement should be weakened in order to confine the influence and control of socially oriented forces such as trade unions.

This cursory overview suggests that the enforcement of austerity politics in the aftermath of the financial crisis in Europe, given the growing dissatisfaction with its economic and distributional effects, has promoted a reorientation of right-wing political parties in the fields of economic and social policy (Afonso and Rennwald 2018; Fenger 2018). Until now, this reorientation is neither complete nor uniform, but rather selective and still contradictory. It is most clearly pronounced in those countries suffering most from the processes of de-industrialization (France and Italy) or still lagging socio-economically behind (Poland and Hungary). However, although the preferences for selective protection, more state intervention and more generous welfare services are perceptible, it remains unclear whether or to what extent they correspond with a hostility to capitalism: to the market and companies. This is even more the case in continental European countries where populist parties have a stronger neoliberal tradition

(Austria, Germany, the Netherlands). These countries often take a structural creditor position in the European division of labour and are normally less confronted with hard austerity pressures. Hence, the sensitivity and resistance of right-wing populists seems to be relatively weak. Moreover, they are rather inclined to subject other EU member states, especially within the eurozone, to a regime of fiscal discipline.

Prospects: right-wing populism and its contradictions

Whether and how the right-wing populists position themselves in the fields of economic and social policy, whether they support, accept or question the austerity agenda, is determined by several factors. A fundamental role is played by the structure and functioning of the respective model of capitalism, including the given welfare state regime (Hopkin and Blyth 2019). The sectoral structure of capitalism and the forms of welfare state regulation determine: 1) how the respective national economy fits into the international or more specifically: European division of labour; 2) the extent to which certain dimensions of globalization (trade, capital markets or labour markets) present themselves as problematic and are politicized; and 3) whether the national economy assumes a structural creditor or debtor position. If a structural creditor position is taken, there is a high probability that the right-wing populists speak out in favour of a restrictive European setting, exert pressures on debt servicing and reject transnational liability claims. It was therefore no surprise that the slogan 'We are not paying for your crisis', formulated by Blockupy and other social movements at the beginning of the financial crisis, was frequently couched in nationalist terms.

The situation is different in those countries that have a structural debtor position. In these countries there is often – sometimes long-lasting – pressure to implement austerity programmes. These programmes in turn have negative economic and social effects – deepening of economic recession, unemployment, reduction of social benefits, decay of public infrastructure and so on – as a result of which social questions often come to the foreground. It is precisely these social questions that more recently have been an important source of the upswing of left- but also right-wing populist parties. In many countries, the latter have increasingly succeeded in taking up the existing fears – for example fears of social falling, of losing cultural traditions or a future worth living (Gidron and Hall 2017) – in public discourses, interpreting them in a welfare-chauvinistic manner by discriminating against minority ethnic and weaker social groups (Fenger 2018). The modification of the neoliberal orientation of earlier years, in some cases even the turning away from it, points in this direction.

The responsiveness of right-wing political forces to urgent social and cultural questions remains, however, ambiguous. As outlined, there are distinct differences between different groups of countries; and often there are still ongoing party-internal struggles about the extent to which they should accommodate the social claims of large parts of their voters. These struggles reflect the contradiction that most right-wing political parties had been founded as organizations of the bourgeois camp – and still having the strategy of forming right-wing bourgeois alliances – but are increasingly electorally supported by people from rural and working-class milieus (Rydgren 2013). In the shadow of the overall nationalist orientation this contradiction was first rather secondary but then became more important under the conditions of stricter austerity. Consequently, most right-wing populist parties tried to balance it by shifting the burden of austerity policy away from the national majority society: in the domestic realm by developing a – nationalist and exclusionary – welfare-chauvinist labour, social and industrial policy; and in the European context by demanding austerity 'for others'.

Whether this strategy of balancing and burden shifting is viable, remains, however, an open question. It proved to be rather successful, as a series of European crises – above all the financial crisis and austerity politics, but also the crisis of the European border and migration regime – reinforced the alienation of large parts of the people from established parties; and for some of them, the nationalist formula was obviously attractive. The more recent COVID-19 pandemic, however, seems to have a different impact. In many countries, mainstream parties in power adopted a fairly strict and comprehensive control strategy flanked by state intervention and the mobilization of public resources in order to moderate the socio-economic consequences of the lockdown (Bergsen et al 2020). This kind of emergency leadership was difficult to top by right-wing populist forces. Obviously, in most countries they had trouble filling the role of an effective political opposition. Instead, their public suggestions for an adequate management of the pandemic were generally seen as ill-conceived and chaotic. Nevertheless, it would be premature to assume that the pandemic represents a turning point and reversal of the ascending trajectory of right-wing populism. For, the fiscal costs of the pandemic are tremendous, and there is some likelihood that in the near future the EU and national governments will turn back towards austerity again.

References

Afonso, Alexandre and Line Rennwald. 2018. 'Social Class and the Changing Welfare State Agenda of Radical Right Parties in Europe', in P. Manow, B. Palier and H. Schwander (eds) *Welfare Democracies and Party Politics. Explaining Electoral Dynamics in Times of Changing Welfare Capitalism*. Oxford: Oxford University Press, pp 171–94.

Albertazzi, Daniele, Arianna Giovannini and Antonella Seddone. 2018. '"No Regionalism Please, We Are *Leghisti*!" The Transformation of the Italian Lega Nord under the Leadership of Matteo Salvini,' *Regional & Federal Studies*, 28(5): 645–71. https://doi.org/10.1080/13597566.2018.1512977

Becker, Joachim. 2018. *Neo-Nationalismus in der EU: Sozio-ökonomische Programmatik und Praxis*, Working Paper No. 179. Wien: AK Wien. http://emedien.arbeiterkammer.at/viewer/pdf/AC15181468/AC15181468.pdf

Bergsen, Pepijn, Alice Billon-Galland, Hans Kundnani, Vassilis Ntousas and Thomas Raines. 2020. *Europe After Coronavirus: The EU and a New Political Economy, Research Paper*. London: Chatham House. www.chathamhouse.org/sites/default/files/2020-06-08-europe-after-coronavirus-bergsen-et-al_0.pdf

Bieling, Hans-Jürgen. 2012. 'EU Facing the Crisis: Social and Employment Policies in Times of Tight Budgets', *Transfer: European Review of Labour and Research*, 18(3): 255–71. https://doi.org/10.1177%2F1024258912448591

Bieling, Hans-Jürgen. 2019. 'Rise of Right-Wing Populism in the Europe of Today – Outlines of a Socio-Theoretical Exploration', *Culture, Practice & Europeanization*, 4(1): 78–91. www.uni-flensburg.de/fileadmin/content/seminare/soziologie/dokumente/culture-practice-and-europeanization/cpe-vol.4-no.1/seeliger-sommer-cpe-2019-vol.4-nr.1.pdf#page=80

Bieling, Hans-Jürgen and Simon Guntrum (eds). 2019. *Alte Segel, neuer Kurs? Die Eurokrise und ihre Folgen für das europäische Wirtschaftsregieren*. Wiesbaden: VS Springer.

Blyth, Mark. 2014. *Austerity: The History of a Dangerous Idea*. Oxford: Oxford University Press.

Collective Foundational Economy. 2018. *Foundational Economy: The Infrastructure of Everyday Life*. Manchester University Press.

D'Alimonte, Roberto. 2019. 'How the Populists Won in Italy', *Journal of Democracy*, 30(1): 114–27. https://doi.org/10.1353/jod.2019.0009

della Porta, Donatella. 2015. *Social Movements in Times of Austerity*. Cambridge: Polity Press.

Dolcini, Filippo. 2018. *Austerity in the Eurozone: A Retrospective Assessment*, MA Thesis. Padua: University of Padua. http://tesi.cab.unipd.it/61782/1/Dolcini_Filippo.pdf

Erben, Sylvia Maria and Hans-Jürgen Bieling. 2020. *Gewerkschaften und Rechtspopulismus. Erfahrungen und Lernprozesse aus Österreich, Schweden und den Niederlanden im Vergleich*, Study 440. Düsseldorf: HBS. http://hdl.handle.net/10419/218736

Fenger, Menno. 2018. 'The Social Policy Agendas of Populist Radical Right Parties in Comparative Perspective.' *Journal of International and Comparative Social Policy*, 34(3): 188–209. https://doi.org/10.1080/21699763.2018.1483255

Fetzer, Thiemo. 2019. 'Did Austerity Cause Brexit?', *American Economic Review*, 109(11): 3849–86. https://doi.org/10.1257/aer.20181164

Foster, Chase and Jeffry Frieden. 2019. 'Compensation, Austerity, and Populism: Social Spending and Voting in 17 Western European Countries'. Working Paper, Center for European Studies, Harvard University, 6 December 2019. https://ces.fas.harvard.edu/uploads/files/events/FosterFriedenCompensationPopulismDec2019.pdf

Freeden, Michael. 1996. *Ideologies and Political Theory. A Conceptual Approach*. Oxford: Clarendon.

Gidron, Noam and Peter A. Hall. 2017. 'The Politics of Social Status: Economic and Cultural Roots of the Populist Right', *The British Journal of Sociology*, 68: S57–S84.

Hayes, Graeme. 2017. 'Regimes of Austerity', *Social Movement Studies*, 16(1): 21–35. https://doi.org/10.1080/14742837.2016.1252669

Hermann, Christoph. 2007. 'Neoliberalism in the European Union', *Studies in Political Economy*, 79(1): 61–90. https://doi.org/10.1080/19187033.2007.11675092

Hopkin, Jonathan and Mark Blyth. 2019. 'The Global Economics of European Populism: Growth Regimes and Party System Change in Europe,' *Government and Opposition*, 54(2): 193–225. https://doi.org/10.1017/gov.2018.43

Ivaldi, Gilles. 2015. 'Towards the Median Economic Crisis Voter? The New Leftist Economic Agenda of the Front National in France,' *French Politics*, 13(4): 346–69. https://doi.org/10.1057/fp.2015.17

Jäger, Johannes and Elisabeth Springler (eds). 2015. *Asymmetric Crisis in Europe and Possible Futures: Critical Political Economy and Post-Keynesian Perspectives*. London, New York: Routledge.

Kriesi, Hanspeter. 2014. 'The Populist Challenge', *West European Politics*, 37(2): 361–78. https://doi.org/10.1080/01402382.2014.887879

Le Pen, Marine. 2016. 'France's Next Revolution? A Conversation with Marine Le Pen', *Foreign Affairs*, 95(6): 2–8. www.jstor.org/stable/43948375

Manow, Philip. 2018. *Die Politische Ökonomie des Populismus.* Frankfurt a.M.: Suhrkamp.

McBride, Stephen and Sorin Mitrea. 2017. 'Austerity and Constitutionalizing Structural Reform of Labour in the European Union', *Studies in Political Economy*, 98(1): 1–23. https://doi.org/10.1080/07078552.2017.1297011

McNamara, Kathleen R. 1998. *The Currency of Ideas. Monetary Politics in the European Union.* Ithaca, London: Cornell University Press.

Mudde, Cas. 2010. 'The Populist Radical Right: A Pathological Normalcy', *West European Politics*, 33(6): 1167–86. https://doi.org/10.1080/01402382.2010.508901

Müller, Jan-Werner. 2016. *Was ist Populismus?* Berlin: Suhrkamp.

Nordensvard, Johan and Markus Ketola. 2015. 'Nationalist Reframing of the Finnish and Swedish Welfare States – The Nexus of Nationalism and Social Policy in Far-Right Populist Parties', *Social Policy and Administration*, 49(3): 356–75. https://doi.org/10.1111/spol.12095

Offe, Claus. 1984. *Contradictions of the Welfare State.* London: Hutchinson.

Peet, Richard. 2011. 'Inequality, Crisis and Austerity in Finance Capitalism', *Cambridge Journal of Regions, Economy and Society*, 4(3): 383–99. https://doi.org/10.1093/cjres/rsr025

Priester, Karin. 2012. *Rechter und linker Populismus. Annäherung an ein Chamäleon.* Frankfurt a.M., New York: Campus.

Rodrik, Dani. 2018. 'Populism and the Economics of Globalization', *Journal of International Business Policy*, 1(1): 12–33. https://doi.org/10.1057/s42214-018-0001-4

Rydgren, Jens (ed). 2013. *Class Politics and the Radical Right.* London, New York: Routledge.

Stubbs, Paul and Noémi Lendvai-Bainton. 2020. 'Authoritarian Neoliberalism, Radical Conservatism and Social Policy within the European Union: Croatia, Hungary and Poland', *Development and Change*, 51(2): 540–60. https://doi.org/10.1111/dech.12565

Szikra, Dorottya. 2018. *Welfare for the Wealthy. The Social Policy of the Orbán-Regime, 2010–2017.* Budapest: Friedrich Ebert Stiftung. http://library.fes.de/pdf-files/bueros/budapest/14209.pdf

Taggart, Paul. 2000. *Populism.* Buckingham, Philadelphia: Open University Press.

van Kessel, Steijn. 2015. 'Dutch Populism During the Crisis', in H. Kriesi and T.S. Pappas (eds) *Populism in the Shadow of the Great Recession.* Colchester: ECPR Press, pp 109–24.

11

Reducing the burden: international struggles against illegitimate debt

Christoph Sorg

Austerity measures have faced one of the biggest and most dynamic waves of protest in recent decades. While a pluralism of issues converged in the occupied squares of 2011, such as stagnating wages, housing rights, political corruption and so on, debt constituted one of the pivotal themes of claim-making. From the sudden contraction of financial markets precipitating household debt traps, bankruptcies and evictions, to the devastating effects of austerity justified by sovereign debt crises, the issue of debt reflected larger questions of democratic decision-making and economic life.

This brief chapter aims to situate debt-centred mobilization and the issue of debt within more and less recent anti-austerity struggles.[1] I will first introduce some general issues, features and concepts of social movement studies, and then trace lineages of debt-centred resistance from the Southern Debt Crisis to mobilization after the North Atlantic Financial Crisis.

Due to lack of space and time, and looking at the variety of interesting chapters by other participants to this publication, this text will centre less on the target of said movements (that is, debt and austerity) than on the movements themselves. Such an approach profits from the field of social movement studies and thereby reminds us to always contextualize our analyses and critiques of austerity with the limits of top-down policy implementation and the resistance of disruptive action against policy consolidation (Huke et al 2015).

[1] By debt-centred movements I mean those social movements that decidedly focus on grievances related to debt – within capitalism in general and within austerity in particular. I perceive debt-centred movements as a sub-group of broader anti-austerity and anti-neoliberal networks.

Social movement studies as a field defines itself by looking at the dynamic margins of established polities for social and political change. The field emerged as a critique of structural functionalism and of (economistic and deterministic readings of) Marxism (Melucci 1980).

Marxism(s) has faced a general crisis in the social sciences since the 1970s, as the diffusion of class compromises and the rise of cultural movements supposedly transformed the material reality in which Marxism emerged. Mainstream Marxism strongly focused on labour-capital relations and the mode of production as the central concepts for social movements, while 'new' social movement scholars argued that the demise of Fordism and industrial capitalism precipitated new societal cleavages, mainly centred on autonomy and identity (Melucci 1980; Touraine 1981; Offe 1985). Additionally, social movement scholars criticized that Marxists tended to assume a relatively automatic translation of the objective realities and contradictions of capitalism into social movements, whereas empirical observations show that grievances do not necessarily precipitate collective action, and that social movements frequently do not primarily attract the actors they would benefit the most. Despite these strong disagreements, early movement scholars remained heavily inspired by Marxist theory (Goodwin and Hetland 2013), and recent years have seen attempts to reintroduce the concepts of capitalism and class into social movement theorizing (for example Barker et al 2014).

In the US, where Marxism was much less rooted in social science, structural-functionalists suggested that protest was mostly irrational and used by marginalized members of society vulnerable to political 'extremism' (Kornhauser 1959, Gurr 1970), contrary to much empirical evidence. They frequently shared a scepticism of mass-based movements, which they associated with fascism, Nazism and Stalinism, and deemed them undesirable, impulsive, pathological responses of the mob to feelings of deprivation.

Far from seeing the protest politics of 'ordinary people' as irrational or even dangerous, new scholars of social movements perceived protest as an important part of regular politics and indeed a potential force for democratization (McAdam et al 2001, 14). Related to this, they challenged the notion that activists were individualized societal outsiders with the empirical observation that members of social movements frequently possess significant material and ideational resources, which tremendously facilitate access to social movement spaces (Caniglia and Carmin 2005, 202). Finally, and perhaps most importantly, new social movement scholars challenged large parts of contemporary Marxism and structural-functionalism in arguing that while grievances are present most of the time, even if fluctuating, affected groups and individuals often do not respond to said grievances (see Olson 1965; McAdam et al 2001, 15; Aslanidis 2012, 61).

As a consequence of these points of critique, SMS argued that other factors were necessary for grievances to precipitate collective action. In this way, they maintained the important role of grievances, but stripped it of its hegemonic causal power. Instead, scholars argued that in the presence of grievances social movements necessitate mobilizing structures, political opportunities and threats, collective action frames, and repertoires of contention. While these concepts are read and weighed differently, social movement studies have seen remarkable agreement that all of these factors are at least relevant for social movements. In other words, in the presence of grievances, social movements:

- need to create formal or informal organizational structures for mobilization;
- translate their perception of the field into effective collective action frames;
- create protest tools to collectively challenge their opponents;
- and their actions are helped or constrained by the existence of threats, opportunities, and constraints in the larger political context.

Without digressing too much about recent developments or internal debates of social movement studies, these ideas might help us approach an analysis of recent anti-austerity struggles as well as the role of debt within them. For the purpose of a book on austerity, we might think about:

- the everyday and collective grievances produced by debt and austerity;
- the threats for individual or collective degradation posed by sudden crises;
- the (im)possibility of progressive institutional politics and new movement parties in late-neoliberal post-democracies;
- as well as the discursive, organizational and action repertoires available to counter-hegemonic actors.

I will use the rest of this chapter to elaborate a couple of features of recent (and less recent) debt-centred movements, drawing from empirical research I carried out for my PhD thesis. I will close with some brief reflections on lessons from these movements on debt and austerity.

Contentious debt politics from the southern debt crisis ...

Social relations of debt have a very long history and, not surprisingly, so does resistance against debt. David Graeber (2011) recently popularized Moses Finley's (1973, 80) assessment of 'the perennial revolutionary program of antiquity, cancel debts and redistribute the land, the slogan of a peasantry, not of a working class'. With the globalizing destruction of pre-capitalist livelihoods and the successive creation and expansion of a 'productive' sphere of formally free wage labour (in Marx's double sense) and a 'reproductive' sphere of feminized care work, reciprocal monetary relations as temporary relations between formally equal entities expanded drastically. In market societies, debts were now excessively calculated and violently enforced along unequal power relations (Graeber 2011). Not paying one's debt thus potentially meant losing said formal equality until the debt was repaid.

The history of debt under capitalism illustrates this transformation, from debtors' prisons to colonial conquests justified by debt, for example British rule in Egypt after 1882. It also reflects that debt is a social relation negotiated under unequal power relations, as rich and powerful people, institutions or states face fundamentally different circumstances, which the London Agreement on German external debt in 1953, US public indebtedness or the socialization of banking losses since 2007 have strikingly illustrated. Accordingly, debtors' claims have to struggle with hegemonic moralities of debt, they have to deconstruct the common sense on debt and re-construct debt as economically inefficient or unsustainable, morally unjust or systemically problematic and thereby divert the discourse from debtors' practices to creditors' practices. Along these lines, debt politics has been a field for redistributive, democratic, anti-colonial and anti-imperial claim-making.

Current debt-centred movement practices, organizations and discourses originated in resistance to structural adjustment across the global South since the 1970s, and especially the 1980s (Reitan 2007; Somers 2014). Keynesian and Developmental statist projects had started to run out of steam since the late 1960s and increasingly faced public debt crises. International financial institutions (and right-wing parties) pushed for harsh austerity measures and thus constructed the foundation upon which widespread mobilization against debt and austerity could be organized (Walton and Ragin 1990; Donnelly 2002; Reitan 2007; Somers 2014).

The 'Volcker Shock' of 1979 severely exacerbated these developments. The FED dramatically increased its interest rates in 1979 due to inflationary pressures on the US dollar, in turn precipitated by the escalating costs of the Vietnam War and the end of Bretton Woods (Arrighi 1994; 2007; Krippner 2011). Large amounts of global financial capital thus headed to the US (and to European states and Japan imitating US financial policies) for high returns and funded ever-increasing US deficits.

The consequences of these developments differed across the global South: East Asian states managed to specialize on cheap commodity exports to Western markets driven by expanding credit, and at the same time re-invested their surpluses especially in the US (Arrighi 2007). Much of the rest of Asia, Latin America and Africa, however, faced sovereign debt crises, with a period of abundant credit being succeeded by dried-up financial markets. An increasing number of states faced balance of payment problems and therefore implemented austerity policies – much like Southern European countries since 2008.

Mobilization against debt and austerity first took the form of protest against national governments' austerity policies and commercial banks, but eventually saw some first counter-summits at large international summits. The 1988 World Bank and IMF Annual General Meeting in Berlin and the G7 summit in Paris a year later were among the first international meetings to spark large-scale protest (Somers 2014). Contentious groups created first transnational links, albeit in the absence of recent breakthroughs in information technology and long-distance travel. Framings often centred on unequal power relations between the global North and global South, linking claims to discourses on the New International Economic Order or liberation theology (Somers 2014, 211).

The Paris protests sparked the formation of the Committee for the Abolition of Third World Debt (CADTM) in Belgium in 1990 (Toussaint and Lemoine 2017, 6) and the Forum on Debt and Development (Fondad) organized the first European conference on debt in the same year, with the important advocacy network Eurodad emerging out of this process (Somers 2014). Illustrated by these groups, two approaches to tackling the debt crises had formed by the end of the 1980s: creating and/or supporting social movements to either push for radical policy changes and/or taking unilateral or coordinated debtor action on the one hand; or coordinated debt campaigning and lobbying with closer contact to individuals and associations internal to debt governance structures on the other. These two approaches largely corresponded to the overlapping cleavages of radical versus reformist, and South versus North, with previous research occasionally understating the former in favour of the latter (for example Ambrose 2005; Tagle and Patomäki 2007; Broome 2009).

Mobilization eventually moved creditor institutions and the G7 to introduce the Toronto Terms in 1988 as well as Brady Bonds in the following year. The UK and France proposed the Toronto Terms as limited debt relief for low-income country debt to bilateral creditors (Somers 2014). While completely inadequate as a solution, the Toronto Terms constituted a shift in the creditors' perspective that the debt crisis was not one of temporary liquidity towards the recognition that debt reduction was necessary. The US government with its geopolitical interests in an increasingly destabilized Latin America was a driving force for the Brady Bonds to deal with commercial debt (Somers 2014). Brady Bonds swap existing loans for dollar-denominated bonds linked to either partial debt write-off or interest rates fixed at below market values. These initiatives precipitated the perception among some at the end of the 1980s that the debt crisis had ended.

Contributing to this, the defeat of really existing state socialism seemed to confirm the neoliberal teleology of representative democracy and capitalist property and market relations as the final or natural form of human civilization. Many debt activists thus reconfigured their strategies away from transgressive tactics and more anti-systemic framings towards closer engagement with their opponents and more technical discourse (Somers 2014, 14). International financial institutions (IFIs) – the World Bank more so than the IMF – contributed to this transformation: With their policies slowly losing legitimacy due to increasing inequality and crises, they strived to include moderate civil society in governance processes (Somers 2014, 75). These encounters remained contentious and complex, with IFIs and governments engaging in reverse lobbying, and civil society groups trying to remain autonomous while exploiting splits in policymaking circles.

Debt campaigning successively spilled over from mainly Latin America to sub-Saharan Africa, where actor constellations differed. Debts were not mainly owed to private commercial banks (of the London Club), but to Northern governments and the multilateral institutions they dominated. National governments remained the preferred target of claims in order to transform international politics. In response to sustained and increasingly sophisticated institutional advocacy, the G7 declared their intention to seek 'comprehensive multilateral debt reduction for qualifying countries' at their summit in Lyon in 1996 (Donnelly 2002, 164). As a consequence, three months later, IMF and World Bank introduced the Heavily Indebted Poor Country (HIPC) Initiative, which promised debt relief and low-interest loans following six years of structural adjustment reforms, for up to 41 designated countries (Somers 2014, 133). Debt politics activists differed in their perception of the HIPC Initiative roughly along above-elaborated cleavages, with some seeing at as a successful first step, and others as perpetuating unequal North-South relations. HIPC remained the dominant framework into the new millennium and was challenged by several campaigns tied to the rising Global Justice Movement.

Among them was the popular UK-based Jubilee 2000 campaign, which demanded debt cancellation for poorer countries. The name related the assumed 2000th anniversary of Christ to the biblical concept of 'jubilee', that is, years when debts are forgiven, slaves freed and land redistributed. The campaign successfully created a broad coalition of a variety of non-religious and religious groups, thereby tapping into both the organizational resources of Global Justice groups as well as into strong transnational religious networks (Donnelly 2007). Similar to, and indeed as constitutive contributors to the alter-globalization movement of movements, debt-centred movement networks increasingly moved from limited forms of international coordination to stronger and more transnational networks (Reitan 2007). In order to keep together its broad coalition, Jubilee 2000 featured a variety of actions, which ranged from raising awareness about debt-related grievances to petitions and large-scale (non-confrontational) mobilization, for example the large human chain surrounding Birmingham City Centre during the 1998 G8 Summit (Reitan 2007, 81). Jubilee 2000 managed to convince creditors, governments and IFIs to make concessions in the 1999 Cologne Debt Deal (also known as HIPC 11 or Enhanced HIPC), which further increased debt reduction of the HIPC Initiative and slightly (!) eased structural adjustment policies. The deal brought structural disagreements between Northern and more reformist groups on the one hand and Southern and more radical groups on the other to the surface. The former interpreted the deal as at least a step in the right direction, whereas the latter perceived 'the offer being too little, too late, and with too many strings attached' (Reitan 2007, 66).

Many Southern groups and individuals thus broke away from the coalition to form an autonomous Jubilee South network oriented more towards direct social justice activism than institutional reform advocacy and with a more radical framing of current debt structures as immoral and illegitimate, since Southern states had paid their debts several times over (due to high interest rates, dollar seignorage and so on). This split did not constitute a definite break, however, but more of a contentious evolution (Somers 2014). Latin American, African and Asian groups felt that autonomous organization was needed, which could then be complemented and strengthened by Northern solidarity networks. South-North dialogue continued via established transnational channels and especially during international (counter-) summits, for example World Social Forums.

In addition to Jubilee South, campaigns and alliances such as Make Poverty History and the Global Call for Action against Poverty (GCAP) continued the Jubilee legacy. The reconfigured Jubilee networks remained active throughout the 2000s and observed further small victories when the G7 announced Multilateral Debt Relief Initiative in 2005, when the Norwegian government (unconditionally) cancelled illegitimate debts of Egypt, Ecuador, Peru, Jamaica and Sierra Leone in 2007 and when Ecuador rejected part of its debt in 2010 (the Argentinian state had struggled with its creditors since 2001 but later agreed to pay part of its debt). Other groups such as the New Economics Foundation, Eurodad (and the German Jubilee campaign Erlassjahr as one of their members in particular) and Afrodad instead turned their focus on the development of a 'Fair and Transparent Arbitration Process' (FTAP) as a structural fix for recurrent debt crises, which they argue would democratize and institutionalize public bankruptcies (Ambrose 2005, 282).

… to the North Atlantic financial crisis

The North Atlantic Financial Crisis (NAFC) provided the critical juncture to herald a new wave of protest, which reconfigured the protest-scape in the field of debt politics. For decades protestors had focused on downward spirals of sovereign debt crises and austerity, odious debt left behind by authoritarian leaders and the heritage of colonialism, and to a smaller extent on household debt and microcredit – all across Latin America, sub-Saharan Africa and Southeast Asia. The NAFC provided the foundation for debt-centred protest and movement organizations to emerge in or reconsider their focus on North Africa and the North Atlantic.

Non-financial corporations had faced diminishing profits since the 1960s and thus turned towards financial markets for returns, thus developing autonomous financial capabilities (Krippner 2005; 2011; Lapavitsas 2011). Financial corporations therefore lost a traditional sector of their activity and in turn increased lending to other banks as well as to households. Financial deregulation fastened this process and so did stagnating wages, which pushed households to increasingly rely on debt for their consumption (Demirović and Sablowski 2013; Lapavitsas 2013). The race for financial yields precipitated increasingly risky financial products, from subprime mortgage-backed securities to collateral debt obligations (Davis 2009). In 2006 a housing crisis developed in the US mortgage market, with low-income and migrant communities being the first to struggle with re-financing. The collapse of the investment bank Lehman Brothers turned the subprime mortgage crisis into a North Atlantic banking crisis, since North American and European banks had lent heavily to each other. Massive government bailouts eventually prevented a complete collapse of global finance, but many households had lost their savings, collapsed financial markets and weakened aggregate demand precipitated economic recession – and governments were now deeply indebted themselves.

Social movements responded to the threats and opportunities deriving from the crisis process. Protests in Iceland since 2008 marked an early point of collective dissent, but a new wave of contention only really took off from 2010 with the Tunisian revolution. North Africa and West Asia saw a series of uprisings against authoritarian structures and increasing social inequality after decades of neoliberal transformation (Hanieh 2013; Beinin 2015). The fall of regimes in Tunisia and Egypt posed the question of what to do with the odious debt left behind by authoritarian leaders, a problematique reminiscent of earlier struggles by the Southern debt movement. IFIs and local elites quickly used increasing sovereign debt as an excuse to maintain or deepen austerity reforms, which emerging debt-centred movement networks contested.

Protest quickly diffused to the North Atlantic (Gerbaudo 2013; Romanos 2016), where social movements challenged political corruption and social inequality. Household debt had soared across the global North for decades, especially in highly financialized Anglo-Saxon economies. Governments unleashed austerity reforms after having socialized private banking losses. In Europe, internal contradictions of the Eurozone exacerbated the sovereign debt crisis especially in peripheral countries, where markets collapsed, living conditions worsened and debt exploded (Streeck 2011; Lapavitsas 2012; Smith 2017).

After the demobilization of the square occupations, new local movement organizations as well as transnational coordination networks formed, thereby linking different scales and territories. In addition, parts of the activists tried to bridge contentious and institutional politics (della Porta et al 2017). Depending on the local context, counter-hegemonic actors formed new movement parties such as Podemos in Spain or Front Populaire in Tunisia, or attempted to appropriate existing parties such as Momentum in the UK or the campaign for Bernie Sanders in the US.

The movements of the squares as well as the new movement organizations and movement parties that formed afterwards managed to mobilize broad heterogeneous coalitions against the grievances of precarity experienced in their everyday life: un- and underemployment, social degradation and insecurity, loss of political rights, increasing taxes, all produced by austerity and debt crises (della Porta 2015). They succeeded in keeping this coalition together by keeping spaces and networks relatively participatory and horizontal so that newcomers could easily enter and organized groups would not hijack the dynamic. In addition, they stressed the broad collective identity shared of those hurt by austerity in the ways mentioned earlier.

Debt-centred movement organizations emerged out of and within this broader wave of anti-austerity struggles. With the help of established debt-centred networks such as CADTM and Eurodad, a younger generation of activists launched new groups such as Debt Resistance UK, Let's audit European debt obligations to Tunisia (ACET) and the Spanish Citizen Debt Audit Platform (PACD). These groups challenged debt-related grievances in their respective countries and eventually launched the International Citizen Debt Audit Platform (ICAN), which linked groups from 12 countries in Europe and North Africa in the aim to '[fight] austerity measures through the implementation of Citizen Debt Audits' (ICAN nd).

Like their predecessors in the Global Justice Movement, they stressed the need for deliberative and participatory democracy, but they put further emphasis on the need for open access to 'regular people' vis-à-vis more experienced activists (see also della Porta 2015). They related constructions of collective identity to broad conceptions of the self (99 per cent, the people, the citizens and so on) and adopted new notions of self-empowering and prefigurative (debt) politics and the form of highly participatory civil debt audits. Debt audits constitute an open process, during which a government, technical experts, civil society reviews, or a combination thereof reviews outstanding credits or debt in order to 'revise all loan contracts looking at specific elements, such as the context of the establishment of the contract, the loan conditions, the interest rates, who the responsible parties are, how democratic the loan process was and borrowing and lending policies in general' (SLUG 2011, 4).

Latin American groups have long experimented with debt audits (Fattorelli 2013), and in 2008 the Ecuadorian government was the first to complete the process, establish a debt commission and suspend a large part of its public debt. One year later, Norwegian civil society groups convinced their newly elected government to launch the first creditor audit to review outstanding debts developing countries have to Norway, after the country had already unilaterally and unconditionally cancelled US$80 million in illegitimate debts to Egypt, Ecuador, Peru, Jamaica and Sierra Leone in 2006 (SLUG 2011). Tunisia and Egypt saw two similar campaigns to audit odious debt after the fall of their respective regimes in 2011, so far without major success.

In 2015, the newly elected Syriza government agreed to launch a 'Greek Truth Committee on Public Debt', which consisted of longstanding civil society experts in debt politics (Truth Committee on the Greek Public Debt 2015). The committee reviewed Greece's finances during and since the crisis and identified debt it considered 'illegitimate, odious, illegal, and unsustainable' (Truth Committee on the Greek Public Debt 2015). Its conclusions and recommendations were radical: partial cancellation of debt as well as an immediate moratorium on further debt payments. CADTM went even further to suggest a complete socialization of Greek banks linked to an exit from the Eurozone, but the capitulation of Syriza in July 2015 put an immediate end to all such proposals.

Younger groups tried to carry the concept of debt audits into local politics. In Spain, PACD created a network of Citizens' Municipal Observatories, which were supposed to observe municipal debt and fiscal policies (for more details, see Martínez and Fresnillo 2013; ICAN 2014; Cutillas 2014). In the UK, DRUK attacked 'lender option borrower option' loans (LOBOs) as a particular exploitative form of local debt (Benjamin 2015; Rogers 2015). LOBOs attract local authorities with initially low interest rates and the possibility to push central government debt off its balance sheets. However, rates may then be increased and include additional fees, which makes it more expensive than public funding and thus ensures a steady flow of public funds into private pockets.

In the US, Strike Debt has produced a Debt Resistors' Operations Manual and Debt Resistors' Organizing Kit, which informs individuals on different ways to resist individual debt. The ideas are inspired by new discourses about the commons and anarchist concepts like mutualism, cooperatives and the gift economy (Strike Debt 2012). Strike Debt has also initiated a Rolling Jubilee as a 'bailout of the people for the people'. Concretely, the group crowdfunded more than US$700,000 and used this money to abolish about US$32 million. The group thereby appropriated financialization's commodification of debt against itself by buying up debt for pennies on the dollar on secondary markets for debt collectors and then abolishing it instead of collecting it (Hern 2012; Rees 2012). The project provided direct help to indebted individuals, contributed to popular education about predatory financial practices and inspired individuals towards collective action.

These organizational, knowledge and action repertoires all contrast the perceived erosion of popular political participation, general morality and societal solidarity under neoliberalism and austerity, as well as the atomizing and demoralizing experience of being in debt ('you are not a loan'; 'ICAN').

What can we learn from debt-centred movements?

So what can we learn from resistance against the Southern Debt Crisis, the Global Justice Movement and recent anti-austerity struggles? Many things, but I shall elaborate a couple of selected aspects in the following lines.

Debt and austerity are heavily interrelated as austerity and neoliberalism produce specific debt-based grievances and conversely debt politics can be one of the tools to implement austerity. Actual or supposed public debt crises constitute an excuse to implement austerity reforms. 'Supposed' refers to the fact that the European Debt Crisis is at the core not a sovereign debt crisis, but a private debt crisis driven by the private debt of financial corporations. This private debt crisis only turned into a sovereign debt crisis once governments decided to socialize private losses and without dispossessing the major shareholders. Debt-centred movements have reminded us that many of the current processes resemble the struggles of the Southern Debt Crisis, with creditors dictating procedures according to their interests and debtors losing sovereignty and facing perpetual austerity and stagnation (for example Toussaint 2011).

Hegemonic 'commons sense' narratives justify austerity via debt: indebted individuals and states have lived beyond their means so now they have to cut back. Debt-centred movements have deconstructed such narratives by reversing the gaze. They have elaborated predatory creditor practices and unequal power relations between debtors and creditors (for example Ellmers 2016), especially in the international realm, which lacks formalized procedures for sovereign bankruptcies (for example Lungu 2004; Afrodad 2010). The main reasons for household debt crises are the privatized Keynesianism of decades-long austerity and neoliberal reforms, not irresponsible behaviour of impoverished classes. The main reasons for sovereign debt crises are unjust regulation of the global financial architecture as well as recurrent transfers of financial-corporate debt onto public shoulders, not a social spending spree of benevolent governments.

As a consequence, austerity for the majority exacerbates the debt problematique. Slashed social services, economic stagnation, unemployment and decreasing social power of labour have increased overall household debt. With poorer social groups consuming a much higher share of their available income, austerity kills economic performance and thereby further increases sovereign debt. In this way, austerity and sovereign debt crises turn into a vicious downward cycle.

Such discursive struggles remind us to not take neoliberal ideology at face value. Free market reforms are not about free markets, but about increasing the social power of large corporations and social elites, and to actually shield them from competition. Fiscal consolidation is not about fiscal consolidation, but about answering the crisis in the interests of the wealthy, which in turn threatens fiscal consolidation.

Looking at the variety of debt-centred social movements and their projects, it becomes clear that they don't suffer a lack of ideas for change, but a lack of power to implement them. Social movements have voiced profoundly reasonable critiques for decades, but reforms were only implemented when policy insiders perceived escalating disruption as a threat – and even then only tiny reforms were introduced. Suggestions by social movements range from debt cancellations to reforms of the financial architecture, the socialization of finance and a democratization of debt politics. I will close this chapter by elaborating these in order to provide food for discussion towards the next potential steps.

Eurodad, its constituents and its allies suggest – among other things – a financial architecture which privileges human over creditor rights, punishes predatory lending and provides for a 'fair and transparent' sovereign insolvency framework (Ellmers and Hulova 2013; Kaiser 2013). A recent effort to push for policy reform within the UN General Assembly with the help of the G77 and China failed due to the resistance of a handful of powerful creditor states, among them the US, Japan, Germany, UK, Canada and Israel (Erlassjahr 2015; Ellmers 2016).

CADTM mainly supports a mixture of national and international financial transformation. In the short term, radical Keynesian measures to regulate the financial sector and re-establish welfare state structures could reconfigure societal property and power relations as well as the financial sector. Concrete reforms could include reducing the size of banks, separating commercial and investment banks, increasing necessary amount of reserves for banks and so on (for example Toussaint et al 2016). In the long term, however, the network aims for new regional financial architectures for debtor states to de-link from the power relations of the current world economy (for example Toussaint 2007; Fattorelli 2013), as well as a complete socialization of the banking sector as a structural fix to capital's excessive structural power (for example Toussaint et al 2016). CADTM distinguishes socialization from nationalization in order to highlight the roles of grass-roots citizen oversight as well as the need to relate democratic self-management of banks to societal needs to finance a transformation towards a social and ecological economy.

Within these processes, citizen debt audits may serve to identify and cancel illegitimate debt (PACD 2013), but also contribute to a wider politicization and democratization of debt politics, especially when institutionalized as a permanent democratic process (Malinen 2015). In this way, citizen debt audits complement the necessity of economic redistribution and re-configuration with the element of transparency and participatory democracy. They reflect the vision of social transformation that does not reproduce statism and does not sacrifice democratic values at the altar of economic equality. Younger generations of activists have stressed this point in particular and are more careful to elaborate concrete measures to be implemented.

None of the networks mentioned earlier perceives debt as an isolated issue. Eurodad works on different financial issues, including taxation, illicit financial flows and development finance. CADTM sees debt cancellation as one measure among many in the transformation towards a social and ecological economic system. ICAN and the new movement organizations interpret debt as one of the many fields of politics, which necessitate popular education, mobilization and democratic experimentation. Any of their visions would be much preferable to the status quo.

References

Afrodad. 2010. *The Case for the Establishment of a Fair and Transparent Arbitration Mechanism on Illegitimate and Odious Debts*. https://opendocs.ids.ac.uk/opendocs/handle/20.500.12413/1665

Ambrose, Soren. 2005. 'Social Movements and the Politics of Debt Cancellation', *Chicago Journal of International Law*, 6(1): 267–85.

Arrighi, Giovanni. 1994. *The Long Twentieth Century: Money, Power, and the Origins of our Times*. London, New York: Verso.

Arrighi, Giovanni. 2007. *Adam Smith in Beijing: Lineages of the Twenty-First Century*. London, New York: Verso.

Aslanidis, Paris. 2012. *Critical Review of Social Movement Literature*. www.academia.edu/2381793/Critical_Review_of_Social_Movement_Literature

Barker, Colin, Laurence Cox, John Krinsky and Alf Gunvald Nilsen (eds). 2014. *Marxism and Social Movements*. Chicago: Haymarket Books.

Beinin, Joel. 2015. *Workers and Thieves: Labor Movements and Popular Uprisings in Tunisia and Egypt*. Stanford, California: Stanford University Press.

Benjamin, Joel. 2015. 'Dispatches: How Local Governments are Being Fleeced by the Banks on £15bn Loans', *Open Democracy*. www.opendemocracy.net/ourkingdom/joel-benjamin/dispatches-how-local-governments-are-being-fleeced-by-banks-for-%C2%A315bn

Broome, André. 2009. 'When do NGOs Matter? Activist Organisations as a Source of Change in the International Debt Regime', *Global Society*, 23(1): 59–78.

Caniglia, Beth and JoAnn Carmin. 2005. 'Scholarship on Social Movement organizations: Classic Views and Emerging Trends', *Mobilization: An International Quarterly*, 10(2): 201–12.

Cutillas, Sergi. 2014. 'Movements Against Spanish State Debt: For a New Social Deal That Can Transform Europe', CADTM. www.cadtm.org/spip.php?page=imprimer&id_article=10421

Davis, Gerald F. 2009. *Managed by the Markets: How Finance Reshaped America*. Oxford: Oxford University Press.

della Porta, Donatella. 2015. *Social Movements in Times of Austerity: Bringing Capitalism Back into Protest Analysis*. Cambridge: Polity Press.

della Porta, Donatella, Joseba Fernández, Chara Kukē and Lorenzo Mosca. 2017. *Movement Parties Against Austerity*. Cambridge, UK, Malden, MA: Polity.

Demirović, Alex and Thomas Sablowski. 2013. *The Finance-Dominated Regime of Accumulation and the Crisis in Europe*. www.rosalux.de/fileadmin/rls_uploads/pdfs/Analysen/Analysen_The_Finance-dominated.pdf

Donnelly, Elizabeth A. 2002. 'Proclaiming Jubilee. The Debt and Structural Adjustment Network', in S. Khagram, J.V. Riker and K. Sikkink (eds) *Restructuring World Politics: Transnational Social Movements, Networks, and Norms*. Minneapolis: University of Minnesota Press, pp 155–80.

Donnelly, Elizabeth A. 2007. 'Making the Case for Jubilee: The Catholic Church and the Poor-Country Debt Movement', *Ethics & International Affairs*, 21(1): 107–33.

Ellmers, Bodo. 2016. *The Evolving Nature of Developing Country Debt and Solutions for Change*. www.eurodad.org/the_evolving_nature_of_developing_country_debt_and_solutions_for_change

Ellmers, Bodo and Diana Hulova. 2013. *The New Debt Vulnerabilities*. https://eurodad.org/files/pdf/5280b0e731441.pdf

Erlassjahr. 2015. *Das "Sovereign Debt Restructuring Liaison Office". Ein greifbares Ergebnis des UN-Prozesses für ein Staateninsolvenzverfahren*. http://erlassjahr.de/wordpress/wp-content/uploads/2016/03/Fachinfo-48.pdf

Fattorelli, Maria Lucia. 2013. *Citizen Public Debt Audit: Experiences and methods*. Genève: CETIM.

Finley, Moses. 1973. *The Ancient Economy*. Berkeley: University of California Press.

Gerbaudo, Paolo. 2013. 'Protest Diffusion and Cultural Resonance in the 2011 Protest Wave', *The International Spectator*, 48(4): 86–101.

Goodwin, Jeff and Gabriel Hetland. 2013. *The Strange Disappearance of Capitalism from Social Movement Studies: The Case of the LGBT Movement*. https://as.nyu.edu/content/dam/nyu-as/faculty/documents/Strange_Disappearance_of_Capitalism.pdf

Graeber, David. 2011. *Debt: The First 5,000 Years*. Brooklyn, N.Y.: Melville House.

Gurr, Ted Robert. 1970. *Why Men Rebel*. Princeton: Princeton University Press.

Hanieh, Adam. 2013. *Lineages of Revolt: Issues of Contemporary Capitalism in the Middle East*. New York: Haymarket Books.

Hern, Alex. 2012. 'Rolling Jubilee: Can a Crowdsourced Bailout of Personal Debt Work?' *New Statesman*.

Huke, Nikolai, Mònica Clua-Losada and David J. Bailey. 2015. 'Disrupting the European Crisis: A Critical Political Economy of Contestation, Subversion and Escape', *New Political Economy*, 20(5): 725–51.

ICAN. 2014. 'OCAX: An Online Tool to Keep Public Budgets under People's Control'. www.citizen-audit.net/ocax-an-online-tool-to-keep-public-budgets-under-peoples-control/

ICAN. nd. 'About ICAN'. www.citizen-audit.net/about-ican/

Kaiser, Jürgen. 2013. *Resolving Sovereign Debt Crises: Towards a Fair and Transparent International Insolvency Framework*. http://erlassjahr.de/wordpress/wp-content/uploads/2016/03/FES-Resolving_Sovereign_Debt_Crises.pdf

Kornhauser, William. 1959. *The Politics of Mass Society*. Glencoe, Ill.: Free Press.
Krippner, Greta. 2005. 'The Financialization of the American Economy', *Socio-Economic Review*, 3(2): 173–208.
Krippner, Greta. 2011. *Capitalizing on Crisis: The Political Origins of the Rise of Finance*. Cambridge, Massachusetts, London, England: Harvard University Press.
Lapavitsas, Costas. 2011. 'Theorizing Financialization', *Work, Employment and Society*, 25(4): 611–26.
Lapavitsas, Costas. 2012. *Crisis in the Eurozone*. London: Verso Books.
Lapavitsas, Costas. 2013. *Profiting Without Producing: How Finance Exploits Us All*. London: Verso.
Lungu, John. 2004. *The Case for the Establishment of a Fair and Transparent Arbitration on Debt*. Afrodad. Lusaka (Discussion paper). https://opendocs.ids.ac.uk/opendocs/handle/20.500.12413/1665
Malinen, Fanny. 2015. 'Debt Audits Challenge the Power of Opaque Finance'. www.opendemocracy.net/can-europe-make-it/fanny-malinen/debt-audits-challenge-power-of-opaque-finance
Martínez Pablo and Iolanda Fresnillo. 2013. 'Breaking Away from Debt at a Municipal Level'. https://auditoriaciudadana.net/2013/09/05/breaking-away-from-debt-municipal-level/
McAdam, Doug, Sidney Tarrow and Charles Tilly. 2001. *Dynamics of Contention*. Cambridge, New York: Cambridge University Press.
Melucci, Alberto. 1980. 'The New Social Movements: A Theoretical Approach', *Social Science Information*, 19(2): 199–226.
Offe, Claus. 1985. 'New Social Movements: Challenging the Boundaries of Institutional Politics'. *Social Research*, 52(4): 817–68.
Olson, Mancur. 1965. *The Logic of Collective Action: Public Goods and the Theory of Groups*. Cambridge, Mass: Harvard University Press.
PACD. 2013. 'What the Spanish Citizen Debt Audit Platform (PACD) means by "Citizen Debt Audit" and "Illegitimate Debt"'. www.cadtm.org/What-the-Spanish-Citizen-Debt
Rees, David. 2012. 'The People's Bailout'. http://howtosharpenpencils.tumblr.com/post/35285338188/the-peoples-bailout
Reitan, Ruth. 2007. *Global Activism*. London, New York: Routledge.
Rogers, Ludovica. 2015. Speech at Assemblée citoyenne européenne sur la dette. www.youtube.com/watch?v=886PnOK4ZaY
Romanos, Eduardo. 2016. 'From Tahrir to Puerta del Sol to Wall Street: The Transnational Diffusion of Social Movements in Comparative Perspective', *Revista Española de Investigaciones* (154): 103–18.

SLUG. 2011. 'The Norwegian Debt Audit from an International Perspective'. https://slettgjelda.no/assets/docs/TheNorwegian-DebtAudit_lowres.pdf

Smith, John. 2017. 'The Global South in the Global Crisis'. *Journal of Labor and Society*, 20(2): 161–84.

Somers, Jean. 2014. *Transnationalism, Power and Change: Three Decades of Debt Campaigning*. Dissertation. Dublin City University. School of Law and Government. www.debtireland.org/download/pdf/20140729115736.pdf

Streeck, Wolfgang. 2011. *The Crisis in Context: Democratic Capitalism and Its Contradictions. MPIfG Discussion Paper* 11/15. www.mpifg.de/pu/dp_abstracts/dp11-15.asp

Strike Debt. 2012. *The Debt Resistors' Operations Manual*. http://strikedebt.org/The-Debt-Resistors-Operations-Manual.pdf

Tagle, Yovana Reyes and Katarina Sehm Patomäki. 2007. *The Rise and Development of the Global Debt Movement: A North-South Dialogue*. http://unrisd.org/80256B3C005BCCF9/%28httpAuxPages%29/2A35FE558DCA39A0C12572C9002F6D79/$file/Reyes.pdf

Touraine, Alain. 1981. *The Voice and the Eye: An Analysis of Social Movements*. Cambridge: Cambridge University Press.

Toussaint, Eric. 2007. *Bank of the South: An Alternative to IMF-World Bank*. www.cadtm.org/Bank-of-the-South-An-Alternative

Toussaint, Eric. 2011. 'A European Brady deal: Austerity for Life'. www.cadtm.org/A-European-Brady-deal-austerity

Toussaint, Eric and Benjamin Lemoine. 2017. *History of the CADTM Anti-Debt Policies*. www.cadtm.org/IMG/pdf/antidette_ENG_web-2.pdf

Toussaint, Eric, Michel Husson, Costas Lapavitsas, Ozlem Onaran, Patrick Saurin, Stathis Kouvelakis et al. 2016. 'What Is To Be Done with the Banks? Radical Proposals for Radical Changes'. www.cadtm.org/What-is-to-be-Done-with-the-Banks,13315

Truth Committee on the Greek Public Debt. 2015. *Preliminary Report of the Truth Committee on Public Debt*. www.cadtm.org/Preliminary-Report-of-the-Truth

Walton, John and Charles Ragin. 1990. 'Global and National Sources of Political Protest: Third World Responses to the Debt Crisis', *American Sociological Review*, 55(6): 876.

12

The crisis next time: the GFC and the continuing fragility of capitalism

Jim Stanford

Capitalism shows an innate tendency to repeated cycles of boom and bust. Many factors can serve as the proximate cause of these cyclical fluctuations: including supply shocks in production of key resources and other inputs, fluctuations in the sentiment and confidence of business leaders and consumers, volatility in the supply of credit (which fuels spending and expansion) or changes in macroeconomic policy (such as interest rates or government spending). Whatever the immediate cause of each cycle, inherent cyclical instability reflects common features embedded within capitalism, including:

- Growth and development are led, first and foremost, by profit-seeking capital investments made by private businesses. If they stop investing, output and employment stop growing or start to shrink.
- But those individual decisions to invest are independent, uncoordinated and subject to volatile shifts in sentiment and expectations.
- This decentralization facilitates coordination failures, whereby individual investors make seemingly rational decisions that damage the whole economy (and hence the collective of businesses).
- Inter-sectoral and international flows of production, trade and investment can spread the effects of any initial sectoral downturn into the broader economy – again facilitated by the lack of coordination of the system.
- Personal consumption is the largest component of total output and spending, but it generally follows economic cycles (rather than leading them) since it depends on the prior existence of employment and labour income. If investment and employment decline, consumer spending also declines – magnifying the resulting shock to total output and employment.
- Fundamental uncertainty exacerbates this instability. Forward-looking investment judgements are inherently uncertain, since future

economic and business conditions are unknowable, and herd-like shifts in expectations about the future further amplify shocks.
- The overdevelopment of financial activities, products and linkages (called financialization[1]) accelerates this volatile mix. Hyperactive and very complex financial linkages amplify shocks and accelerate their contagion.

Given this volatile mix, the question is not whether capitalism will experience another crisis – but when, where and specifically why. Indeed, the history of neoliberalism is one of regular crises (Duménil and Lévy 2011; Boyer 2013), marked by increasing rapidity of onset, amplitude and global reach. Every few years since neoliberal macroeconomic policies became ascendant, the global and regional economies have been wracked by repeated episodes of contagious, financialized crisis, recession, displacement and then reconstruction. The first of these episodes signalled the onset of the neoliberal era: the shock from Paul Volcker's interest rate hikes (and explicit abandonment of full employment as the central goal of macroeconomic policy) caused a global recession in the early 1980s. That crisis signalled to all segments of society that the economic rules had fundamentally changed.[2]

Every few years since then, the advanced capitalist economies have experienced subsequent episodes of recession, financial collapse and dislocation. And the intensity of these crises has tended to worsen over time:

- the crisis in the US savings and loan industry in the mid-1980s;
- the global recession in the early 1990s, sparked by the first Gulf War and a spike in energy prices;
- Japan's real estate meltdown and subsequent 'lost decade' in the 1990s;
- a series of regionally focused financial crises in the 1990s, including in the Nordic countries, Mexico, east Asia and Russia;

[1] See Epstein (2005) and Sawyer (2013) on the nature, causes and consequences of financialization.

[2] The former Research Director of the IMF Michael Mussa explained the historic importance of the Volcker shock this way: 'To establish its credibility, the Federal Reserve had to demonstrate its willingness to spill blood, lots of blood, other people's blood.' Cited in Glyn (2006), p 24.

- the meltdown in dot-com stocks in 2000, and subsequent recession in the US and other countries.

All these intermittent crises paled in comparison, however, to the GFC and subsequent 'Great Recession' that began in 2008. The GFC was by far the worst and widest downturn since the 1930s. It sparked unprecedented interventions by governments, central banks and international institutions. Yet despite that dramatic response, leading capitalist countries remained bedevilled by underutilization, macroeconomic stagnation, large government deficits and other symptoms of macroeconomic dysfunction for years afterwards. Indeed, even a decade later, the advanced capitalist countries had still not fully recovered. But if history is any guide, another crisis would be along soon.

Of course, we now know what that next crisis would be. While it was safe to assume another crisis would emerge, few could imagine the dramatic repercussions of this one: the outbreak of COVID-19, the deliberate shutdown of economic activity in entire sectors and regions and the onset of a truly global recession that was as deep as the Great Depression of the 1930s in depth, but faster. While the current COVID-19 recession is unique, for many reasons, it reflects the same underlying vulnerability to instability that facilitated previous crises. And it is increasingly clear that the present crisis is more than epidemiological in nature. The initial health-ordered shutdowns of specific customer-facing industries (like retail, hospitality and transportation) spread into an economy-wide recession, with conventional features like collapsed business investment, shattered confidence and permanent job losses. Moreover, the financial, macroeconomic and political shockwaves from COVID-19 are made worse by the weak state of global capitalism when the virus first erupted. The economies of most OECD economies were already limping, long before the novel COVID-19 arrived on the scene.

This chapter will look back at the GFC of 2008–09, and the painful decade of stagnation and halting recovery that followed it, to glean several key lessons that aid in understanding and responding to this latest, more dramatic conflagration. First it briefly reviews the major causes and features of the GFC, identifying commonalities with previous crises. The next section describes several empirical indicators attesting to the failure of global capitalism to recover from the GFC, even a decade afterwards. Because of this failure, the system was badly prepared for whatever next crisis came along. The final section considers the relevance of the 2008–09 experience and its aftermath for the development of progressive responses to the current crisis – and, indeed, to the continuing and predictable general instability of capitalism. Rather than waiting for some final crisis that brings the system down, a pro-active and ambitious response needs to be readied: one that *pushes* the economic and political system towards transformative change. The major elements of such a response are identified and briefly discussed.

The GFC and the Great Recession

In 2008 and 2009, the world economy slipped into a crisis unlike any it had experienced before. The GFC had lasting and painful consequences: economic, political, even cultural. And it starkly exposed both the weaknesses, and the strengths, of the neoliberal order. Even compared to the escalating fluctuations of previous neoliberal downturns, the GFC was unique. The history of the GFC and its aftermath have been well documented and analyzed.[3] This section reviews the major features of that history, with a focus on how they left the advanced capitalist countries[4] in a weakened and fragile state.

The GFC began with a downturn in the US housing industry, and a subsequent meltdown in the highly leveraged and weakly regulated US mortgage lending industry. The US housing sector had expanded dramatically in previous years, fuelled by very low interest rates and lax lending by US banks and mortgage brokers. New construction boomed, and average housing prices across the US tripled between 1999 and 2006. Speculative pressures accentuated the inflation of property prices. But starting in 2006 and 2007, many US households (mostly lower-income families) defaulted on their mortgages. This was partly a consequence of unethical lending practices, including manipulative contracts and ultra-low-interest introductory rates (which were later ratcheted up to unaffordable levels). The securitization of mortgage loans allowed lenders to shift the risk of these fragile mortgages to unknowing investors. Credit rating agencies either ignored these risks, or in some cases participated in the deception (lured by rich commissions from bond issuers).

These defaults sparked a self-fulfilling collapse of the bubble in real estate prices (pulled down by a flood of foreclosures), causing huge

[3] Mirowski (2013) and Foroohar (2016) provide useful critical overviews.

[4] Of course, many developing countries were hit even harder; the empirical focus of this chapter, however, is on the industrialized countries of the OECD.

losses for holders of mortgage-linked securities bonds. Those losses then caused panic on several fronts: consumer and business lending dried up as banks conserved cash to protect against loan losses, the interbank lending system started to freeze up, and several banks and shadow banks collapsed. Financial regulators (led by the US Federal Reserve) tried to save some crumbling firms. But in September 2008 the Federal Reserve allowed the collapse of Lehman Brothers (a major investment bank), and the full tidal wave of the GFC was unleashed. Panic spread rapidly to financial centres around the world, banks stopped lending and the credit money system decelerated rapidly. Banks in many countries collapsed in the following months: hardest hit were the US, the UK and the Eurozone. The IMF (2010) pegged the cumulative value of bank failures from 2008 to 2010 at $2.3 trillion.

The GFC spread further and faster than any previous downturn, transmitted via hyperactive and global financial linkages. The financial panic was also transmitted into the real economy (that is, affecting the production of actual goods and services not just financial valuations) through various channels: including a sharp downturn in construction,[5] reduced spending on business investment and consumer durables as banks cut back their lending, and a retrenchment of international trade. All OECD countries except Australia suffered a recession in 2009, and in most cases the decline of output and employment was steeper than any downturn since the 1930s. In fact, 2009 marked the first year since the end of World War II that total global GDP declined.

And where a typical recession lasts for a few quarters, followed by a rebound in GDP, the consequences of the GFC on output and employment lasted for years. The initial plunge in GDP was halted by mid-2009 in most places, thanks largely to aggressive government fiscal and monetary policy interventions. Once real GDP began growing again, it could be claimed that the economy was in 'recovery' (at least according to the narrow definition favoured by economists). But the rebound was slow, halting and incomplete. And the political and fiscal aftershocks of the crisis continued for years. The moniker 'Great Recession' was coined to describe this condition of continuing stagnation.

The fallout for government finances from the GFC was dramatic, for several reasons: the recession was very deep, recovery was very

[5] Baker (2018) shows residential construction activity fell by four percentage points of GDP in the US between 2006 and 2009, enough to single-handedly spark an economy-wide recession.

slow and many governments faced enormous extra costs to bail out private banks. Public debt grew rapidly, sparking a second chapter of the crisis in the Eurozone. Plunging investor confidence, speculative pressures in bond markets and the austere response of EU institutions to fiscal imbalanced in peripheral EU countries all combined to cause continuing, intermittent recession.

Monetary policy also changed dramatically after the GFC. Interest rates were quickly reduced to near-zero (normally considered their lower limit) in most countries. Some jurisdictions (including the ECB and the Bank of Japan) experimented with negative interest rates (on overnight holdings of commercial banks) in an effort to prod banks to lend more. Many central banks also invoked quantitative easing (QE), whereby central banks purchased financial assets (including government bonds, corporate bonds and equities, and others) with money they themselves created. The goal was to increase cash reserves of major financial agents (especially banks) in hopes they would lend that excess cash and thus stimulate spending. Central banks created over US$5 trillion in new money through QE from 2008 to 2013 (Ojeda-Sierra and Coulton 2020).[6] But the effectiveness of these unprecedented interventions was muted. Businesses and consumers remained pessimistic, and aggregate demand conditions remained weak; hence lower borrowing costs and greater availability of credit made produced only modest improvements in spending and growth. Even mainstream economists began to conclude[7] that fiscal spending (which more directly spurs spending, production and employment) was more effective than monetary easing in fighting the long post-GFC stagnation.

Staggering to the next crisis

This section reviews several key empirical indicators of the performance of OECD economies in the decade after the GFC, compared to its condition and momentum when the GFC hit. By virtually every measure, the leading capitalist economies had not fully recovered from the GFC even a decade later. Economic growth (and its key components) remained weaker through the whole decade after the GFC than during the decade

[6] For perspective, central banks created more than $6 trillion in additional new money through QE injections in just the first few months of the COVID-19 pandemic (Ojeda-Sierra and Coulton 2020).

[7] Surveyed by Stone (2020).

Figure 12.1: Average annual growth in real GDP, 1998–2018

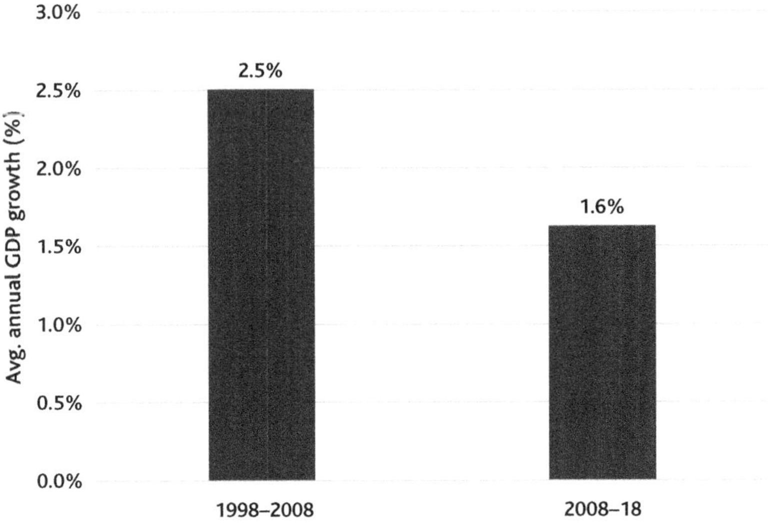

Source: Author's calculations from OECD Economic Outlook database

preceding it (see Figure 12.1). Government fiscal imbalances were larger, and monetary policy remained highly accommodative even a decade after the crisis – suggesting an erosion of the power of conventional macroeconomic stabilization policy. Continuing social and political stresses in most OECD countries, including growing inequality and alienation, and the rise of populist and authoritarian political movements, also attested to the failure to re-establish a stable political-economic regime. The leading capitalist countries were clearly in weaker shape to confront the next crisis – whenever and however it might arrive.

Real GDP across the OECD countries fell over 3 per cent in 2009, by far the biggest one-year drop since demobilization after World War II. Positive real GDP growth recommenced in 2010; but the rebound was slow and intermittent, held back by the aftershocks of the GFC. The Eurozone was particularly bedevilled by continuing financial instability and austerity. But even in other major economies, growth never regained pre-GFC norms.[8] Average annual growth in the OECD in the decade after 2008 was 1.6 per cent – over one third slower than

[8] And even the pre-GFC performance of the OECD economies was far weaker than gains in GDP, productivity and incomes recorded prior to the ascendancy of neoliberal policies in the 1980s.

the decade prior to the GFC, and the slowest sustained growth of the entire post-war era.

In a capitalist economy, private business capital accumulation is supposed to be the leading engine of growth. Yet a persistent slowdown in private capital investment has been a defining feature of the neoliberal era.[9] Gross fixed capital spending in OECD countries declined by about four percentage points of GDP from the 1970s to the 2000s; net fixed capital spending (after depreciation) fared even worse.[10]

But this sustained slowdown in business capital spending worsened dramatically after the GFC. As indicated in Figure 12.2, gross investment declined by over 4 points of GDP from the pre-crisis peak in 2007 to 2010. Only one quarter of that lost ground was regained in the subsequent decade. The post-GFC weakness of business capital spending reflects many factors, including continuing macroeconomic and financial uncertainty, the shift of capital spending towards emerging economies (especially China) and a structural shift towards sectors and business models (like digital and internet companies) with relatively smaller fixed capital requirements. In some OECD countries (including Japan), new investment has not even kept up with depreciation, so that the real net capital stock has actually declined. In several other countries, growth of the net capital stock has been slower than growth in employment, causing a surprising decline in the average capital intensity of production.[11]

Whatever its causes, the weakness of business capital spending has been a chronic drag on the macroeconomic performance of the advanced capitalist economies, and throws into question their traditional reliance on profit-seeking investment as the core engine of growth. Business profit margins, it should be noted, did recover strongly after the GFC – reaching post-war records as a share of GDP in some countries (including the US). So it is not a shortage of incentive or cash flow that explains weak capital spending. The combination of strong profitability with weak reinvestment fuelled excessive corporate

[9] See Stanford (2020a) for a more comprehensive review of the dimensions and consequences of weak business capital investment.

[10] Depreciation charges have become relatively larger, in part due to the shift towards more technologically sophisticated machinery and equipment (which depreciates more quickly).

[11] This unexpected decline in capital intensity, which contradicts the common narrative about accelerating technological change and workers being 'replaced' by machines, is explored further in Stanford (2020b).

Figure 12.2: Gross fixed capital spending as share of GDP, 2000–18

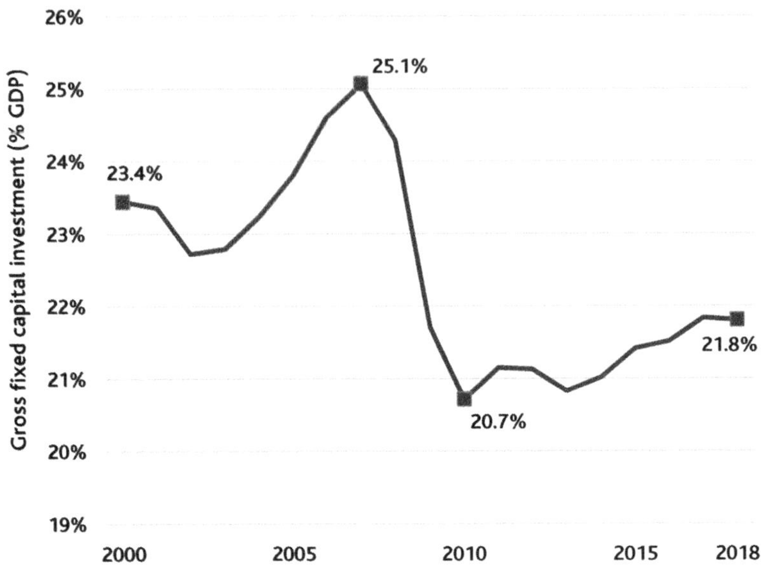

Note: Unweighted average of 35 countries (data unavailable for Chile and Turkey)

Source: Author's calculations from OECD National Accounts Database

saving, retained earnings and payouts to shareholders (in dividends and share buybacks) that further undermined macroeconomic momentum.

In the neoliberal vision of globalization, international trade is supposed to constitute another leading source of private sector growth. Opening up global markets for more trade (in goods and services) and foreign investment is claimed to facilitate mutual gains in efficiency and incomes, and spur growth and innovation. But a marked and sustained slowdown in global trade flows occurred after the GFC. Real exports of goods and services from OECD countries fell by 11 per cent in 2009, rebounding the following year. In subsequent years the expansion of exports remained far more modest than in the years preceding the GFC.

Figure 12.3 illustrates average annual growth in the real value of exports before and after the GFC. Prior to the GFC, trade had been growing at a robust annual rate of over 5 per cent per year – much faster than the expansion of output. This growth decelerated by over 2 percentage points after the GFC. Trade still grew faster than GDP (which was even more stagnant), but this growth in trade was muted compared to the pre-crisis period. Various factors held back the growth of exports, including rising protectionism and uncertainty in

Figure 12.3: Average annual growth in real exports of goods and services, 1998–2018

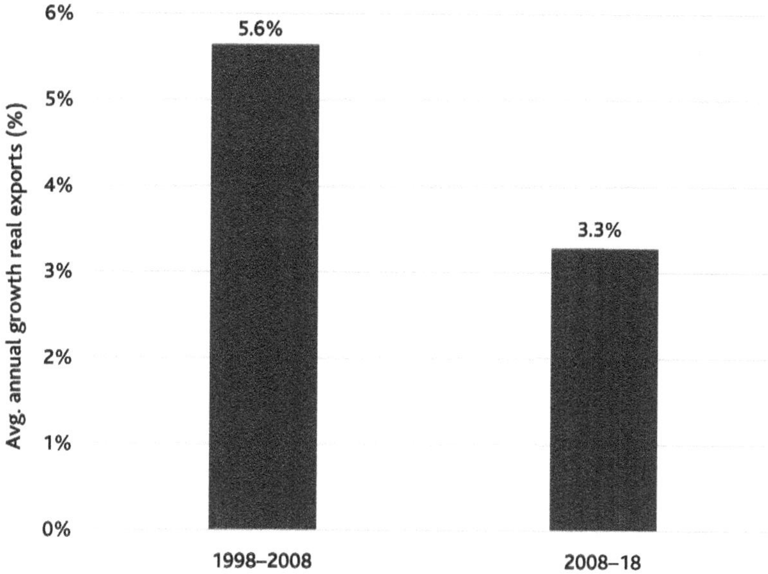

Source: Author's calculations from OECD Economic Outlook database

trade policy (especially after the election of Donald Trump), weak aggregate demand in most countries and uncertainty from the European debt crisis.

Again, whatever its specific causes, the slowdown in trade after the GFC negated another core claim of neoliberal economic governance: namely that ongoing liberalization of trade and capital flows would accelerate growth and generate mutual gains in efficiency and prosperity. Neither profit-led business investment nor the continued expansion of globalization could seem to solve the OECD's lasting post-crisis stagnation.

Surprisingly, one dimension of the real economy which seemed to recover more completely after the GFC was unemployment (see Figure 12.4). The unemployment rate spiked across the OECD after the GFC, reaching an average of 8.5 per cent in 2010 (up from 6 per cent in 2008). Unemployment remained above 8 per cent through 2013, including the worst years of European financial instability, but then began to decline steadily. By 2019, average unemployment in the OECD zone fell to 5.4 per cent – somewhat lower than it had been in 2008, and lower still than at the turn of the century (before the dot-com crisis and 2001 recession).

Figure 12.4: Average unemployment rate, OECD countries, 2000–19

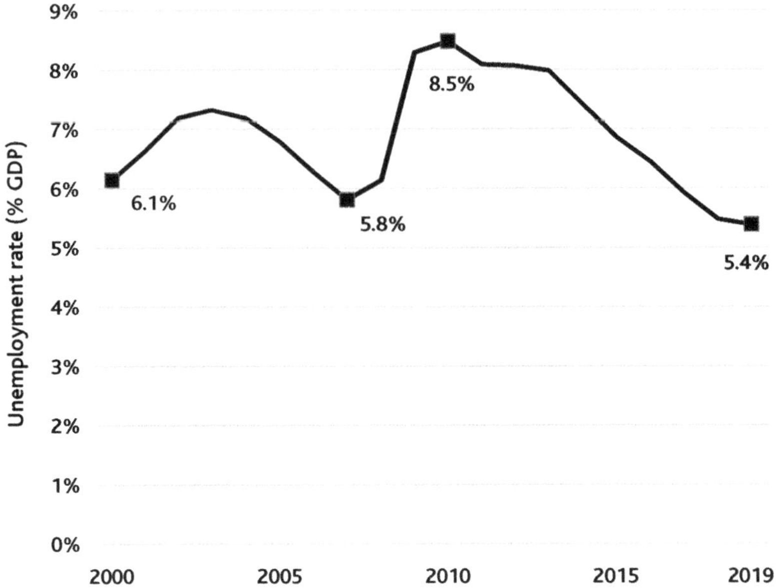

Source: OECD Economic Outlook database

However, this decline in official unemployment did not reflect any acceleration in real economic growth, nor was it the result of strong job-creation. As indicated earlier, GDP growth remained sluggish for a decade after the GFC. Job creation was also weak: total employment grew just 0.9 per cent per year after 2008 (and even slower for full-time positions). That compares poorly to average annual employment growth of 1.6 per cent across the OECD in the decade prior to the GFC. However, despite slow job creation, labour markets 'tightened' (by official measures, anyway) due to demographic changes. With a growing proportion of adults reaching retirement age, labour supply was suppressed, and hence formal unemployment measures declined despite generally weak employment growth.

Another important labour market trend since the GFC has been the expansion of non-standard or precarious employment arrangements, facilitated by the flexibilization of employment laws and regulations in most jurisdictions (Weil 2014). The expansion of part-time, irregular and 'gig'-style employment may boost the total number of new jobs, but the income and benefits associated with those non-standard roles is typically inferior. And the precarious nature of these new employment relationships meant that jobs could disappear more quickly and seamlessly when business conditions became unfavourable – as occurred in the COVID-19 pandemic.

The weakness of macroeconomic conditions across the OECD forced macroeconomic policy to remain strongly stimulative for most of the decade after the GFC. This is especially evident with respect to monetary policy and interest rates. The remarkable decline in interest rates after the GFC is illustrated in Figure 12.5, which shows policy rates for the four largest OECD central banks. Even a decade after the 2008 shock, nominal interest rates were still negative in the Eurozone and Japan, and under 1 per cent in the UK. Only the US central bank succeeded in imposing even moderate tightening on interest rates, as the American 'recovery' gained some momentum late in the decade – with rates there eventually rising to 2.5 per cent.

As discussed earlier, central banks supplemented low interest rates (which lost stimulative power, being at or near their effective lower bound) with massive QE injections. Figure 12.6 illustrates the near-monotonic growth in central bank balance sheets, which swelled over the decade to pay for continued QE programmes. In theory, central bank asset purchases were supposed to be 'unwound' once the economy regained its footing and inflation began to pick up. By selling back

Figure 12.5: Central bank interest rates, 2005–19

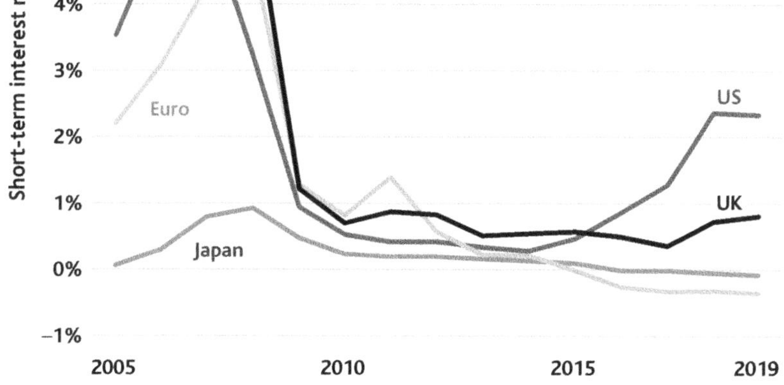

Source: OECD Economic Outlook Dataset

Figure 12.6: Balance sheets, six central banks, 2004–18

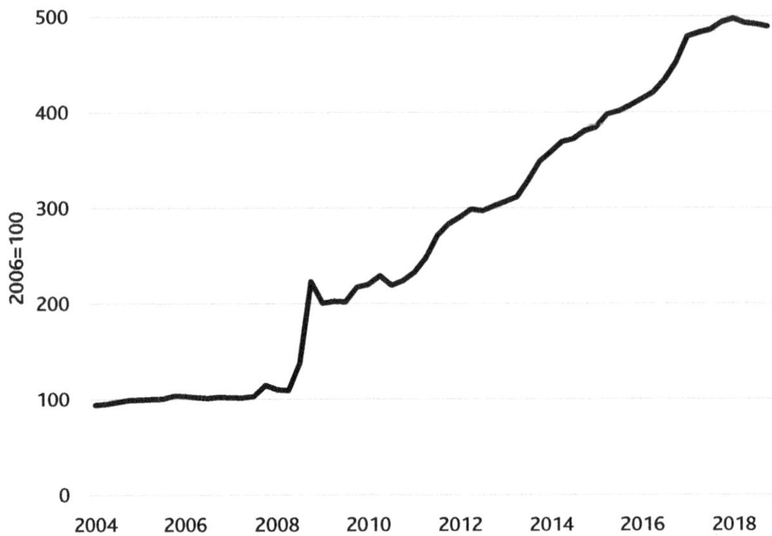

Source: Bank of International Settlements (2019). Includes US Fed, ECB, Bank of Japan, Bank of England, Swiss National Bank and Sveriges Riksbank.

assets they had purchased earlier (with created money), central banks could reduce cash holdings in the economy and prevent excess demand from pushing up inflation. As time went on, however, it was clear the macroeconomic system remained too fragile for any such reversal.

After doubling in the initial months of the GFC, central bank balance sheets doubled again by end-2015. They kept growing until 2018, when most QE programmes were suspended (but not significantly reversed). The need for seemingly permanent support from central banks for credit-creation attests to the continuing fragility of financial and demand conditions. Of course, much larger QE interventions started up again in 2020 (this time including central banks which had sat out the initial trend to QE, like Canada and Australia) with the COVID-19 pandemic.

Fiscal policy also revealed continuing macroeconomic weakness throughout the decade. Most OECD countries entered the GFC with relatively modest deficits – usually below the 3 per cent of GDP criteria established by the now-abandoned Maastricht criteria of the EU. That was consistent with broad stability in public debt (measured as a share of GDP). After all, modest continuing deficits can be offset by ongoing GDP growth, with little impact on the debt share of GDP. With the onset of the GFC, deficits increased rapidly, reaching more than 8 per cent of GDP across the OECD in 2009 and 2010 (Figure 12.7).

Figure 12.7: Government deficits as share of GDP, 2005–19

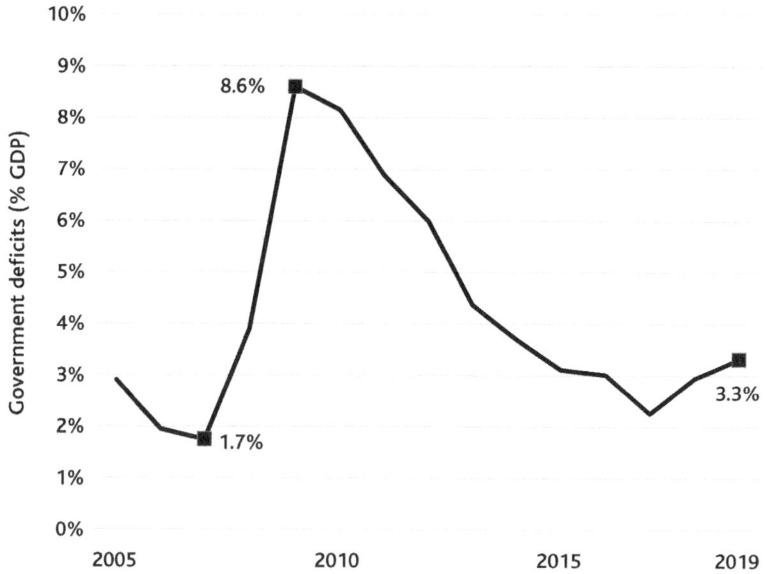

Source: OECD Economic Outlook database

Movement towards fiscal balance after the trough of the crisis was slow and painful – particularly in the Eurozone, where fiscal policy in several smaller, more fragile economies (especially Portugal, Italy, Ireland, Greece and Spain) was handcuffed by the absence of a national currency and by increasingly stringent restructuring edicts from the EU. Average OECD government deficits did not reach 3 per cent of GDP until 2017 – but even within Europe, the significance of that threshold had long-since evaporated, given the effective collapse of the Maastricht criteria. Average OECD deficits then began increasing again after 2017, even before the COVID-19 pandemic – led by huge US deficits caused by the Trump tax cuts. That the advanced capitalist countries remained so dependent on continual fiscal injections, even at the 'peak' of a decade-long recovery, is another startling indicator of the fragility of macroeconomic conditions across the advanced capitalist world.

It must be noted that the mere presence of large deficits does not, in and of itself, imply that fiscal policy was necessarily 'stimulative'. In several countries, especially the Eurozone and the UK, fiscal policy became very austere once the immediate GFC had passed. Governments cut spending for many public and social programmes, invoking the need to reduce deficits. The peripheral economies in the Eurozone suffered most dramatically from austerity. Greece experienced a huge decline in output, employment and incomes, driven down by strong austerity measures imposed by the EU and its 'Troika' partners (the IMF and the ECB) as conditions of emergency financial support. Greece experienced contracting GDP in eight of the nine years following the initial GFC, and GDP shrank by a cumulative 27 per cent to 2017. Portugal, Spain and Italy also experienced repeated years of economic contraction.

Despite spending cuts, deficits remained substantial throughout the OECD economies, and the accumulated level of public debt continued to grow. By weakening aggregate demand and stalling recovery, austerity actually prolonged recession in many countries – in turn reinforcing the weakness in public finances. As indicated in Figure 12.8, accumulated gross public debt across the OECD jumped by about 40 percentage points of total GDP in the five years after the crisis: from just over 70 per cent of GDP to around 110 per cent of GDP by 2013. It then stayed at that elevated level, with hardly any reversal even in the latter years of the 'recovery'. Continued deficits and the sluggishness of macroeconomic recovery ensured that the rise in public debt (like the fall in interest rates) was a 'one-way street'.

As a share of GDP, accumulated gross public debt in 2019 exceeded 100 per cent in five of the G7 economies. As indicated in Figure 12.9, Japan had by far the largest accumulated debt burden, equal to 225 per cent of GDP: the legacy of decades of sputtering recovery from that country's 'lost decade' recession in the 1990s. Japan's huge debt accumulation has been supported by ongoing QE by the Bank of Japan; this ensured the growing debt remained mostly domestically owned, financed (and refinanced) with virtually no interest costs. Proponents of austerity warn that large public debt will cause future financial instability or even national bankruptcy, but these fears are overblown: national governments (especially in countries with a national currency) can sustain large debts indefinitely.[12] Nevertheless, the continuing dependence of advanced capitalist on continuing fiscal injections, and the inability of governments in most jurisdictions to

[12] Radical, post-Keynesian and other heterodox traditions in economics have long recognized that real productive capacity, not 'money' or deficits, poses the ultimate constraint on output and employment. Recent public discussion on this point has also been spurred by proponents of 'Modern Monetary Theory' (for example Kelton 2020). However, the broader heterodox critique of balanced-budget fiscal policies and the falsity of neoliberal concepts of 'scarcity' is older and more general than MMT critiques.

Figure 12.8: Accumulated gross debt, 2005–19

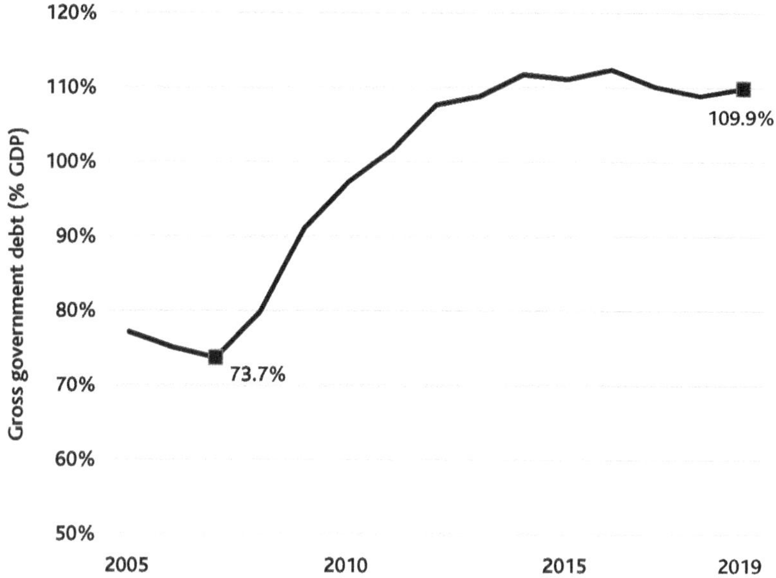

Source: OECD Economic Outlook database

Figure 12.9: Gross public debt, G7 economies, 2019

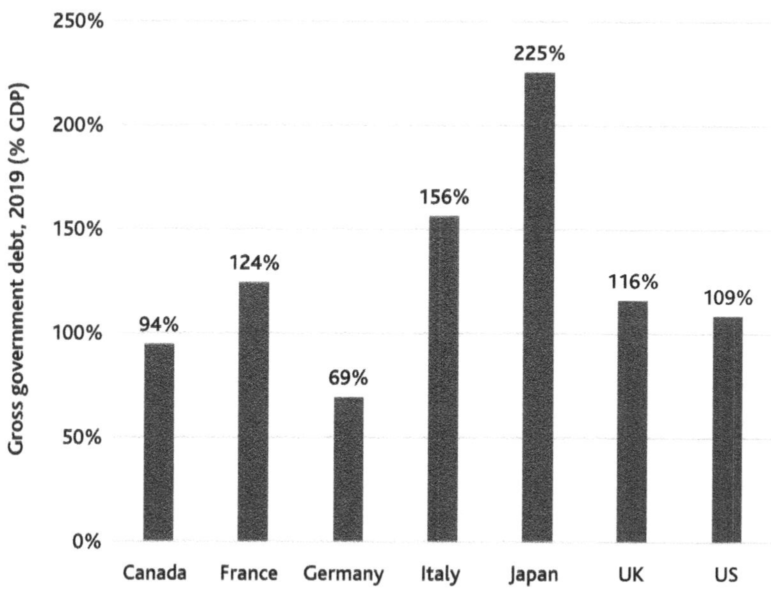

Source: OECD Economic Outlook database

collect sufficient revenues to cover public programme expenses – even at the 'peak' of a long 'recovery' – are telling signs of the loss of underlying dynamism of the overall system.

In sum, the OECD economies were in an obviously weakened state a full decade after the unprecedented events of the GFC. Growth was weak. The traditional drivers of capitalist expansion – business capital accumulation and globalization – were sputtering. Labour markets remained underutilized – and official unemployment rates did not tell the full extent of that underutilization. The overall macroeconomy was addicted to continual support from monetary and fiscal policy. But the efficacy of this support (particularly via low interest rates) waned as stagnation endured.

Given the history of capitalism in the neoliberal era, it was a foregone conclusion that another crisis would soon arrive. But the OECD economies were obviously not well-prepared for it. And while the onset of another crisis was no surprise, the nature, speed and severity of that next crisis certainly was.

The response next time: learning the lessons from the GFC

Despite the mass suffering and dislocation which the GFC caused, and its obvious connection to neoliberal policies and structures, progressive movements in most countries were not ready with a forceful, coherent and convincing set of alternative policies. This is one reason why neoliberalism managed to quickly recapture political leadership. This was ironic, given that the GFC was obviously facilitated by the financialization, deregulation and inequality that neoliberalism itself produced. To be sure, some popular resistance broke out against the worst effects of the crisis. The early days of the GFC featured often spontaneous public protests against bankers and speculators (like the global 'Occupy' movement). Strong campaigns against austerity were mounted, even achieving electoral realignments in some countries (such as Greece and Spain). But in general, progressive movements were caught flat-footed by the GFC, and have been on the political defensive since. Hence, despite a weak and incomplete economic recovery, in political terms neoliberalism has been perversely strengthened. Enduring underemployment, lost incomes and declining public services have not translated into sufficiently powerful movements for progressive change. More often, the GFC seems to have spawned right-wing populist, racist and authoritarian sentiments – even among those who suffered from its effects the worst.

In economic terms, global capitalism enters this next crisis in a weakened state, and this is another factor which should shape progressive responses to the next crisis. The structural drivers of capitalist expansion – in particular, business capital spending – have been underperforming for many years. That puts even more onus on pro-active interventions from government to support spending and spur recovery. But conventional stabilization levers are themselves exhausted from more or less continual engagement over the last decade; the usual tools of 'stimulus' will be ineffective after this overuse. In that light, there is both a need and an opportunity for progressives to advance more powerful, transformative responses to this latest, deeper crisis.

In designing progressive strategies for responding to the frightening times ahead, there are several key lessons from the economic and political aftermath of the GFC that should be contemplated:

- *Neoliberalism will not collapse of its own accord.* Some progressives hoped the economic chaos of the GFC would be enough to decisively and permanently destroy its credibility, legitimacy and power.[13] Without a consistent and coherent narrative to explain systemic failure, and without consistent and powerful movements to demand transformative change, progressive responses have been fragmented and dissipated. Grass-roots anger was channelled into populist and authoritarian directions. Progressives need a compelling analysis of what's gone wrong in the economy, an ambitious, consistent vision of how to fix it – and then powerful movements to win those changes.
- *Governments are not constrained by money.* After years of justifying austerity on grounds of fiscal constraints, governments opened the fiscal taps after the GFC to save banks, stabilize financial markets and support limited macroeconomic recovery. The resulting deficits were unprecedented in the post-war era – only to be quickly surpassed (by an order of magnitude) during the COVID-19 pandemic. So long as the mechanisms of credit creation remain subject to national authority, and countries retain their own currencies and central

[13] Australia's then Prime Minister Kevin Rudd (2009) wrote a now-infamous essay celebrating the assumed collapse of the neoliberal order, that stands as one of the more triumphalist (and premature) of these views. Harvey (2009) took the opposite view, arguing that the class project represented by neoliberalism would outlast the GFC, unless it was defeated politically.

banks,[14] there is no financial constraint on government actions. The productive capacity of the economy, which in turn depends first and foremost on our collective capacity to work, is the only ultimate constraint on what governments can do.

- *The private banking system is privileged and protected, yet unstable.* Many conservative critics dislike QE on the grounds that it is akin to governments 'creating money'. Yet that is exactly what private banks do every day they are open for business. And one unintended consequence of the GFC has been a belated recognition of the unique powers of the private banking system to create money, whenever it issues new loans. Contrary to outdated fables about 'fractional reserve' banking (a system that no longer exists), it is more widely understood that private banks (and quasi-banks) literally create money out of thin air through their own lending activity.[15] This power is central to their profitability and influence, but it also explains their continuing instability. Even after the modest tightening of prudential regulations after the GFC (through national and international reforms, including the Basel process), private banks have no 'real money' underpinning the vast majority of their total outstanding loans. They thus remain inherently vulnerable to future shocks in confidence. This helps explain the continuing volatility of financialized neoliberal economies. It also opens the door to more fundamental critiques of private banking, and to developing proposals to socialize credit-creation in the interests of job creation, well-being and sustainability (through public or social ownership of banks and other reforms[16]).

The need for a broader, comprehensive counter-vision is especially apparent in the wake of the COVID-19 pandemic and recession. So we conclude by considering some of the possible elements of such a comprehensive alternative. This list is informed by our analysis of the reasons for the failure of the advanced capitalist economies to recover

---

14 Sub-national governments and countries which use a supranational currency (like the Euro) do not have the same flexibility; this is a problem that was not adequately contemplated by countries that joined the Eurozone.

15 A refreshingly blunt acknowledgement of this reality was provided in the wake of the GFC by the Bank of England: 'Whenever a bank makes a new loan, it simultaneously creates a matching deposit in the borrower's bank account, thereby creating new money' (McLeay et al 2014, 14).

16 See Dutt (2017) and Stanford (2015, Chapter 29) for further discussion of these alternative models of credit and finance.

from the GFC – a failure which now pales in comparison to the much deeper crisis arising from COVID-19. This failure confirms that the challenge of economic reconstruction must go far beyond cyclical stabilization.[17] Given these deeper structural failings and vulnerabilities of the neoliberal order, we need a more transformative vision, that should include the following themes:

1. *Re-establish full employment as the over-arching economic goal.* The internal logic of austerity falls apart whenever there are large numbers of people un- or underemployed: the claim that 'we can't afford it' disappears when employing more people would *allow* us to 'afford it'. By creating opportunities for unemployed people to work, produce, generate incomes and pay taxes, new resources are generated which can then be allocated to the full range of economic, social and environmental priorities. The failure of neoliberal policies to employ all willing and able workers disproves traditional claims that unregulated markets are the best tools for allocating and employing productive resources. And it opens the door to a more fundamental challenge to the profit-led economy.
2. *Use public and social investment as an engine of sustainable growth.* Highlighting the failures of private business capital accumulation also informs and motivates a focus on developing alternative forms of investment. A progressive economic alternative need to specify alternative methods (beyond reliance on private business capital spending) for mobilizing resources, starting new ventures and creating new opportunities for work and production. Expanded government investment in physical infrastructure is now widely advocated by mainstream policy makers as a sensible response to recession, and this is useful as far as it goes.[18] But 'hard' capital projects like roads, transit and utilities do not address the deeper failure of profit-driven investment as the engine of broader economic growth. Therefore, a more comprehensive alternative vision of expanded public and social investment is needed. It would aim to expand the realm of public investment into other activities typically assigned to the private sector. Avenues for expanding the footprint of public and social investment could include housing,

[17] See Pennington and Stanford (2020) for discussion of why the COVID-19 pandemic demands more than a standard counter-cyclical response.

[18] See Wheatley (2020) for discussion of how even international financial institutions are now advocating more public investment.

human and caring services (discussed later), energy and utilities, and strategic or socially significant industries (like food, arts and media, manufacturing or transportation).

3. *Direct expansion of public sector work.* In past recessions and depressions, direct government job creation and make-work projects have been important in rebuilding employment. After the COVID-19 crisis, direct public sector jobs will need to play an even larger and more permanent role. At a structural level, demand for human and caring services in the OECD economies is growing: in part because these societies are ageing, and in part because demand for these services tends to rise with income (they are considered 'superior' goods, so a greater proportion of total income is devoted to them as income levels rise). Public sector hiring can be targeted at regions or communities that face especially challenging employment barriers (including racialized or immigrant workers, youth and less developed regions).
4. *Harness the power of credit for public and social good.* The private credit system creates purchasing power out of thin air through its lending activity – credit which is often used for useless or even destructive purposes (like inflating housing prices or fuelling financial speculation). Regulated, directed and even publicly owned credit vehicles should be mobilized to provide the purchasing power for more productive and beneficial priorities: including funding public investment, human and caring services, and the transformation of the energy system. Central banks already do this, in a narrow fashion, through their QE policies. But the power of public credit should be harnessed more broadly and permanently: underwriting subnational and municipal bonds (as well as national public debt), capitalizing public or sector-specific investment banks, the pro-active use of sovereign wealth and pension funds, and other strategies.
5. *Prioritize energy and climate transitions.* Preventing and adapting to climate change must now shape all economic policymaking. Therefore, investments in transforming the energy system, and making the most of the accelerating shift to renewable energy forms, must be a central element of the overall plan for economic reconstruction. There are enormous opportunities for new work associated with renewable energy developments, sustainable transportation, energy conservation and environmental remediation.
6. *Actively manage distribution to broadly share the gains of reconstruction.* The breakdown of the post-war social contract and falling living standards for masses of working people created fertile soil for the

> spread of populist and racist sentiments. A progressive plan to achieve full employment, driven by expanded public, social and environmental investments, can help to repair those fractures. But this strategy must also feature pro-active efforts to reshape the distribution of income and opportunity, and ensure that the economic gains from reconstruction and full employment are broadly shared. This must include measures to empower workers and unions, lift wages, open opportunity for traditionally marginalized groups and generally strengthen the regime of labour and social standards. Strong active labour market policies, including vocational training, higher education and adjustment programmes, will also help attain a fine balance between workers and jobs as the economy approaches full employment.

After the long, hard decade following the GFC, some examples of ambitious progressive visions which imagine the re-establishment of full employment, shaped by parallel commitments to social equality and sustainability, began to emerge from progressive movements in various countries. Even before COVID-19, American social movements resuscitated Roosevelt's vision of a New Deal from the 1930s, and modernized it to include environmental and social justice priorities in a so-called 'Green New Deal'.[19] Similar proposals have been advanced in other countries, including a European version proposed by the DiEM25 (2020) campaign, and one in Canada (MacArthur et al 2020). This call for full employment, social inclusion and sustainability will become all the more urgent in the wake of the health and economic catastrophes resulting from the pandemic. By learning from the GFC and the painful decade which followed it, progressive movements will hopefully be more successful in articulating and fighting for that ambitious but necessary vision.

References

Baker, Dean. 2018. *The Housing Bubble and the Great Recession: Ten Years Later.* Washington: Centre for Economic and Policy Research.

Bank for International Settlements. 2019. *Large Central Bank Balance Sheets and Market Functioning.* Basel: BIS, October.

[19] The original Green New Deal was described in a 2019 motion to the U.S. House of Representatives from Alexandra Ocasio-Cortes (2019), and echoed in proposals advanced by U.S. presidential candidate Bernie Sanders (2020).

Boyer, Robert. 2013. 'The Global Financial Crisis in Historical Perspective: An Economic Analysis Combining Minsky, Hayek, Fisher, Keynes and the Regulation Approach', *AEL: A Convivium*, 3: 93–139.

DiEM25. 2020. *European New Deal: A Comprehensive Economic & Social Policy Framework for Europe's Stabilisation, Sustainable Recovery and Democratization*. https://diem25.org/wp-content/uploads/2017/03/European-New-Deal-Complete-Policy-Paper.pdf

Duménil, Gérard and Dominique Lévy. 2011. *The Crisis of Neoliberalism*. Cambridge, MA: Harvard University Press.

Dutt, Devika. 2017. *Does Greater Public Ownership in the Financial System Promote Superior Performance?* Amherst: Political Economy Research Institute, University of Massachusetts.

Epstein, Gerry (ed). 2005. *Financialization and the World Economy*. Cheltenham and Northampton: Edward Elgar.

Foroohar, Rana. 2016. *Makers and Takers: How Wall Street Destroyed Main Street*. New York: Crown.

Glyn, Andrew. 2006. *Capitalism Unleashed: Finance, Globalization, and Welfare*. Oxford: Oxford University Press.

Harvey, David. 2009. 'Is This Really the End of Neoliberalism?', *Counterpunch*, 13 March.

International Monetary Fund. 2010. *Meeting New Challenges to Stability and Building a Safer System*. Global Financial Stability Report, April.

Kelton, Stephanie. 2020. *The Deficit Myth: Modern Monetary Theory and the Birth of the People's Economy*. New York: Public Affairs.

MacArthur, Julie L., Christina E. Hoicka, Heather Castleden, Runa Das and Jenny Lieu. 2020. 'Canada's Green New Deal: Forging the socio-political foundations of climate resilient infrastructure?', *Energy Research and Social Science*, 65: 101442.

McLeay, Michael, Amar Radia and Ryland Thomas. 2014. 'Money Creation in the Modern Economy', *Bank of England Quarterly Bulletin*, 2014(Q1): 14–27.

Mirowski, Philip. 2013. *Never Let a Serious Crisis Go to Waste: How Neoliberalism Survived the Financial Crisis*. London: Verso.

Ocasio-Cortes, Alexandra. 2019. *Recognizing the Duty of the Federal Government to Create a Green New Deal*. Resolution to the 116th Congress 1st Session. https://ocasio-cortez.house.gov/sites/ocasio-cortez.house.gov/files/Resolution%20on%20a%20Green%20New%20Deal.pdf

Pennington, Alison and Jim Stanford. 2020. 'Rebuilding After Covid-19 Will Need a Sustained National Reconstruction Plan', *Journal of Australian Political Economy*, 85: 164–74.

Robert Ojeda-Sierra, Robert and Brian Coulton. 2020. *Economics Dashboard: Central Bank Balance Sheets*. New York: Fitch Ratings.

Rudd, Kevin. 2009. 'The Global Financial Crisis', *Monthly*, 42: 20–9.

Sanders, Bernie. 2020. 'The Green New Deal'. https://berniesanders.com/issues/green-new-deal/

Sawyer, Malcolm. 2013. 'What Is Financialization?', *International Journal of Political Economy*, 42(4): 5–18.

Stanford, Jim. 2015. *Economics for Everyone: A Short Guide to the Economics of Capitalism*. London: Pluto Press.

Stanford, Jim. 2020a. 'Dimensions and Implications of the Slowdown in OECD Business Investment', in L-P. Rochon and H. Bougrine (eds) *Essays in Honour of Marc Lavoie and Mario Seccareccia*. Cheltenham: Edward Elgar, pp 261–83.

Stanford, Jim. 2020b. *The Robots are NOT Coming*. Canberra: Centre for Future Work.

Stone, Chad. 2020. *Fiscal Stimulus Needed to Fight Recessions: Lessons from the Great Recession*. Washington: Center on Budget and Policy Priorities. April.

Weil, David. 2014. *The Fissured Workplace: How Work Became So Bad for So Many and What Can be Done to Improve It*. Cambridge, MA: Harvard University Press.

Wheatley, Jonathan. 2020. 'Borrow to Fight Economic Impact of Pandemic, Says World Bank's Chief Economist', *Financial Times*, 8 October.

13

Austerity after COVID-19: from emergency pragmatism to inclusive economic governance in Europe

Hans-Jürgen Urban and Sebastian Kramer

Following the outbreak of COVID-19 in early 2020, the European Union is still in the midst of one of the biggest economic crises after World War II. While it is still too early to get a full picture of the economic impact of the lockdowns imposed in order to stop the spread of the virus, the immediate consequences are already quite severe. For 2020, the European Union expects its economy to shrink by 6.4 per cent (Eurostat 2021a). The EU-27 unemployment rate rose from 6.5 per cent in February 2020 before the crisis to 7.5 per cent in December 2020 (Eurostat 2021b). The most important reason why Europe has not seen an even more dramatic increase – especially when compared to the United States with a peak of over 40 million unemployed – is the widespread support of workers through short-time work programmes. At the end of April, businesses in the European Union had submitted roughly 42 million applications to support workers through short-time work programmes. That is equivalent to nearly 27 per cent of all EU employees (Müller and Schulten 2020a). Lockdowns and business closures have hit workers and welfare recipients especially hard, and they are the ones who will have the toughest time finding new jobs or compensating for lost income.

The immediate policy responses of many European countries have focused on a combination of bailout packages for businesses and different social policy measures to support workers and in some cases welfare recipients. In addition, the EU member states have agreed to set up a recovery fund of €750 billion, allowing the EU commission to take on a large amount of shared debt on financial markets and distributing half of the money via non-repayable grants and the other half in the form of loans. In the immediate aftermath of the COVID-19 crisis, most governments had to act as a 'lender of last resort' and drastically increased their short-term public spending. Consequently, according to the European Commission's Spring 2020 Economic Forecast, the euro area budget deficit is expected to increase to 8.5 per cent of GDP in 2020 from 0.6 per cent of GDP last year. The euro area aggregated debt-to-GDP ratio is expected to rise from 16.7 per cent in 2019 to a staggering 102.7 per cent in 2020, with large differences across countries. While only a few countries, such as Estonia or Luxembourg, are expected to stay below the 60 per cent benchmark, others, such as Spain or Italy, will likely end up with ratios well above 120 per cent (European Commission 2020).

The economic impact of the COVID-19 pandemic, herefore, has huge implications for fiscal and economic policies in the EU, at least in the short term. In March 2020, the European Commission announced the activation of the general escape clause of the SGP, in order to allow member states to depart from the strict budgetary requirements that would normally apply. A few days later, the German parliament passed a decision to suspend the 'debt brake', a constitutional rule requiring the federal government to keep its structural deficit below 0.35 per cent of GDP as well as permit German states to run any structural deficit at all. The SGP of the EU as well as the German 'debt brake' have been central institutions promoting austerity in Europe over the last couple of years. They are the pillars of a constitutionalized form of fiscal policy that is based on the assumption that voluntary deflation, which in the case of the EU is achieved by cutting public spending and reducing government debt, will stimulate growth and prosperity (Blyth 2013; Matthjis and Blyth 2015; Streeck 2017).

While the suspension of those fiscal mechanisms is certainly a remarkable decision, a temporary suspension should not be mistaken with a permanent change of the core institutional rules of austerity. It is rather a kind of 'emergency-pragmatism' by political elites with the aim of preventing an economic meltdown. In fact, the constitutional rules underlying the paradigm of austerity have been designed in such a way that short-term deviations in case of an economic crisis are permitted, while at the same time keeping the long-term commitments to austerity policies in place. Even though the EU as well as many national governments have increased their short-term public spending as a reaction to the current economic crisis, the institutional setting of European Economic Governance not only dictates a rapid return to austerity, it also hampers more radical and long-lasting policy changes.

Given the structural problems European economies are facing as well as the severity of the current economic crisis, short-term adjustments and one-time stimulus policies are increasingly insufficient. There is a huge misfit between the problem-solving capacities of the current institutional setting and the challenges that need to be addressed by the EU and its member states, such as rising levels of social inequality, the growing legitimacy problems of European Governance and first and foremost the indispensable social-ecological transformation of the European economy. Given such an obvious misfit, it is somewhat puzzling why we have not seen more radical policy changes in the field of European Economic Governance in recent years and how it is possible for austerity to persist despite its devastating social and economic effects.

The chapter aims at providing a theoretically grounded and empirically informed answer to this question and contributes to a debate about alternatives to austerity. Our arguments are based on those variants of International Political Economy in which theories of classical political economy, regulation theory and a historically actor-oriented institutionalism intersect (Scharpf 1997; Gill 1998; 2017; Bieling et al 2016). The regulation theory approach systematically reflects on the interplay between basic political-economic structures, regulatory institutions and corresponding political norms and cultures. It views itself as a social-economic theory of overall social development and is based on the assumption that capitalist economies are, structurally speaking, crisis-prone. This crisis potential becomes virulent on a dimension that goes above and beyond normal economic cycles when basic social-economic structures (accumulation regimes) and the system of institutional and normative forms of mediation regulating them no longer 'align'. The regulation model comprises the ensemble of social mediation of basic social-economic relations, but above all the totality of institutional structures and norms that provide the development model its stability. In order to avoid the danger of a functionally truncated understanding of the relationship between politics and the economy as well as a fixation on nation-state units, regulation theory concepts have been expanded to include fragments of theory borrowed from neogramscian International Political Economy (IPÖ). The notions of hegemony, historical bloc and passive revolution constitute three basic analytical categories in this tradition (Gill 1998; 2017; Cox and Schlechter 2002;). The concept of hegemony integrates class constellations, societal consensus structures as well as political and everyday cultures into the mechanisms of domination and control. The category of the 'transnational historical bloc' encompasses temporal constellations in which a relatively coherent interplay between civil society actors and discourses that transcends national spaces begins to emerge; and the theorem borrowed from 'passive revolution' analyses processes in these community spaces in which hegemonic states involve other states in relations of domination and dependence or promote transformations in their social structures for their own benefit 'from above' and 'from outside'.

This theoretical context highlights three key findings in the further debate: First, respective institutional settings upon whose foundations political practices, paradigms and strategies rest are on the one hand functionally related to the requirements dictated by the respective accumulation regime. On the other hand, these materialize institutional logics of their own, social power relations and social constellations of hegemony. At the same time, this means that socially desired transformations in the 'economic base' can hardly be realized without corresponding changes in the institutional regulatory system and thus require political reforms. Second, institutional changes, however, usually continue to have an impact over longer periods of time. All ideas aiming to transform institutional settings must bear in mind that change 'takes place in the long shadow cast by the past, in turn casting a long shadow into the future' (Schimank 2007, 170). Third, changes in institutional settings and changes in the trajectory of institutional developments are nevertheless possible. However, these usually take place under specific conditions (Baumgartner and Jones 1993; Pierson 2004; Baumgartner et al 2014; Blyth, Helgottir and Kring 2016). They are more likely to occur in acute crisis situations than in undisturbed phases of development, and above all: they require appropriate constellations of actors in which they are willing and able to push through changes in line with their own interests and preferences.

From this theoretical perspective, the formation and the possibilities of changing the institutional austerity regime in the EU must be analyzed in the context of the changes in the transnational accumulation regime that took place in the transition from national welfare state capitalism to global financial market capitalism. In the context of the New Economic Governance, actors in the arenas of nation-states lost political weight, while those in the spheres of global (financial) economy gained weight. As a reaction to the financial market crisis of 2008 and the efforts to stabilize the euro, 'disciplining neoliberalism' (Gill 2017, 638) increasingly took on the features of a 'post-democratic executive federalism' in order to channel the 'imperatives of the market to national budgets' (Habermas 2011, 81). The reduction of public expenditures in the course of imposed budgetary discipline as well as the deregulation of labour markets and flexibilization of labour to strengthen national competitiveness constituted the central pillars of EU policy (Schäfer and Streeck. 2012; McBride and Mitrea 2017; Urban 2018).

The process of European integration needs to be directed towards a fundamentally new path if the EU wants to surmount the economic, social and environmental problems it is facing. On the one hand, this necessity emanates from the legacy of the damage caused by the EU's austerity and structural adjustment policies. At the same time, it is indispensable, because the growth model prevailing in the EU is reaching its social and environmental limits and has become a real obstacle for sustainable prosperity. A partial correction, in the form of a neo- or post-Keynesian fiscal and demand policy, would not be sufficient. What is needed is a transition to a mode of economic governance that not only opens up scope to overcome austerity and structural reform policies, but which also offers a functional framework for the indispensable social-ecological transformation of the economy. A decarbonization of the European development model not only compels political intervention in the material dimension of economic value-creation, it also requires intervention in the control and decision-making structures of companies. If they are to have democratic legitimacy, this will have to mean democratizing the economy. Such an objective calls for inclusive economic governance, which, in overcoming the austerity regime, combines environmental, social as well as democratic policy objectives.

The remainder of this chapter is structured as follows: based on the premises of our institutional and regulation theoretical approach, we first argue that the European institutional structure represents an essential pillar of the European austerity regime, which acts as an obstacle towards a more inclusive economic governance in Europe (Section 2). With this in mind, we outline the contours of an institutional setting that could facilitate an alternative to the devastating social and ecological consequences of the current austerity regime (Section 3). Since the transition to an inclusive mode of economic governance presupposes the constitution of an actor with sufficient transformational power, our considerations conclude with a brief outlook at some of the works that deal with the demanding development of a corresponding European reform alliance (Section 4.)

The constitutionalization of austerity in Europe

Despite growing empirical evidence against the effectiveness of austerity with regard to its stated objectives (Blyth 2013) as well as a host of experiences with the devastating social and economic effects in those countries where it was imposed by the Troika (IMF, ECB and European Commission), austerity remains one of the central pillars of fiscal and economic policymaking in the EU. Understanding austerity in the context of the trend towards 'authoritarian neoliberalism' (Anderson 2012; Tansel 2016) reveals how austerity policies have become constitutionalized over time and thereby removed from the realm of public deliberation about appropriate economic policy goals and instruments (McBride 2016). Balanced budgets and low public debt ratios are no longer a matter of policy choice, but are instead constitutional requirements. The constitutionalization of austerity in Europe not only explains the surprising resilience of austerity over the last few decades, it also shows why it is so notoriously difficult to implement alternative fiscal and economic policies across Europe.

While austerity as an intellectual idea has been around for quite some time (Blyth 2013; on the importance of ideas and think tanks see Plehwe, Neujeffski and Krämer 2018), it was the Maastricht Treaty (MT) in 1993 that provided the first legal framework for the implementation of austerity policies in the EU. The MT set in place budgetary rules for member states with a target of 60 per cent of GDP as a maximum debt level and a maximum yearly budget deficit of no more than 3 per cent of GDP. In line with the general trend towards transferring political authority in the area of economic and fiscal policies from the national to the European level, the MT also provided some tools for enforcing those rules. The EC and the Economic and Financial Affairs Council (ECOFIN) monitored and evaluated the fiscal policies of member states and could even impose sanctions in the case of rule violations (McBride 2016).

The SGP extended the initial legal framework of the MT a few years later. The SGP enhanced the fiscal rules laid out in the MT. More specifically, it strengthened the monitoring and coordination of national fiscal and economic policies to enforce the deficit and debt limits established by the MT. After the 2005-reform, the SGP consists of a so-called 'preventive arm' defining country-specific medium-term budgetary objectives as well as a 'correcting arm' defining the concrete steps of the excessive deficit procedure for states not complying with the deficit and debt limits. While the SGP strengthened the existing fiscal rules, it did not implement a mechanism for automatic sanctions in case of rule violations (McBride 2016).

It was not until the introduction of the European Fiscal Compact in 2012 and the subsequent ratification of the agreement by most EU member states that austerity has become constitutionalized as a quasi-automatic policy with strict and enforceable compliance mechanisms (Bugaric, Bojan and Matjaz Nahtigal 2015). Under the Fiscal Compact, states must keep structural deficits to 0.5 per cent of GDP if their debt-to-GDP ratio is exceeding 60 per cent, and deficits must be kept to 1 per cent of GDP for states below the 60 per cent threshold. Additionally, the fiscal compact implements strict debt reduction procedures. Member states whose debt-to-GDP ratio exceeds the 60 per cent are required to reduce it at an average rate of 5 per cent per year. The most important part of the Fiscal Compact pertains to the so-called automatic correction mechanism. In case of a significant deviation from the budgetary objectives, the European Commission is allowed to open an Excessive Deficit Procedure (EDP), which requires states to detail necessary structural reforms to ensure a timely return towards a balanced budget. Although it is politically difficult to enforce, the Commission can even impose financial sanctions in case of repeated deviations in the form of interest bearing-deposits or a fine of up to 0.5 per cent of GDP (McBride 2016; Thygesen et al 2019).

While the Fiscal Compact is up until now not formally part of EU law, the treaty provisions are binding under International Law, and member states agreed to adopt the general principles into their national constitutions (Burret and Schnellenbach 2014). Thus, the substantial rules detailed in the Fiscal Compact as well as the provisions of the SGP are legally binding and ensure the perpetuation of austerity policies within the EU. Furthermore, the Fiscal Compact has been complemented by other reforms that provide the European Commission with a lot of leeway to monitor and evaluate the fiscal and economic policies of member states. Especially relevant in this context is the establishment of the European Semester in 2010, which has become the central framework for coordinating fiscal and economic policies between the EU and its member states (McBride 2016). It consists of three different pillars – budgetary surveillance, macroeconomic surveillance and socio-economic coordination – and combines a mix of non-binding processes as well as legally binding procedures. Based on the aforementioned legislative acts and treaties, the European Commission uses the European Semester in order to monitor and evaluate national budgets and force member states to comply with the budgetary rules. While there is no provision on what kinds of policies have to be implemented in order to reach the objective of a balanced budget, the Commission utilizes the European Semester to orient states towards the adoption of a neoliberal policy agenda, including structural reforms of labour markets, privatization and cutting of social expenditures (McBride and Mitrea 2017).

The constitutionlization of austerity in the EU over the last decades has created a dense network of different institutions not only promoting the idea of fiscal discipline and internal devaluation, but at the same time supporting a more general turn towards a neoliberal policy agenda. Economic governance in the EU is mainly geared towards two objectives – financial stability and competitiveness – with little regard for social as well as environmental concerns. The fact that austerity has become deeply constitutionalized within the EU over time and thus effectively shielded from public deliberation makes changes towards a more integrative mode of economic governance quite challenging. The recent countertrend of a rise in short-term public spending as a reaction to the economic aftermath of the COVID-19 pandemic is covered by the exceptional clauses within the existing institutional framework. It is an anticipated exception from the rule and not a departure from austerity. At present, it seems unlikely that the current crisis will lead to a reversal of constitutionalized austerity in Europe.

The politicization of austerity: towards social, sustainable and democratic economic governance

When constitutionalization has been the strategy for implementing austerity policies promoting a form of 'authoritarian neoliberalism' that effectively shields certain policies from public scrutiny, politicization is the strategy available to those actors promoting social, sustainable and democratic alternatives. In brief, 'politicization means making collectively binding decisions a matter or an object of public discussion' (Zürn et al 2012, 74). Whereas constitutonalization promotes a technocratic mode of decision-making behind closed doors, politicization is about public communication and contestation. For political actors interested in a more integrative form of European economic governance, which takes environmental, social and democratic concerns serious, politicization of austerity is the only available strategy for a substantive policy change. Research on the politicization of the EU at least shows that it can be quite effective under certain circumstances promoting substantial policy changes (Hartlapp et al 2014; Rauh 2019). For this to happen in the case of austerity, what is needed is a substantial public mobilization of demands for an alternative policy and a genuine effort of contestation of the existing institutional arrangements by a powerful coalition of actors.

It has not only been since the COVID-19 pandemic that critical analyses insisting on the dysfunctionality and need for reform of the EU fiscal regime's austerity-policy rule have become increasingly frequent (for example Pescatori, Leigh and Guajardo 2011; EuroMemo Group 2019 and 2020; Scharpf 2019; Blanchard et al 2020, Dullien et al 2020). If the EU wants to make prospects for a stable future a possibility for itself, however, more is needed than merely overcoming the governance of austerity policy and a crisis of growth as a result of external shocks (financial market crisis 2018 and after, COVID-19 pandemic). The entire socio-economic development model of the EU and its member states has manoeuvred itself into an 'economic-ecological pincer crisis' (Dörre 2019). Above all, the current type of growth, once a central factor in defusing economic problems and social distribution conflicts, has mutated from a problem-solver to a problem-driver. On the one hand, the societies of developed capitalism are suffering structural growth weaknesses and declining growth in productivity, which is associated with old and new problems in economic cycles, on labour markets and, not least, in the financing of government expenditures on infrastructure. On the other hand, the resource- and emission-intensive mode of economic growth is exacerbating the situation and increasingly jeopardizing the reproductive capacity of global ecosystems. And under the aegis of the austerity regime, this is at the same time promoting social division by causing unemployment and social precariousness while, also, avoiding any exploitation of major wealth and corporate profits to finance the necessary countermeasures. Contemporary European capitalism (and not only this brand of capitalism) is thus suffering at once from too little and too much growth.

Under status quo conditions, traditional, Keynesian-inspired strategies for stimulating growth cannot lead the way out of the crisis, but rather are propelling societies deeper into it. But a general departure from any kind of growth, as is called for by the different variants along the de-growth spectrum, would also be a short-sighted answer.[1] They overlook the fact that contemporary societies are not only societies of plenty but also societies beset with deficits. Environmentally harmful production of luxury on the one hand, underinvestment in social security, health and care, education and culture, as well as the mobility of people and goods on the other. Rectification of these deficits still requires the material production of goods and social services. It requires the creation of economic value, which must be redistributed through public investment in public goods and infrastructure.

A development model would therefore be expedient in which the economy is not subject to the dictates of capitalist accumulation, and can instead be oriented towards socially and ecologically sustainability goals. A socially and environmentally responsible growth model differs fundamentally from the current one (Galbraith 2014). Growth would

[1] For scenarios under discussion in the debate critical of growth, see Victor 2012.

probably be flatter, since it would not be promoted at the expense of all other objectives, but only when societal benefits can be expected; it would be more sustainable, since it would accept the constraints of nature as a constraint on growth; and it would have to be more equitable, since it would not force losers in processes of structural change into unemployment or poverty, but would open up new prospects for them by means of social investments. Such a balanced, controlled and democratized growth model would be at the core of an alternative economic system that can be described as a type of ecological-social economic democracy (see, for example, Urban 2018; 2019a, 183). Its realization requires fundamental corrections in production and distribution relations and hence far-reaching political interventions in various policy fields (see, for example, Hyman 2013). At the same time, it would presuppose transformation of the institutional structures of economic governance.

This involves an inclusive reform project that does not stop at merely overcoming the austerity regime, but rather seeks to drive the transformation process in the direction of a social-ecological development model. The formulation of such an inclusive reform project without a doubt constitutes a mega-project. Critical social science could and should contribute analysis, evidence-based findings and an impetus for discourse. It is with this in mind that we sketch out some essential economic, social and environmental policies that could be the starting point of collective work on such a project. Whereas the current model of economic governance in the EU narrowly focuses on competitiveness and financial stability, integrative economic governance takes the overall interests of the general public into account and includes social, environmental as well as democratic policy objectives.

First, it would undoubtedly be crucial to overcome the deficits in EU fiscal rules and economic governance. Key reforms of institutional fiscal rules and the procedure for avoiding macroeconomic imbalances have been outlined by economists close to the trade union movement. The guiding principle is a:

> reform focused on appropriate fiscal rules that promote short-term macroeconomic stabilisation and the long-term modernisation of the public capital stock, while still keeping the sustainability of public debt in mind. We propose an expenditure rule for non-investment expenditure that takes the sustainability of public debt into account [...], coupled with a Golden Rule for public investment [...] A reform of the Macroeconomic Imbalance Procedure (MIP) is equally

> important. A key element of such a reform would be the establishment of a Macroeconomic Dialogue for the euro area as a whole and in the individual member states, in order to ensure compliance with the reformed rules and consistency of the national strategies. (Dullien et al 2020, 3)

Additionally, instead of cutting wages, public investments and social benefits, the EU should commit to a more progressive and coordinated tax policy. Among other things, this would include a reform of the corporate tax system, increasing taxes on wealth, financial transactions and high incomes as well as a serious effort to shut down tax havens and eliminating tax loopholes.

Second, an active fiscal policy outfitted with new leeway for public investments must go hand in hand with the transformation of the material basis of the European value-added chain. A point of reference can be the 'Green Deal', which the EU Commission has presented as a core project for the coming years. It spells out an ambitious goal:

> It is a new growth strategy that aims to transform the EU into a fair and prosperous society, with a modern, resource-efficient and competitive economy where there are no net emissions of greenhouse gases in 2050 and where economic growth is decoupled from resource use. It also aims to protect, conserve and enhance the EU's natural capital, and protect the health and well-being of citizens from environment-related risks and impacts. At the same time, this transition must be just and inclusive. (European Commission 2019, 2)

The general ambition of ecological transformation is translated into individual measures in various policy fields, such as industrial, environmental or transport policies. At the same time, the Green Deal is to be integrated into macroeconomic coordination:

> As part of the Green Deal, the Commission will refocus the European Semester process of macroeconomic coordination to integrate the United Nations' sustainable development goals, to put sustainability and the well-being of citizens at the centre of economic policy, and the sustainable development goals at the heart of the EU's policymaking and action. (European Commission 2019, 3)

The EU's Green Deal has been criticized for being not ambitious enough in terms of its potential for a decarbonization of the economy and for remaining stuck in the paradigm of economic growth and market competition:

> The proposed amounts of funding are limited, subject to political agreement with member states and overemphasize private sector contributions. The policies for securing a fair transition, leaving no one behind, remain vague. The international dimension remains stuck in a competitiveness paradigm and prioritizes the EU's interest in securing free access to raw materials at the expense of concrete proposals for fostering international cooperation. Ultimately, a longer-term process of socioecological transformation will eventually have to overcome the expansionist dynamics of capitalism. (EuroMemo Groupe 2020, 2)

While the Green Deal has its obvious shortcomings and will not lead to a substantive social-ecological transformation, it nevertheless signals the willingness of the European Commission for incremental changes in the field of environmental and economic governance. Actors interested in a more radical transformation may find at least some point of reference for debates about further policy changes.

Third, initiatives to transform the economic structures in terms of its material basis are key. But without moving beyond the constraints imposed by the austerity regime, ecological transformation will lack an important social dimension. The reform of fiscal rules outlined earlier would also create new scope for national and European social policy. To be able to leverage this, however, Europe would have to free itself from the 'progressive regression' it has been going through for decades (Streeck 2018). Under the pressure of competition from different models of capitalism and consolidation policies within the framework of European austerity, European social policy has mutated into an instrument with which to open new markets and enhance competitiveness by any means necessary. Its strategic orientation has not been characterized by corrective regulation of national markets and the EU single market or de-commodification of labour by hedging market risks, but rather by the opening of the market along the lines of the 'four freedoms' of the single market (free movement of goods, labour, capital and services). EU social policy has been put at the yoke of structural adjustments of labour markets, wage-setting models and social-protection systems ('structural reforms') imposed by the policy of budgetary consolidation in general, and Troika conditions in the so-called 'programme countries' in the wake of the financial crisis. This all resulted not only in cuts in public social spending, but also deregulation of labour markets and increased flexibility of labour. The focus of social policy on the 'social investment paradigm' (European Commission 2013) complemented this set of policy priorities (for a critical view of this, see EuroMemo Groupe 2020, 19). Throughout implementation of this course, the labour market and social policy lost their ability to counteract social poverty, precarious work and unemployment.

In its 2020 memorandum, the EuroMemo Groupe proposed a number of measures to move social policy away from this orientation and to link the Green Deal project with social protection policies. One measure in the fight against unemployment and social poverty:

> is the job guarantee, to cover social needs and provide useful jobs, defined locally and collectively. The central principle [...] is that of the state as the 'employer of last resort'; where the central state or local authorities pledge to provide employment for all those who are prepared to work at the basic public sector wage rate (and possibly above that rate, depending on the qualifications required for the jobs offered). (EuroMemo Groupe 2020, 20)

A Europe-wide minimum wage can be an additional element on the way towards a more integrative economic governance. In January 2020, the European Commission published a consultation document with a view to taking legislative action to establish fair minimum wages in Europe (Müller and Schulten 2020b). The point of departure is a patchwork of different institutional and normative rules for wage determination and the safeguarding of minimum wage levels in the EU member states. This heterogeneous starting position has repeatedly been seen as an obstacle to the coordination of trade union wage policies and institutional harmonization (Höppner and Lutter 2018). Addressing this challenge, a new proposal has been put forward that is based on a:

> pragmatic approach [...] of taking the 'in-work-poverty-wage' threshold of 60 per cent of the national full-time gross median wage as the reference to assess the adequacy of minimum wages. In countries, in which a high proportion of workers earn very low wages, the whole wage structure, and therefore the median wage, is very low; therefore, a

> minimum wage of 60 percent of the national median wage may still not be enough to ensure a decent living standard. (Müller and Schulten 2020b, 1) The limits and minimum levels thus specified constitute an attempt to find a viable solution in the institutional and cultural jungle of individual national regulations.

Finally and without a doubt, the most extensive need for politico-economic and sociological research is with regard to the democratization of economic governance, in particular at the European level. Eric O. Wright's understanding of the core structures of different economic systems 'as [a] way of organizing the power relations through which economic resources are allocated, controlled and used' (Wright 2009, 72) offers an analytical approach to the topic of economic democracy. A democratic model of economic activity is thus based on 'conditions in which social power, organised through the active participation and empowerment of ordinary people in civil society, exerts direct and indirect democratic control over the economy' (Wright 2009, 92). The central challenge facing a social-ecological brand of economic democracy is to achieve economic efficiency, environmental sustainability and democratic legitimacy at the same time. To achieve this, the economy must be transformed into a field with a new constellation of actors, rules and institutions. In this field, economic entities are confronted with new incentive structures, options for action and sanction rules. The aim would be to empower society (and democratically legitimized politics) vis-à-vis the economy. This empowerment implies a socialization of central production and distribution decisions and would require institutionally secured channels of influence, without which the linkage of economic value creation to the needs of society and nature cannot be ensured. Here it might prove useful to recall, for example, trade union demands for intervention in the capitalist system of property and for the establishment of economic and social advisory councils. As institutions for the democratization of the economy, these need to be endowed with robust rights and competences and participate as actors in regional economic and structural planning processes. With regard to ownership structures and allocation mechanisms, a social and ecological economic democracy would need to be conceived as a new model of a 'mixed economy'. Its basis would consist of a combination of private, public/state and cooperative ownership. Learning from the experience of failed bureaucratic state planning economies offers an argument for using market-based processes to enable individual needs to be satisfied more flexibly, while at the same integrating markets into an institutional framework regulating which economic actors must repeatedly reach agreement in a democratic and communicative manner.

Conclusion

The demands facing a new institutional setting that not only overcomes the challenges of austerity and structural adjustment policies, but also enables a transition to a social, ecological and democratized development model, are tremendous. An inclusive reform project in such a sense is a prerequisite. Its realization requires a new regime of fiscal and economic policy institutions and rules that open up new scope for counter-cyclical economic and inclusive social policies. This would have to fit into the concepts and strategy for a social-ecological transformation, at the heart of which is a new type of economic growth. What is needed are minimum social standards that guarantee a minimum of social protection and an industrial and regional policy, which promotes the decarbonization of the industrial value-added chain. At the same time, intervention in markets and business decisions and thus progress in the democratization of the economy are proving to be indispensable.

Research from the perspective of international political economy and historical institutionalism repeatedly draws attention to the actor and power-political preconditions required for such a change of direction. Overcoming the inertia of institutional arrangements acting to preserve structures requires actors who are willing and able to initiate and direct institutional transformation in a targeted manner. This is especially true for the transformation of basic capitalist structures. It is precisely this transformation that will be fraught with fierce power struggles due to institutional rigidities (such as the stability of state-guaranteed property rights) and economic conflicts of interest (between capital, labour and state bureaucracies). Therefore, transformational power is needed if this change is to take place in the direction outlined earlier. This calls for a coalition of civil society actors, social movements and trade unions to put forward alternative policies and politicize the existing mode of technocratic decision-making (see also Busch et al 2013).

However, recent research also shows that both 'new' (for example anti-globalization movements) and 'old' social movements (trade unions) have difficulties when it comes to organizing lasting counter-hegemonic public contestation and debate (Peterson et al 2015). As far as social or political protest can serve as an indication, it is borne by a multitude of economic, social and political actors, which differ according to socio-demographic, cultural and (class) political factors and orientations (della Porta 2015). Cross-class and cross-cultural as well as transnational movements are apparently made considerably more difficult as a result. At the same time, the potential for conflict is activated in a spatially and temporally uneven manner (for example between Southern and Northern European countries), usually remaining in the arenas of nation-state politics without developing resilient transnational communication structures. Wherever, for example, relevant activities against the regime of precariousness have been observed, these have not gone beyond a 'fragmented conflict dynamic'. The new pan-European protest cycle expected in the wake of the 2008 financial crisis did not materialize. Moreover, there is still no credible protest movement justifying the hope of some analysts that 'post-growth concepts' can be turned into a 'resource for a European Union of sustainability' (Loske 2017, 570 and 568). While the activities of the Fridays-for-Futures movement have been quite successful in terms of putting climate change back on the agenda, they are at the same time not very much integrated with the economic and social concerns of the broader public. So far, at any rate, the economic, social and ecological consequences of austerity and structural adjustment policies have not led to any broad, stable and effective resistance movement. Hence, the prospects for European socioecological reformism are certainly not the best (Gill 2017).

Neither the social actors involved nor a critical social science should accept the current situation without comment. Both should agree on the specific contribution that they each could make to solve the problems at hand. In civil society and trade union contexts, the prospects for a 'mosaic left' (Urban 2019b) that is socially and politico-culturally heterogeneous and still capable of action have been under discussion for some time. Critical social science is also once again debating its social responsibility and contribution to solving contemporary problems. Moving the social sciences into the direction of a 'public sociology' as proposed by the former president of the American Sociological Association and the International Sociological Association Michael Burawoy (2005), could improve the prospects for a successful cooperation between critical social scientists and civil society actors for more inclusive economic governance in Europe considerably.

References

Anderson, Gavin. 2012. 'Beyond Constitutionalism Beyond the State', *Journal of Law and Society*, 39: 359–83.

Baumgartner, Frank and Bryan D. Jones. 1993. *Agendas and Instability in American Politics*. Chicago: University of Chicago Press.

Baumgartner, Frank, Bryan D. Jones and Peter B. Mortensen. 2014. 'Punctuated Equilibrium Theory: Explaining Stability and Change in Public Policymaking,' in P. Sabatier and C. Weible (eds) *Theories of the Policy Process*. Routledge, pp 59–103.

Bieling, Hans-Jürgen, Johannes Jäger and Magnus Ryner. 2016. 'Regulation Theory and the Political Economy of the European Union', *Journal of Common Market Studies*, 54(1): 53–69.

Blanchard, Olivier, Álvaro Leandro and Jeromin Zettelmeyer. 2020. *Revisiting the EU Fiscal Framework in an Era of Low Interest Rates*. Paper draft. https://ec.europa.eu/info/sites/info/files/s3-p_blanchard_et_al_0.pdf

Blyth, Mark. 2013. *Austerity: The History of a Dangerous Idea*. Oxford: Oxford University Press.

Blyth, Mark, Oddny Helgadottir and William Kring. 2016. 'Ideas and Historical Institutionalism'. in O. Fioretos, T.G. Falleti and A. Sheingate (eds) *The Oxford Handbook of Historical Institutionalism*. Oxford: Oxford University Press, pp 142–62.

Bugaric, Bojan and Matjaz Nahtigal. 2015. *The EU Fiscal Compact: Constitutionalization of Austerity and Preemption of Democracy in Europe*. Paper draft. http://matjaznahtigal.com/ENGpage/wp-content/uploads/2013/03/The-EU-Fiscal-Compact_March2013.final2_.pdf

Burawoy, Michael. 2005. 'For Public Sociology'. *American Sociological Review*, 70: 4–28.

Burret, Heiko T. and Jan Schnellenbach. 2014. *Implementation of the Fiscal Compact in the Euro Area Member States: Expertise on Behalf of the German Council of Economic Experts*. Working Paper No. 08/2013e. Wiesbaden: German Council of Economic Experts.

Busch, Klaus, Christoph Hermann, Karl Hinrichs and Thorsten Schulten. 2013. *Euro Crisis, Austerity Policy and the European Social Model. International Policy Analysis*. Friedrich Ebert Stiftung. www.socium.uni-bremen.de/about-the-socium/members/karl-hinrichs/publications/en/?publ=4832&print=1

Cox, Robert W. and Michael G. Schechter. 2002. *The Political Economy of a Plural World: Critical Reflections on Power, Morals and Civilization*. New York: Routledge.

della Porta, Donatella. 2015. *Social Movements in Times of Austerity. Bringing Capitalism Back into Protest Analysis*. Cambridge: Polity Press.

Dörre, Klaus. 2019. 'Risiko Kapitalismus. Landnahme, Zangenkrise, Nachhaltigkeitsrevolution', in K. Dörre, H. Rosa, K. Becker, S. Bose and B. Seyd (eds) *Große Transformation? Zur Zukunft moderner Gesellschaften*. Wiesbaden: Jumper VS, pp 3–33.

Dullien, Sebastian, Christoph Paetz, Andrew Watt and Sebastian Watka. 2020. *Proposals for a Reform of the EU's Fiscal Rules and Economic Governance. IMK Report* 159, June.

EuroMemo Groupe (European Economists for an Alternative Economic Policy in Europe). 2019. *Prospects for a Popular Political Economy in Europe*. www2.euromemorandum.eu/uploads/euromemorandum_2019.pdf. Last accessed 10 August 2020.

EuroMemo Groupe (European Economists for an Alternative Economic Policy in Europe). 2020. *A Green New Deal for Europe – Opportunities and Challenges*. www2.euromemorandum.eu/uploads/euromemorandum_2020.pdf

European Commission. 2013. *Towards Social Investment for Growth and Cohesion – Including Implementing the European Social Fund 2014–2020*. COM (2013) 83 final.

European Commission. 2019. *The European Green Deal*. Brussels, COM (2019) 640 final.

European Commission. 2020. *European Economic Forecast. Summer 2020 (Interim)*. European Economy Institutional Paper 132. https://ec.europa.eu/info/sites/info/files/economy-finance/ip132_en.pdf

Eurostat. 2021a. 'Preliminary Flash Estimate for the Fourth Quarter of 2020'. https://ec.europa.eu/eurostat/documents/portlet_file_entry/2995521/2-02022021-AP-EN.pdf/0e84de9c-0462-6868-df3e-dbacaad9f49f. Last accessed 20 February 2021.

Eurostat. 2021b. 'Unemployment Statistics'. https://ec.europa.eu/eurostat/statistics-explained/index.php/Unemployment_statistics. Last accessed 20 February 2021.

Galbraith, James K. 2014. *The End of Normal. The Great Crisis and the Future of Growth*. New York: Free Press.

Gill, Stephen. 1998. 'New Constitutionalism, Democratisation and Global Political Economy', *Pacifica Review: Peace, Security & Global Change*, 10(1): 23–38.

Gill, Stephen. 2017. 'Transnational Class Formations, European Crisis and the Silent Revolution'. *Critical Sociology*, 3(4–5): 635–51.

Habermas, Jürgen. 2011. *Die Verfassung Europas. Ein Essay*. Frankfurt/M.: Suhrkamp.

Hartlapp, Miriam, Julia Metz and Christian Rauh. 2014. *Which Policy for Europe? Power and Conflict Inside the European Commission*. Oxford: Oxford University Press.

Höppner, Martin and Mark Lutter. 2018. 'The Diversity of Wage Regimes: Why the Eurozone Is Too Heterogeneous for the Euro', *European Political Science Review*, 10(1): 71–96.

Hyman, Richard. 2013. 'Democratisation of the Economy', *Warsaw Forum of Economic Sociology*, 4:2(8): 59–74.Loske, Reinhard. 2017. 'Postwachstumskonzepte als Ressource für eine Europäische Union der Nachhaltigkeit', *Leviathan*, 45(4): 553–73.

Matthjis, Matthias and Mark Blyth. 2015. *The Future of the Euro*. Oxford: Oxford University Press.

McBride, Stephen. 2016. 'Constitutionalizing Austerity: Taking the Public Out of Public Policy', *Global Policy*, 7(1) (2016): 5–14.

McBride, Stephen and Sorin Mitrea. 2017. 'Austerity and Constitutionalizing Structural Reform of Labour in the European Union', *Studies in Political Economy*, 98(1): 1–23.

Müller, Torsten and Thorsten Schulten. 2020a. *Ensuring Fair Short-Time Work – A European Overview*. ETUI Policy Brief No. 7. www.etui.org/sites/default/files/2020-06/Covid-19%2BShort-time%2Bwork%2BM%C3%BCller%2BSchulten%2BPolicy%2BBrief%2B2020.07%281%29.pdf

Müller, Torsten and Thorsten Schulten. 2020b. *The European Minimum Wage on the Doorstep*. ETUI Research Paper – Policy Brief (1).

Pescatori, Andrea, Daniel Leigh and Jaime Guajardo. 2011. *Expansionary Austerity New International Evidence*. IMF Working Paper No. 11/158.

Peterson, Abby, Magnus Wahlsröm and Matthias Wennerhag. 2015. 'European Anti-Austerity Protests. Beyond "Old" and "New" Social Movements?', *Acta Sociologica*, 58: 293–310.

Pierson, Paul. 2004. *Politics in Time: History, Institutions, and Social Analysis*. Princeton: Princeton University Press.

Plehwe, Dieter, Moritz Neujeffski and Werner Krämer. 2018. 'Saving the Dangerous Idea: Austerity Think Tank Networks in the European Union', *Policy and Society*, 37(2): 188–205.

Rauh, Christian. 2019. 'EU Politicization and Policy Initiatives of the European Commission: The Case of Consumer Policy', *Journal of European Public Policy*, 26(3): 344–65.

Schäfer, Armin and Wolfgang Streeck. 2012. *Politics in the Age of Austerity*. Cambridge: Polity Press.

Scharpf, Fritz W. 1997. *Games Real Actors Play. Actor-centered Institutionalism in Policy Research*. Boulder: Routledge.

Scharpf, Fritz W. 2019. 'Multilevel Democracy: A Comparative Perspective', in N. Behnke, J. Broschek and J. Sonnicksen (eds) *Configurations, Dynamics and Mechanisms of Multilevel Governance. Comparative Territorial Politics*. Cham: Palgrave Macmillan.

Schimank, Uwe. 2007. 'Neoinstitutionalismus', in A. Benz, S. Lütz, U. Schimank and G. Simonis (eds) *Governance. Theoretische Grundlagen und empirische Aushandlungsfelder*. Wiesbaden: VS Verlag für Sozialwissenschaften, pp 161–75.

Streeck, Wolfgang. 2017. *Buying Time: The Delayed Crisis of Democratic Capitalism*. Verso.

Streeck, Wolfgang. 2018. *European Social Policy: Progressive Regression*. MPIfG Discussion Paper 18/11.

Tansel, Cemal Burak. 2016. *States of Discipline: Authoritarian Neoliberalism and the Contested Reproduction of Capitalist Order*. London: Rowman and Littlefield.

Thygesen, Niels, Roel Beetsma, Massimo Bordignon, Sandrine Duchêne and Mateusz Szczurek. 2019. *Assessment of EU Fiscal Rules with a Focus on the Six and Two-Pack Legislation*. Brussels: Report of the European Fiscal Board.

Urban, Hans-Jürgen. 2018. 'Ausbruch aus dem Gehäuse der European Governance. Überlegungen zu einer Soziologie der Wirtschaftsdemokratie in transformatorischer Absicht', *Berliner Journal für Soziologie*, 28(1–2): 91–122.

Urban, Hans-Jürgen. 2019a. *Gute Arbeit in der Transformation. Über eingreifende Politik im digitalisierten Kapitalismus*. VSA Verlag.

Urban, Hans-Jürgen. 2019b. 'Vorlauf zu einem HKWM-Artikel "Mosaik-Linke"', *Das Argument*, 61(1): 19–32.

Victor, Peter E. 2012. 'Growth, Degrowth and Climate Change: A Scenario Analysis', *Ecological Economics*, 84: 206–12.

Wright, Eric O. 2009. *Envisioning Real Utopias*. London: Verso.

Zürn, Michael, Martin Binder and Matthias Ecker-Ehrhardt. 2012 'International Authority and Its Politicization', *International Theory* (2012) 4(1): 69–106.

Conclusion

Stephen McBride, Dieter Plehwe and Bryan Evans

Austerity, defined broadly as a compound of fiscal consolidation, public sector restructuring and labour market flexibilization, has played a key role in the decades-long hegemony of neoliberalism, and in its subsequent crisis. After a brief period of fiscal stimulus after the Great Financial Crisis of 2007–08, there was an intensification of austerity, albeit with some variety within a common theme (see Whiteside et al 2021). Its effects have influenced experience of the COVID-19 pandemic.

Considered as a 'solution' to the financial and economic crisis austerity policies were an abject failure. In a global system experiencing multiple crises austerity had nothing positive to contribute. Its intellectual rationale was subjected to lethal critique (Stiglitz 2011; Blyth 2013; Herndon et al 2013; Krugman 2013;). Yet the national and international economic and political elites, international organizations and national governments remained in lockstep, imposing austerity as a necessary and productive response.

Though clearly not directly responsible for the health crisis that emerged as a result of the spread of the COVID-19 virus in early 2020, some effects of austerity (and of neoliberal globalization more generally) exacerbated the situation. These included diminished public services, a precarious and low-waged labour force in affected sectors such as long-term care, the intrusion of the profit motive into such facilities where returns could be maximized through over-crowding, labour economies involving a just-in-time workforce often working in several facilities and therefore liable to spread the infection, eroded capacity of national governments and diminished industrial capacity where 'advanced' industrial societies were unable to supply protective equipment in a timely fashion. Austerity thus contributed to the severity of the pandemic and the lived experience of it for many.

Driven by finance and producing extreme inequality of wealth and income, austerity sustained its own economic crisis for a decade after the GFC and contributed to the multiple other crises the world is experiencing – environmental-ecological, food security, dislocation of peoples and migration, stagnant economies and now health. Compounding all this is the failure of institutions to represent popular will and respond democratically. Instead the unaccountable application of rules by remote institutions, or the opaque machinations of network governance produce an empty politics in which trust is eroded and political leaders, regardless of political party, speak from similar texts.

We can broadly summarize the empirically rich and detailed contributions to this volume under four themes: finance, labour and dissenting voices, public services, and democracy. In each case years of austerity have had profound effects. In each case austerity practices have been embedded into state structures and practices. This gives rise for concerns that even the severity of the pandemic, its exposure of the poverty of austerity policies and its intersection with other crises will make it difficult to dislodge. However, as most of our contributors note, crises also present opportunities, and there are prospects for change that will be touched on in more detail later in the chapter.

In the area of finance the use of PPPs (P3s) to provide state infrastructure and other services has become normalized. Heather Whiteside (Chapter 1) presents a damning picture of the problems associated with reliance on private finance in the provision of public goods. These include bankruptcies and bailouts, contrary to the rationale that risk is transferred from the public purse to private investors, long-run public financial commitments that far outweigh any initial benefits, and inefficiencies of all kinds. These all run contrary to the claimed benefits of harnessing private funds for public purposes, and the greater efficiency and know-how that it supposedly mobilized. Yet P3 promotion units are often embedded within state bureaucracies.

If P3s are still poorly understood by the general public, they are still more visible than some of the mechanisms that serve to institutionalize austerity. Sebastian Botzem (Chapter 2) lifted the veil on a set of accounting practices that privilege the information needs of capital, reduce democratic accountability and at an apparently technical level entrench the logic of austerity. As in many other areas of governance, ostensibly technical rules obscure deliberately pro-market politics. In a later chapter (11), Christoph Sorg, dealing with the role of debt in triggering anti-austerity protests, outlines the debt repayment and debt transfer agenda under austerity. In this analysis predatory creditors evade responsibility while debtors must assume the full burden of their obligations. This is a classic moral hazard situation where the interests of unwise, irresponsible or simply corrupt lenders are protected.

Voices of opposition to the austerity agenda can be found in labour organizations, the academic community and in various, often localized, social movements. Steffen Lehndorff (Chapter 3) documents the systematic weakening of trade unions in the European Union. This process, re-enforced by some structural factors, has been underway throughout the neoliberal period, but has intensified over the last decade of austerity. EU governance practices, such as the 'European Semester' and 'country-specific recommendations', have been a constant source of pressure to decentralize and weaken collective bargaining processes. The intention has been to lower labour unit costs, a version of internal devaluation, constraining wages and lowering living standards. Though not without opportunities for resistance the effect has been to make the playing field for capital versus labour even less level than it was before. In a similar vein, Evans, McBride and Watson (Chapter 8) show how the crisis diminished the voice labour had expressed in institutions of social dialogue or social partnership. In the wake of the GFC these institutions were closed down (in some cases), bypassed or diverted to a much narrower range of issues than they had dealt with previously. Without exaggerating the former influence of labour in these venues, there is no doubt it has been reduced or eliminated over the last decade. And, Dieter Plehwe and Moritz Neujeffski (Chapter 7), in a chapter pertinent also to the democracy theme, note the exclusion of heterodox and diverse voices from important advisory boards in Germany.

Public services have been a major target of austerity cutbacks and privatization initiatives. In Chapter 4 Donna Baines, Ian Cunningham, Philip James and Chandrima Roy explore the ramifications of marketized social programmes. Their case studies note sacrifices imposed on the largely female work forces through increased precarity and low wages, and on service users, through poor-quality care due to underfunding and privatization. In Chapter 5, Meghan Joy, John Shields, Sharon Broughton and Sui Mee Cheng analyzed innovative ways of private sector intrusion into social provision through Social Innovation Laboratories and Social Innovation Bonds. They conclude that these have proven 'woefully inadequate'. Certainly, the impact of the pandemic has highlighted that only the state can respond adequately to ameliorate loss of income and provide other supports.

In the democracy theme a number of the developments discussed earlier play a role – the exclusion of alternative perspectives from economic decision-making (Plehwe and Neujeffski), the marginalization of labour's voice (Lehndorff; Evans et al), and the sense of anti-debt campaigners that while they may win the argument they lack sufficient power to implement change (Sorg). The institutional obstacles to change were taken up by McBride and Schnittker (Chapter 6). They outlined a policy of 'constitutionalizing' important policy areas rendering them remote from democratic influence. Such matters (much of fiscal, monetary, trade and investment, and increasingly labour) are regarded as settled or fixed and thus beyond debate in official circles. In their chapter (13) Hans-Jürgen Urban and Sebastian Kramer made the case for major institutional reform within the EU to overcome these obstacles.

In 2020 the explosion of a new, immediately life-threatening crisis with huge economic ramifications led to austerity, at least the fiscal ingredient of the compound, being unceremoniously ditched. Just as in an earlier time, when World War II succeeded the Great Depression, previously unavailable money flowed without apparent limit so, during the pandemic, resources previously declared non-existent or unobtainable, appeared as if by magic, and neoliberal dogma was temporarily cast aside. In the brief period of post-GFC stimulus after 2008 many assumed, or hoped, that this implied a permanent change from a crisis-plagued and increasingly polarized system. These hopes were to be dashed. From 2010 austerity became the order of the day, and neoliberalism was re-established as the dominant creed. Now many wonder and hope that if the tragedy of COVID-19 might have any positive side effect, it could lie in the re-invention of public purpose, and the development of real alternatives leading to a more just and sustainable society.

Nothing is certain. Indeed, quite the reverse – everything is uncertain. In the Introduction to this book, and in many of the chapters, we have identified opportunities that might lead to real change, and obstacles that might prevent it. In particular we outlined three alternative scenarios: (1) a return to the status quo (of neoliberal globalization and austerity) before the pandemic struck; (2) selective deviation from the austerity model, probably most pronounced in the health sector which most would expect, whatever else happens, to be more public, more regulated and better resourced; and (3) a transformative change leaving the world of austerity capitalism and neoliberalism behind.

This book was drafted in the midst of the long-running austerity disaster, but before the COVID-19 virus struck. It is primarily about austerity in the 12 years since the GFC. Yet it seemed useful, where appropriate, to add some consideration of the connection between the two crises and what that might imply for the prospects for change. The last five chapters in the book address these issues more directly but the earlier chapters engage to some extent, and vary in degrees of optimism, about whether real change will emerge.

Where do we go from here? How do we get there?

The chapters on public services privatization (in various ways, through P3s, Social Impact Bonds or transferring care activities into private hands) demonstrate clearly their disastrous nature (for all but those enriched as a result of these initiatives). The COVID-19 crisis has exacerbated all the pre-existing fault lines involved in the marketization of state activities. In general terms the solution is easy to identify: a re-assertion of the public role, including public ownership democratically controlled. What was already evident before the COVID-19 virus struck became even more evident after it did. Opportunities to reverse these measures exist. But obstacles to doing so – institutional and ideological – remain formidably entrenched.

A great deal of work has been done on the ideational front. Much well-marshalled evidence has been compiled on the failures of neoliberal austerity. Many well-thought-out alternatives have been developed.

Organizationally things do not look so good. Opposition exists, but a coherent organized bloc capable of demanding and achieving change has yet to materialize.

Trade unions which are potentially a central part of such a bloc have been weakened through the systematic if gradual decentralization and fragmentation of collective bargaining systems. Social concertation institutions which had provided a platform for exerting some influence in the policy system have similarly seen their role reduced. Yet without underestimating the obstacles in any way, Steffen Lehndorff sees some evidence of successful resistance (examples being campaigns and labour court victories in Southern Europe that defended some aspects of the collective bargaining systems – see his chapter (3) for details). He also identifies concrete proposals that could obstruct the further unfolding of the neoliberal agenda at the European level. This would involve embedding binding standards into the European governance system that would have to be observed by European elites. Possibilities include a European minimum wage and structures to extend collective bargaining coverage. Although far from easy to achieve, these are the types of issues on which unions could organize Europe-wide campaigns with some prospect of success. Once there, such measures would function as 'social foreign body' within the EU policymaking machine. Efforts to recalibrate failed policies by making better advice available through changing and diversifying the composition of advisory councils, as suggested by Plehwe and Neujeffski should, in principle, be an easier sell in these times.

There has, of course, been considerable resistance to austerity. Podemos in Spain, Sinn Fein in Ireland, the Corbyn and Sanders phenomena in the UK and US respectively, all mobilized a considerable number of people looking for real alternatives. These cases show the potential for system change. The fact that only limited gains were made show its limits. In some ways protesting *against* austerity may have been easier than the task of organizing *for* an alternative.

Then, existing institutions, banks, governments and supranational entities provided a target. Now, the exogenous cause of the pandemic is perhaps less in focus, and therefore the solutions that must be devised and implemented are similarly broader.

Even with a relatively confined issue there are difficulties in bridging from critique to alternatives. Christoph Sorg's historical survey of debt and the protests that have mobilized against it demonstrates the problem. The anti-debt movements have been very successful in exposing existing narratives as enablers of predatory relationships between creditors and debtors. Exposing the reality that public/sovereign debt that was used to justify austerity was really a private debt crisis of financial corporations that were rescued, bailed out, or whose debt was socialized, can lead to a far-reaching re-assessment of capitalist political economy.

The critique of the existing hegemonic conventional wisdom has led to the development of plausible ideas for transformation involving reforms to financial architecture, socialization of the financial sector and the democratization of debt politics. Still, as Sorg observes, although there is no lack of ideas for change, there is a lack of power to achieve it.

Ingo Schmidt turns to the problem of how ideas do, or do not, get adopted and implemented. He argues that economic liberals were able to construct an historic bloc capable of implementing their policies. This bloc – market populism – was constructed around a blend of neoliberal economics and social liberalism – the latter encompassing individual self-actualization, cosmopolitanism and based in a new middle class of well-educated symbolic analysts in the new technology-grounded knowledge economy.

This bloc has disintegrated as a result of the two crises – the GFC and the pandemic – and its evident inability to deal with the multiple crises affecting contemporary capitalism. But no new bloc has been assembled. Right populism has emerged but is far from achieving a real breakthrough. On the left, divisions on the priority to be accorded class on the one hand, and various forms of identity on the other, and lingering ideological divisions between old and new lefts, impede any sort of unity. According to Schmidt a stalemate or interregnum exists. His rather sombre conclusion, as far as left prospects are concerned, is that notwithstanding sometimes impressive protest movements during the austerity period, such as Podemos in Spain, no firm institutional roots were established, an indication that the road to forming a left historic bloc may well be a long one.

The complexities and contradictions within the populist phenomena received a detailed analysis in Hans-Jürgen Bieling's chapter. In particular he notes how right-wing populist formations, firmly within the bourgeois blocs of their respective countries have in some cases responded to the pressures of austerity by advocating protective social policies, and have mobilized considerable working-class support as a result. The chapter probes why this has occurred in some countries and not in others. But in any case, the protection is selectively targeted and exclusionary towards minority ethnic and weaker social groups. To some extent this process has been undermined by the impact of COVID-19, as mainstream parties and governments expanded social spending and in the process addressed some of the economic and social difficulties of the populists' base. In the not unlikely event that the fiscal costs of the crisis response lead to a return to austerity, then the interrupted rise of right populism may resume.

In Chapter 12, Jim Stanford outlines the depth of the crisis we face as a result of the COVID-19 pandemic, not least in terms of the long-term ability of democratic institutions to cope with the hardship, polarization and populist movements that have posed challenges to their legitimacy. As a result, strengthening these capacities must be a central part of a progressive response.

Hans-Jürgen Urban and Sebastian Kramer (Chapter 13) point to the EU's entanglement in the multiple crises – economic, social and environmental – that we all face. They argue that any further European integration must be transformational, combining environmental, social, economic and democratic objectives, and must close the book on the austerity and structural adjustment policies that have so far predominated. Like McBride and Schnittker (Chapter 6), they consider the obstacles posed by the 'constitutionalization' in the EU, the nature of the rules adopted, and of European governance, and the temporary nature of the suspension of some of these during the current crisis.

These obstacles led McBride and Schnittker to posit greater potential for change if integration is loosened and greater scope for action at the national level empowered democratic forces. Urban and Kramer recognize the difficulty of achieving institutional change at the European level (a necessary condition for adoption of a more progressive economic-social-environment model) but explore the possibilities, even while conceding that it is not probable under existing conditions.

That said, their proposal adds up to a detailed and exciting vision of what a progressive European vision might look like. It would include a green economic deal, including decarbonization, job guarantees and an EU-wide minimum wage, and inclusive and democratic governance structures.

Overcoming institutional inertia and resistance, and achieving the necessary institutional transformation necessary to achieve such a programme will be complex and fraught with fierce power struggles. A limited departure from austerity might generate somewhat better public health systems in some places, or more rapid decarbonization in others. In many countries, though by no means in all, government has learned how to cope with a temporary crisis through short-time work schemes and support for small businesses and the self-employed. Increased interest in and widespread discussion of larger schemes like the green new deal indicate a longing for new developments leading to a different society. This volume shows in how many different places, more and less arcane, groups interested in alternatives have to organize: public interest groups in privatization struggles and norm setting institutions of finance, trade unions in collective bargaining and minimum wage legislation and transformative industrial policy, democracy movements and traditional parties in struggles to turn parliaments and public discourse in meaningful and powerful arenas again, wrenching control from government bureaucracies and public private network lobby circuits, heterodox and female economists, critical legal scholars and progressive social scientists in academic disciplines and consulting gambits dominated by old boy networks austerity voices. Austerity politics combines all these spaces and yet social struggles need to proceed in each of the different corners in their own right and at their own pace. More communication across these different realms is necessary to ascertain common objectives and directions. It has been noted in past austerity studies how well connected the right has become across borders and sectors (Plehwe et al 2018), which should be read as a call for more horizontal and vertical networking on the other side. Otherwise there is a risk of yet another progressive vision disowned. Much like sustainability has been transformed into the business-friendly concept of sustainable growth, the green new deal can also mutate into the continuation of many old deals under the new green label. A significant indicator of the extent to which we will see a departure from austerity politics as usual will be the way in which progressive goals will be linked: social equality, ecological healing and stability and economic sustainability can, but should not, be played off against each other. Old trade unions and new social movements may find it interesting to listen to each other, or find themselves marching alone.

To prevail will require a powerful coalition of civil society actors, social movements and trade unions. Although there is little sign of such a coalition at the present moment, if it were true that 'necessity is the mother of invention', the task of creating one is the foremost task, if we as societies are to overcome the multiple crises in which we are mired.

References

Blyth, Mark. 2013. *Austerity: The History of a Dangerous Idea*. Oxford: Oxford University Press.

Herndon, Thomas, Michael Ash and Robert Pollin. 2013. *Does High Public Debt Consistently Stifle Economic Growth: A Critique of Reinhart and Rogoff* Amherst: University of Massachusetts, Political Economy Research Institute, Working Paper 322.

Krugman, Paul. 2013. *End this Depression Now!* New York: W.W. Norton.

Plehwe, Dieter, Moritz Neujeffski and Werner Krämer. 2018. 'Saving the Dangerous Idea: Austerity Think Tank Networks in the European Union', *Policy and Society*, 37(2): 188–205.

Stiglitz, Joseph E. 2011. 'Rethinking Macroeconomics: What Went Wrong and How to Fix It', *Global Policy*, 2(2): 165–75.

Whiteside, Heather, Stephen McBride and Bryan Evans. 2021. *Varieties of Austerity*. Bristol: Bristol University Press.

Index

References to footnotes show both the page number and the note number (for example, 231n3).

C

H

I

U

V

W

X

Y

Z

Printed and bound by CPI Group (UK) Ltd, Croydon, CR0 4YY

15/09/2026

14962384-0006